PAGE 38
ON THE ROAD
YOUR COMPLETE DESTINATION GUIDE
In-depth reviews, detailed listings and insider tips

Accommodation p162

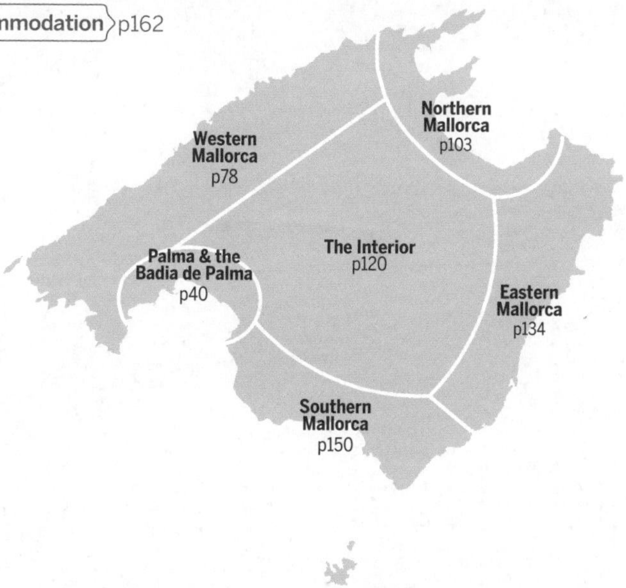

PAGE 199
SURVIVAL GUIDE
VITAL PRACTICAL INFORMATION TO HELP YOU HAVE A SMOOTH TRIP

Directory A–Z 200
Transport 207
Language & Glossary 211
Index 218
Map Legend 223

THIS EDITION WRITTEN AND RESEARCHED BY

Anthony Ham

welcome to Mallorca

Stirring Landscapes

Contrary to what you may have heard about tourism overdevelopment on the island, Mallorca is one of the great natural destinations of the Mediterranean. Majestic limestone cliffs plunge into the translucent sapphire- and turquoise-hued waters of the Mediterranean for the length of the island's western and northern coasts. Vast plains carpeted with almonds, carobs, olives and vineyards stretch luxuriantly across the interior. And yachts drop anchor in idyllic inlets that are otherwise accessible only on foot all along the eastern and southern coasts. Wherever you find yourself, the best way to explore all of this natural splendour is under your own steam, with a fantastic portfolio of hiking and cycling trails; they range from one-day escapes from the rigours of resort life to soulful days spent traversing the Serra de Tramuntana as you move from one pretty village to the next.

Coastal Living

There are many reasons why Mallorca has become one of Europe's premier summer destinations, but one ranks above all others: this is one beautiful coast. The island's resorts have colonised many lovely coves, but there are many more again that serve as reminders of why the world long ago fell in love with the island's beaches. On many of these, pine forests provide a picturesque backdrop and the space to put your towel is

HOLGER LEUE/LONELY PLANET IMAGES ©

Like a movie star settling comfortably into middle age, Mallorca has matured, wedding stunning natural beauty with an appreciation for the finer things in life without ever losing its glamour.

(left) Cala Sant Vicenç (p109).
(below) Els Calderers (p130), Sant Joan.

HOLGER LEUE/LONELY PLANET IMAGES ©

such as to send many other Mediterranean destinations, including on the Spanish mainland, into paroxysms of envy. But the Mallorcan summer is about so much more than beaches: Mallorca has perfected the art of coastal living, with Mallorcan food (including the freshest seafood), wine (vineyards are rarely more than an hour away) and natural attractions (ditto) at the centre of the whole experience.

Return to Tradition

All across the island, locals are returning to their cultural roots, and it's one of the most exciting things to happen on Mallorca for decades. Forsaking quantity for quality, the island's old manor houses, country estates and long-abandoned farms have sprung back to life as refined rural retreats. Food is also at the heart of this revival, with the island's chefs – inspired as much by their Mallorquin grandmothers as by the innovative trends of Mediterranean nouvelle cuisine – revitalising the mainstays of the Mallorcan kitchen. Spending at least a part of your holiday in such a supremely comfortable place, apart from being the ultimate in rural relaxation, will take you deep into the Mallorquin world. And like so many visitors to the island before you, you'll never want to leave.

› Mallorca

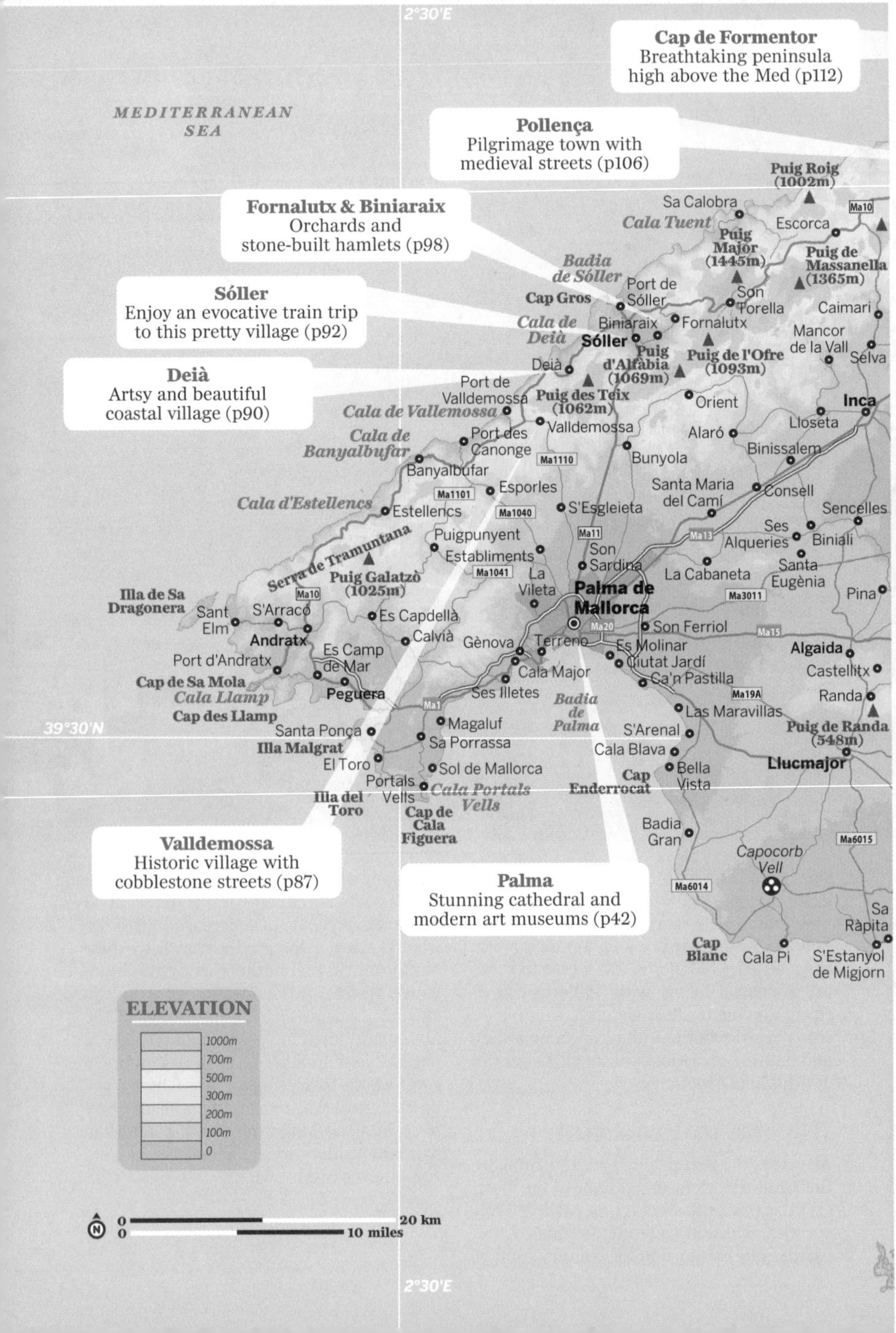

Cap de Formentor
Breathtaking peninsula high above the Med (p112)
Pollença
Pilgrimage town with medieval streets (p106)
Fornalutx & Biniaraix
Orchards and stone-built hamlets (p98)
Sóller
Enjoy an evocative train trip to this pretty village (p92)
Deià
Artsy and beautiful coastal village (p90)
Valldemossa
Historic village with cobblestone streets (p87)
Palma
Stunning cathedral and modern art museums (p42)
MEDITERRANEAN SEA
2°30'E
39°30'N
Puig Roig (1002m)
Sa Calobra
Cala Tuent
Escorca
Puig Major (1445m)
Puig de Massanella (1365m)
Badia de Sóller
Port de Sóller
Cap Gros
Son Torella
Caimari
Cala de Deià
Biniaraix
Fornalutx
Sóller
Mancor de la Vall
Selva
Deià
Puig d'Alfàbia (1069m)
Puig de l'Ofre (1093m)
Port de Valldemossa
Puig des Teix (1062m)
Orient
Inca
Cala de Vallemossa
Valldemossa
Lloseta
Cala de Banyalbufar
Port des Canonge
Alaró
Bunyola
Binissalem
Banyalbufar
Esporles
Santa Maria del Camí
Consell
Cala d'Estellencs
Estellencs
S'Esgleieta
Sencelles
Serra de Tramuntana
Puigpunyent
Ses Alqueries
Biniali
Establiments
Son Sardina
Santa Eugènia
La Cabaneta
Puig Galatzò (1025m)
La Vileta
Pina
Illa de Sa Dragonera
Sant Elm
S'Arraco
Palma de Mallorca
Es Capdellà
Son Ferriol
Andratx
Calvià
Gènova
Terreno
Es Molinar
Algaida
Port d'Andratx
Es Camp de Mar
Ciutat Jardí
Castellitx
Cala Major
Ca'n Pastilla
Cap de Sa Mola
Cala Llamp
Peguera
Ses Illetes
Randa
Badia de Palma
Las Maravillas
Cap des Llamp
Magaluf
Puig de Randa (548m)
Santa Ponça
S'Arenal
Sa Porrassa
Illa Malgrat
Cala Blava
Llucmajor
El Toro
Sol de Mallorca
Bella Vista
Portals Vells
Cap Enderrocat
Illa del Toro
Cala Portals Vells
Cap de Cala Figuera
Badia Gran
Capocorb Vell
Sa Ràpita
Cap Blanc
Cala Pi
S'Estanyol de Migjorn
Ma10
Ma1110
Ma1101
Ma1040
Ma11
Ma13
Ma1041
Ma3011
Ma20
Ma15
Ma19A
Ma1
Ma6015
Ma6014
ELEVATION
1000m
700m
500m
300m
200m
100m
0
0
20 km
0
10 miles

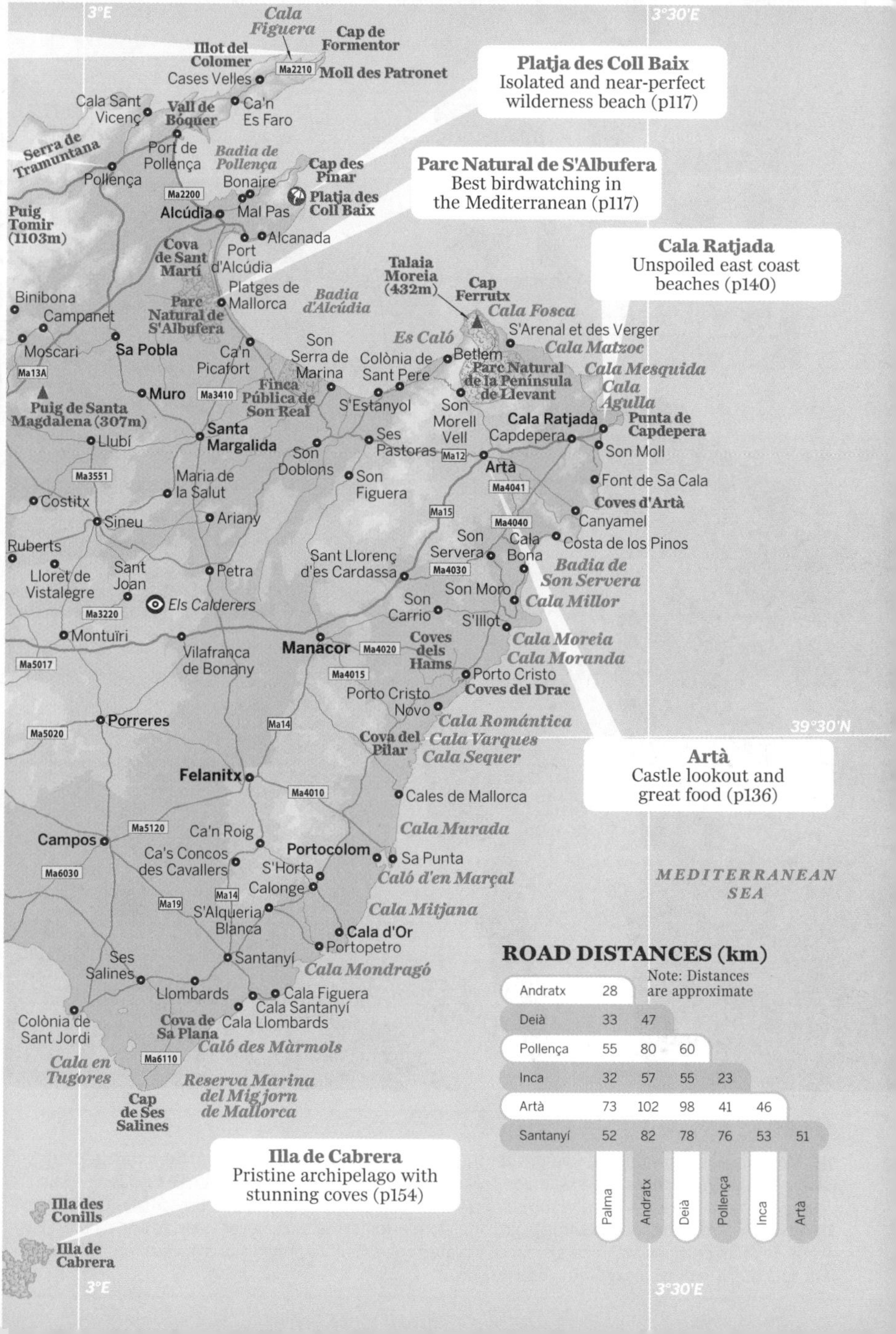
Platja des Coll Baix
Isolated and near-perfect wilderness beach (p117)
Parc Natural de S'Albufera
Best birdwatching in the Mediterranean (p117)
Cala Ratjada
Unspoiled east coast beaches (p140)
Artà
Castle lookout and great food (p136)
Illa de Cabrera
Pristine archipelago with stunning coves (p154)
3°E
3°30'E
39°30'N
Cala Figuera
Cap de Formentor
Illot del Colomer
Ma2210
Moll des Patronet
Cases Velles
Cala Sant Vicenç
Vall de Bóquer
Ca'n Es Faro
Serra de Tramuntana
Port de Pollença
Badia de Pollença
Cap des Pinar
Pollença
Bonaire
Ma2200
Platja des Coll Baix
Puig Tomir (1103m)
Alcúdia
Mal Pas
Alcanada
Cova de Sant Martí
Port d'Alcúdia
Platges de Mallorca
Badia d'Alcúdia
Talaia Moreia (432m)
Cap Ferrutx
Cala Fosca
Binibona
Campanet
Parc Natural de S'Albufera
S'Arenal et des Verger
Moscari
Sa Pobla
Ca'n Picafort
Son Serra de Marina
Es Caló
Colònia de Sant Pere
Betlem
Cala Matzoc
Ma13A
Parc Natural de la Península de Llevant
Cala Mesquida
Puig de Santa Magdalena (307m)
Muro
Ma3410
Finca Pública de Son Real
S'Estanyol
Son Morell Vell
Cala Agulla
Cala Ratjada
Punta de Capdepera
Santa Margalida
Llubí
Son Doblons
Ses Pastoras
Ma12
Capdepera
Son Moll
Artà
Ma3551
Maria de la Salut
Son Figuera
Ma4041
Font de Sa Cala
Costitx
Coves d'Artà
Ma15
Sineu
Ariany
Ma4040
Canyamel
Ruberts
Son Servera
Cala Bona
Costa de los Pinos
Lloret de Vistalegre
Sant Joan
Petra
Sant Llorenç d'es Cardassa
Ma4030
Badia de Son Servera
Els Calderers
Son Moro
Cala Millor
Ma3220
Son Carrio
S'Illot
Montuïri
Vilafranca de Bonany
Manacor
Ma4020
Coves dels Hams
Cala Moreia
Cala Moranda
Ma5017
Ma4015
Porto Cristo
Coves del Drac
Porto Cristo Novo
Porreres
Ma14
Cala Romántica
Ma5020
Cova del Pilar
Cala Varques
Cala Sequer
Felanitx
Ma4010
Cales de Mallorca
Ma5120
Cala Murada
Campos
Ca'n Roig
Portocolom
Ca's Concos des Cavallers
Sa Punta
S'Horta
Ma6030
Calonge
Caló d'en Marçal
MEDITERRANEAN SEA
Ma19
S'Alqueria Blanca
Cala Mitjana
Cala d'Or
Portopetro
Santanyí
Ses Salines
Cala Mondragó
Llombards
Cala Figuera
Cala Santanyí
Colònia de Sant Jordi
Cova de Sa Plana
Cala Llombards
Caló des Màrmols
Ma6110
Cala en Tugores
Reserva Marina del Migjorn de Mallorca
Cap de Ses Salines
Illa des Conills
Illa de Cabrera

ROAD DISTANCES (km)

Note: Distances are approximate

	Palma	Andratx	Deià	Pollença	Inca	Artà
Andratx	28					
Deià	33	47				
Pollença	55	80	60			
Inca	32	57	55	23		
Artà	73	102	98	41	46	
Santanyí	52	82	78	76	53	51

17 TOP EXPERIENCES

HOLGER LEUE/LONELY PLANET IMAGES ©

Scenic drive to Sa Calobra

1 Mallorca has numerous candidates for the title of 'most breathtaking drive', from the descent to Port de Valldemossa to the sinuous road the length of Cap de Formentor. But nothing rivals the seemingly endless twists and turns from the main Ma10 down to Sa Calobra (p101). The hairpin bends, hewn from the rock of some weird and wonderful formations, never seem to end as the road leads down to perhaps Mallorca's most celebrated cove. Built to provide land access for tourists, it attracts them in droves, and with good reason.

Deià

2 Of all the villages that cling to the western slopes of the Serra de Tramuntana, Deià (p90) does so with the greatest charm. Its wonderfully preserved stone buildings climb the pyramid-shaped hill crowned by a church – when seen from a distance against the backdrop of impossibly high mountains, the scene rivals anything Tuscany has to offer. Not surprisingly, Deià has always drawn an artsy crowd, not least among them the poet Robert Graves (whose house can be visited), while its beach at Cala de Deià is one of western Mallorca's prettiest.

Palma Catedral

3 Resembling a vast ship moored at the city's edge as it surveys the Mediterranean from a gentle rise, Mallorca's premier place of worship (p42) dominates the city's skyline and is the island's most spectacular architectural treasure. On the seaward side, the flying buttresses are extraordinary, while astonishing stained-glass windows and an intriguing flight of fancy by Gaudí inhabit the interior alongside a striking rendering of a biblical parable by contemporary artist Miquel Barceló. You'll find yourself returning here, either to get your bearings, or simply to gaze in wonder.

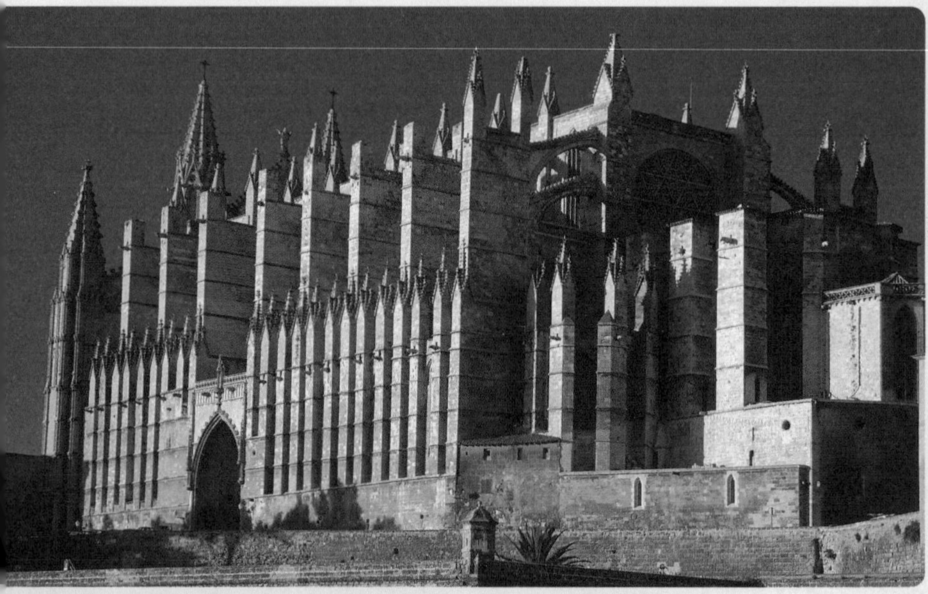

DAVID TOMLINSON/LONELY PLANET IMAGES ©

HOLGER LEUE/LONELY PLANET IMAGES ©

Biniaraix & Fornalutx

4 Beautiful stone-built villages appear in the foothills and valleys of the Serra de Tramuntana with anything but monotonous regularity, but the journey to reach Biniaraix (p98) and Fornalutx (p98) is every bit as rewarding as the villages themselves. Narrow snaking paths wind along the valley floor, passing stone walls and fields of fragrant fruit trees en route to idyllic hamlets; the former village is timeless and tranquil, the latter well aware of its beauty with fine restaurants, hotels and little shops to welcome you at journey's end. Biniaraix

DAVID TOMLINSON/LONELY PLANET IMAGES ©

Pollença

5 Of all the towns of the Mallorcan interior, it is Pollença (p106) that rises above the rest. Its two hilltop sanctuaries and pilgrimage points look down on a medieval roofscape of stone and terracotta, while at ground level this city has one of the island's largest weekly markets, some lovely churches and traffic-free lanes. You'll also eat wonderfully well here, its tidy little boutiques will detain you longer than you plan and, with some outstanding hotels, most day visitors regret not having chosen the town for their northern Mallorcan base.

East Coast Beaches

6 Amid the overdevelopment that blights so much of eastern Mallorca, a number of beautiful little beaches serve as reminders of why people have always come here in search of the perfect stretch of sand. The beaches within striking distance of Cala Ratjada – particularly Cala Agulla, Cala Mesquida and those of the Parc Natural de la Península de Llevant – are some of the best on the island with white sand and turquoise waters set against a backdrop of pine trees and sand dunes. Cala Mesquida

GRAND TOUR/CORBIS

HOLGER LEUE/LONELY PLANET IMAGES ©

Staying in a Rural Hotel

7 Ranking high among the lesser-known charms of travelling in Mallorca are the countless rural properties that have been converted into places to stay all across the island, particularly inland and in the coastal hinterland. These places capture the rustic spirit of rural Mallorcan life, combining peaceful locations with stylishly renovated rooms, and many have an attached restaurant serving traditional local cuisine. Some are palatial and five-star in facilities and price, but many more are readily accessible to those on a midrange budget. Agroturisme Monnàber Vell

Coastal Scenery of Cap de Formentor

8 The narrow, precipitous peninsula of Cap de Formentor (p112) is one of the most dramatic mountain ranges in southern Europe. Here, peaks thrust upwards like the jagged ramparts of some epic Mediterranean fortress, while forests of Aleppo pines add light and shadow to austere rocky outcrops that drop abruptly to some of the most beautiful and most isolated beaches and coves on the island. However you travel the road running its length, the drama of the natural world dominates at every turn.

HOLGER LEUE/LONELY PLANET IMAGES ©

OLIVER STREWE/LONELY PLANET IMAGES ©

Fresh Seafood

9 Visiting Mallorca is a pleasure for gastronomes, not least because the island's chefs have mastered the art of preparing fish and seafood. For the most part forsaking sauces to let the flavours speak for themselves, Mallorcan kitchens consistently produce perfectly grilled renditions of the freshest catch of the day. But if it's sauces that you want, the range of seafood rice dishes and (especially lobster) stews has few rivals in a country renowned for its paellas. And don't leave the island without tasting the prawns from Port de Sóller (p92).

Palma's Art Museums

10 The crisp Mediterranean light drew some of Europe's most respected painters throughout the 20th century, but two in particular – Joan Miró and Mallorquin Miquel Barceló – will be forever associated with the island. Miró's former home contains a fine range of his works, while Barceló adorned Palma's cathedral with flair and distinction. Elsewhere, Picasso and Dalí seem perfectly at home in Palma's galleries, whether in Es Baluard (p54) the Palau March (p48) or the Museu Fundación Juan March (p52). Es Baluard

HOLGER LEUE/LONELY PLANET IMAGES © ARCHITECTS: JAIME & LUIS GARCÍA RUIZ, ÁNGEL SÁNCHEZ-CANTALEJO AND VICENTE TOMÁS

HOLGER LEUE/LONELY PLANET IMAGES ©

11

Train to Sóller

11 Palma and Sóller rank highly as attractions in their own right, but the antique wooden train (p63) that ambles between them is an utterly charming way to travel. The train forsakes the clamour of city life, passing through quiet scenes of rural Mallorca before climbing into the foothills, looking for a way through the Serra de Tramuntana. Traversing tunnels and narrow valleys before emerging high above pretty Sóller, the train takes you at once across the island and back in time, a reminder that sometimes it's the journey itself that matters.

ROBERT HARDING WORLD IMAGERY/ALAMY

Illa de Cabrera

12 The only national park in the Balearics is a special place and Illa de Cabrera (p154) is the jewel in its crown. The largest of 19 uninhabited islands that make up the marine park, Cabrera is blissfully peaceful – its wild headlands and secluded beaches are protected by laws that limit the number of daily visitors to sustainable levels. Boat excursions to the island from Colònia de Sant Jordi stop off at Sa Cova Blava, an exquisitely blue marine cave of rare beauty.

Parc Natural de S'Albufera

SEBASTIÀ TORRENS/PHOTOLIBRARY

13 One of the Mediterranean's premier birdwatching sites at any time of the year, this park (p117) is home to over 300 species, including 64 who breed here. Waterbirds are the park's forté and easily accessible trails wind amid the wetlands. Such is its appeal that it's likely to convert even the most ambivalent visitor into an avid twitcher. Just when the high-rise towers of holiday resorts threaten to overwhelm your experience of the Mallorcan coast, this wonderful protected area restores one's faith in the power of the natural world to endure.

MZJ/IMAGEBROKER

Water Sports

14 The Mallorcan summer may be famous for long lazy days by the beach, but those needing more than the occasional dip in the turquoise waters are well catered for. There are some outstanding diving and snorkelling possibilities, from the Illa de Sa Dragonera in the south to the northern Badia de Pollença; the latter is considered by experienced divers to be the gateway to Mallorca's best diving. There are professional dive centres all around the island, and operators who arrange sea kayaking, windsurfing, sailing and more-sedate boat trips. Port de Pollença

Medieval Artà

15 Set back from eastern Mallorca's busy summer coast, Artà (p136) has enduring year-round charms. Its stone buildings line narrow streets that gently climb up a hillside before ascending steeply to one of the island's most unusual church-castle complexes. The views here are sweeping and simply wonderful, while back in town fine restaurants, hotels and an agreeably somnambulant air make it an ideal base for your exploration of the island, including nearby Parc Natural de la Península de Llevant (p138).

HOLGER LEUE/LONELY PLANET IMAGES ©

PETER WIDMANN/PHOTOLIBRARY

Valldemossa

16 In any poll of the prettiest villages in the Balearics, Valldemossa (p87) is sure to make the shortlist. Draped like a skirt down the eastern foothills of the Serra de Tramuntana, Valldemossa has the usual cobblestone lanes and a pretty church. But the village is given added cachet by having its very own saint and a former royal monastery which once housed Frédéric Chopin and George Sand; apart from giving Valldemossa's residents something to gossip about in perpetuity, their stay bequeathed to the town one of Mallorca's most uplifting festivals.

PEP ROIG/ALAMY

Platja des Coll Baix

17 Isolated coves remote from roads and resorts are something of a secret Mallorcan speciality, but few can rival the Platja des Coll Baix (p117). Accessible only on foot or by sea, this hidden beach on the uninhabited eastern side of Cap des Pinar is a small slice of paradise. There's no problem finding space to spread your towel and the soundtrack is an increasingly rare one these days in the Mediterranean – water lapping against the shore, the trill of birdsong and ringing silence.

need to know

Currency

» Euro (€)

Languages

» Spanish, Catalan and Mallorquin

When to Go

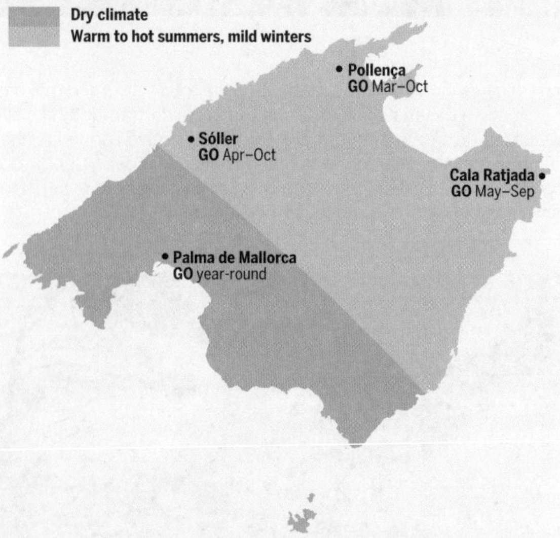

High Season

(Jun–Aug)

» Expect clear skies and warm temperatures.

» Accommodation is often booked months in advance in coastal areas.

» Accommodation prices are high but there are often good deals online.

Shoulder

(Easter–May, Sep & Oct)

» Most hotels and restaurants open by Easter and stay open until October; some resorts open in May.

» Cool evening temperatures in April and October.

» Grape harvest falls in late September.

Low Season

(Nov–Easter)

» Many hotels and restaurants close, either for one month or the entire winter; some may reopen briefly for Christmas/New Year.

» Cooler-than-expected night-time temperatures and cool-to-mild days.

Your Daily Budget

Budget less than

€100

» Doubles in *hostales*: €45–€60

» Cheaper stays possible at all-inclusive resorts

» Breakfast in hotel, three-course *menú del día* lunch

» Travel by public transport

Midrange

€100–€200

» Double room in midrange hotel (including some boutique hotels): €60–€170

» Most meals at decent local restaurants

» Car rental: from €30 per day

Top end over

€200

» Double room in top-end hotel: €170 and up

» Lunch and dinner in decent local restaurant

» Travel by rental car

Money
» ATMs are widely available. Credit cards are accepted in most hotels, restaurants and shops.

Visas
» Generally not required for stays of up to 90 days (or not at all for members of EU or Schengen countries). Some nationalities will need a Schengen visa.

Mobile Phones
» Local SIM cards are widely available and can be used in European and Australian mobile phones. Other phones may need to be set to roaming.

Driving
» Drive on the right; steering wheel is on the left side of the car.

Websites

» **Consell de Mallorca** (www.infomallorca.net) Excellent website from the island's regional tourist authorities.

» **LonelyPlanet.com** (www.lonelyplanet.com/mallorca) Destination information, hotel bookings, traveller forums and more.

» **Top Fincas** (www.topfincas.com) Directory and booking service for Mallorca's rural properties.

» **ABC Mallorca** (www.abc-mallorca.com) Lifestyle portal for both residents and tourists.

» **Mallorca Web** (www.mallorcaweb.com) Articles, upcoming events and listings.

Exchange Rates

Australia	A$1	€0.74
Canada	C$1	€0.71
Japan	¥100	€0.86
New Zealand	NZ$1	€0.57
UK	UK£1	€1.12
USA	US$1	€0.70

For current exchange rates see www.xe.com.

Important Numbers

There are no area codes in Spain.

International access code	☎0
Spain country code	☎34
International directory inquiries	☎11825
Emergency	☎112
Policía Nacional	☎91

Arriving in Mallorca

» **Son Sant Joan Airport, Palma**

Bus – Bus 1 runs every 15 minutes from the airport to Plaça d'Espanya in central Palma (€2, 15 to 30 minutes); buy tickets from the driver

Taxi – €16 to €21, 15 minutes

» **Ferry Port, Palma**

Bus – Bus 1 (the airport bus) runs every 15 minutes from the ferry port (Estació Marítima) to Plaça d'Espanya (€1.50, 10 to 15 minutes)

Taxi – €7 to €10 (10 minutes)

Adiós or Adéu?

As in some other Spanish regions, language is a sensitive topic on Mallorca. In their dealings with each other, Mallorquins wear their language as a badge of honour and an expression of cultural independence, conducting most conversations, whether for business or pleasure, in the local language. Most bookshops are also dominated by titles in Catalan. All of that said, Spanish is universally spoken and we're yet to meet a Mallorquin working in the tourist industry (or elsewhere) who expects visitors to the island to speak the Mallorquin dialect of Catalan. In most areas, a little bit of Spanish will get you a long way, and English and/or German are widely spoken. Of course, locals will certainly appreciate it if you greet them with a hearty *bon dia* (good day) and bid them on their way with *adéu* (goodbye).

if you like...

Hidden Coves

Mallorca's rocky coastline is riven with inlets lapped by waters of an indescribable blue (somewhere between turquoise and sapphire). Known as *cales*, they're among the Mediterranean's prettiest coves and are protected by the fact that many can only be reached on foot.

Cala Magraner Antidote to eastern Mallorca's resorts (p146)

Platja des Coll Baix Pebbles and sand on remote Cap des Pinar (p117)

Cala Figuera Idyllic and way down below the Cap des Formentor road (p111)

Cala Matzoc Beautiful beach among many near Cala Ratjada (p144)

Platja de Ses Roquetes Virgin beach near Cap de Ses Salines (p158)

Cala Llombards Encircled by cliffs in Mallorca's south (p157)

Cala Carbó Quietest of Cala Sant Vicenç's four lovely coves (p109)

Cala Sa Nau Almost-deserted east-coast cove (p147)

Scenic Drives

Mallorca is a great place to drive. Yes, you'll find yourself having to pull over time and again to let other vehicles pass as the tarmac narrows to single lane, but the rewards are quite simply extraordinary. The roads that shadow the western and northern coasts rank among the Mediterranean's most breathtaking.

Andratx to Monestir de Lluc Mallorca's drive among drives, tracing the Serra de Tramuntana high above the Mediterranean (p97)

Sa Calobra Bucks and weaves down, down to this once-isolated cove (p101)

Cap de Formentor Eighteen kilometres of sheer and splendid beauty (p112)

Artà to Ermita de Betlem A 9km route incorporating pine forests, fine views and a soulful hermitage (p139)

Port de Valldemossa A short but seemingly impossible steep descent, then back up again (p90)

Sóller to Alaró Through mountainous foothills and quiet rural hamlets (p99)

Pretty Towns & Villages

Stone-built Mallorcan villages that seem to have grown out of the landscape itself are an island speciality, with the most beautiful to be found on the slopes of the Serra de Tramuntana or just inland from the northern coast.

Valldemossa Wonderfully preserved village rich in history (p87)

Orient Near-perfect stone *pueblo* in a quiet valley between Sóller and Alaró (p99)

Deià Mallorca's most famous village, perched against a mountainous backdrop (p90)

Fornalutx Bijoux light-stone village close to Sóller (p98)

Biniaraix Fornalutx's neighbour and alter ego, and largely unchanged in decades (p98)

Binibona On the road from nowhere to nowhere with fine rural retreats (p127)

Sóller Gorgeous architecture and spectacular Serra de Tramuntana backdrop (p92)

Pollença An ancient core that rises to one of Mallorca's most famous places of pilgrimage (p106)

Alcúdia Enclosed within medieval walls with quiet streets and old mansions (p112)

HOLGER LEUE/LONELY PLANET IMAGES ©

» Interior at Jardins d'Alfàbia (p99)

Coastal Walks

Mallorca's deeply fissured and textured coastline is superb from any perspective, but unless you're travelling by boat the only way to explore much of it is on foot. Numerous day hikes quickly leave behind the madding crowds, while the multiday traverse of western Mallorca's Serra de Tramuntana is one of *the* great hikes in southern Europe.

Ruta de Pedra en Sec From one end of Mallorca to another, through the island's best scenery (p83)

Cap de Ses Salines to Colònia de Sant Jordi Stunning reminder that not all of southern Mallorca has disappeared under concrete (p158)

Parc Natural de la Península de Llevant Trails connect beaches and pine valleys far from the nearest road (p138)

Cap de Formentor The jaw-dropping northern finale of the Serra de Tramuntana (p112)

Finca Can Roig to Cala Magraner Trails lead past four of eastern Mallorca's prettiest and least-visited coves (p148)

Art Galleries

Mallorca's artistic heritage includes the best that 20th-century Spanish art has to offer. Pablo Picasso and Joan Miró both had deep attachments to the island, while Catalan master Salvador Dalí can seem like an adopted Mallorquin son. These big names provide a great starting point for your artistic wanderings.

Es Baluard Mallorquin landscape painters and big names in cleverly adapted Palma ramparts (p54)

Palau March Dalí, Eduardo Chillida, Henry Moore, Auguste Rodin in Old Palma (p48)

Museu Fundación Juan March Picasso, Miró, Dalí, Juan Gris and Mallorquin native Miquel Barceló (p52)

Fundació Pilar i Joan Miró Miró's former home filled with his works and spirit (p75)

Ca'n Prunera – Museu Modernista Modernista architecture and a roll-call of painting greats (p92)

Catedral Palma's cathedral has extraordinary contributions by Gaudí and Miquel Barceló (p42)

Sa Torre Cega Cala Ratjada mansion with 70 eminent sculptures (p140)

Grand Mallorcan Estates

After the 13th-century Christian Reconquest of the island, Mallorca's newly powerful nobility were rewarded for their loyalty with sprawling country estates crowned by elegant and large-scale manor houses. Known collectively as *possessions*, many were abandoned for centuries only to be restored in recent decades. Others are now high-end hotels.

La Granja Glorious gardens and interiors presented like a theme park to Mallorcan history (p86)

Els Calderers Tucked away on quiet country back roads in Mallorca's interior, it's a classic of the genre (p130)

Jardins d'Alfàbia Intriguing Christian-Moorish hybrid in the Serra de Tramuntana foothills (p99)

Raixa Recently restored to its former glory with gardens and cloisters the highlight (p99)

Miramar Coastal mansion with views to bid you silent (p88)

Son Marroig A similar deal with vertiginous foot access to this stirring stretch of coast (p88)

If you like...learning about Mallorca's marine environment before you set off snorkelling or diving, visit the outstanding Palma Aquarium (p73) or the Centro de Visitantes Ses Salines (p153) in Colònia de Sant Jordi.

Unspoiled Nature

Mallorca's pristine and extraordinarily beautiful natural areas more than cancel out the infamy attached to some of the island's concrete-jungle tourist resorts. Most of these areas are protected, either by government fiat or thanks to the indignation of local residents determined not to spoil the island's remaining semiwilderness.

Parc Nacional Marítim-Terrestre de L'Arxipèlag de Cabrera Mallorca's only national park, the offshore Illa de Cabrera is an island paradise (p155)

Cap de Formentor Stunning combination of mountains, forests and coast (p112)

Parc Natural de la Península de Llevant Rugged peninsula entered by just one road and criss-crossed by trails (p138)

Parc Natural de Mondragó Another mercifully protected area in southeastern Mallorca (p159)

Parc Natural de S'Albufera Prime birdwatching country, clocking numerous species (p117)

Platja des Trenc Mallorca's longest and least-developed beach in the least likely corner of the island (p155)

Ruins & Castles

The Romans and Muslims may be the best-known occupiers of ancient Mallorca, and both civilisations left small but fascinating signposts to their presence here. But before either of these were the little-understood Talayotic cultures, named after the watchtowers that watch over the rubble of these long-vanished cultures.

Ses Païsses Large and well-preserved Talayotic site in the shade (p137)

Capocorb Vell Similarly intact Talayotic site with five watchtowers (p152)

Pol·lentia Sprawling Roman ruins with an eye-catching theatre amid the trees (p112)

Castell de Capdepera Arguably the finest castle complex on the island (p139)

Torre des Verger Vertigo-inducing 16th-century tower dizzyingly high above the coast (p85)

Castell d'Alaró Evocatively ruined castle of 10th-century, Muslim origin (p100)

Castell de Santueri Scene of the Muslims' last stand (p133)

Necròpolis de Son Real Hundreds of tombs in the shape of minitowers (p118)

Underground Caves

Hidden beneath the earth, Mallorca's cave complexes are vast underground palaces. Stalactites and stalagmites, sculpted by the waters seeping through the earth's crust, have here taken on the strangest forms, prompting gasps of disbelief from all who visit. Most of the caves are along the coast and are visited on guided tours – this is not hard-core spelunking, but a gentle walk through the creatively lit depths, sometimes with a classical-music concert at the end.

Coves del Drac The undoubted king of Mallorcan caves (p145)

Coves d'Artà Glorious coastal setting and features such as the 'Queen of Columns' and 'Chamber of Hell' (p143)

Coves de Campanet Rare inland cave with fewer crowds and fine formations (p127)

Coves dels Hams Beautiful if overpriced neighbour to Coves del Drac (p145)

Cova des Pas de Vallgornera The Balearics' longest cave at over 6.5km; a more DIY experience (p152)

month by month

Top Events

1 **Sa Fira**, May

2 **Es Firó**, May

3 **Nit de Sant Joan**, June

4 **Festes de la Patrona**, August

5 **Festes de la Verema**, September

January

The depths of winter are agreeably mild across most of Mallorca, although you'll often struggle to find hotels and restaurants that open at this time.

Bless the Animals

The Festes de Sant Antoni Abat (16 and 17 January) are celebrated with concerts, prancing demons, huge pyres and fireworks, and parading farm animals get a blessing. It's celebrated with particular gusto in Sa Pobla and Artà.

February

In February, Mallorca is lovely, quiet and almost completely asleep. Thankfully, the high spirits of Carnaval mark the island's emergence from hibernation, although many places are still closed.

Carnaval

Across Mallorca, the high point of February (sometimes March) is Carnaval. In Palma a children's procession, Sa Rueta, is followed by the grown-ups' version, Sa Rua, which is the biggest Carnaval procession on the island.

March

March is one of our favourite months in Mallorca with solemn Easter celebrations, wildflowers in bloom and fantastic birdwatching in the Parc Natural de S'Albufera.

Holy Week

Follow the Semana Santa (Easter Week) processions around the island. Begin in Palma on Holy Thursday evening, then head to Pollença for its moving Good Friday Davallament (bringing down; p107). On Easter Sunday, head to Montuïri's S'Encuentro (p131).

April

Mallorcan hotels and restaurants truly dust off the cobwebs, and the resorts start to fill. There's still a chill in the air in the evenings.

May

If it hasn't opened by May, then it's probably closed for good. Coastal Mallorca has a real spring in its step as resorts come to life.

Sineu's Ancient Market

Since 1318, Sineu has been the setting for Sa Fira (p128), the island's largest livestock and produce market, held on May's first Sunday. The secret to its longevity lies in authenticity, in the confirmation that some traditions never change.

Pirate Attack

On the second weekend of May, Sóller stages Es Firó, during which the town's heroic defenders, led by the so-called Valiant Women, fight off Muslim pirates as in 1561, doing so amid much merriment.

Corpus Christi

Corpus Christi (on the Thursday of the ninth week after Easter) is a major celebration in Palma. The weeks leading up to it are marked by concerts in the city's baroque courtyards.

June

Mallorca moves into top gear in June. Patron saints' festivals, where religious tradition mixes with good old-fashioned pagan partying, are the excuse for many a knees-up.

Fiery Fiestas

The feast day of St John (24 June) is preceded the night before by fiery partying on the Nit de Sant Joan (p59). In Palma, there's *correfoc* (fire running), concerts and partying on the beaches until dawn.

July

In July there's little to interrupt the long lazy days on the beach and long liquid nights. But midmonth there's one festival close to coastal Mallorca's heart.

Of Sailors & Fisherfolk

Before tourism there were fishing fleets and before yacht marinas there were sailors of a very different kind. On 16 July, many coastal towns stage processions for the Festa de la Verge del Carme, the patron saint of fishers and sailors.

Dance with the Devil

On 25 July, the inland town of Algaida sees *cossiers* do traditional dances in the streets of Algaida for the Festa de Sant Jaume. Six men and one woman dance alongside a demon, who ultimately comes unstuck.

August

A full calendar of festivals provides a diversion from beaches or wineries. Baking summer temperatures ensure you won't want to stray too far from cooling waters.

Pirates of the Mediterranean

One of the most colourful festivals, culminating in a staged battle between townsfolk and invading Moorish pirates, takes place in Pollença during the weeklong Festes de la Patrona (p107).

Classical Chopin

Valldemossa's one-time resident, composer Frédéric Chopin, and his stately one-time residence, the Real Cartuja de Valldemossa, come together for high-quality classical concerts devoted mostly to Chopin throughout August during the Festival Chopin (p88).

Mallorca Jazz

Sa Pobla is an unlikely setting for one of the Mediterranean's most celebrated jazz festivals. Of course you won't think so if your visit coincides with the Mallorca Jazz Festival (p129) and some of the genre's big names.

September

September remains a busy month, but it's like the joyous last drink before the hangover. Autumn is good for migrating birds in the Parc Natural de S'Albufera.

Wine & Dine

Mallorca's wine centres celebrate the grape harvest with the Festes de la Verema (aka Festa d'es Vermar; p124). Binissalem's celebrations are the best known and grandest, stretching over the last nine days of September.

October

Last drinks! People bid tearful farewells to newfound friends at resorts across the island. For those left behind, it's time for a well-earned rest.

November

As the weather turns cold, much of the island breathes a long sigh of relief, and many restaurants and hotels close. A quiet month in all.

December

The few festivals at this time are overwhelmingly geared towards local residents. Nights (and even some days) can be colder than you might expect.

itineraries

Whether you've got six days or 60, these itineraries provide a starting point for the trip of a lifetime. Want more inspiration? Head online to lonelyplanet.com/thorntree to chat with other travellers.

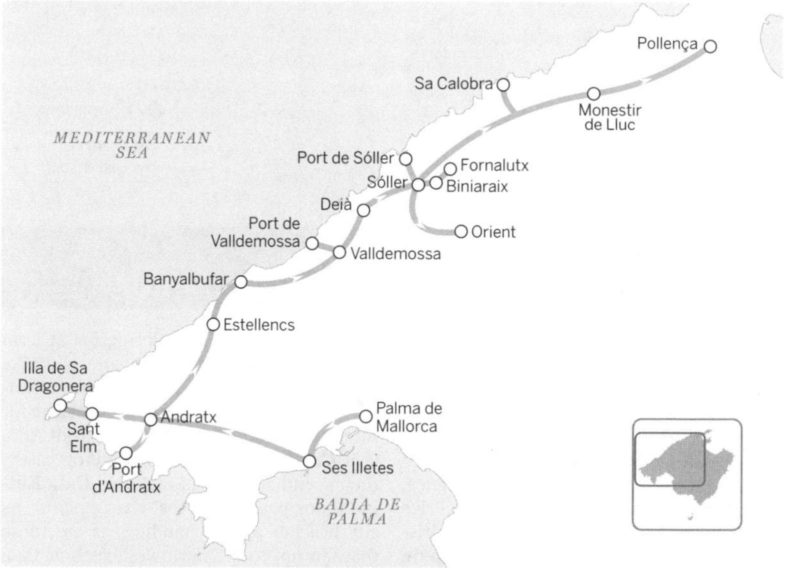

One Week

The West Coast

Begin with a couple of nights in **Palma**, the island's lively and architecturally distinguished capital, before sampling the resorts of the southwest in three of our favourites: **Ses Illetes**, **Port d'Andratx** and **Sant Elm**; from the latter, make time for a boat-and-snorkelling excursion to the offshore **Illa de Sa Dragonera**. One of the Mediterranean's most beautiful drives begins in **Andratx**, and as the road climbs high above the coast, pause in the lovely villages of **Estellencs** and **Banyalbufar**, before continuing on to **Valldemossa**, which rewards those who stay overnight after the day-tripping coachloads have departed. Drop down off the precipice to **Port de Valldemossa**, before returning to the main road and heading north towards **Deià**, another gorgeous village rich in history; don't miss Cala de Deià while you're here. Next stop is **Sóller**, a wonderful stop in its own right or a fine base for detours inland to charming **Orient**, **Fornalutx** or **Biniaraix**, or a tram trip down to the coast at **Port de Sóller**. As the Ma10 drifts inland, make the vertiginous side road to **Sa Calobra** en route to the **Monestir de Lluc** before continuing on to lovely **Pollença**.

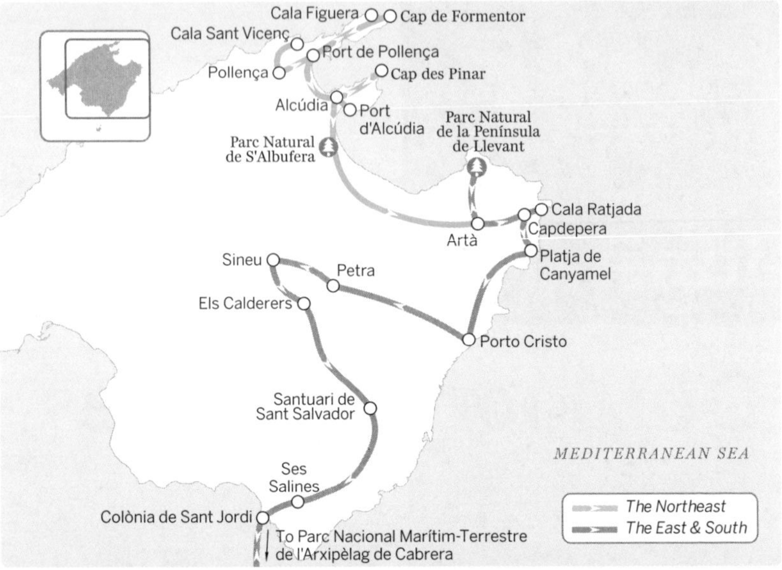

One Week

The Northeast

Pollença is one of the loveliest towns on the island: allow at least two nights and a day to wander its old streets and climb the 365 steps to Calvari; try to be here on Sunday for a lively market day, but stay overnight to see both sides of Pollença life. From Pollença, drive to **Cala Sant Vicenç** for a meal of rice overlooking the turquoise coves before driving the glorious road to the tip of **Cap de Formentor** and back again; allow time to hike down off the road to **Cala Figuera**. If watersports are your thing, spend a night or two in **Port de Pollença** or **Port d'Alcúdia**. Otherwise, make for **Alcúdia** and sleep within the town's medieval walls. **Cap des Pinar** has numerous attractions, among them lunch at the Restaurante Mirador de La Victòria or a hike down to the beach at Platja des Coll Baix. As you continue east, engage in a spot of birdwatching in the wetlands of **Parc Natural de S'Albufera**, then make for **Artà**, like Pollença a lovely medium-sized medieval town with a slew of fine restaurants.

10 Days

The East & South

Artà is worth exploring for at least half a day, and make sure you take the road north into the **Parc Natural de la Península de Llevant** for some splendid views. Moving on from Artà, visit **Capdepera** and its fine hilltop castle, then spend a couple of nights in **Cala Ratjada**, our pick of the east-coast resorts; its city beaches are outstanding, as are those that fan out to the northwest, such as Cala Mesquida and Cala Matzoc. From Cala Ratjada, don't miss the Coves d'Artà, Torre de Canyamel or a meal at Porxada de Sa Torre; all are in or around **Platja de Canyamel**. Away to the south, enjoy the Coves del Drac in **Porto Cristo**, then venture inland to the lovely inland towns of **Petra** and **Sineu**, stopping off at wineries along the way. On the journey back to the coast, stop off in **Els Calderers**, climb the heights of the **Santuari de Sant Salvador**, then head for artsy **Ses Salines**, detouring via pretty beaches such as Cala Mondragó and Cala Llombards for a quick swim. Finally, continue on to **Colònia de Sant Jordi**, the ideal base for visiting nearby Platja des Trenc and the must-see **Parc Nacional Marítim-Terrestre de l'Arxipèlag de Cabrera**.

Outdoor Activities

Best Boat Excursion
Port d'Alcúdia to Cala Sant Vicenç (May–Sep)

Best Canyoning
Gorg Blau-Sa Fosca & Monument Nacional Torrent de Pareis (May–Oct)

Best Caving
Cova des Pas de Vallgornera (May–Oct)

Best Cycling Route
Cap de Formentor (Apr, May, Sep & Oct)

Best Day Hike
Parc Natural de la Península de Llevant (Apr, May & Sep)

Best Multiday Hike
Ruta de Pedra en Sec (Apr, May & Sep)

Best Horse Riding
Cala Ratjada to Cala Mesquida (Apr–Oct)

Best Sailing
Port d'Andratx to Port d'Alcúdia (May–Sep)

Best Scuba Diving
Badia de Pollença (Apr–Oct)

Best Snorkelling
Parc Nacional Marítim-Terrestre de l'Arxipèlag de Cabrera (May–Sep)

Mallorca is all about the great outdoors. Its mild climate and undoubted natural beauty provide the perfect conditions for exploring the island under your own steam. A favourite walking destination for a generation, Mallorca is now garnering fame as a cycling hot spot and from Easter until autumn the hilly country roads are filled with pelotons of avid cyclists, both amateur and professional alike. With 550km of coastline, Mallorca makes it easy to enjoy the Mediterranean and you'll find ample opportunities to go sailing, kite surfing, sea kayaking and windsurfing. Or head inland for more adventurous pursuits such as caving or canyoning.

Planning Your Trip

When to Go

Mallorca's outdoor activities are, in theory, possible year-round thanks to the island's relatively mild winters. That said, most organised activities that depend on local operators will only be doable roughly from Easter to October. For the rest of the year, most guides and operators head off for sunnier climes to ply their trade elsewhere.

The ideal conditions for most activities, particularly hiking and cycling, is in spring and autumn. Daytime temperatures in summer can be uncomfortably warm and the traffic on the roads can make cycling a stop-start affair. These drawbacks are partly compensated for by the long daylight hours.

What to Take

Most activities operators in Mallorca can provide you with all of the necessary equipment, while high-quality bicycles are available for rent from cycle shops across the island. Whether you bring your own bicycle is a question of cost and convenience, in which you'll need to balance the costs of getting your bicycle to Mallorca and back with the costs of rental, while the comfort of riding your own bike tips the balance for most.

Although professional-standard equipment is available for purchase on Mallorca, anyone planning on hiking should bring their own boots – the trails of the Serra de Tramuntana are not the place to be breaking in new footwear.

Activities

Balloon Rides

Operators offer the chance to get a bird's-eye view of the island in all its glory:

» **Illes Balears Ballooning** (☎607 647 647; www.ibballooning.net) Balloons for charter.

» **Mallorca Balloons** (☎971 596 969; www.mallorcaballoons.com; 30/60min ride adult €140/160, child €60/90; ⏲Mar-Oct) Early morning flights from a launch site east of Manacor.

Boat Excursions

Glass-bottomed boats drift up and down the eastern coast and can be a fun way to enjoy the water without having the responsibility of sailing your own boat. Most are day trips only and rarely last longer than half a day. Most operate only from Easter or May to October. All sell return tickets, but on some east-coast routes you can travel one way.

Boat Excursion Routes

There's almost nowhere you can't go by boat along the eastern coast, but if we had to choose just three routes, they would be these:

» **Transportes Marítimos Brisa** (p114) Port d'Alcúdia to Cala Sant Vicenç and back, via Cap de Formentor.

» **Barcos Azules** (p96) Port de Sóller to Sa Calobra.

» **Excursions a Cabrera** (p155) Round-trip tours by speedboat or slower boats from Colònia de Sant Jordi to the Parc Nacional Marítim-Terrestre de l'Arxipèlag de Cabrera.

Boat Excursion Resources

The Consell de Mallorca publishes the useful brochure *Excursions en Barca* (Boat Excursions), which should be available from the **Consell de Mallorca tourist office** (p72) in Palma, or its branch office at Palma's airport. The pamphlet lists 43 different boat trips around the island, with contact details for operators.

Canyoning

Perhaps the ultimate Mallorcan adrenaline rush, canyoning – jumping into ravines or simply trudging down gorges and gullies – can be dangerous if you're not well prepared (going with a guide is essential), but it can also be exhilarating.

Canyoning Routes

The best places for canyoning are concentrated in the central Serra de Tramuntana between Valldemossa and Sa Calobra. It's here that you'll find two of our favourite sites:

» **Gorg Blau-Sa Fosca** Tough, 2.5km route with freezing waters and stretches of total darkness.

» **Monument Nacional Torrent de Pareis**

Canyoning Guides

Mallorca has some extremely professional canyoning companies, among them:

» **Escull Aventura** (☎691 230 291; www.escullaventura.com)

» **Mallorca Canyoning** (p100)

» **Món d'Aventura** (p100)

» **Rocksport Mallorca** (☎629 948 404; www.rocksportmallorca.com) British-run operator with courses or guides in caving, canyoning or rock-climbing from its base in Port de Pollença.

» **Tramuntana Tours** (p96) In Port de Sóller and Sóller.

Caving

Mallorca's pocked limestone terrain means caving conditions are fantastic. That said, most of Mallorca's caves are fairly sedate affairs with staircases, lighting, guides with torches and even the occasional classical-music concert. While this approach has the advantage of the island's stunning underground cave complexes accessible to just about anyone, serious cavers will find it all rather tame.

There are numerous cave complexes that burrow into the cliffs of the southern and eastern coasts, but the pick is undoubtedly the **Cova des Pas de Vallgornera** (p152), which at 6345m is the longest cave in the Balearics and it'll probably be yours to explore without the crowds. **Jose Antonio Encinas** (☎609 372 888) is an expert local guide. There are also countless more explorable caves on the island with more being discovered and catalogued each year.

Cycling

Nearly half of Mallorca's 1250km of roads have been 'adapted' for cycling, with measures ranging from simple signposts to separate bike lanes (such as the excellent lanes along Palma's waterfront). The better roads are just one more draw for cyclists, who descend in droves to sample Mallorca's hilly terrain and peaceful countryside, especially from March to May and late September to November, when the weather is refreshingly cool.

Mountain bikers will find plenty of trails here as well, ranging from flat dirt tracks to rough-and-tumble single-track climbs. Be sure to get a good highway or trekking map before you set out on any cycling expedition.

Bike-rental agencies abound across the island and maintenance standards are generally high. We've listed many such places throughout the book, but check local tourist offices for route information and details about the nearest bike-rental agency. Prices can vary between €8 per day for a basic touring bike and €30 for a high-end mountain or racing bike. Kids bikes and kiddie seats are also widely available.

Cycling Routes

There is no 'best' area for biking; trails cover the island like a web and, depending on your skills and interests, anywhere can be the start of a fabulous ride. That said, here are some of our favourites:

» **Ecovies** (Eco Trails; p109) Bicycle trails between Pollença and Artà (Northern Mallorca)

» **Palma to Capocorb Vell** (Palma & Southern Mallorca)

» **Andratx to Monestir de Lluc** (Western Mallorca)

» **Parc Natural de la Península de Llevant** (Eastern Mallorca)

» **Cap de Formentor** (Northern Mallorca)

» **Port d'Alcúdia & Cap des Pinar** (Northern Mallorca)

Cycling Resources

The **Federació de Ciclisme de les Illes Balears** (Cycling Federation of the Balearic Islands; ☎971 757 628; www.webfcib.es) can provide contact information for local cycling clubs. A growing number of hotels cater specifically to cyclists, with garages and energy-packed menus.

Golf

Palma is a popular golfing destination, which is not surprising given the mix of warm Mediterranean climate and fine natural setting. At last count there were around 20 golf courses scattered around the island. Green fees for 18 holes start from €30 and can go as high as €130, although the average is €40 to €75. Cart rental costs €30 to €45. Prices dip in summer when it's often simply too hot to have fun, and can soar in spring and autumn.

Golfing Resources

Useful resources on golfing in Mallorca:

» **Mallorca Golf** Annual publication available from some tourist offices and golf courses with brief coverage of all 20 courses.

» The **Consell de Mallorca** tourist authority publishes a similar brochure entitled *Mallorca Golf* with much the same information. Its website (www.infomallorca.net) also has links to each course's website; click on 'Tourist Information', then 'Themes', then 'Sports', then 'Golf'.

» **Federació Balear de Golf** (Balearic Golf Federation; ☎971 722 753; www.fbgolf.com) General golfing info.

Hiking

From the bald and dramatic limestone peaks in the west to the rocky coastal trails of the east, trekkers have their pick of numerous splendid walks on Mallorca. The Consell de Mallorca has become serious about marking and maintaining the island's trails, many of which have been used for centuries.

Day Hikes

Just about every tourist office in even Mallorca's smallest villages can dispense a brochure or advice on local day hikes in the area. We've covered our favourites at length, but these are just the beginning:

» **Cap de Formentor** (Northern Mallorca)

» **Cap de Ses Salines to Colònia de Sant Jordi** (Southern Mallorca)

» **Finca Can Roig to Cala Magraner** (Eastern Mallorca)

» **Parc Natural de la Península de Llevant** (Northern Mallorca)

Multiday Hikes

There are two main long-distance hiking trails in Mallorca. As in the rest of Spain, the two GR (long-distance) trails are signposted in red and white.

» Keen hikers can tackle the **Ruta de Pedra en Sec** (Route of Dry Stone, GR 221), which is a four- to seven-day walk running from Port d'Andratx to Pollença, crossing the Serra de Tramuntana. At a few points along the GR 221 there are *refugis de muntanya* (rustic mountain huts) where trekkers can stay the night.

» Signposting is currently under way on the **Ruta Artà-Lluc** (GR 222), which will eventually link the two towns, although progress on this route is slow.

Hiking Maps & Guides

The best hiking maps are the 1:25,000 *Tramuntana Central*, *Tramuntana Norte* and *Tramuntana Sur* maps by Editorial Alpina. While these can be picked up at many bookshops around the island, your best bet is to head to the source at **La Casa del Mapa** (p70) in Palma.

If you need more than a good map, there are some reputable guides on the island:

» **Rich Strutt** (☎609 700 826; www.mallorcanwalkingtours.puertopollensa.com) An English-speaking guide based in Port de Pollença with (at last count) 63 day hikes or longer treks to choose from for groups of four or more.

» **Tramuntana Tours** (p94) Respected activities operator based in Sóller and Port de Sóller; its focus is on the Serra de Tramuntana.

Other Hiking Resources

The Consell de Mallorca publishes two excellent brochures, both of which should be available from the **Consell de Mallorca tourist office** (p72) in Palma, or its branch office at Palma's airport. In both cases, the brochures' maps are orientative in scope and you'll need to supplement them with detailed hiking maps:

» **Rutes per Mallorca (Mallorca Itineraries)** Six treks ranging from 33.2km to 113.5km.

» **Caminar per Mallorca (Walking in Mallorca)** Twelve day hikes from 4.5km to 14km.

Horse Riding

With its extensive network of rugged trails making their way over the hilly countryside and alongside the Mediterranean, Mallorca is a magnet for equestrians. Many towns and resorts also have stables where you can sign up for a class (€10 to €20) or join a group for an excursion (about €15 for the first hour, with two-/five-hour rides generally costing around €25/60 per person. Longer trips are also possible. Some stables also offer pony rides for small children.

And for something a little different, you could always try ostrich riding at **Artestruz Mallorca** (p156)...

Horse-riding Routes

Cala Ratjada, Colònia de Sant Jordi and Pollença are all popular riding areas; ask at local tourist offices for the nearest stables. Cala Ratjada in particular allows you to ride along a largely undeveloped coast towards Cala Mesquida. Cala Ratjada's two main stables are German-run:

» **Eddi's Reitstall** (p141)

» **Rancho Bonanza** (p141)

Horse-riding Resources

Get more information from the **Federació Hipica de les Illes Baleares** (Equestrian Federation of the Balearic Islands; ☎971 154 225; www.fhbalear.com, in Spanish; Carrer de Uruguay, Palma de Mallorca). Its website lists 14 stables in Mallorca under 'Clubes Illes Balears'.

Paragliding

As you approach Port d'Alcúdia you'll often see paragliders drifting high on the thermals. If you're keen to join them, try **Parapente Alfabia** (p115). In addition to tandem flights for beginners, there are also beginners' and intermediate courses year-round.

Sailing

Among the 35 marinas that ring Mallorca's coast, many offer yacht charters, sailboat rentals and sailing courses. There are large sailing schools in Palma, Port de Pollença and other resorts; expect a nine-hour course to cost €120 and up; **Voyage** (p58) in Palma is the most professional outfit.

MALLORCA'S PARKS

The creation of protected wildlife areas has helped stabilise Mallorca's wildlife and make it accessible to visitors. Now a full 40% of the island falls under some form of official environmental protection status.

PARK	FEATURES	ACTIVITIES	WHEN TO VISIT
Parc Nacional Marítim-Terrestre de l'Arxipèlag de Cabrera	Archipelago of 19 islands and islets; home to 130 bird species and diverse marine life	Hiking, scuba diving, snorkelling and swimming	Easter to October
Parc Natural de S'Albufera	Vital wetland sheltering 400 plants and 230 species of birds, many of them on migration paths between Europe and Africa	Birdwatching (including 80% of the birds recorded on the Balearic Islands), cycling	Spring and autumn
Parc Natural de Mondragó	Rolling dunes, juniper groves, vibrant wetlands and unspoilt beaches close to east-coast resorts	Strolling through forests and near wetlands, picnicking on unspoiled beaches	May–Sep
Parc Natural de la Península de Llevant	Flora and fauna	Walking, birdwatching	May–Sep
Parc Natural de Sa Dragonera	Two small islets and the 4km-long Dragonera island, with its harrowing cliffs, pristine coves and countless caves; endangered gull population	Snorkelling and scuba diving	May–Sep

One place that rents yachts is **Llaüts** (p82) in Port d'Andratx; prices start at €170 per day.

Sailing Routes

If you charter or bring your own yacht, your options for sailing are unlimited. Popular routes:

» **Palma to Illa de Cabrera** To enter the national park, you'll need prior permission.

» **Port d'Andratx to Port de Sóller** The best of the Serra de Tramuntana coast.

» **Cala Sant Vicenç to Port d'Alcúdia** Round the inspiring Cap de Formentor.

Sailing Resources

Sailing is a serious busines in Mallorca and there are plenty of organisations to promote the sport and provide information or to ensure that sailors leave the environment as they found it.

» **Harbours & Marinas Guide** Free guide to moorings and marinas published annually by Tallers de Molí; available from tourist offices or marinas.

» **Conselleria de Medi Ambient** (☎971 176 800; www.caib.es; Avinguda de Gabriel Alomar i Villalonga 33, Palma de Mallorca) Contact this organisation for guidelines for anchoring your yacht in open water to protect the sea floor.

» **Federación Balear de Vela** (Balearic Sailing Federation; ☎971 402 412; www.federacionbalearvela. org, in Spanish) Another good source of information.

Scuba Diving & Snorkelling

Mallorca is one of the premier diving and snorkelling destinations in southern Europe, the combination of superclear waters and professional dive centres making this an excellent place for a leisure dive or even the open-water PADI diving-accreditation course.

First dives start from €27, but the per-dive rate falls markedly the more dives you take. Diving equipment and insurance are sometimes, but not usually, included in the quoted prices, so always ask. Snorkelling starts from €15 per hour.

We've listed numerous dive centres throughout this guidebook, but one useful resource is www.mallorcadiving.com, which covers 10 centres around the island.

Scuba-diving & Snorkelling Sites

The options around the Mallorcan coast are close to endless, from Port d'Andratx in the southwest to Cala Ratjada in the northeast. Generally, the diving is at its best on the northern and western coasts. Recommended:

» **Badia de Pollença** Experienced divers rank this the island's best diving, with caves and decent marine life along the southern wall of the Cap de Formentor peninsula or the southern end of the Cap des Pinar.

» **Parc Nacional Marítim-Terrestre de l'Arxipèlag de Cabrera** A national park, so special permission required for scuba diving, but great snorkelling.

» **Illa de Sa Dragonera** The best underwater views off the island's southwest.

Sea Kayaking

The craggy coast and generally calm conditions of Mallorca make it well suited to sea kayaking, a sport that's beginning to attract a loyal following.

Sea-kayaking Routes

Guide and rental companies are clustered around Alcúdia and Port de Pollença.

» **Escola d'Esports Nàutics Port de Sóller** (p96) Port de Sóller

» **Kayak Mallorca** (p110) Port de Pollença

» **Piraguas Mix** (p154) Colònia de Sant Jordi

» **Skualo Adventure Sports Centre** (p147) Portocolom

» **Skualo Adventure Sports & Dive Centre** (p146) Porto Cristo

» **Tramuntana Tours** (p96) Port de Sóller

» **Xplore Mallorca** (p160) Cala d'Or

Sea-kayaking Resources

For details on courses for kids and adults, as well as a list of nautical clubs with a kayak presence, check out the **Federación Balear de Piragüismo** (Balearic Federation of Canoeing & Kayaking; ☎971 792 019; www.fibp.org, in Spanish).

Windsurfing & Kite Surfing

While the relatively calm wind and waves of Mallorca don't make the island a natural hot spot for fans of windsurfing or kite surfing (aka kite boarding), there are a few places to ride the waves; Port de Pollença and Port d'Alcúdia are the main locations. Four-day beginners' windsurfing courses cost around €190/160 per adult/child, with hourly rental starting from €15.

» **Sail & Surf Pollença** (p110) Sailing and windsurfing courses and rental in Port de Pollença.

» **Wind & Friends** (p115) Windsurfing and kite surfing in Port d'Alcúdia.

Eat Like a Local

Best Celler

Mallorca's traditional *cellers* (former wine cellars) are atmospheric dining experiences, with numerous choices in Inca, Sineu and there's even one in Palma

Best Gourmet Temples

Of the island's Michelin-starred chefs, we particularly like the home kitchens of Marc Fosh – Simply Fosh (p61) and Tasca de Blanquerna (p60) in Palma – and Josef Sauerschell's Es Racó d'es Teix (p91) in Deià

Best Local Pastries

For *ensaïmades*, those feather-light whirls topped with a puff of icing sugar, our two favourite places are Ca'n Joan de S'Aigo (p61) and Horno San Antonio (p61)

Best Local Snack

Pa amb oli (literally 'bread with oil'): they don't do much else at S'Esponja Café (p62) in Palma

Best Traditional Mallorcan Cuisine

Porxada de Sa Torre (p144), Canyamel

Best Lobster Rice

Son Tomás (p85), Banyalbufar

Best Picnic Snack

Sobrassada

The Mallorcan kitchen is one of the most revered in Spain, famously making use of some of the freshest produce grown under the Mediterranean sun. Mallorquin cooking is a world away from the pizzerias that dominate so many resorts; the latter can be difficult to escape, but the rewards are wonderful.

Dependent on the land and the surrounding sea, Mallorcan cuisine at its best is a delicious reflection of the island's climate, terrain and history. In centuries past, a stream of invaders and conquerors crossed the island bringing with them new fruits and vegetables, spices and recipes, leaving a culinary legacy that lingers today. Arabian influences include apricots, pine nuts, capers, honey, almonds and spices; Catalans encouraged pork farming and winemaking.

Mallorcan cuisine has become more daring in recent years. Young chefs, as part of a trend seen throughout the Mediterranean, are bringing a revival to Balearic food. The combination of local ingredients, age-old recipes and international flair is the basis of oftentimes surprisingly original dishes.

When to Go: Food Seasons

Easter to October is undoubtedly the best time for a gastronomic visit to the island, not least because most restaurants are open and ready for business. Some close for a month, typically in December, January or parts thereof, while some shut for the entire period from November to Easter.

PRICE INDICATORS

Throughout this guidebook, the order of Eating listings is by author preference, and each place to eat is accompanied by one of the following symbols (the price relates to mains per person):

CATEGORY	PRICE
€ budget	<€20
€€ midrange	€20-50
€€€ top end	>€50

The island's grape harvest usually takes place in late September, and this is a fine time to be on the island. Numerous wine-producing villages and regions celebrate this time with a festival, the largest of which is the Festes de la Verema (p124) in Binissalem.

In early autumn, locals head to the hills in search of tasty *esclata-sang*, a mushroom of the milk-fungus family that's called *rovellon* in Catalonia. In summer it's time to pick the slender green asparagus that grows in rocky, shrub-filled areas. You can also pick *fonoll marí* (samphire), a leafy coastal herb that's marinated and used in salads.

What to Eat: Local Specialities

Pa amb oli

No meal in Mallorca begins without a dish of olives and Mallorca's most widely served dish: a hunk of *pa amb oli* (bread with oil), made with traditional *pa moreno* (rye bread). It's usually topped with chopped tomatoes, but many restaurants have learned to riff on the theme and there seems to be no limit to the toppings you'll find. Some are a meal in themselves.

Rice & Seafood

Paella may have its origins just across the water in Valencia on the mainland, but this and other rice dishes have been taken to heart by Mallorquins to the extent that some of Spain's best paellas are found on the island. Seafood paella in its many varieties is ubiquitous. *Arroz negro* (black rice), cooked in and coloured by squid ink, is widespread, but Mallorca's most traditional rice dish is *arros brut* (literally 'dirty rice'), a soupy dish made with pork, rabbit and vegetables.

Whereas the rice grains absorb much of the sauce in a paella, *arros caldoso* (moist rice) is filled with juice and flavour – the *arroz bogavante* (lobster rice) is one such dish and one of the island's star turns.

It's true that much of the fish eaten on Mallorca is flown in from elsewhere, but many species still fill the waters near the island. *Besugo* (sea bream) and *rape* (monkfish) are some of the most common fish caught here. Especially appreciated is *cap roig*, an ugly red fish found around the Illa de Cabrera.

Although you'll find fish and seafood cooked in a variety of sauces, this is largely a nod to foreign tastes. Mallorquins long ago learned that fresh seafood is best served grilled with just a bit of salt and lemon. Another delicious way to eat it is *'a la sal'*, or baked in a salt crust. A *marisquada* is a heaped tray of steamed shellfish – plan to share. One dish in which sauces actually enhance the flavours of the seafood is the Catalan favourite *suquet*, a stew cooked in rich fish stock and filled with fish and/or seafood.

Meat

Pork is found in some measure in countless sausages, stews, soups and even some vegetable dishes and desserts. The centuries of hunger Mallorquins endured taught them to appreciate every part of the pig; even today, they use everything but the squeal. Other favourite meat dishes include *frit Mallorquí*, a fried mix of tasty lamb parts; it too was born out of a desperate need for protein.

Dried Mallorcan sausages are iconic. Traditionally made by families as a way to keep meat year-round, *sobrassada* (tangy pork sausage flavoured with paprika) is the best-loved product. There are numerous ways to make it, but most involve chopped pork being ground with red pepper and sea salt, and then left to age for a couple of months. *Botifarra* (flavourful pork sausage) and *botiffarón* (a larger version of *botifarra*) are some of the best island sausages.

Vying with *sobrassada* and *frit Mallorquí* for the title of Mallorca's most widely served local speciality is *lechona* (roast suckling pig); it's sometimes called *porcella*. Grilled rabbit (usually cooked with onions) is widely enjoyed as well.

Desserts

The Mallorcan pastry par excellence is the beloved *ensaïmada,* a soft round bun made with a spiral of sweet dough and topped with powdered sugar. Sometimes, *ensaïmades* are filled with cream, chocolate or a sugary paste called *pasta de angel.* Every Mallorquin has their favourite bakery for *ensaïmades.*

Other local pastry desserts include *gató Mallorquí* (a dense almond cake), *quarts* (cake topped with meringue and sometimes also chocolate) and *coca de patata* (a bread-like pastry dusted with sugar and particularly famous in Valldemossa).

Mallorca also has its very own traditional, family-owned ice-cream manufacturer: Sa Fàbrica de Gelats (p94) in Sóller. Not surprisingly in this orchard town, orange is its special flavour.

Mallorcan Wine

Mallorca has been making wine since Roman times but only in recent years has it earned a reputation for quality. Just over 30 cellars, with 2500 hectares between them, make up the island's moderate production, most of which is enjoyed in Mallorca's restaurants and hotels. The wineries are huddled in the island's two DOs (Denominaciones de Orígen), Binissalem and an area in the interior of the island that includes towns such as Manacor, Felanitx and Llucmajor, where growing conditions are ideal. International varieties like cabernet sauvignon are planted alongside native varieties, like Manto Negro, Fogoneu and Callet. Local white varieties include Prensal Blanc and Giró Blanc, which are blended with Catalan grapes like Parellada, Macabeo and moscatel or with international varieties like chardonnay.

Wine production also takes place on the seaward slopes of the Serra de Tramuntana, particularly around Banyalbufar where the Malvasia grape is enjoying a revival.

Tourist offices across the wine country generally have a list of local wineries and their opening hours.

How to Eat Like a Local

Stopping to sit down and slowly savour a meal is one of the best things about eating in Mallorca. Lunch is the biggest meal of the day, and for Mallorquins, eating is not a functional pastime to be squeezed in between other more important tasks; instead it's one of life's great pleasures, a social event always taken seriously enough to allocate hours for the purpose and to be savoured like all good things in life. On Sundays, the midday family meal may last until late afternoon. Social dinners are equally drawn out, with each step from appetisers to post-dinner drinks being relished to the fullest. If you're extended the honour of being invited to dine in someone's home, bring a small gift of wine or chocolates and prepare yourself for a feast. A Mallorquin host will go all-out to entertain guests.

When to Eat

Mallorquins eat late, no matter what the meal, although the large foreign population on the island means that restaurants

GOOD TO GO: GOURMET MALLORCAN FOODS

Palma and Western Mallorca have numerous shops selling gourmet foods and local foods, usually packaged for easy transportation home. The Consell de Mallorca tourist office at the airport and downtown Palma should have the excellent brochure *Productes de Mallorca*, listing wineries and other food stores around the island. Apart from the wineries listed throughout the book, some of our favourite shops:

» **Fet a Sóller** (p95)
» **Tramuntana Gourmet** (p98)
» **Cassai Gourmet** (p157)
» **Colmado Manresa** (p69)
» **Colmado Santo Domingo** (p69)
» **Malvasia de Banyalbufar** (p86)

tend to open an hour or more earlier than they do on the mainland. Lunch, the most important meal of the day, is served from 1pm to 4pm, although many kitchens close by 3.30pm. For dinner, there's usually something open in most towns by 7.30pm; for most Mallorquins, the appropriate dinner time is around 9pm. Nearly all close their kitchens by midnight.

Breakfast

Most people start the day with a simple coffee at home, but it's also common to head out to *esmorzar* ('breakfast' in Catalan) midmorning. This is the ideal time to try a sugary *ensaïmada* and wash it down with a *café con leche* (espresso with milk) or a *zumo de naranja natural* (freshly squeezed orange juice); the orange juice is a particular treat in Sóller where the oranges are rightfully famous. Other coffees options include a *café solo* (black espresso) or a *cortado* (espresso served with a splash of milk).

In touristy areas expect to see restaurants advertising 'full English breakfast'. Many hotels and guesthouses take a more German approach, serving muesli and yogurt, toast with sliced cheese, processed meats and fruit.

Lunch

The best value at lunch is the *menú del día*, a fixed-price lunch menu that offers several options each for *primeros platos* (starters), *segundos platos* (mains) and *postres* (desserts), bread and a drink (including wine or beer) for as little as €10. Even when not ordering a *menú*, Mallorquins generally order two courses and a dessert when they go out for lunch.

Dinner

Mallorquins' stomachs start growling by 7pm or so. This is a great time to stop for tapas. An import from the mainland, tapas aren't as widespread here as in other Spanish cities, but many bars and cafes will have a small selection of snacky things to choose from. Olives, potato chips or a dish of almonds are the ideal accompaniment to a *caña*.

A meal usually begins with *pa moreno* and perhaps a *pica pica*, when many small appetisers are put out for everyone to share. Next comes the *primer plato*, which may be a salad, pasta, grilled-vegetable plate or something more creative. Desserts are most often a simple *helado* (ice cream), flan or fruit.

Types of Eateries

No Mallorcan town is without its fair share of cafes and restaurants. Cafe culture is very much a part of life here, and any excuse is a good one to meet for coffee, go for drinks or get a group of friends together for dinner.

It's often hard to distinguish between a cafe, a bar and a restaurant. Any may serve food and a single establishment might morph from a low-key morning cafe to a lunchtime bistro to a lively bar after dark. Also, bars come in several forms. *Cervecerías* are more or less the Spanish equivalent of a pub, while anything actually called 'pub' is likely to serve stout and show lots of football. *Tabernas* are generally rustic and may also serve tapas or meals. In any of the above you might be charged more if you get a table or sit outside.

Restaurants have a similar gamut of styles. Anything with *ca'n* or *ca's* in its name serves traditional fare in a family-style atmosphere, while anything dubbed a *celler* evokes the image of a country wine-cellar-turned-restaurant, although some of these traditional eateries were never actual cellars. A *marisquería* will specialise in seafood.

Vegetarians & Vegans

Being a vegetarian on Mallorca is difficult but not impossible. The island is especially proud of its fava broad beans, peppers, aubergines, artichokes, cauliflowers and green asparagus, which grows wild across the islands. Figs, apricots and oranges (especially around Sóller) are abundant.

Be aware that many traditional vegie dishes are prepared with salted pork, bacon, meat broth or lard. For example, the bean stew *fava pelada pagesa* is cooked with bacon, and *ensaïmades* are made with lard. *Sopas Mallorquins,* which are hearty vegetable stews, may or may not include pork fat.

Safe bets for vegetarians include *tortillas,* thick omelettes made with potatoes or vegies, and *tumbet,* the typical sautéed vegetable dish similar to ratatouille. Many restaurants offer a grilled-vegetable plate and fresh salads such as *trampó,* a cold dish made with tomato, onion, special pale-green Mallorcan peppers and olives. The Spanish *gaspacho* (cold tomato soup) is popular, too.

Organic food is sold at some local fresh markets, at health food stores and at farm shops such as **Finca Son Barrina** (☎971 504 540; www.mallorcaorganics.com; Carretera Inca-Llubí Km6; ⊙9am-8pm Fri & Sat).

Travel with Children

Best Regions for Kids

Palma & the Badia de Palma

The island's capital is the ideal base, with a wide range of attractions – including castles, theme parks and an aquarium – in the vicinity, as well as beaches and diverse restaurants to suit all tastes. Plus, nowhere else on the island is more than two hours away.

Eastern Mallorca

With vast cave complexes, endless beaches, snorkelling and boat trips along the coast, eastern Mallorca has all the ingredients for a fun-filled summer.

Northern Mallorca

More wonderful beaches and boat trips, with the added incentive of water sports that will appeal especially to older kids.

Mallorca for Kids

Mallorca is a fantastic destination for kids – distances are relatively small, beaches and family-friendly attractions are never far away, restaurants and bars are now smoke-free and the island's hotels and restaurants are accustomed to catering for families.

Beaches in abundance are the most obvious attraction and most have relatively calm waters; those that don't usually have a lifeguard on duty and warning flags on display. Most coastal hotels have swimming pools.

Beyond the beaches, theme parks and zoos are found across Mallorca, particularly in the hinterland of the major resorts. Some of these are good-old-fashioned water parks with water slides and rides, while there are also minizoos, nature parks and aquariums. Other child-friendly attractions include castles, which you'll find from Palma to Capdepera.

Getting around can also become an attraction in itself, with the historic train ride from Palma to Sóller and glass-bottomed-boat trips. Many of the latter allow time for snorkelling, a pastime that's easy to organise in most coastal towns.

On dry land, rent bikes and make the most of the island's bike paths, like the flat stretch running along Palma's waterfront. Horse riding is a thrill for older kids, and even toddlers will enjoy the pony rides available at many of the stables.

Just off the highways of the Serra de Tramuntana are two dozen or so public recreational areas, parks and rural estates that now have barbecues and play areas.

Please note that many family-focused sights and activities are open only from May to October.

Children's Highlights

Boat Trips

» **Port de Sóller to Sa Calobra** Beautiful trip to a fine beach

» **Illa de Sa Dragonera** Snorkel without the crowds in the southwest

» **Parc Nacional Marítim-Terrestre de l'Arxipèlag de Cabrera** The Blue Cave always draws gasps of surprise

» **Cala Ratjada** Glass-bottomed maritime forays along the east coast

» **Port de Pollença to Playa de Formentor** Deposits you on a fine beach

Castles

» **Castell de Bellver** Near-perfect fortress high above Palma

» **Castell de Capdepera** Evocative, sprawling hilltop perch above Capdepera

» **Santuari de Sant Salvador** Compact church-castle complex above Artà

» **Castell d'Alaró** Kids and adults will need to have decent fitness to reach this one, but views are worth it

» **Torre de Canyamel** Free-standing tower in excellent state of preservation

» **Medieval Walls** Walk atop ancient walls encircling Alcúdia

» **Torre des Verger** Watchtower perched on western Mallorca's cliffs

Caves

» **Coves del Drac** Mallorca's most spectacular caves

» **Coves d'Artà** A glorious setting

» **Coves de Campanet** Plenty to let the imagination roam free

» **Coves dels Hams** Less busy Porto Cristo alternative

» **Coves de Gènova** The closest caves to Palma

Zoos & Amusement Parks

» **Palma Aquarium** One of southern Europe's best

» **Safari-Zoo** Drive amid wildlife close to Cala Millor

» **Aqualand** S'Arenal water park with rides for all ages

» **Natura Parc** Kangaroos and flamingos southwest of Santa Eugènia

» **Western Water Park** Flashy themed water park in Magaluf

» **Hidropark** Port d'Alcúdia water park

Other Highlights

» **La Granja** Grand old estate with gardens and staff in period dress

» **Museo de Muñecas** Intriguing little doll museum in Old Palma

TIPS FOR TRAVELLING WITH CHILDREN

Some of our authors have travelled through Mallorca with their children. Here are a few of their tips:

» Be prepared for the fact that any child whose hair is less than jet black will be dubbed *rubio/rubia* (blonde)

» Expect your children to be kissed, offered sweets, have their cheeks pinched and their hair ruffled at least once a day

» Ask for extra tapas in bars, such as olives or raw carrot sticks

» Adjust your children to Spanish time (ie late nights) as quickly as you can – otherwise they'll miss half the fun

» Unlike in the USA, crayons and paper are rarely given out in restaurants – bring your own

» Kids who share your bed won't incur a supplement – extra beds usually cost €20 to €30

» Ask the local tourist office for the nearest children's playgrounds

» **Tourist Train** Cutesy train-on-wheels in Cala Ratjada

» **Palma to Sóller train journey** Train travel as it used to be

Planning

Accommodation

In hotels, cots are invariably available but few in number – make sure you reserve a cot when making your booking. We recommend ringing the hotel a couple of days in advance of your arrival to confirm.

Many hotels, particularly in coastal resorts, offer apartments and these come in a range of styles – some have two bedrooms and ample shared spaces, others are one-bedroom suites with a small sitting area and sofa bed. As they're all called 'apartments', make sure you know precisely what you're getting.

Although we're no fan of the all-inclusive resorts that dominate the southern, eastern and (to a lesser extent) northern coastline, they do one thing very well: most places employ teams of young Spaniards or Germans to organise children's activities, from games and concerts to craft-based activities.

Baby Food

You can buy baby formula in powder or liquid form, as well as sterilising solutions such as Milton, at *farmacias* (pharmacies). Disposable nappies (diapers) are widely available at supermarkets and *farmacias*. Fresh cow's milk is sold in cartons and plastic bottles in supermarkets in big cities, but can be hard to find in small towns, where UHT is often the only option.

If you've brought baby food with you, just ask for it to be warmed up in the kitchen; most restaurants will have no problem with this.

Babysitters

Some of the better hotels can generally arrange childcare. You could also check out the website **Canguroencasa** (www.canguroencasa.com, in Spanish), where you can search for English-speaking babysitters *(canguros)*; click on 'Canguros Baleares'. You'll also find ads at www.loquo.com (search under Mallorca, then 'canguros').

RESOURCES

For general advice on travelling with children, consider the following:

» Lonely Planet's *Travel with Children*

» www.travelwithyourkids.com

» www.familytravelnetwork.com

Car Hire

You can hire car seats for infants and children (usually for a per-day fee) from most car-rental firms, but book them well in advance.

Discounts

Discounts are available for children (usually aged under 12) on public transport and for admission to sights. Those under four generally go free.

Restaurants

You cannot rely on restaurants having high chairs, although many have at least one – getting there early increases your chances of snaffling one. Very few have nappy-changing facilities. That said, you'll get lots of smiles if you have cute kids with you and letting a kid wander around a restaurant – as long as they're not breaking wine bottles or bothering anyone – is usually OK.

Childrens menus are reasonably widespread, especially in coastal areas. Those restaurants without the latter are generally happy to improvise to suit children's tastes and appetites. Simple grilled meats, French fries, spaghetti and *tortillas* are all common kids plates.

regions at a glance

Palma & the Badia de Palma

Architecture ✓✓✓
Galleries ✓✓✓
Food ✓✓

Medieval Architecture
Exploring Palma is like a journey through the Mediterranean's architectural history. The cathedral is the showpiece, but it's in the surrounding old town that you'll find Modernista masterpieces, medieval mansions and elegant *patis* (patios).

Miró, Picasso & Dalí
Palma has always been a magnet for Spain's (and particularly Catalonia's) premier artists of the 20th century. Miró spent much of his life here, Miquel Barceló is from here, and the works of Picasso and Dalí fill the city's numerous museums.

The Mallorcan Kitchen
The depth of Mallorcan cuisine comes together in Palma, from the island's best seafood restaurants to the expanding coterie of restaurants overseen by Michelin-starred Marc Fosh, from wonderful little tapas bars around Plaça Major to pastry shops *par excellance.*

p40

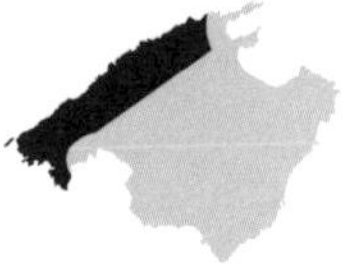

Western Mallorca

Villages ✓✓✓
Landscapes ✓✓✓
Hiking ✓✓✓

Stone-built Hamlets
Western Mallorca is home to the island's prettiest villages inhabiting the mountain foothills. The finest: Valldemossa, Deià, Fornalutx, Binaraix and Orient.

Mallorca's Spine
The Serra de Tramuntana is one of the most beautiful mountain ranges in the Mediterranean, rising from the water's edge in the most dramatic fashion, creating sea and mountain views of rare beauty.

Hike the High Country
Yes, you could take any number of day hikes, but the minimum-four-day Ruta de Pedra en Sec is one of Europe's great walks, taking you the length of the island's western coast. Utterly unforgettable.

p78

Northern Mallorca

Landscapes ✓✓✓
Old Towns ✓✓
Beaches ✓✓

Cap de Formentor
The northern crescendo of the Serra de Tramuntana is a peninsula of Tolkienesque mountain summits, plunging cliffs and sheltered coves of heartbreaking beauty. Drive, cycle or hike it.

The Coast's Alter Ego
In northern Mallorca's coastal hinterland reside two of Mallorca's most engaging midsized towns: Pollença with its cobblestone streets and 365 steps to Calvari, and Alcúdia with Roman ruins and defensive walls.

Something for Everyone
If you're after sandy beaches backed by resorts, look no further. But we like northern Mallorca for the quiet coves of Cala Sant Vicenç, Cap de Formentor or Cap des Pinar.

p103

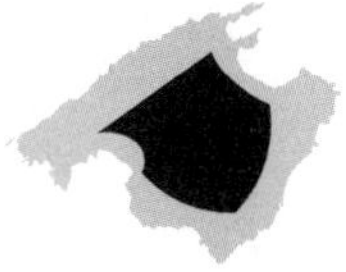

The Interior

Wines ✓✓✓
Food ✓✓
Architecture ✓✓✓

Wines & Wineries

Mallorca's wine-producing areas range across the island's interior, some of the numerous vineyards offering tInterior, the ours, most with just cellar-door sales.

Hearty Inland Fare

From the *celler* restaurants of Inca and Sineu, which inhabit old wine cellars, to the rural properties transformed into hotels and restaurants, eating in the Mallorcan interior is all about authenticity.

Monasteries & Medieval Towns

Almost every hilltop in inland Mallorca was long ago colonised by a monastery from where the views are cinematic in scope, while towns like Sineu and Petra are places of quiet, underrated charm.

p120

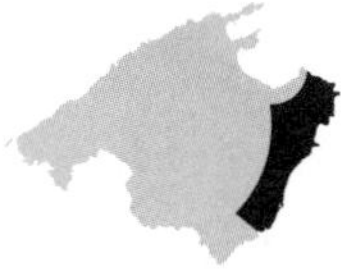

Eastern Mallorca

Beaches ✓✓✓
Caves ✓✓✓
Landscapes ✓✓

Beyond the Resorts

Make for the wild beaches northeast of Cala Ratjada, which are some of Mallorca's most desirable stretches of coastal real estate. The quiet *cales* (coves) south of Porto Cristo are similarly lovely.

Underground Cathedrals

The epic formations of eastern Mallorca's caves rank among the island's most eye-catching natural phenomena – try Coves del Drac, Coves d'Artà and Coves dels Hams.

Protected Peninsula

North of pretty Artà, the Parc Natural de la Península de Llevant is paradise for birdwatchers and hikers with beaches accessible only on foot. Cap Ferrutx is the endpoint, while the Ermita de Betlem is a soulful place.

p134

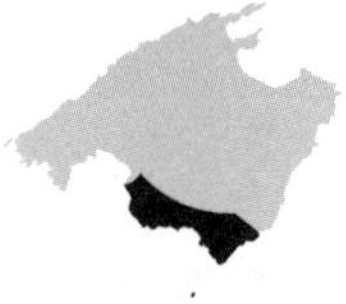

Southern Mallorca

Beaches ✓✓✓
Scenery ✓✓✓
Archaeology ✓

Unspoiled Sands

Head for the sweeping sands of scarcely developed Platja des Trenc, or the picturesque coves of Cala Pi, Cala Llombards or the Parc Natural de Mondragó.

Coastal Ramparts

Large swaths of southern Mallorca's coast have been saved from developers' bulldozers by the high cliffs of the coast, especially from Cap Blanc to Cap de Ses Salines, though the real treasure is the offshore Illa de Cabrera.

Mallorca's Mysterious Past

The island's prehistoric history is shrouded in uncertainty, and Talayotic sites such as Capocorb Vell and those close to Ses Salines offer intriguing insights into pre-Roman Mallorca.

p150

Look out for these icons:

TOP CHOICE Our author's recommendation

A green or sustainable option

FREE No payment required

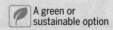

See the Index for a full list of destinations covered in this book.

On the Road

PALMA & THE BADIA DE PALMA 40

PALMA DE MALLORCA 42
BADIA DE PALMA 72
East of Palma 73
West of Palma 75

WESTERN MALLORCA 78

THE SOUTHWEST 79
To Cap de Cala Figuera 79
Andratx 79
Port d'Andratx 79
Sant Elm 83
SERRA DE TRAMUNTANA .. 84
Andratx to Valldemossa .. 84
Valldemossa 87
Port de Valldemossa 90
Deià & Around 90
Sóller 92
Port de Sóller 95
Biniaraix 98
Fornalutx 98
Road from Sóller to Alaró 99
Cala de Sa Calobra & Cala Tuent 101
Monestir de Lluc & Around 102

NORTHERN MALLORCA 103

Pollença & Around 106
Pollença 106
Cala Sant Vicenç 109
Port de Pollença 110
CAP DE FORMENTOR 112
BADIA D'ALCÚDIA 112
Alcúdia 112
Port d'Alcúdia 114
Cap des Pinar 115
Parc Natural de S'Albufera 117
SOUTH OF ALCÚDIA 118
Ca'n Picafort & Around ... 118
Son Serra de Marina 119
Colònia de Sant Pere 119

THE INTERIOR 120

THE CENTRAL CORRIDOR 121
Santa Maria del Camí & Around 121
Binissalem 121
Santa Eugènia 124
Inca 125
Around Inca 126
Sineu 128
Sa Pobla & Muro 129
THE SOUTHEAST 129
Algaida 129
Montuïri & Around 130
Petra 131
Manacor 131
Felanitx 133

EASTERN MALLORCA 134

ARTÀ & AROUND 136
Artà 136
Parc Natural de la Península de Llevant 138
Capdepera 139
Cala Ratjada 140
Coves d'Artà & Platja de Canyamel 143
CALA MILLOR TO PORTOCOLOM 144
Cala Millor & Around 144
Porto Cristo 145
Portocolom 147

SOUTHERN MALLORCA 150

FROM CAP ENDERROCAT TO SA RÀPITA 152
Cala Pi & Around 152
Sa Ràpita & Around 152
COLÒNIA DE SANT JORDI & AROUND 153
Colònia de Sant Jordi 153
Platja des Trenc 155
Ses Salines 155
SANTANYÍ TO CALA D'OR 157
Santanyí & Around 157
Cala Figuera 159
Parc Natural de Mondragó 159
Portopetro 159
Cala d'Or 160

ACCOMMODATION .. 162

PALMA DE MALLORCA ... 164
WESTERN MALLORCA 165
NORTHERN MALLORCA .. 169
THE INTERIOR 171
EASTERN MALLORCA 172
SOUTHERN MALLORCA .. 174

Palma & the Badia de Palma

Includes »

Palma de Mallorca....42
Badia de Palma 72
East of Palma........73
West of Palma 75

Best Places to Eat

- » Caballito de Mar (p64)
- » Tasca de Blanquerna (p60)
- » Las Olas (p60)
- » La Bodeguilla (p60)
- » Aramís (p62)

Best Places to Stay

- » Puro Oasis Urbano (p165)
- » Hotel Born (p164)
- » Hostal Brondo (p164)
- » Hotel Dalt Murada (p164)
- » Hotel San Lorenzo (p165)

Why Go?

Palma de Mallorca, Mallorca's only true city, is among the most agreeable of all Mediterranean towns, arrayed around the Badia de Palma and backed by not-so-distant mountains. Surveying it all from a gentle rise, the old quarter, crowned by the Catedral, is an attractive blend of tree-lined boulevards and cobbled laneways, Gothic churches and baroque palaces, designer bars and slick boutiques. Mallorca's renowned culinary sophistication also finds its most diverse expression here. The Badia, extending either side of Palma, is a pretty arc of bay, albeit dominated by unappealing resorts; there are exceptions including the quiet coves of Ses Illetes or the upscale charms of Es Portitxol. But above all, Palma is a beguiling port city with glamour and more earthy charms in just the right balance.

When to Go

Scarcely a month passes in Palma without a festival of some kind and, unlike the rest of the island, Palma's energy levels remain fairly constant throughout the year; most sights, hotels and restaurants remain open year-round. That said, the city does have an irresistible feel-good atmosphere when the weather's warm, the yacht harbour's filled with masts and one of the numerous sailing regattas brings the beautiful people to town – this applies from April to October. The beach resorts of the Badia de Palma effectively shut down in winter.

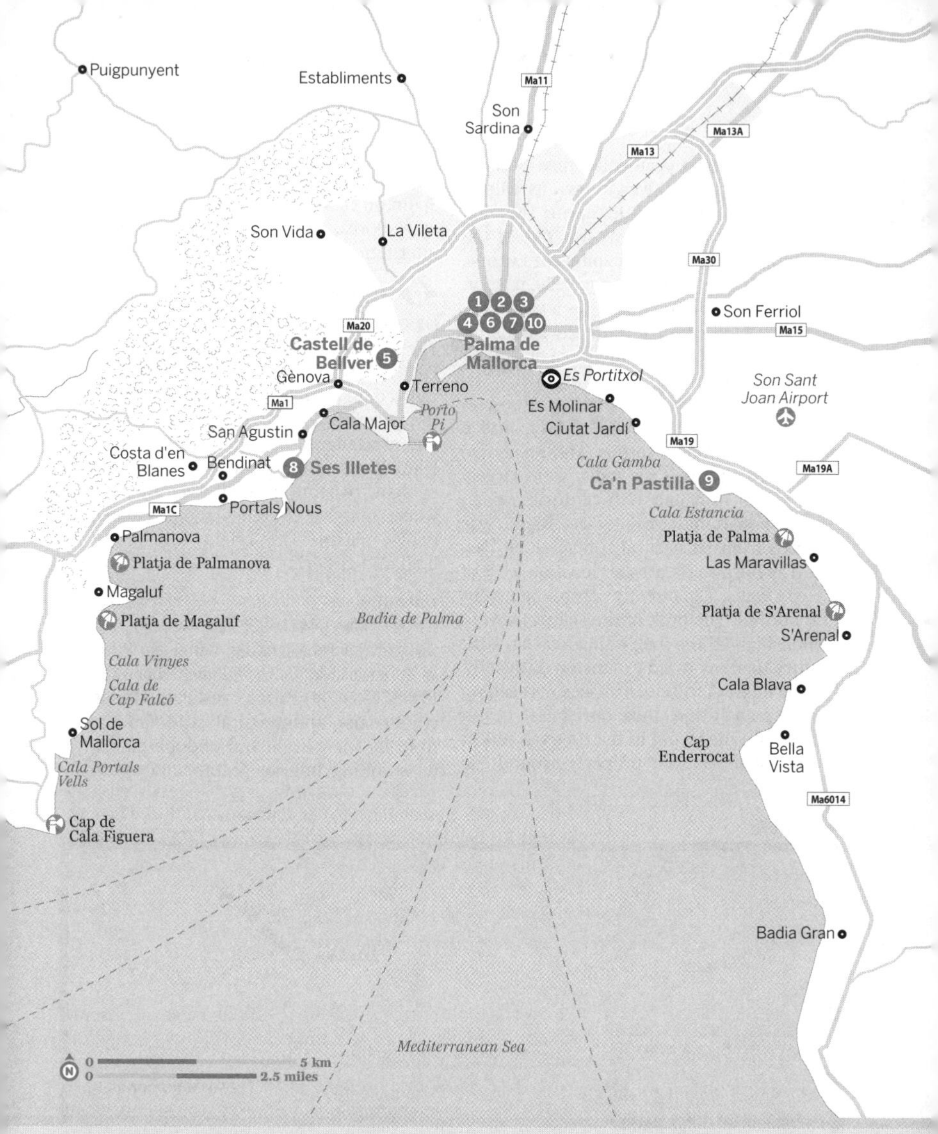

Palma & the Badia de Palma Highlights

1 Admire the fantasy of Barceló and Gaudí at the Gothic **Catedral** (p42)

2 Take in the contemporary art inside the one-time city walls at **Es Baluard** (p54)

3 Get lost in Old Palma's labyrinth, discovering the baroque courtyards and resting in the **Banys Àrabs** (p49)

4 Sample Picasso, Miró and Dalí at the **Museu Fundación Juan March** (p52)

5 Survey the Badia de Palma from the hilltop **Castell de Bellver** (p56)

6 Return to Santa Catalina's roots at **Hostal Cuba Colonial** (p67), then savour its makeover at **Room** (p63)

7 Absorb the irresistible energy of Sa Gerreria, starting with **L'Ambigú** (p65)

8 Escape the crowds with a drink at **Virtual Club** (p76)

9 Soak up the style of **Puro Beach** (p75), in Ca'n Pastilla

10 Sample fine seafood at **Ca'n Eduardo** (p64) or **Nautic** (p64)

PALMA DE MALLORCA

POP 404,681

History

Palma has been occupied since Roman times, when the city was known as Palmeria or Palma. By the 12th century, Medina Mayurka (City of Mallorca) was one of the most flourishing Muslim capitals in Europe. After the Christian conquest in 1229, it again entered a period of prosperity as a trade centre in the 14th century – the Christians renamed the city Ciutat de Mallorca or Ciudad Capital (City Capital).

By the 16th century, along with the rest of the island, the city was sinking into a protracted period of torpor. The great seaward walls that you see today were largely built in the 16th and 17th centuries, when the city's seasonal torrent, the Riera, was diverted from its natural course along Passeig d'es Born to its present location west of the city walls. The old city centre then went into decline. The bulk of the sea walls were demolished at the beginning of the 20th century to allow rapid expansion of the city. But the heart of the city has been spruced up beyond recognition since tourist cash began to flow into the island in the 1960s. A report in 2007 claimed that property around the Dalt Murada was among the most expensive in all Spain.

The planting of bombs by the Basque separatist group ETA in July and August 2009, which was reportedly linked to the impending arrival of the King and Queen of Spain on their annual summer holiday visit to Mallorca, thrust the city briefly into the international spotlight.

Sights

OLD PALMA

The heart of the old city (the districts of Sa Portella and Sa Calatrava) has always been centred on its main place of worship (where the Catedral now stands) and the one-time seat of secular power opposite it. The bulk of Palma's sights are jammed into this warren of tight, twisting lanes and sunny squares, where massive churches abound alongside noble houses. The bright Mediterranean light and glittering sea are never far away.

Catedral CATHEDRAL
(La Seu; Map p44; ☎902 022 445, 971 723 130; www.catedraldemallorca.org; Carrer del Palau Reial 9; adult/child €4/3; ⏲10am-6.15pm Mon-Fri, 10am-2.15pm Sat) Palma's vast cathedral is the city's major architectural landmark. Aside from its sheer scale and undoubted beauty, its stunning interior features, designed by

Palma

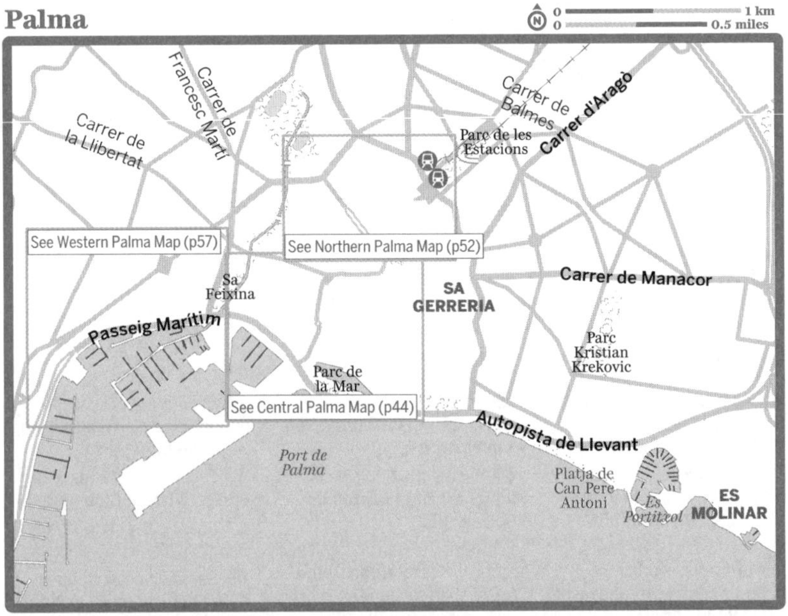

PALMA IN TWO DAYS

Palma makes a great city break and with a will to cram you can do a lot in a weekend. Start touring with the obvious: the **Catedral** and the **Palau de l'Almudaina**. You could spend hours wandering the old town lanes and, to add a little structure, throw in visits to **Casa-Museu Joaquim Torrents Lladó** and the **Banys Àrabs**. Lunch at **Las Olas**. Restart touring with the **Basílica de Sant Francesc** and **Es Baluard**, where you can stop for a snack alongside the battlements. For a night out, make for nearby Santa Catalina, with dinner at **Fàbrica 23**, drinks at **Idem Café** and clubbing along **Passeig Marítim**. The following day, head east out of town up to **Castell de Bellver** and the **Fundació Pilar i Joan Miró**, book lunch at **Ca'n Eduardo** and spend the afternoon exploring the **Museu Fundación Juan March**, then end with a drink at **Guiness House**. Later, have an *ensaïmade* at **Ca'n Joan de S'Aigo**, dinner at **Simply Fosh** or **Misa Braseria**, then hit the bars of Sa Gerreria, beginning at **L'Ambigú**.

Antoni Gaudí and renowned contemporary artist Miquel Barceló, make this unlike any cathedral elsewhere in the world.

The Catedral occupies the site of what was the central mosque of Medina Mayurka, capital of Muslim Mallorca for three centuries. Although Jaume I and his marauding men forced their way into the city in 1229, work on the Catedral (La Seu in Catalan), one of Europe's largest, did not begin until 1300. Rather, the mosque was used in the interim as a church and dedicated to the Virgin Mary. Work wasn't completed until 1601.

The awesome structure is predominantly Gothic, apart from the main facade. The main facade is startling, quite beautiful and completely mongrel. The original was a Renaissance cherry on the Gothic cake, but an earthquake in 1851 (which caused considerable panic but no loss of life) severely damaged it. Rather than mend the original, it was decided to add some neo-Gothic flavour, which with its interlaced flying buttresses on each flank and soaring pinnacles forms a masterful example of the style. The result is a hybrid of the Renaissance original (in particular the main doorway) and an inevitably artificial-feeling, 19th-century pseudo-Gothic monumentalism.

Entry to the church is from the north flank. You get tickets in the first room and then enter a sacristy, which hosts the main part of the small **Museu de la Catedral**, at the centre of which is a huge gold-plated monstrance. Interesting items include a portable altar, thought to have belonged to Jaume I. Its little compartments contain saints' relics. Other reliquaries can be seen, including one purporting to hold three thorns from Christ's crown of thorns. Next come two chapter houses, one Gothic (by Guillem Sagrera) and the second baroque. The latter is dominated by a *relicario de la vera cruz* (reliquary of the true cross).

On passing through one of the side chapels into the cathedral itself, your gaze soars high to the cross vaults, supported by slender, octagonal pillars. The broad nave and aisles are flanked by chapels. The walls support three levels of exquisite stained glass, including five magnificent rose windows. The grandest (the *oculus maior* or 'great eye') is above the main altar and is said to be the largest in the world. Visit in the morning and see the stunning effect of its coloured light and shapes reflected on the west wall. This spectacle is at its best in February and November.

Gaudí carried out renovations from 1903 to 1914. His most important contribution was opening up many of the long bricked-up windows, adding new stained glass and improving lighting. What most people notice today, however, is the strange baldachin that hovers over the main altar. Topped by a fanciful sculpture of Christ crucified and flanked by the Virgin Mary and St John, it looks like the gaping jaw of some oversized prehistoric shark dangling from the ceiling of an old science museum. Some 35 lamps hang from it and what looks like a flying carpet is spread above it. The genius of Barcelona Modernisme seems to have left behind an indecipherable pastiche, but then this was supposed to be a temporary version. The definitive one was never made.

Not content with this strangeness, the parish commissioned contemporary Mallorquin artist Miquel Barceló (an agnostic) with the remake of the Capella del Santíssim i Sant Pere, at the rear of the south aisle. Done in 15 tonnes of ceramics, this dreamscape

Central Palma

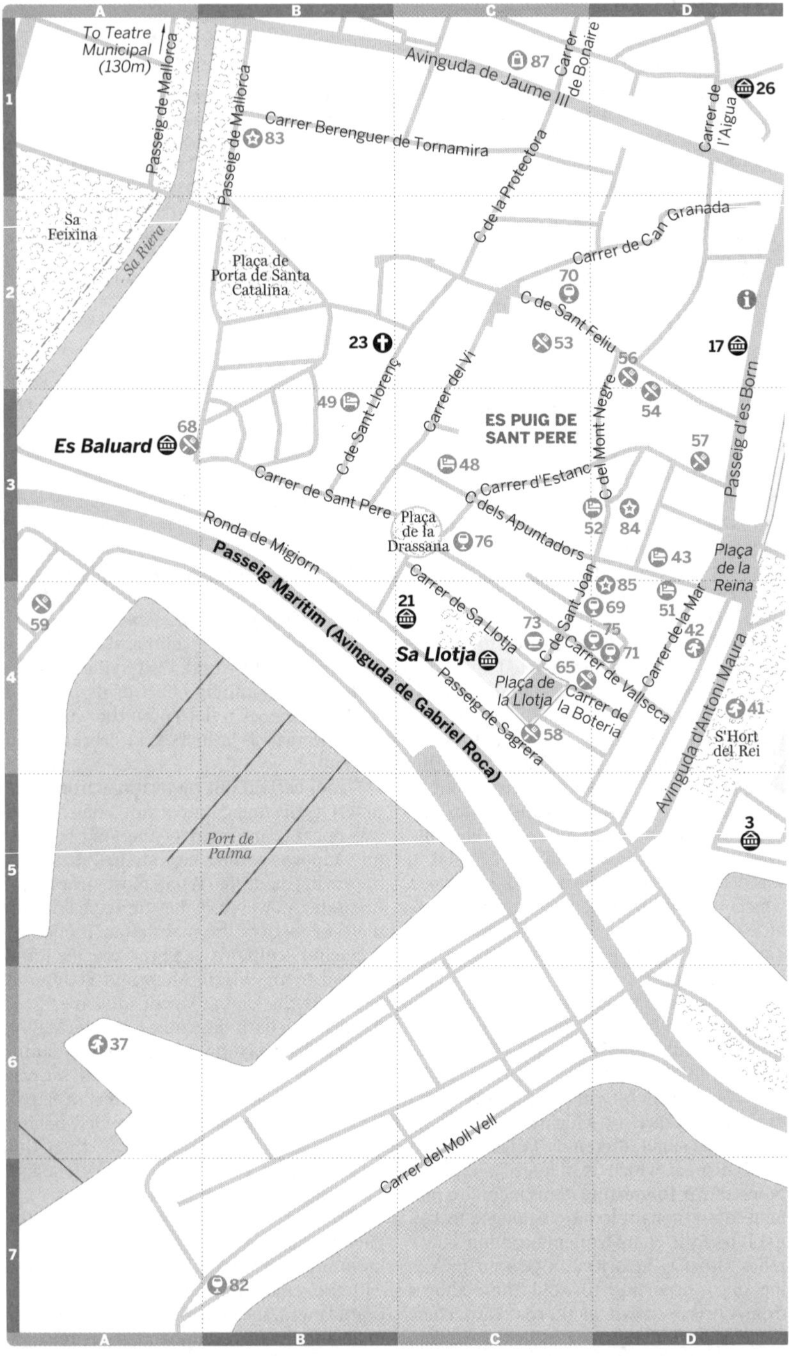
To Teatre Municipal (130m)
Avinguda de Jaume III
Carrer de Bonaire
Carrer Berenguer de Tornamira
Passeig de Mallorca
Carrer de l'Aigua
C de la Protectora
Sa Feixina
Sa Riera
Plaça de Porta de Santa Catalina
Carrer de Can Granada
C de Sant Feliu
Carrer del Vi
C de Sant Llorenç
ES PUIG DE SANT PERE
C del Mont Negre
Passeig d'es Born
Es Baluard
Carrer de Sant Pere
Carrer d'Estanc
C dels Apuntadors
Plaça de la Drassana
Ronda de Migjorn
Passeig Marítim (Avinguda de Gabriel Roca)
Plaça de la Reina
Carrer de Sa Llotja
C de Sant Joan
Carrer de la Mar
Sa Llotja
Carrer de Vallseca
Plaça de la Llotja
Carrer de la Boteria
Passeig de Sagrera
Avinguda d'Antoni Maura
S'Hort del Rei
Port de Palma
Carrer del Moll Vell
87
26
83
70
23
53
17
56
54
49
68
57
48
52
84
76
43
85
21
51
59
69
73
75
42
71
65
41
58
3
37
82
A
B
C
D
1
2
3
4
5
6
7

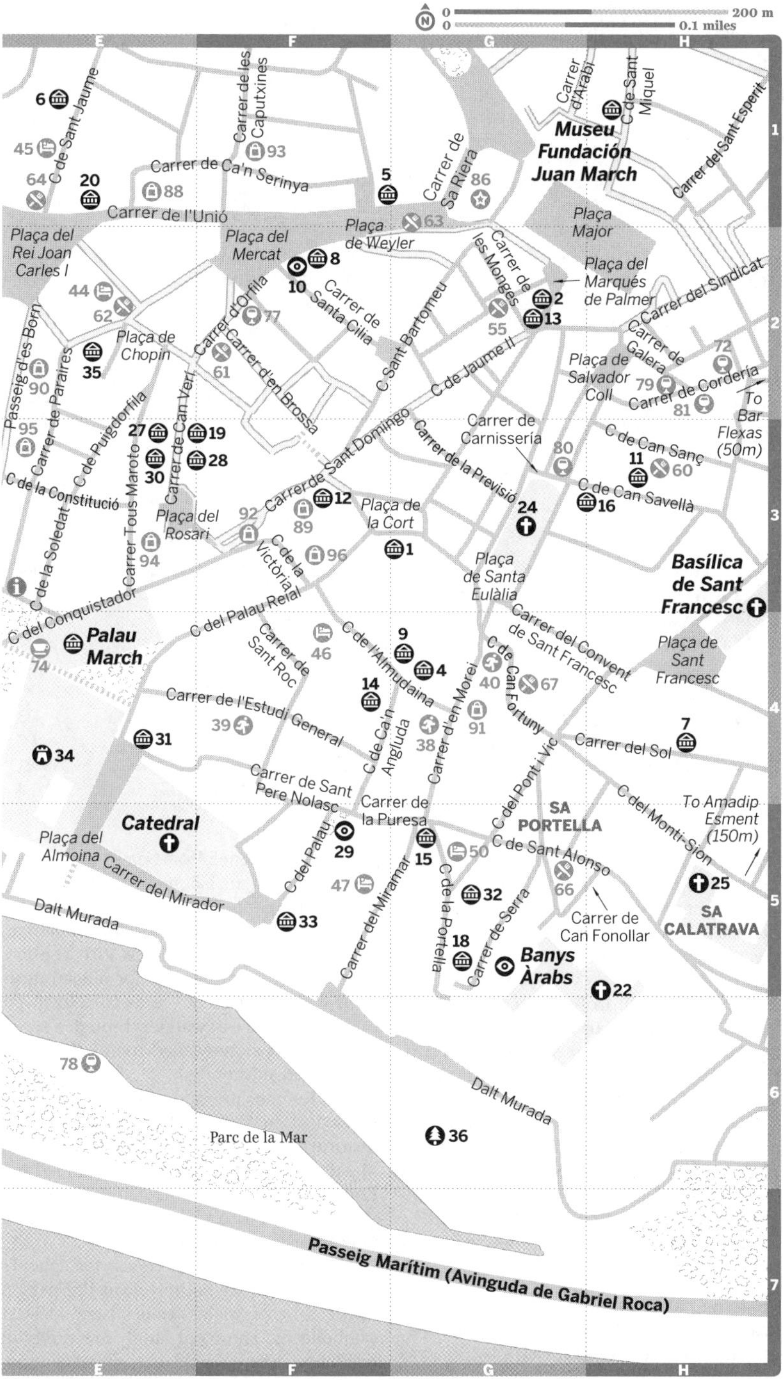
0 200 m
0 0.1 miles
Museu Fundación Juan March
Basílica de Sant Francesc
Palau March
Catedral
Banys Àrabs
Carrer de Ca'n Serinya
Carrer de l'Unió
Carrer de les Caputxines
Carrer de Sa Riera
Carrer d'Arabí
C de Sant Miquel
Carrer del Sant Esperit
C de Sant Jaume
Plaça del Rei Joan Carles I
Plaça del Mercat
Plaça de Weyler
Plaça Major
Plaça del Marqués de Palmer
Carrer de les Monges
Carrer de Santa Cilia
Carrer d'Orfila
Carrer d'en Brossa
C Sant Bartomeu
C de Jaume II
Carrer del Sindicat
Carrer de Galera
Carrer de Cordería
Plaça de Salvador Coll
To Bar Flexas (50m)
Plaça de Chopin
Passeig d'es Born
Carrer de Paraires
C de Puigdorfila
Carrer de Can Verí
Carrer Tous Maroto
C de la Constitució
C de la Soledat
Plaça del Rosari
Carrer de Sant Domingo
Carrer de la Previsió
Carrer de Carnissería
C de Can Sanç
C de Can Savellà
Plaça de la Cort
C de la Victòria
Plaça de Santa Eulàlia
C del Conquistador
C del Palau Reial
Carrer de Sant Roc
C de l'Almudaina
Carrer del Convent de Sant Francesc
Plaça de Sant Francesc
C de Can Fortuny
Carrer d'en Morei
Carrer de l'Estudi General
C de Ca'n Angluda
Carrer del Sol
C del Pont i Vic
Carrer de Sant Pere Nolasc
Carrer de la Puresa
C del Palau
SA PORTELLA
C del Monti-Sion
To Amadip Esment (150m)
C de Sant Alonso
Plaça del Almoina
Carrer del Mirador
Dalt Murada
Carrer del Miramar
C de la Portella
Carrer de Serra
Carrer de Can Fonollar
SA CALATRAVA
Parc de la Mar
Passeig Marítim (Avinguda de Gabriel Roca)

Central Palma

Top Sights

Banys Àrabs ... G5
Basílica de Sant Francesc ... H3
Catedral ... E5
Es Baluard ... A3
Museu Fundación Juan March ... H1
Palau March ... E4
Sa Llotja ... C4

Sights

1 Ajuntament ... G3
2 Almacenes El Águila ... G2
3 Arc del Wali ... D5
4 Arco de l'Almudaina ... G4
5 CaixaForum ... F1
6 Cal Comte de San Simón ... E1
7 Cal Marquès del Palmer ... H4
8 Can Berga ... F2
9 Can Bordils ... G4
10 Can Casasayas ... F2
11 Can Catlar del Llorer ... H3
12 Can Corbella ... F3
13 Can Forteza Rey ... G2
14 Can Marquès ... F4
15 Can Salas ... G5
16 Can Vivot ... H3
17 Casal Solleric ... D2
18 Casa-Museu Joaquim Torrents Lladó ... G5
19 Centre Cultural Contemporani Pelaires ... F3
20 Círculo de Bellas Artes ... E1
21 Consolat de Mar ... C4
22 Convent de Santa Clara ... H5
23 Església de Santa Creu ... B2
24 Església de Santa Eulàlia ... G3
25 Església del Monti-Sion ... H5
26 Fundació Sa Nostra ... D1
27 Galeria K ... E3
28 Galeria La Caja Blanca ... F3
29 Jardí del Bisbe ... F5
30 Joan Guaita Art ... E3
31 Museo de Muñecas ... E4
32 Museu de Mallorca ... G5
33 Museu Diocesà ... F5
34 Palau de l'Almudaina ... E4
35 Sala Pelaires ... E2
36 Walls & Parc de la Mar ... G6

Activities, Courses & Tours

37 Cruceros Marco Polo ... A6
38 Die Akademie ... G4
39 Estudi Lul·lià de Mallorca ... F4
40 Mallorca Rutes ... G4
41 Palma City Sightseeing ... D4
42 Palma on Bike ... D4

Sleeping

43 Hostal Apuntadores ... D3
44 Hostal Brondo ... E2
45 Hotel Born ... E1
46 Hotel Dalt Murada ... F4

representing the miracle of the loaves and fishes was unveiled in 2007. Slabs of clay seem to have been plastered onto the chapel walls. On the left, fish and other marine creatures burst from the wall. The opposite side has a jungle look, with representations of bread and fruit. In between the fish and palm fronds, and standing above stacks of skulls, appears a luminous body that is supposed to be Christ but is modelled on the short and stocky artist.

Other notable elements of the interior include the giant organ, built in 1798 (free recitals are held at noon on the first Tuesday of each month), and the two pulpits, the smaller of which was partly redone by Gaudí.

Mass times vary, but one always takes place at 9am.

Palau de l'Almudaina PALACE

(Map p44; ☎971 214 134; www.patrimonionacional.es; Carrer del Palau Reial; adult/child €4/2.30, audio guide €2.50; ⏱10am-5.45pm Mon-Fri, 10am-1.15pm Sat) Originally an Islamic fort, this mighty construction opposite the Catedral was converted into a residence for the Mallorcan monarchs at the end of the 13th century. It is still occasionally used for official functions when King Juan Carlos is in town. At other times you can wander through a series of cavernous stone-walled rooms that have been lavishly decorated.

The Romans are said to have built a *castrum* (fort) here, possibly on the site of a prehistoric settlement. The Wālis (governors) of Muslim Mallorca altered and expanded the Roman fort, while Jaume I and his successors modified it to such an extent that little of the Muslim version remains.

Now, as in medieval times, the island's maximum secular authority (in the person of the King of Spain) resides here, at least symbolically. The royal family are rarely in residence, except for the occasional ceremo-

47 Hotel Palacio Ca Sa Galesa F5
48 Hotel Palau Sa Font C3
49 Hotel San Lorenzo B3
50 Hotel Santa Clara G5
51 Hotel Tres D4
52 Puro Oasis Urbano D3

Eating
53 13% C2
54 Aramís D3
55 Bar España G2
56 Bon Lloc D2
57 Bruselas D3
58 Caballito de Mar C4
59 Ca'n Eduardo A4
60 Ca'n Joan de S'Aigo H3
61 Confitería Frasquet F2
62 Forn del Santo Cristo E2
63 Forn des Teatre G1
64 La Bodeguilla E1
65 La Bóveda C4
66 La Taberna del Caracol G5
67 Las Olas G4
68 Restaurant Museu Es Baluard A3

Drinking
69 Abaco D4
70 Atlantico Café C2
71 Bodeguita del Medio D4
72 Ca La Seu H2
73 Café La Lonja C4
74 Cappuccino E4
75 Es Jaç D4
76 Escape Bar C3
77 Gibson F2
78 Guiness House E6
79 Jamón Jamón H2
80 L'Ambigú G3
81 Quina Creu H2
82 Varadero B7

Entertainment
83 Blue Jazz Club B1
84 Bluesville D3
85 Jazz Voyeur Club D4
86 Teatre Principal G1

Shopping
87 Camper C1
88 Carmina E1
89 Colmado Santo Domingo F3
90 Farrutx E2
91 Fine Books G4
92 La Casa del Mapa F3
93 Lust Universe F1
94 Món E3
95 Quesada E3
Típika ..... (see 40)
96 Vidrierias Gordiola F3

ny, as they prefer to spend summer in the Palau Marivent (in Cala Major).

The first narrow room you enter has a black-and-white ceiling, symbolising the extremes of night and day, darkness and light. You then enter a series of three grand rooms. Notice the bricked-in Gothic arches cut off in the middle. Originally these three rooms were double their present height and formed one single great hall added to the original Arab fort and known as the Saló del Tinell (from an Italian word, *tinello*, meaning 'place where one eats'): this was once a giant banqueting and ceremonial hall. The rooms are graced by period furniture, tapestries and other curios. The following six bare rooms and terrace belonged to the original Arab citadel.

In the main courtyard, or Patio de Armas, troops would line up for an inspection and parade before heading out into the city. The lion fountain in its centre is one of the palace's rare Arab remnants. Up the grand Royal Staircase are the royal apartments, a succession of lavishly appointed rooms (look up to the beautiful coffered timber *artesonado* ceilings), whose centrepiece is the Saló Gòtic, the upper half of the former Saló del Tinell, where you can see where those Gothic arches wind up. Next door to the apartments is the royal Capella de Sant'Anna, a Gothic chapel whose entrance is a very rare Mallorcan example of late Romanesque in rose and white marble.

After the death of Jaume III in 1349, no king lived here permanently again.

In the shadow of the Almudaina's walls, along Avinguda d'Antoni Maura, is S'Hort del Rei (the King's Garden).

Museu Diocesà MUSEUM
(Map p44; ☎971 723 860; www.bisbatdemallorca.com; Carrer del Mirador 5; adult/child €3/free; ⊙10am-2pm Mon-Sat) Opened in 2007 in its

magnificent new home of the Palau Episcopal (bishop's residence), the Museu Diocesà, behind the cathedral to the east, is a fascinating excursion for those interested in Mallorca's Christian artistic history.

The first thing you see upon entering is a mind-boggling *retaule* (*retablo* in Spanish, an altarpiece) depicting the Passion of Christ (c 1290–1305) and taken from the Convent de Santa Clara. The episodes are shown with effusive detail: Palm Sunday, the Last Supper, St Peter's kiss of betrayal. Christ flailed looks utterly unperturbed, while the image of his being nailed to the cross is unsettling. Off to the right, a key work is Francesc Comes' *St Jaume de Compostela* (St James, known to the Spaniards as the Moor-slayer). Pere Niçard's *Sant Jordi* (St George), done around 1468–70, is remarkable for its busy detail. The City of Mallorca (Palma) is shown in the background as St George despatches the dragon. Below this painting is a scene by Niçard and his boss Rafel Mòger depicting the 1229 taking of Palma. The final room in this wing is the Gothic Oratori de Sant Pau, a small chapel. The stained-glass window was a trial run done by Gaudí in preparation for the windows he did in the Catedral.

Otherwise, a succession of rooms showcases Mallorquin artists such as Pere Terrencs and Mateu López (father and son), while upstairs is a thin collection of baroque art, ceramics and some lovely views out over the bay.

Palau March MUSEUM

(Map p44; ☎971 711 122; www.fundacionbmarch.es; Carrer de Palau Reial 18; adult/child €3.60/free; ⏲10am-6pm Mon-Fri, 10am-2pm Sat) This house, palatial by any definition, was one of several residences of the phenomenally wealthy March family. Sculptures by 20th-century greats, such as Henry Moore, Auguste Rodin, Barbara Hepworth and Eduardo Chillida, grace the outdoor terrace. Within lie many more artistic treasures from some of Spain's big names in art.

Entry is through an outdoor terrace display of modern sculptural works. Centre stage is taken by the enormous *Orgue del Mar* (1973) by Barcelona's Xavier Corberó.

Inside, more than 20 paintings by Salvador Dalí around the themes 'Alchemy and Eternity' catch the eye, as does the extraordinary 18th-century Neapolitan baroque *belén* (nativity scene). Hundreds of incredibly detailed figures, from angels to kings, shepherds to farm animals and market scenes, make up this unique representation of Christ's birth.

Upstairs, the Barcelona artist Josep Maria Sert (1874–1945) painted the main vault and music room ceiling. The vault is divided into four parts, the first three representing three virtues (audacity, reason and inspiration) and the last the embodiment of those qualities in the form of Sert's client Juan March. One of the rooms hosts an intriguing display of medieval maps of the Mediterranean by Mallorcan cartographers.

Museo de Muñecas MUSEUM

(Museu de Nines Antigues; Map p44; ☎971 729 850; mallorcadollsmuseum@gmail.com; Carrer del Palau Reial 27; adult/child €3.50/2.50; ⏲10am-6pm Tue-Sun) Near the cathedral, this fascinating niche shop-cum-museum is dedicated to old dolls, with more than 500 examples from over 50 countries, from Ashanti fertility dolls to Shirley Temple. At the top of the steep stairs, you buy a ticket and are ushered through the back to two rooms jammed with old dolls, made of anything from cardboard to porcelain.

In the first room, countless versions of a popular Spanish doll, Mariquita Pérez, which first appeared in 1938 in San Sebastián, steal the show. Many of the dolls in the second room date to the 19th or early 20th centuries and the aim is to show you how dolls have evolved down through the decades. Cardboard Spanish dolls from the 1940s, for example, show how tough times were after the Civil War. Or what about the utterly un-PC gollywogs? And what are the tiny dolls with the huge bare breasts all about? The museum will appeal as much to collectors as to children.

FREE Jardí del Bisbe GARDENS

(Map p44; Carrer de Sant Pere Nolasc 6; ⏲9am-1pm & 3-6pm Mon-Fri, 10am-3pm Sat May-Oct, 9am-3pm Mon-Fri, 10am-3pm Sat Nov-Apr) Adjoining the Palau Episcopal is the Jardí del Bisbe; this modest botanic garden is an oasis of peace. Have a quiet stroll among the palms, pomegranates, water lilies, thyme, artichokes, cumquats, orange and lemon trees, and more. Or just sit on a bench and contemplate.

Can Marquès HISTORIC BUILDING

(Map p44; ☎971 716 247; www.canmarquescontemporaneo.net; Carrer de Ca'n Angluda 2A; ⏲10am-3pm Mon-Fri) This exquisitely furnished mansion, the only one of its kind in Palma open to visitors, retains elements dating to the 14th century. It gives a fascinating insight into how the well-to-do lived around the turn of the 20th century. The building shows elements of Gothic, baroque and even Modernista influences. It hosts contemporary art exhibitions, but was closed for restoration at the time of research.

Once it reopens, enter the main *pati* (courtyard) where the family coach once clattered in, and climb the Modernista stairway to the main floor of the house, where the public can undertake a circuit through 10 rooms.

The immense Sala d'Entrada was a formal reception area and designed to impress the visitor with the owner's evident wealth. Next come three rooms, each used for entertaining guests of differing importance. The last of these, reserved for special guests, connected with the *alcoba,* an opulent-looking bedroom that was for show only. Perhaps most interesting are the kitchen (fully equipped and ready for the servants to come and prepare the masters' meals) and dining room (with its washbasin in the corner for cleaning greasy hands).

Can Bordils HISTORIC BUILDING
(Map p44; Carrer de l'Almudaina) This 16th-century mansion with a 17th-century courtyard is home to the Arxiu Municipal, which sometimes holds temporary exhibitions.

Arco de l'Almudaina HISTORIC BUILDING
(Map p44; Carrer de l'Almudaina) The arch down the street (east) of Can Bordils is intriguing for history buffs, part of a rare stretch of defensive wall and tower. It is said to have been in use from antiquity until about the 13th century. Although largely medieval in appearance, it is almost certain that this was part of the Roman wall.

Museu de Mallorca MUSEUM
(Map p44; ☎971 717 540; www.museudemallorca.es; Carrer de la Portella 5) This excellent city museum will be worth worth a visit, but will remain closed for extensive renovations until at least 2014. Once it reopens, you'll find a museum that inhabits a rambling ensemble of 17th-century mansions and has an extensive collection of archaeological artefacts, religious art, antiques and ceramics.

Casa-Museu Joaquim Torrents Lladó GALLERY, HISTORIC BUILDING
(Map p44; ☎971 729 835; www.jtorrentsllado.com; Carrer de la Portella 9; adult/child €4/2.50; ⏲10.30am-2.30pm Tue-Sat) This fine old house, with a timber gallery overlooking a courtyard, belonged to the Catalan artist Joaquim Torrents Lladó (1946–93), who moved to Mallorca in the 1960s. The 1st and 2nd levels feature timber floors, 19th-century furniture and a changing display of the painter's work, ranging from portraits to labels for Codorniu champagne. Occasional temporary exhibitions are staged here, too.

Banys Àrabs BATHHOUSE
(Map p44; ☎971 721 549; Carrer de Serra 7; adult/child €2/free; ⏲9.30am-8pm) These modest Arab baths are the single most important remaining monument to the Muslim domination of the island, although all that survives are two small underground chambers, one with a domed ceiling supported by a dozen columns, some of whose capitals were recycled from demolished Roman buildings.

The site may be small, but the two rooms – the caldarium, or hot bath, and the tepidarium (warm bath) – evoke a poignant sense of abandonment. Normally there would also have been a third, cold bath, the frigidarium. As the Roman terms suggest, the Arabs basically took over a Roman idea, here in Mallorca and throughout the Arab world. These ones probably were not public but attached to a private mansion. The baths are set in one of Old Palma's prettiest gardens, where you can sit and relax.

FREE **Església de Santa Eulàlia** CHURCH
(Map p44; ☎971 714 625; Plaça de Santa Eulàlia 2; ⏲9am-noon & 6.30-8.30pm Mon-Fri, 10.30am-1pm & 6.30-8.30 Sat, 9.30am-1.30pm, 6.30-7.30pm & 9-10pm Sun) One of the first major churches raised after the 1229 conquest, the Església de Santa Eulàlia is a soaring Gothic structure with a neo-Gothic facade (a complete remake was done between 1894 and 1924). It is the only such church in Mallorca, aside from the Catedral, with three naves. The baroque *retablo* is rather worn and you can't get to the chapels in the apse.

Basílica de Sant Francesc CHURCH
(Map p44; ☎971 712 695; Plaça de Sant Francesc 7; admission €1.50; ⏲9.30am-12.30pm & 3.30-6pm Mon-Sat, 9.30am-12.30pm Sun) One of Palma's oldest churches, the Franciscan Basílica de Sant Francesc was begun in 1281 in Gothic style and its baroque facade was completed in 1700. It's best known for its beautiful, two-tiered, trapezoidal cloister.

PALMA'S HISTORIC COURTYARDS & MODERNISTA GEMS

Born of the necessities of a hot Mediterranean climate, the typical privileged Roman *domus* (house) and the *pati andaluz* (Andalucian courtyard) of Muslim Arab Spain was built around one or more cool courtyards. In Mallorca nobles and wealthy merchants from the time of Jaume I's conquest onward adopted the tradition and made it their own.

In Palma, the Gothic houses of the well-to-do maintained the idea of a cool, plant-filled central courtyard, around which the rest of the house was built. Access from the street was via a narrow entrance, and a stone external staircase led up to the first (or noble) floor of the house. In the 17th and 18th centuries, the baroque influence saw entrances widened to allow the entry of coaches and horses, and designs were more extravagant. The houses and the *pati* (courtyard) in particular were the preserve of Mallorca's elite and marked the intersection between public and private life – guests were received here while the rest of the house remained off-limits.

There are around 150 such homes in Palma. Today the doors to quite a few *patis* are opened by day, although it's rare that you're allowed to walk in far off the street. In late spring around 50 are opened for guided visits and concerts during the Corpus Christi celebrations.

Among the more interesting *patis* to look out for:

» **Can Salas** (Can Jordà; Map p44; Carrer de la Puresa 2)

» **Can Catlar del Llorer** (Map p44; Carrer de Can Savellà 15)

» **Can Vivot** (Map p44; Carrer de Can Savellà 4)

» **Can Berga** (Map p44; Plaça del Mercat 12)

» **Cal Marquès del Palmer** (Map p44; Carrer del Sol 7)

» **Cal Comte de San Simón** (Map p44; Carrer de Sant Jaume 7)

» **Can Caldès** (Carrer del Monti-Sion 3)

Others open to the public because they house museums, public offices and the like:

» **Can Marqués** (p48)

» **Museu de Mallorca** (p49)

» **Centre Cultural Contemporani Pelaires** (p51)

» **Fundació Sa Nostra** (p53)

» **Casal Solleric** (p55)

» **Can Bordils** (p49)

Palma is also sprinkled with eye-catching buildings that resulted from the strange and fecund, if brief, period of architectural imagination known as Modernisme. Examples include the following:

» **CaixaForum** (p53)

» **Forn des Teatre** (p61)

» **Almacenes El Águila** (p53)

» **Can Casasayas** (Map p44; Plaça del Mercat 13 & 14)

» **Can Corbella** (Map p44; Plaça de la Cort 6)

» **Can Forteza Rey** (Map p44; Carrer de les Monges 2)

In the splendid, sunny Gothic cloister – a two-tiered, trapezoid affair – the elegant columns in various styles indicate it was some time in the making. Inside the lugubrious church, the fusion of styles is clear. The high vaulted roof is classic Gothic, while the glittering, curvaceous high altar is a baroque lollipop, albeit in need of a polish.

In the first chapel (dedicated to Nostra Senyora de la Consolació) on the left in the apse is the church's pride and joy, the tomb of and monument to the 13th-century scholar and evangelist Ramon Llull. He is Mallorca's favourite son (apart perhaps from the tennis genius Rafael Nadal). Llull's alabaster tomb is high up on the right. Drop a few coins in the slot for the campaign to have him canonised (he has only made it to beatification). Check out the Capilla de los Santos Mártires Gorkomienses, on the right side of the apse. In 1572, 19 Catholics, 11 of them Franciscans, were martyred in Holland. In this much faded portrayal of the event, you can see them being hanged, disembowelled, having their noses cut off and more.

Remnants of 12th-century Arab wall RUIN
(Carrer de Mateu Enric Lladó) One block east of the Església de Sant Jeroni, you strike a portion of the 12th-century Arab city wall (with some heavy blocks from the Roman wall at the base), beyond which is a park named after the city gate that once stood here: Porta d'es Camp (Gate of the Countryside). The Muslims knew it as Bab al-Jadid (the New Gate).

Església del Monti-Sion CHURCH
(Map p44; Carrer del Monti-Sion; ⌚5.15-7pm) The gaudy baroque facade of the Església del Monti-Sion was converted from a Gothic synagogue. It got a serious baroque makeover, inside and out, in the 16th to 17th centuries.

As you wander in, a priest sitting in a booth by the entry may flip a switch and light up the curves-and-swirls baroque *retablo* at the back of the church. Gothic giveaways include the ogive arches in front of the chapels, the key vaulting in the ceiling and the long, low Catalan Gothic arch just inside the entrance.

Convent de Santa Clara CONVENT
(Map p44; Carrer de Can Fonollar 2; ⌚9am-12.30pm & 4.15-6.15pm) This church is a gloomy baroque affair. It was closed for renovation when we were here, but, in any event, locals prefer to pop into the adjacent building, because the handful of cloistered nuns maintain a centuries-old tradition of baking sweets for sale.

You will see a *torno,* a kind of timber turnstile set in a window. Ring for a nun, order what you want and put money into the turnstile. This swivels around and out come your *bocaditos de almendra* (almond nibbles) or *rollitos de anís* (aniseed rolls), at €3 for 200g.

Ajuntament HISTORIC BUILDING
(Town Hall; Map p44; Plaça de la Cort 1) Dominating the square that has long been the heart of municipal power in Palma is the *ajuntament.* The baroque facade hides a longer history: the town hall building grew out of a Gothic hospital raised here shortly after the island's conquest. On the top floor of the main facade sits En Figuera, as the town clock is affectionately known.

The present mechanism dates to 1863 and was purchased in France, but a clock has tolled the hours here for centuries. You can generally enter the foyer only, in which you will see a Gothic entrance, a fine sweeping staircase and, probably, half a dozen *gegants* (huge figures of kings, queens and other characters that are paraded around town on people's shoulders during fiesta) in storage.

Centre Cultural Contemporani Pelaires CULTURAL CENTRE, GALLERY
(Map p44; ☎971 720 375; www.pelaires.com; Carrer de Can Verí 3; ⌚10am-1.30pm & 4.30-8pm Mon-Fri, 10am-1.30pm Sat) This private cultural centre is as interesting for its architecture as for its content (changing art exhibitions). The building, Can Verí, is a beautiful 17th-century town house that was also used for a while as a convent. This narrow pedestrian lane is rather chichi, home to galleries, antique shops and fashion boutiques.

Arc del Wali HISTORIC BUILDING
(Map p44; off S'Hort del Rei) A grand arch, the Arc del Wali is one of the city's few reminders of its Arab past. When the Riera, the city's river, coursed along what is now Passeig d'es Born and the sea lapped the city walls, this was the seaward entrance into the Arab palace and early shipyards.

Walls & Parc de la Mar CITY WALLS, PARK
(Map p44) Most of Palma's defensive walls were destroyed in the late 19th century to allow easier expansion of the city. Only a section of the Renaissance sea wall, the Dalt Murada (begun in 1562, finished in 1801), remains impressively intact. In 1984 the Parc de la Mar (with its artificial lake, fountain and green spaces) was opened.

Looking tatty in parts, it is still a pleasing part of the view from the stout walls, and a pleasant place for a breezy drink at a terrace cafe in summer.

PLAÇA MAJOR & AROUND

Plaça Major is a typically Spanish central square, lined with arcades, shops and cafes. Lively by day, it falls eerily silent at night. To the east, Carrer del Sindicat spokes out towards the avenues that mark the limits of historic Palma. It crosses a district known

Northern Palma

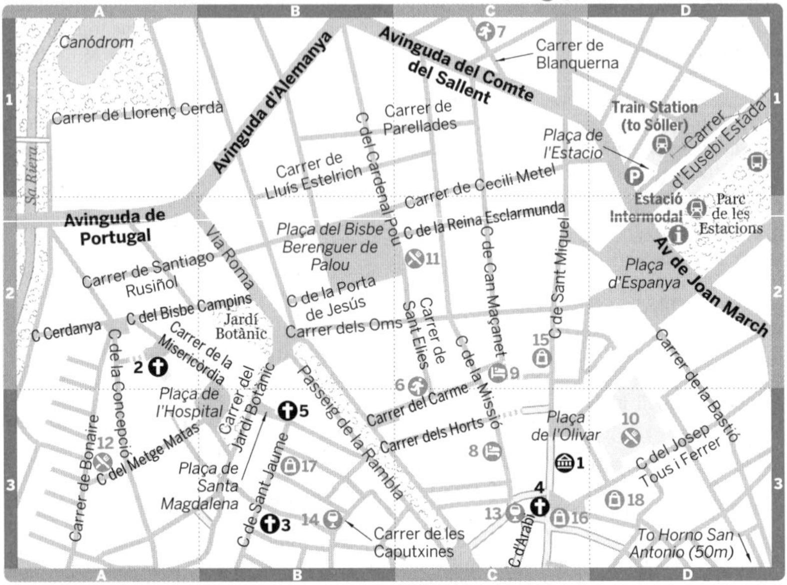

as Sa Gerreria. For decades run-down and slightly dodgy, Sa Gerreria is enjoying a revival and it's becoming a trendy hub of the city's nightlife. Off Plaça Major, the shopping boulevard, Carrer de Sant Miquel, leads north towards the vast **Plaça d'Espanya**. Plaça Major and Carrer de Sant Miquel are on high ground that falls away to the west down to shady Passeig de la Rambla.

FREE Museu Fundación Juan March — MUSEUM

(Museu Fundació Juan March; Map p44; ☎971 713 515; www.march.es/arte/palma; Carrer de Sant Miquel 11; ⏰10am-6.30pm Mon-Fri, 10.30am-2pm Sat) This 17th-century mansion makes a good introduction to Spanish contemporary art. On permanent display are some 70 pieces held by the Fundación Juan March. Together they constitute a veritable who's who of mostly 20th-century artists, including Picasso, Miró, Juan Gris (of cubism fame), Dalí and the sculptor Julio González.

After starting with the big names, the collection moves through various movements in Spanish art, such as that inspired in Barcelona by the *Dau al Set* review (1948–53) and led by Antoni Tàpies. Meanwhile, in Valencia, Eusebi Sempere and Andreu Alfaro were leading the way down abstract paths. Sempere's *Las Cuatro Estaciones* (1980) reflects the four seasons in subtle changes of colour in a series of four panels with interlocking shapes made of fine lines. Other names to watch for are Manuel Millares, Fernando Zóbel and Miquel Barceló, who is represented by a huge ceramic pot with bulging skull shapes (*Grand Pot avec Crânes sur une Face*, 2000) and a canvas, *La Flaque* (The Puddle, 1989).

Església de Sant Miquel — CHURCH

(Church of St Michael; Map p52; Carrer de Sant Miquel 21; ⏰9.30am-1.30pm & 5-7.30pm) Raised after the conquest of Mallorca, this church is a striking mix. It was one of the first four churches built on the site of a mosque where the island's first Mass was celebrated on 31 December 1229. The facade and entrance, with its long, low arch, is a perfect example of 14th-century Catalan Gothic. The squat, seven-storey bell tower is also a Gothic creation.

Otherwise, the church, with its barrel-vaulted ceiling, is largely the result of a baroque makeover. Note the statue of Pope John Paul II on the right as you enter.

FREE Claustre de Sant Antoniet — GALLERY

(Map p52; Carrer de Sant Miquel 30; ⏰10am-2pm & 3.30-8pm Mon-Fri, 10am-1.30pm Sat) The Claus-

Northern Palma

Sights

1 Claustre de Sant Antoniet C3
2 Església de Sant Crist de la Sang A2
3 Església de Sant Jaume B3
4 Església de Sant Miquel C3
5 Església de Santa Magdalena B3

Activities, Courses & Tours

6 Dialog C2
7 Fosh Food C1

Sleeping

8 Convent de la Missió C3
9 Misión de San Miguel C2

Eating

10 Mercat de l'Olivar D3
Misa Braseria .... (see 9)
11 Restaurant Celler Sa Premsa C2
12 S'Esponja Café A3
Simply Fosh .... (see 8)

Drinking

13 Café L'Antiquari C3
14 Es Pincell B3

Shopping

15 Addaia C2
16 Bordados Valldemossa C3
Dialog .... (see 6)
17 Rosario P B3
18 Xocoa D3

tre de Sant Antoniet is a baroque gem that belongs to the BBVA bank. The two-tiered, oval-shaped enclosure was built in 1768 and is now used for temporary art exhibitions. It was originally attached to the **Església de Sant Antoni de Viana**, which was closed for restoration when we visited, next door.

Almacenes El Águila HISTORIC BUILDING
(Map p44; Plaça del Marqués de Palmer 1) Gaspar Bennàssar (1869–1933), one of the most influential architects in modern Palma, his native city, played with various styles during his long career, including Modernisme. An outstanding example of this is the Almacenes El Águila, built in 1908. Each of the three floors is different and the generous use of wrought iron in the main facade is a herald of the style.

Círculo de Bellas Artes GALLERY
(Map p44; ☎971 723 112; Carrer de l'Unió 3) Casal Balaguer – with the grand if unevenly cobbled courtyard, graced by four thin, leaning palms – is home to a faded but weighty art institution, the Círculo de Bellas Artes. The site was closed for much-needed major renovations at the time of our visit. When it reopens, it will host art exhibitions.

CaixaForum GALLERY
(Map p44; ☎971 178 500; www.lacaixa.es/ObraSocial; Plaça de Weyler 3; ⏲10am-9pm Mon-Sat, 10am-2pm Sun) This exhibition centre is run by one of Spain's biggest building societies, the Barcelona-based La Caixa. CaixaForum is housed in the wonderful Modernista building (the island's first) that was once home to the Grand Hotel. Pick up a free program at reception and flick through it at the ground-level cafe. There's also an excellent bookshop.

The Grand Hotel was once a city landmark that was built in 1900–03 by the Catalan master architect Lluís Domènech i Montaner and the first building in Palma with electricity and a lift. The hotel was shut down during the Civil War and never recovered. As well as the art exhibitions, other frequent activities put on here include lectures, workshops, film cycles and concerts.

FREE **Fundació Sa Nostra** GALLERY, CULTURAL CENTRE
(Map p44; ☎971 725 210; www.obrasocialsanostra.com; Carrer de la Concepció 12; ⏲11am-9pm) The big Balearics building society, Sa Nostra, has a cultural foundation in Can Castelló, where it stages exhibitions. It is worth popping by just to check out the fine 18th-century courtyard, which now hosts a hip cafe. The temporary exhibitions at the centre are always worth a look.

The original house dates to the previous century, and it even has a few Modernista touches from renovation work done in 1909. Just in front of it is **Font del Sepulcre**, a Gothic baptismal font left over from a long-disappeared church. Inside it is a 12th-century Muslim-era well. Carrer de la Concepció used to be known as Carrer de la Monederia, as the Kingdom of Mallorca's mint was on this street.

FREE **Església de Sant Jaume** CHURCH
(Map p52; Carrer de Sant Jaume 10; ⏲11.30am-1.30pm & 5.30-8.30pm) Despite its baroque facade, this is one of Palma's older surviving Gothic churches, a grey soaring eminence, and one of the first four parish churches to be built, from 1327 'under the protection

of the Royal House of Mallorca'. It is said that the Bonapart family (later Bonaparte) lived around here until they moved to Corsica in 1406. Napoleon could have been a Mallorquin!

FREE **Església de Santa Magdalena** CHURCH
(Map p52; Plaça de Santa Magdalena; ⌚9am-12.30pm & 5.30-7.30pm Mon-Sat) The main claim to fame of the baroque Església de Santa Magdalena is as being the resting place of Santa Catalina Thomàs of Valldemossa. Her clothed remains are visible through a glass coffin held in a chapel to the left of the altar and are an object of pilgrimage.

It is said that the future saint sat weeping by a great clump of stone one day as none of the convents would accept her because she was too poor. Then someone told her that the convent once attached to the Església de Santa Magdalena would take her in. She was overjoyed. The stone in question is now embedded in the rear wall of the 14th-century **Església de Sant Nicolau** on Plaça del Mercat.

FREE **Església de Sant Crist de la Sang** CHURCH
(Map p52; Plaça de l'Hospital; ⌚7.30am-1pm & 4-8pm Mon-Fri, 7.30am-1pm & 5-8pm Sat, Sun & holidays) Within the Hospital General (founded in the 16th century), you can behold the Gothic facade of this church. It is the object of pilgrimage and devotion, since the *paso* (a sculpted image used in processions) of 'Holy Christ of the Blood' is considered to be miraculous.

If you happen on a Mass, it's moving to see the devotion of the faithful who climb up behind the altar to venerate the image of Christ crucified, with long, flowing *real* hair and embroidered loincloth. Just on your left as you enter the church is a 15th-century nativity scene, probably imported from Naples.

HAVE YOUR SAY

Found a fantastic restaurant that you're longing to share with the world? Disagree with our recommendations? Or just want to talk about your most recent trip?

Whatever your reason, head to lonelyplanet.com, where you can post a review, ask or answer a question on the Thorntree forum, comment on a blog, or share your photos and tips on Groups. Or you can simply spend time chatting with like-minded travellers. So go on, have your say.

ES PUIG DE SANT PERE

Passeig d'es Born is capped by Plaça del Rei Joan Carles I (named after the present king and formerly after Pope Pius XII), a traffic roundabout locally known as Plaça de les Tortugues, because of the obelisk placed on four bronze turtles. A block from here on the east side of the avenue, on the corner of Carrer de Jovellanos, the distorted black face of a Moor, complete with white stone turban, is affixed high on the corner of a building. Known as the **Cap del Moro** (Moor's Head), it represents a Muslim slave who is said to have killed his master, a chaplain, in October 1731. The slave was executed and his hand lopped off and reportedly attached to the wall of the house where the crime was committed. Chronicles claim the withered remains of the hand were still in place, behind a grille, in 1840!

Es Baluard GALLERY, MUSEUM
(Museu d'Art Modern i Contemporani; Map p44; ☎971 908 200; www.esbaluard.org; Porta de Santa Catalina 10; permanent exhibition adult/child €6/4.50, temporary exhibitions €4/3; ⌚10am-9pm Tue-Sun) Built with flair and innovation into the shell of the Renaissance-era seaward walls, this contemporary art gallery is one of the finest on the island. While its temporary exhibitions are always worth checking out, the core of the permanent collection – works by Joan Miró, Miquel Barceló and Picasso – and the setting are what give the gallery its cachet.

The 21st-century concrete complex has been cleverly built in and among the fortifications, which include the partly restored remains of an 11th-century Muslim-era tower (on your right as you arrive from Carrer de Sant Pere). The effect is a playful game of light, surfaces and perspective.

Inside, the ground floor houses the core of the permanent exhibition, starting with a section on Mallorcan landscapes by local artists and others from abroad; the big names here include Valencia's Joaquín Sorolla, Mallorca's own Miquel Barceló and the Catalan Modernista artist Santiago Rusiñol; the latter did a lot of work in and around the town of Bunyola. A broad swath of local and mostly Catalan landscape artists is also

GALLERY ALLEY

Contemporary-art enthusiasts will get a buzz out of the plethora of galleries that populate the narrow streets just west of the Passeig d'es Born. Top places:

» **Sala Pelaires** (Map p44; ☎971 723 696; www.pelaires.com; Carrer de Pelaires 5; ⏲10am-1.30pm & 4.30-8pm Mon-Fri, 10am-1.30pm Sat)

» **Galeria La Caja Blanca** (Map p44; ☎971 722 364; www.lacajablanca.com; Carrer de Can Verí 9; ⏲11am-2pm & 5-8pm Mon-Fri, 11.30am-2pm Sat)

» **Joan Guaita Art** (Map p44; ☎971 715 989; www.joanguaitaart.com; Carrer de Can Verí 10; ⏲11am-2pm & 5-8pm Mon-Fri, 11.30am-2pm Sat)

» **Galeria K** (Map p44; ☎680 207 207; www.galeria-k.com; Carrer de Can Verí 10; ⏲10.30am-2pm & 5-8pm Mon-Fri, 10.30am-2pm Sat)

on show here. Also on the ground floor and part of the permanent collection is a room devoted to the works of Joan Miró, while on the top floor is an intriguing collection of ceramics by Pablo Picasso; after viewing the latter, step out onto the ramparts for fine views. In sum, it's an impressive rather than extraordinary collection that's well worth a couple of hours of your time.

Casal Solleric CULTURAL CENTRE, HISTORIC BUILDING
(Map p44; ☎971 722 092; Passeig d'es Born 27; ⏲10am-2pm & 5-9pm Tue-Sat, 10am-1.30pm Sun) This grand 18th-century baroque mansion with the typical Palma courtyard of graceful broad arches and uneven stone paving is at once a cultural centre with temporary exhibitions, bookshop and tourist information office. Displays are usually free and found over a couple of floors. The part facing Passeig d'es Born was actually the rear of the original house, built in 1763. Archduke Ludwig Salvador thought its courtyard 'one of the most beautiful in Palma'.

FREE **Sa Llotja** HISTORIC BUILDING
(Map p44; ☎971 711 705; Plaça de la Llotja; ⏲11am-1.45pm & 5-8.45pm Tue-Sat, 11am-1.45pm Sun) The gorgeous, if weather-beaten, 15th-century sandstone Gothic Sa Llotja, opposite the waterfront, was built as a merchants' stock exchange and is used for temporary exhibitions. It was closed for renovations at the time of writing.

Designed by Guillem Sagrera, it is the apogee of civilian Gothic building on the island and was completed in 1450. Inside, six slender, twisting columns lead to the lofty vaulted ceiling. In each corner of the building rises a fanciful octagonal tower. The flanks are marked with huge arches, fine tracery and monstrous-looking gargoyles leaning out overhead.

Consolat de Mar HISTORIC BUILDING
(Map p44; Passeig de Sagrera) Virtually next door to Sa Llotja (Plaça de la Llotja), the Consolat de Mar was founded in 1326 as a maritime tribunal. The present building, one of Mallorca's few examples of (albeit impure) Renaissance design, was completed in 1669. It was tacked onto, and faces, a late Gothic chapel completed around 1600 for the members of Sa Llotja. The Consolat de Mar houses the presidency of the Balearic Islands regional government.

Església de Santa Creu CHURCH
(Map p44; ☎971 712 690; Carrer de Sant Llorenç 4; admission €3; ⏲11am-1pm Mon, Tue, Thu & Fri) Work on this Gothic church began in 1335. The main entrance (Carrer de Santa Creu 7) is a baroque addition. What makes it interesting is the Cripta de Sant Llorenç (crypt of St Lawrence), an early-Gothic place of worship dating possibly to the late 13th century. Some paintings by Rafel Mòger and Francesc Comes are scattered about the interior.

SANTA CATALINA & AROUND

A curious district of long, grid-pattern streets and traditional low-slung one- and two-storey houses, Santa Catalina was once a down-at-heel sailors' district and for a long time a somewhat raggedy part of town. As early as the 17th century, windmills were raised in the area (still known as Es Jonquet) south off Carrer de Sant Magí, the oldest street in the *barri*. In recent years it has been transformed into a bohemian place to find great bars and restaurants.

PASSEIG MARÍTIM & WESTERN PALMA

Western Palma boasts a handful of sights. The Castell de Bellver is the most worthwhile, not least for the views.

Castell de Bellver CASTLE
(Bellver Castle; ☎971 730 657; Carrer de Camilo José Cela 17; adult/child €2.50/1, Sun & public holidays free; ⏲8.30am-8.30pm Mon-Sat, 10am-6.30pm Sun) Set atop a pleasant park, the Castell de Bellver is a 14th-century circular castle (with a unique round tower), the only one of its kind in Spain. Jaume II ordered the castle built atop a hill known as Puig de Sa Mesquida in 1300 and it was largely complete 10 years later. The views from here of Palma and the Badia de Palma are spectacular.

The castle was conceived above all as a royal residence but seems to have been a white elephant, as only King Sanç (in 1314) and Aragón's Joan I (in 1395) moved in for any amount of time. In 1717 it became a prison. The best part of a visit is the chance to mosey around the castle and enjoy the views over the surrounding woods to Palma and out to sea. Climb to the roof and check out the prisoners' graffiti etched into the stonework.

The ground-floor **Museu d'Història de la Ciutat** (City History Museum) consists of some explanatory panels and a modest collection of pottery. Upstairs you can visit a series of largely empty chambers, including the one-time kitchen. These are kept closed (no great loss) on Sundays, when admission is free.

About the nearest you can get to the castle by bus (3, 46 or 50) is Plaça de Gomila, from where you'll have to hoof it about 15 minutes (1km) up a steep hill. Instead, combine it with the Palma City Sightseeing open-top bus, which climbs to the castle as part of its circuit of the city.

Poble Espanyol ARCHITECTURE MUSEUM
(Map p57; ☎971 737 070; Carrer del Poble Espanyol 55; adult/child €8/5; ⏲9am-7.30pm) This 'Spanish Village' is a copy of bits of Spanish towns from all over the country. It's cheesy but intriguing and contains replicas of everything from typical Andalucian streets to Canary Islands houses, from the grand Bisagra gate of Toledo to Granada's Muslim Alhambra. Buses 5, 29 and 46 take you close (alight at Avinguda d'Andrea Doria 41).

ES PORTITXOL, ES MOLINAR & CIUTAT JARDÍ

A 1km walk from the city centre end of the Platja de Can Pere Antoni brings you to Es Portitxol. The 'little port' has a quiet abundance of pleasure craft and is closed off inland by the motorway (at a discreet distance). You can walk, cycle or rollerblade here along the Passeig Marítim from central Palma.

From Es Portitxol, continue walking around the next point and enter **Es Molinar**. This simple, waterfront 'suburban' district of low fishing folks' houses has become a dining haunt, with a handful of places at the Es Portitxol end. Over the bridge is **Ciutat Jardí**, a low-key residential area with a broad, sandy beach.

Museu Krekovic MUSEUM
(☎971 219 606; Carrer de Ciutat de Querétaro 3; adult/child €1.80/0.45; ⏲9.30am-1pm & 3-6pm Mon-Fri, 10.30am-1pm Sat, closed Aug) This museum looks on to the somewhat dishevelled Parc Kristian Krekovic, east of the centre, and is dedicated to the work of eccentric Bosnian artist Kristian Krekovic (1901–85), who spent the last 25 years of his life in Mallorca after a long period studying the Incas and Peruvian indigenous groups. The result is three rooms of monumental canvases in a thunder-and-lightning crash of colour depicting ancient warriors, chiefs, virgins, musicians and masked figures. Bus 12 runs close by.

Activities

Marenostrum BOAT TRIPS
(Map p57; ☎971 456 182; www.marenostrum-catamarans.com; Passeig Marítim 8; with/without hotel pick-up €56/48) Marenostrum puts on daily five-hour catamaran tours (from May to October) to either Cala Portals Vells or Cala Vella (depending on wind direction), just east of the Badia de Palma. The price includes food on board and snorkelling gear.

Cruceros Marco Polo BOAT TRIPS
(Map p44; ☎647 843 667, 971 426 643; www.crucerosmarcopolo.com; off Passeig Marítim; 1hr cruise €10; ⏲hourly 11am-4pm Mon-Sat Mar-Oct) This operator offers a one-hour whiz around the bay up to six times daily.

Palma on Bike BICYCLE RENTAL
(Map p44; ☎971 718 062; www.palmaonbike.com; Avinguda d'Antoni Maura 10; city/mountain bike per day €12/16, per week €49/75, rollerblades per

Western Palma

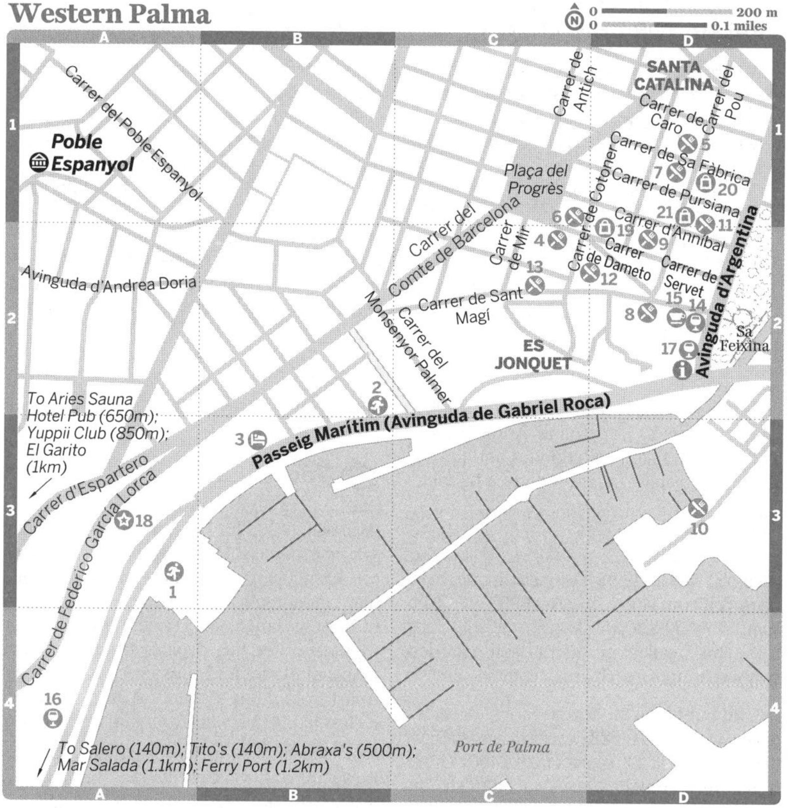

Western Palma

Top Sights
Poble Espanyol A1

Activities, Courses & Tours
1 Marenostrum A3
2 Voyage B2

Sleeping
3 Hotel Mirador B3

Eating
4 Afrikana C2
5 Diecisiete Grados D1
6 Fàbrica 23 .... C1
7 Hórreo Veinti3 .... D1
8 La Baranda D2
9 Mercat de Santa Catalina D2
10 Nautic D3
11 Restaurante a Todo Vapor D1
12 Room D2
13 Ummo C2

Drinking
Café Lisboa .... (see 8)
14 Hostal Cuba Colonial D2
15 Idem Café D2
16 Made in Brasil A4
17 Soho D2

Entertainment
18 Auditòrium A3

Shopping
19 B Connected Concept Store D2
20 Colmado Manresa D1
21 Trading Place D1

PALMA FOR CHILDREN

With the city's beaches and related water activities (including boat tours) a simple option, Palma should be stress-free for kids and their adult guardians. Children will love to explore the Castell de Bellver (p56) and **Castell de Sant Carles** (☎971 402 145; Carretera del Dic de l'Oest; admission free; ⊙9am-1pm Mon-Sat); you can also combine art with fun on the ramparts at Es Baluard (p54); and young girls and boys might find the Museo de Muñecas (p48) intriguing. Palma Aquarium (p73), east of Palma in Platja de Palma, is also outstanding and you could easily spend half a day there.

Sets of swings, climbing things and other diversions for young children are scattered about town. There is an immense assortment in Parc de les Estacions, near the bus station, and another good set in Sa Feixina park near Es Baluard. You'll stumble across more swings in the shadow of Palau de l'Almudaina and further along near the walls just east of Parc de la Mar.

day €10; ⊙10am-2pm & 4-8pm) Palma on Bike has city bikes to get around Palma, as well as mountain bikes, rollerblades and kayaks. Bike rates include insurance and a helmet.

Courses

Dialog LANGUAGE
(Map p52; ☎971 719 994; www.dialog-palma.com; Carrer del Carme 14; 2-week course €395; ⊙9.30am-2pm & 4.30-8.30pm Mon-Fri, 10am-1.30pm Sat) This bookshop offers well-regarded, two-week intensive Spanish courses.

Estudi Lul·lià de Mallorca LANGUAGE
(Map p44; ☎971 711 988; www.estudigeneral.com; Carrer de Sant Roc 4; courses from €400) Offers intensive summer courses in Spanish language and culture.

Die Akademie LANGUAGE
(Map p44; ☎971 718 290; www.dieakademie.com; Carrer de Morei 8; per week €175-195; ⊙9am-1.30pm & 5-7.30pm Mon-Fri) Housed in a late-Gothic mansion, Die Akademie runs a variety of Spanish-language courses.

Fosh Food COOKING
(Map p52; ☎971 290 108; www.marcfosh.com; Carrer de Blanquerna 6; per person from €50) Marc Fosh, who runs some of Palma's most celebrated eateries, also heads up the gourmet laboratory Fosh Food. Cooking classes by various chefs, both local and international, are held most days of the week and start from €50. Book ahead, as groups often take over the calendar.

Voyage SAILING
(Map p57; ☎971 222 907; www.voyageseaschool.com; Avinguda de Gabriel Roca 4) Want to learn to be a yacht or catamaran skipper in the Med? Voyage runs courses in conjunction with the UK Royal Yachting Association. Contact it for prices.

Tours

Palma City Sightseeing GUIDED TOUR
(Map p44; ☎902 101 081; www.mallorcatour.com; Avinguda d'Antoni Maura; adult/child €13/6.50; ⊙9.30am-10pm) This hop-on-hop-off bus has (moderately interesting) commentary in various languages. Tickets are valid for 24 hours. The bus departs from Avinguda d'Antoni Maura and runs every 20 minutes. Apart from doing a circuit of the city centre, it runs along the waterfront and even climbs up to the Castell de Bellver.

Mallorca Rutes WALKING TOUR
(Palma VIP; Map p44; ☎971 728 983; www.mallorcarutes.com; Carrer de Morei 1; per person €25; ⊙10.30am Sat) These privately run city walking tours take in the best of the old city, enabling you to enter some of otherwise closed patios and there's also a gastronomic theme running through. The tours can be booked through Típika, next to Plaça de Santa Eulalia, and the tours leave from Plaça de la Reina, at the southern end of Passeig d'es Born.

Festivals & Events

Festa de Sant Sebastiá MUSIC
(19-20 Jan) On the eve of the feast day of Palma's patron saint, concerts (from funk to folk) are staged in the city squares, along with flaming pyres and the *aiguafoc*, a fireworks display over the bay. It's a big (if chilly) night.

Sa Rueta & Sa Rua CARNAVAL
(Feb-Mar) Palma's version of Carnaval (celebrated in the last days before Lent starts)

involves a procession for kids (Sa Rueta) followed later by a bigger one (Sa Rua) with floats and the like.

Semana Santa RELIGIOUS
(Holy Week; Mar-Apr) Processions dot the Easter Week calendar, but the most impressive are those on Holy Thursday evening. In the Processó del Sant Crist de la Sang (Christ of the Blood), robed and hooded members of *confraries* (lay brotherhoods) parade with a *paso* (heavy sculpted image of Christ, borne by a team of men). It starts at 7pm in the Església del Crist de la Sang, where the *paso* is kept, and returns hours later.

Festival Mundial de Danses Folklòriques DANCE
(☎971 736 060; www.worldfolkdance.com; Apr) The world comes to Palma for five days, with folk dancers performing in central Palma's streets and squares.

MUST FASHION
(www.dissenymallorca.com; Apr) A three-day fashion fest held around central Palma.

Saló Naùtic BOAT FAIR
(www.firesicongressos.com; May) Usually held around the first week of May, this is a major boat fair held at the Moll Vell docks.

Corpus Christi RELIGIOUS
(May-Jun) The feast of the Body of Christ (the Eucharist) falls on the Thursday of the ninth week after Easter, although the main procession from the cathedral takes place on the following Sunday at 7pm. On that day, carpets of flowers are laid out in front of the Catedral and in Plaça de la Cort. Concert cycles (many held in the city's *patis*, which can also be visited at this time) add a celebratory note for about a month around the feast day.

Nit de Sant Joan MUSIC
(23 Jun) The night before the feast of St John (24 June) is celebrated with fiery feasting. As night falls, the *correfoc* (fire running) begins in the Parc de la Mar. People dressed up as demons, and armed with pyrotechnical gear that would probably be illegal in hell, leap and dance in an infernal procession. Locals then head for the beaches, where wandering musical groups and pyres add flaming cheer to a partying crowd until dawn.

Estiu de Cultura MUSIC
(www.imtur.es; Jul & Aug) Palma's Castell del Bellver hosts the Estiu de Cultura, a series of musical events through July and August ranging from classical to jazz.

Nits a la Fresca MUSIC
(www.imtur.es; Jul & Aug) Catch the open-air cinema, folk music and theatre at a stage set up in Parc de la Mar.

Festes de Sant Magí NEIGHBOURHOOD
(19 Aug) A local event in Santa Catalina with music, street theatre and fireworks.

Palma de Mallorca Surf Action SURF
(www.mallorcasurfaction.net; Aug) Since 2005, Platja de Palma has been the stage for the annual Palma de Mallorca Surf Action event, which attracts demos, stands and leading figures in windsurfing, kite surfing, wakeboarding, light sailing, skating and more.

SAILING EVENTS IN PALMA

Sailing is a big deal in Palma and numerous regattas are held in the course of the year. In addition to those listed, the **Real Club Náutico** (www.realclubnauticopalma.com), the most prestigious of Palma's yacht clubs, organises more than 20 events (some in collaboration with other clubs) throughout the year.

Copa del Rey (King's Cup) Held over eight days in July and August, and is a high point. The king, Juan Carlos I, and his son Felipe frequently race on competing boats.

PalmaVela (www.palmavela.com) Held in April, the PalmaVela has hundreds of yachts of all classes from around the world.

Trofeo SAR Princesa Sofía (www.trofeoprincesasofia.org) Held in April, this is one of six regattas composing the World Cup Series, attracting Olympic crews from all over the world.

The Superyacht Cup (www.thesuperyachtcup.com) Held over three days in October, this is one of the major races for superyachts of anything from 25m to 90m in size.

Ciutat de Palma-Regata Nova IX A huge event for smaller boats, held over four days in December.

DIY MEALS

Palma's produce markets are a great way to get under the skin of the city as you bustle about the fresh-produce stands. You can stock up on all you need to put together your own meals, from cheeses and cold meats to fruit and veg (and plenty more if you have access to cooking facilities). The most engrossing is the central **Mercat de l'Olivar** (Map p52; Plaça de l'Olivar; ⏲8am-2pm & 5-8pm Mon-Fri, 8am-2pm Sat), while equally busy and with few tourists are the **Mercat de Santa Catalina** (Map p57; Plaça de la Navegació; ⏲8am-2pm & 5-8pm Mon-Fri, 8am-2pm Sat) and **Mercat de Pere Garau** (Plaça de Pere Garau; ⏲8am-2pm & 5-8pm Mon-Fri, 8am-2pm Sat).

Nit de l'Art CONTEMPORARY ART
(Sep) An established art event; galleries and institutions all over town throw open their doors to expose the latest trends in art.

Christmas Market MARKET
(Plaça Major; ⏲10am-8pm) The Christmas market takes over the Plaça Major from 16 December to 5 January.

Eating

OLD PALMA

Las Olas MEDITERRANEAN, VIETNAMESE €€
(Map p44; ☎971 214 905; www.lasolasbistro.com; Carrer de Can Fortuny 5; meals €25-30, tapas €1.50-7; ⏲12.15-3.45pm & 8.15-11pm Tue-Sat, 12.15-3.45pm Mon) Now here's something special. Run by an Irish-Cambodian couple, Las Olas divides the day into two: lunch is all about fresh Mediterranean flavours with international twists, while dinner is a Vietnamese-Cambodian affair. Other innovations include *tapas sefardis* (Jewish tapas), in recognition of the fact that the restaurant's location is on the cusp of Palma's old Jewish Quarter.

Confitería Frasquet CAKES, SWEETS €
(Map p44; ☎971 721 354; www.confiteriafrasquet.com; Carrer d'Orfila 4; ⏲9.30am-2pm & 4.45-8pm Mon-Fri, 9.30am-2pm Sat) This distinguished sweetshop with its 19th-century decor has an astonishing range of sweets and specialises in chocolates and *embatumats* (a cake and chocolate confection); everything's tempting. There's been a sweetshop here since the 17th century.

La Taberna del Caracol SPANISH €€
(Map p44; ☎971 714 908; Carrer de Sant Alonso 2; meals €20-25, tapas €4-16.50; ⏲7.30-11.30pm Mon-Sat) Descend three steps into this high-ceilinged Gothic basement. Through a broad vault at the back you can see what's cooking – tasty tapas that include grilled artichokes, snails and a host of other Spanish delicacies. Amid soothing background music, a broad assortment of tapas (four choices for €14, minimum of two people) makes a great start to the evening.

Amadip Esment INTERNATIONAL €
(S'illa Verda; ☎971 722 505; www.amadipesment.org; Plaça es Pes de sa Palla 3; mains €5-10; ⏲8am-5.30pm Mon-Fri, 10am-5.30pm Sat) This agreeable place east of the old town combines numerous spaces – an organic food store with attached cafe serving sandwiches and salads, and a lively cafe-restaurant with mains costing as little as €5. There's little that's too imaginative in the cooking, but the tastes are fresh and the international dishes well-prepared. The outdoor tables are lovely when the weather's warm.

Forn del Santo Cristo PASTRIES €
(Map p44; ☎971 712 649; www.hornosantocristo.com; Carrer de Paraires 2; ensaïmades from €1.30; ⏲8am-8.15pm Mon-Sat, 8am-1pm Sun) Staff here has been baking up *ensaïmades* (a light, spiral pastry emblematic of the island) since 1910; also good for all sorts of traditional goodies.

PLAÇA MAJOR & AROUND

Tasca de Blanquerna SPANISH, MEDITERRANEAN €€
(☎971 290 108; www.tascadeblanquerna.com; Carrer de Blanquerna 6; mains €12-22.75; ⏲1-4pm & 8-10.30pm Mon-Sat) Perfectly presented tapas that combine Spanish staples (cheeses and cured meats from around the country) with other more creative takes on the genre (such as pork and mushroom terrine with onion and apricot chutney) at this tapas bar run by celebrity chef Marc Fosh. There are bite-sized morsels, larger *raciones* and a handle of main dishes, as well as a lunchtime *menú del día.*

La Bodeguilla SPANISH €€
(Map p44; ☎971 718 274; www.la-bodeguilla.com; Carrer de Sant Jaume 3; mains €9-18; ⏲1-11.30pm

Mon-Sat; 🚭) This gourmet restaurant does creative interpretations of dishes from across Spain; try the *cochinillo* (suckling pig) from Segovia or the *lechazo* (young lamb, baked Córdoba-style in rosemary). Also on offer is an enticing range of tapas – the marinated cubes of salmon with dill chutney caught our eye.

Simply Fosh MEDITERRANEAN FUSION €€€
(Map p52; ☎971 740 114; www.simplyfosh.com; Carrer de la Missió 7A; mains €14.50-27.50; ⏰1-3.30pm & 7.30-10.30 Mon-Sat; 🚭) Lovingly prepared Mediterranean grub with a special touch is the order of the day in the convent refectory, one of the home kitchens of Michelin-starred chef Marc Fosh. The range of set menus is a wonderful way to sample high-quality cooking at a reasonable price, but there are also à la carte choices. There's a three-course lunchtime *menú del día* (€19.50) as well as a five-course *menú degustación* (tasting menu; €58).

Misa Braseria MEDITERRANEAN FUSION €€€
(Map p52; ☎971 595 301; www.misabraseria.com; Carrer de Can Maçanet 1; mains €14-34.50; ⏰1-3.30pm & 7.30-10.30pm Mon-Sat) The latest addition to Marc Fosh's ever-expanding restaurant empire, this attractive place consists of a basement restaurant adorned with famous restaurant menus on the walls, or offers lunchtime dining upstairs in its modern courtyard. The food is slickly presented and tastes are typically fresh with dishes that change weekly and with the seasons. The *menú del día* (€17.50) is outstanding.

Forn des Teatre PASTRIES €
(Map p44; ☎971 715 254; www.forndesteatre.com; Plaça de Weyler 9; ensaïmades from €1.30; ⏰8am-8pm) This pastry shop does featherweight *ensaïmades* and is a historic landmark. Larger ones are prepared to order, but smaller, takeaway ones start from €1.30. Also on offer is a mean almond cake.

TOP CHOICE **Horno San Antonio** PASTRIES €
(☎971 715 932; Plaça Sant Antoni 6; ensaïmades from €1.30; ⏰8am-8.30pm Mon-Fri, 8am-3pm Sat, 8am-2pm Sun) Considered by most Mallorquins to be the best of the best when it comes to *ensaïmades*, this wonderfully traditional old pastry shop does a roaring trade in all sizes and types, from plain to chocolate, with cream or apricot filling. You can get them nicely packed if you plan on taking one home.

Restaurant Garage Rex SPANISH €€
(☎871 948 947; www.garagerex.com; Carrer de Pablo Iglesias 12; mains €11-21; ⏰1.30-4pm & 8.30pm-midnight Mon-Fri, 8.30pm-midnight Sat; 🚭) Housed in what was Mallorca's car-washing garage in the 1960s, this minimalist lounge restaurant serves up cooking with some creative touches. Think slices of sole rolled up and stuffed with prawns in an almond sauce or boneless quail stuffed with mushrooms and Iberian ham on a warm lentil salad.

Ca'n Joan de S'Aigo CAFE €
(Map p44; ☎971 710 759; Carrer de Can Sanç 10; hot chocolate €1.70; ⏰8am-9pm Mon & Wed-Fri, 8am-9.15pm Sat & Sun) Dating from 1700, this is *the* place for a hot chocolate in what can only be described as an antique-filled milk bar. The house speciality (apart from chocolate thick enough to stand your spoon in) is *quart*, a feather-soft sponge cake that children love, with almond-flavoured ice cream. The *ensaïmades* also have a devoted following.

Bar España SPANISH €€
(Map p44; ☎971 724 234; Carrer de Ca'n Escurrac 12; meals €15-25; ⏰6pm-midnight Mon, noon-4pm & 6pm-midnight Tue-Sat) Happening upon this

THE BEST ENSAÏMADES

Most Mallorquins and just about every Spanish visitor to the island has one culinary favourite above all others – the humble *ensaïmada*, a delicate, feather-light croissantlike pastry dusted with icing sugar, and sometimes filled with cream. Getting them to agree on where to buy the best is surprisingly simple. We've road-tested them and we're inclined to agree that these are the best you'll find in Palma, and possibly the entire island:

» **Horno San Antonio** (p61)

» **Ca'n Joan de S'Aigo** (p61)

» **Forn des Teatre** (p61)

» **Forn del Santo Cristo** (p60)

place in the evening when everything else in the vicinity is closed is like discovering some hidden secret. Hugely popular and deservedly so, this place has stone walls and an agreeable hum of conversation accompanies the fine *pintxos* (Basque tapas), which are lined up along the bar or chalked up on a board.

S'Esponja Café SPANISH, MEDITERRANEAN €€
(Map p52; ☎971 723 701; www.sesponja.com; Carrer del Metge Matas 2; mains €7-13; ⏰8.30pm-midnight Mon-Sat, closed Mon in Aug) A jug of *sangría* and *pa amb oli* (with unusual variants on the theme, such as the *capresse,* a mozzarella and tomato combo), perhaps followed by a little cake, is not a bad way to start the night at this funky eatery. It also does terrific salads and the service is attentive yet casual.

Restaurant Celler Sa Premsa SPANISH €€
(Map p52; ☎971 723 529; www.cellersapremsa.com; Plaça del Bisbe Berenguer de Palou 8; mains €9-14; ⏰noon-4pm & 7.30-11.30pm Mon-Sat Sep-Jun, closed Sat & Sun Jul & Aug; 🚭) A visit to this local institution is almost obligatory. It's a cavernous tavern filled with huge old wine barrels and has walls plastered with faded bullfighting posters – you find plenty such places in the Mallorcan interior but they're a dying breed here in Palma. Mallorcan specialities dominate the menu. Come here for the well-prepared roast lamb, *tumbet, frito mallorquín*, pork with cabbage, and rabbit with onion. But it's the atmosphere that you'll really remember.

ES PUIG DE SANT PERE

Aramís SPANISH €€
(Map p44; ☎971 725 232; aramis.palma@terra.es; Carrer de Sant Feliu 7; mains €11-15; ⏰1-3.30pm & 7.30-10.30pm Mon-Fri, 7.30-10.30pm Sat; 🚭) This carefully orchestrated gourmet hideaway, with dark-timber floors and art on the walls, is surprisingly well priced. The creative cooking includes dishes like sautéed calamari with *sobrassada* (spicy Mallorcan sausage) and pine nuts. The midday *menú del día* is similarly good value at €14.

Bon Lloc VEGETARIAN €
(Map p44; ☎971 718 617; www.bonllocrestaurant.com; Carrer de Sant Feliu 7; menú del día €14.50; ⏰1-4pm Mon-Sat; 🖉) This 100% vegetarian place is light, open and airy with a casual but classy atmosphere. All produce is organic and you're in assured hands here – this was Palma's first vegetarian restaurant and there are no agonising decisions, just a satisfying, take-it-or-leave-it four-course *menú*. It's hugely popular, so do ring to reserve.

La Bóveda SPANISH €€
(Map p44; ☎971 720 026; Carrer de la Boteria 3; mains €8.50-16; ⏰1.30-4pm & 8pm-12.30am; 🚭) You have to love this place, one of the few to transmit an essential Spanish boisterousness in this heavily touristed district. You'll find Andalucian wall tiles, high ceilings from which hang slow-turning fans, Spanish *jamón*, and people crammed in to munch on generous tapas and larger *raciones.*

13% TAPAS, INTERNATIONAL €
(Map p44; ☎971 425 187; www.13porciento.com; Carrer de Sant Feliu 13A; mains €8-11; ⏰noon-midnight Mon-Sat, 6pm-midnight Sun; 🚭🖉👪) At the quieter end of the old town, this L-shaped barn of a place is at once a wine and tapas bar, bistro and delicatessen. Most items are organic and there's plenty of choice for vegetarians. Wines are displayed on racks (both bar and takeaway prices are quoted, so you know the exact mark-up). You'll find everything from canapés, salads and carpaccio of smoked ostrich with cranberry jam to fresh sardine fillets in *cava*. The *menú del día* is a choice selection of three tapas.

Bruselas SPANISH €€
(Map p44; ☎971 710 954; www.restaurantebruselas.com; Carrer d'Estanc 4; mains €8.50-24; ⏰1-4pm & 8pm-midnight Mon-Sat; 🚭) Once a Belgian-owned piano bar (hence the name), this is all about red meat for aesthetes, with pleasantly contemporary decor in the stone-vaulted basement and Argentine steaks – such as *solomillo con foie* (sirloin with foie gras) – dominating the menu. There are also gourmet hamburgers and it all goes down particularly well with a throaty Mallorcan red, such as Son Bordils Negre.

Restaurant Museu Es Baluard INTERNATIONAL €€
(Map p44; Porta de Santa Catalina 10; mains €11.50-15; ⏰10am-9pm Tue-Sun; 🚭) The terrace cafe of Es Baluard is as good for a snack (€2.90 to €9.95) or *bocadillo* (filled roll; €3.45 to €5.50) as for a more substantial meal. The former include tandoori wraps, nachos and noodles, but you can also just order a drink and enjoy the view that stretches from the Castell de Bellver to the Catedral.

THE SLOW CHUG NORTH TO SÓLLER

Welcome to one of the most rewarding excursions in Mallorca. Since 1912 a narrow-gauge train has trundled along the winding 27.3km route north to Sóller (one way/return €10/17). The fragile-looking timber-panelled train, which replaced a stagecoach service, departs from Plaça de l'Estació seven times a day (five times from November to February) and takes about 1¼ hours; there are between four and five return trains every day. The route passes through ever-changing countryside that becomes dramatic in the north as it crosses the Serra de Alfàbia, a stretch comprising 13 tunnels and a series of bridges and viaducts.

The trip starts out heading through the streets of Palma but within 20 minutes you're in the countryside. At this stage the view is better to the left towards the Serra de Tramuntana. The terrain starts to rise gently and to the left the eye sweeps over olive gardens, the occasional sandy-coloured house and the mountains in the background. Half an hour out of Palma you call in at Bunyola. You could board here to do just half the trip (one way/return €5/10) to Sóller.

Shortly after Bunyola, as the mountains close in (at one point you can see Palma and the sea behind you), you reach the first of a series of tunnels. Some trains stop briefly at a marvellous lookout point, the Mirador Pujol de'n Banya, shortly after the Túnel Major (or main tunnel, which is almost 3km long and took three years to carve out of the rock in 1907–10). The view stretches out over the entire Sóller valley. From there, the train rattles across a viaduct before entering another tunnel that makes a slow 180-degree turn on its descent into Sóller, whose station building is housed in an early-17th-century noble mansion. Return tickets are valid for two weeks.

At the train station in Palma, you can buy packages that include a tram from Sóller to Port de Sóller, and then a boat from there to Sa Calobra, and then all the way back to Palma again. It costs between €37 and €44, depending on which train you take. For more information, call ☎900 600 555 or visit www.vallsollerservices.com.

SANTA CATALINA & AROUND

Fàbrica 23 SPANISH €€

(Map p57; ☎971 453 125; fabrica23restaurant.com; Carrer de Cotoner 42; meals €45-55; ⏱1-3.30pm & 8.30-11pm Tue-Sat; ⊖) For good market-based Med cooking, this gourmand fave (long since moved from Carrer de Sa Fàbrica) is hard to beat. The menu changes regularly and generally there is only a handful of dishes each day, covering meat, fish and vegetarian tastes. There's a *menú del día* for €21 and it is usually a good idea to book ahead.

Room SPANISH €€

(Map p57; ☎971 281 536; www.theroompalma.com; Carrer de Cotoner 47; mains €8.50-16.50; ⏱8am-midnight; ⊖) Be taken right through the day, from breakfast to cocktails, at this stylish and very contemporary collaboration between the two owners, a chef and a pastry chef. You'll find a few fish and meat mains, but this is more about a lighter touch, with pasta dishes, tapas, salads and homemade desserts.

Afrikana AFRICAN €€

(Map p57; ☎971 287 007; malayka@teleline.es; Carrer de Dameto 17; mains €8-12; ⏱noon-midnight Mon-Sat; ⊖✎) Get your fingers messy in this pan-African delight, with dishes extending from Madagascar to Morocco, from Ethiopia to Benin and around 20 other African countries. There's a good vegetarian selection, like the Angolan beans, coconut cream and curry mix. For a whiff of the sea, try *gombo* (from Benin): prawn and shrimp mixed with okra and other vegetables. Wash it down with hibiscus or tamarind juice.

Diecisiete Grados SPANISH, MALLORCAN €€

(Map p57; ☎871 943 368; Carrer de Sa Fàbrica 12; mains €8-15; ⏱1.30-3.45pm & 8.30-11.45pm) A pleasingly modern restaurant with a few pavement tables and lots of original tapas and small dishes, but it also does a mean *chuletón* (huge steak). Our favourite dish is risotto with *sobrassada*, wild mushrooms and *butifarrón*. The list has some good wines, unfortunately at exorbitant prices.

La Baranda ITALIAN €€

(Map p57; ☎971 454 525; Carrer de Sant Magí 29; mains €9-19; ⏱8pm-midnight Mon-Fri, 1-3.30pm & 8pm-midnight Sat & Sun) An easygoing Italian – with exposed stone, warm-yellow-hued walls, and simple timber furniture and art scattered about – this is a good choice for wood-fired pizzas, pasta dishes, and a range of homemade cakes for dessert. You can also get tapas downstairs.

Ummo SPANISH, BASQUE €€
(Map p57; ☎871 953 873; Carrer de Sant Magí 66; mains €10-18; ⏰1.30-3.30pm & 8.30-11.30pm Tue-Fri, 8.30-11.30pm Sat & Sun; 🚭) Choose between Basque dishes or *pintxos* at this relaxed little restaurant. The chef, from San Sebastián, has worked in numerous prestigious restaurants around Palma and elsewhere. Fresh vegetables and *bacalao* (dried cod) feature in his ever-changing menu.

Hórreo Veinti3 MEDITERRANEAN €€
(Map p57; ☎649 033 806; restaurantehorreoveinti3@hotmail.com; Carrer de Sa Fàbrica 23; mains €9-22; ⏰1pm-12.30am Thu-Mon, 7pm-12.30am Tue & Wed; 🚭) One of numerous good options along this pedestrian street, this trendy place is especially good if you're hungry in the early evening or late afternoon. Dishes range from risotto and grilled fish to duck breast with apple and shallots.

Restaurante a Todo Vapor SPANISH €€
(Map p57; ☎971 451 845; Carrer d'Annibal 9; mains €9-17; ⏰1-3.30pm & 7.30-10.30pm Thu-Sat, 1-3.30pm Sun, Tue & Wed ; 🖉) This original place has a simple philosophy: all of its ingredients must come from the nearby Mercat de Santa Catalina and all dishes are steamed to ensure the goodness remains locked in. We especially enjoyed the couscous.

PASSEIG MARÍTIM & WESTERN PALMA

Nautic SEAFOOD €€€
(Map p57; ☎971 726 383; www.nautic-restaurant.com; Muelle San Pedro 1; mains €16-29; ⏰1-3.30pm & 8-11.30pm Tue-Sat, 1-3.30pm Mon) One of Palma's standout seafood options in the Royal Sailing Club, Nautic does all the usual grilled fishes and shellfish, as well as rice dishes, but you'll also find surprises such as zucchini stuffed with lobster in a *sobrassada* sauce. It's a classy place and an easy walk from central Palma.

Caballito de Mar SEAFOOD €€
(Map p44; ☎971 721 074; www.caballitodemar.info; Passeig de Sagrera 5; mains €15.39-23.22; ⏰1-11.30pm Sun-Thu, 1pm-midnight Fri & Sat Jun-Sep, closed Mon Oct-May; 🚭) One of Palma's seafood beacons, the 'Little Seahorse' presents its fruits of the sea in a contemporary key. There are monkfish medallions, *sobrassada* (spicy Mallorcan sausage) and *butifarrón* (blood sausage) wrapped in cabbage leaves in a nut sauce, for example. Or you could go for something more traditional, such as the fresh fish of the day, rice dishes or red shrimp from Sóller. Grab a seat on the sunny terrace.

Ca'n Eduardo SEAFOOD €€€
(Map p44; ☎971 721 182; www.caneduardo.com; 3rd fl, Travesía Contramuelle; mains €23-29; ⏰1-11.30pm; 🚭) What better place to sample fish than here, right above the fish market? With its bright, contemporary decor and picture windows overlooking the fishing port, Ca'n Eduardo has been in business since the 1940s and has a loyal clientele. Black-vested waiters serve up grilled fish and seafood and some fantastic rice dishes (minimum of two) – the *arroz bogavante* (lobster rice) is a favourite.

Casa Jacinto SPANISH, MALLORCAN €€
(☎971 401 858; www.rtecasajacinto.com; Camí de la Tramvía 37; mains €8-24; ⏰1pm-12.30am Mon-Sat, 1-5pm & 7pm-12.30am Sun) A classic since the 1980s, this huge and no-nonsense eatery far from the centre of town attracts Mallorquins from far and wide for copious servings of mainland Spanish and local food, especially grilled meats, including game cuts such as venison and wild boar.

ES PORTITXOL, ES MOLINAR & CIUTAT JARDÍ

Ca'n Jordi SEAFOOD €€
(☎971 491 978; www.restaurantecanjordi.es; Carrer de l'Illa de Xipre 12; meals €45-55; ⏰1-3.30pm & 8-11pm Mon-Sat, 1-3.30pm Sat; 🚭) One of the classic seafood restaurants in Palma, Ca'n Jordi attracts local businessfolk and seafood-lovers of every ilk. On your way into the over-lit but otherwise tastefully presented dining area you'll see fresh fish (sold by weight) awaiting your choice. It doesn't have views (it's a block inland), but its seafood more than makes up for it.

Casa Fernando SEAFOOD €€
(☎971 265 417; www.restaurantecasafernando.com; Carrer de Trafalgar 27; mains €18-25; ⏰1-4pm & 7pm-midnight Tue-Sun, closed mid-Dec–mid-Jan; 🚭) No sea views here, but countless photos of local and more distant celebs grin at you from the walls of this ordinary-looking restaurant. Basic linen graces the timber tables in this fishy, ill-lit den, providing a style counterpoint to Ca'n Jordi but virtually the

same recipe – well-prepared catch of the day, sold by weight.

Es Mollet SEAFOOD €€€
(☎971 247 109; Carrer de la Sirena 1; mains €25-35; ⌚1-3.30pm & 7.30-10.30pm Mon-Sat) With its covered veranda just over the road from a little bay (Cala Portitxolet), this is a classic seafood joint, where your main course, the freshest catch of the day, is sold by weight (€45 to €60 per kg). There's a price to pay, but the produce here is selected direct from local fishers and grilled to utter perfection.

Can Mito MENORCAN €€
(☎971 274 644; www.canmito.com; Carrer de Vicario Joaquín Fuster; mains €16-23; ⌚1pm-midnight) With a well-earned reputation for getting the basics right, Can Mito is well priced and has a pleasant outdoor terrace. It's best known for its rice dishes and lobster stews.

Drinking

Palma will never be voted Spain's party capital, but there's always plenty going on and dozens of appealing little bars. For the truly raucous summer tourist scene, head for Platja de Palma or Magaluf.

OLD PALMA

Gibson BAR
(Map p44; ☎971 716 404; Plaça del Mercat 18; ⌚8am-3am) This chirpy cocktail bar with outside seating is still busy with (mostly local) punters on a weekday night when everything else around has pulled the shutters down.

Cappuccino CAFE
(Map p44; ☎971 717 272; www.grupocappuccino.com; Carrer del Conquistador 13; ⌚8.30am-10pm Mon-Wed, 8.30am-11pm Thu & Sun, 8.30am-midnight Fri & Sat) You'll pay more for your coffee fix here, but the coffee's good, the atmosphere sophisticated and the setting the perfect place to pause on your exploration of downtown. This is one of nearly a dozen hyperhip coffee houses belonging to Cappuccino, a Mallorcan chain, which also produces its own lounge-music CDs.

PLAÇA MAJOR & AROUND

L'Ambigú TAPAS BAR
(Map p44; ☎971 572 151; Carrer de Carnissería 1; ⌚7pm-midnight Mon-Sat) Tucked in behind the Església de Santa Eulalia, this irresistible little bar rocks on Tuesday and Wednesday nights when you can scarcely see the tapas perched atop the bar, but we like it any night for its sense of a tiny hub of modern, casual sophistication beneath the high stone walls of medieval Palma.

Bar Flexas BAR
(☎971 425 938; www.barflexas.com; Carrer de la Llotgeta 12; ⌚1-5pm & 8pm-1am Mon-Fri) This place took up residence long before the streets southeast of the Plaça Major became trendy and that whiff of aunthenticity remains. It's a lively locals' bar with a whiff of grunge and is a great spot for a noisy chat far from the tourist haunts. You'll find art exhibitions, occasional live acts and bar staff with just the right sort of attitude. The image of the Virgin Mary near one door is a contrast with the provocative erotic image at the back.

Café L'Antiquari BAR
(Map p52; ☎971 719 687; www.facebook.com/cafeantiquari; Carrer d'Arabi 5; ⌚noon-2am Mon-Sat) This old antique shop has been transformed into one of the most original places in Palma to nurse a drink or two. Antiques adorn every corner and inch of wall space, and even the tables and chairs belong to another age. It also has occasional live music and the coffee is unbeatable.

LA RUTA MARTIANA

The Sa Gerreria neighbourhood of Palma, southeast of the Plaça Major, has undergone an extraordinary transformation, from the no-go area of central Palma to one of its hippest places to go out at night. Part of the momentum is attributable to the inexplicably named **La Ruta Martiana** (The Martians' Route; www.rutamartiana.com), whereby over 20 bars clustered tightly around these streets offer a small morsel to eat (known as a tapa, or a *pintxo*) and a drink for €2 on Tuesday and Wednesday from 7.30pm to 1am. Apart from being great value and allowing you to go on a tapas crawl without breaking the bank, it has breathed life into this long-neglected corner of town. There's a full list of participating bars on the website. Among the bars taking part are L'Ambigu (p65), Jamón Jamón (p66) and Ca La Seu (p66).

Ca La Seu TAPAS BAR
(Map p44; ☎871 572 157; Carrer de Cordería 17; ⊙8pm-2am Mon-Sat Jun-Aug, 6pm-2am Mon-Sat Sep-May) Set in an artfully converted 500-year-old barn of a place, this is one of our favourite bars in Palma with marble-top tables, creative tapas to accompany your drinks and an agreeable buzz most nights. If other places come and go in the neighbourhood, we reckon this place is destined to last the distance.

Es Pincell BAR
(Map p52; ☎971 227 361; Carrer de les Caputxines 13; ⊙6pm-1am Tue-Thu, 7pm-2.30am Fri & Sat, 7pm-midnight Sun) No sign reveals the existence of this deep-vaulted cellar where locals gather for a *pomada* (Menorcan gin and lemon soft drink) at long timber tables. Young rebels with causes, such as independence from the Spanish state, often gather for animated discussion.

Quina Creu BAR
(Map p44; ☎971 711 772; Carrer de Cordería 24; ⊙noon-midnight Mon-Sat) A newcomer riding the wave of popularity in this new nighttime hub, Quina Creu has more sophistication than most. The bar has a designer feel, as do the tapas lined up along the bar and chalked up on the blackboard. But above all, it's a funky place to nurse a drink or two and watch the crowds streaming past outside.

Jamón Jamón TAPAS BAR
(Map p44; ☎971 753 675; www.jamonjamonpalma.com; Carrer de Galera 4; ⊙8pm-midnight Mon-Sat) It may lack the obvious personality of some of the other bars in the area, but this place packs them in most nights, not least because the €2 offer from La Ruta Martiana for a drink and a tapa is not restricted here to Tuesday and Wednesday.

ES PUIG DE SANT PERE

TOP CHOICE **Abaco** DESIGNER BAR
(Map p44; ☎971 715 947; www.bar-abaco.com; Carrer de Sant Joan 1; cocktails €15-16; ⊙8pm-1am Sun-Thu, 8pm-3am Fri & Sat) Behind a set of ancient timber doors is this extraordinary bar. Inhabiting the restored patio of an old Mallorcan house, Abaco is filled with ornate candelabra, elaborate floral arrangements, cascading towers of fresh fruit, and bizarre artworks. It hovers between extravagant and kitsch, but the effect is overwhelming whatever your opinion. Paying this much for a cocktail is an outrage, but one might just be worth it here.

Atlantico Café BAR
(Map p44; ☎971 722 882; Carrer de Sant Feliu 12; ⊙10pm-3am Mon-Sat) This is one of the most enticing bars in town. Think cocktails (€7), 'Hotel California' for the music and US car number plates on the walls (along with generous and ever-expanding swaths of graffiti).

Bodeguita del Medio BAR
(Map p44; ☎971 717 832; Carrer de Vallseca 18; ⊙9pm-3am) For a taste of Cuba, head in here for a *mojito* (rum, lemon, mint and ice, one of Hemingway's favourites) or three. The walls are covered in punters' scribblings and the music usually has a Caribbean swing to keep things sexy.

Es Jaç COCKTAIL BAR
(Map p44; ☎666 830 345; Carrer de Vallseca 13; ⊙8pm-1am Thu & Sun, 8pm-3am Fri & Sat) This designer cocktail bar is slick in all the right places, with stunning decor and bar staff who know their cocktails and are adept at helping those who aren't really sure what they want.

Café La Lonja CAFE
(Map p44; ☎971 722 799; Carrer de Sa Llotja 2; ⊙10am-1am Mon-Thu, 10am-3am Fri, 11am-3am Sat Easter-Nov) With its curved marble bar, tiled-chessboard floor and smattering of tables and benches, this place is as appealing for breakfast as it is for a very generous *pomada* (Menorcan gin and lemon soft drink). Many choose to sit outside in the shadow of Sa Llotja.

Escape Bar BAR
(Map p44; ☎971 724 968; Plaça de la Drassana 13; ⊙bar 5pm-1am Mon, 10am-1am Tue-Thu & Sun, 10am-3am Fri & Sat) A largely international crowd (with Brits generally well represented) fills up the two rooms of this small bar in the early stages of the evening. Grab one of a couple of tables out the front for an afternoon refreshment or come along in the morning for a full English breakfast (€10). It also whips up some imaginative dishes (the *menú del día* costs €12.50) at lunchtime.

SANTA CATALINA & AROUND

Soho BAR
(Map p57; Avinguda d'Argentina 5; ⊙6.30pm-2am Mon-Thu, 6.30pm-2.30am Fri & Sat; wi-fi) This self-proclaimed 'urban vintage bar' has a green-lit beer fridge, red walls (with some 1960s

decor), low white ceilings, fabulous velour sofas and an otherwise wonderfully retro look. The music's mostly indie and the laid-back crowd mostly seems oblivious to the traffic pounding past the footpath tables.

Idem Café CAFE
(Map p57; ☎971 280 854; www.idemcafe.es; Carrer de Sant Magí 15A; ⏰9pm-3am) A deep, dark-red baroque feel attracts cocktail-drinking night owls. Past the front bar and deeper inside are two separate spaces. Some of the wall art is risqué and the place has something of the air of an old-style but gay-run bordello.

Hostal Cuba Colonial BAR
(Map p57; ☎971 452 237; Carrer de Sant Magí 1; ⏰8am-2am Sun-Thu, 8am-4am Fri & Sat) Inhabiting an early-20th-century Santa Catalina landmark for sailors passing through Palma, this place has been reborn as a watering hole of a more sophisticated kind. You'll find everything from coffee to full meals, and a chill-out zone on the 1st floor.

Café Lisboa MUSIC BAR
(Map p57; Carrer de Sant Magí 33; ⏰11pm-4am Thu-Sat, 10.30pm-2am Sun-Wed) The curved timber bar gives this place homey appeal. When some Latin and bossa-nova sounds get thrown on, it gets even better; check out Brazil night on Wednesdays from midnight. It fills up quickly on evenings that live music is staged.

PASSEIG MARÍTIM & WESTERN PALMA

Varadero BAR
(Map p44; ☎971 726 428; Carrer del Moll Vell; ⏰9am-2am Sun-Thu, 9am-4am Fri & Sat) This bar's splendid fore position makes it feel as though you've weighed anchor. The squawking of seagulls mixes with lounge sounds as you sip your favourite tipple and gaze east across the bay or back to a splendid cathedral from the sprawling terrace.

Guiness House BAR
(Map p44; ☎971 717 817; Parc de la Mar; ⏰8am-midnight Sun-Thu, 8am-2am Fri & Sat) It's all about location here between the Catedral and the sea. The views of the former are unrivalled, especially whe floodlit at night. It's at its best for an early-morning coffee before the crowds arrive, or after dark.

Made in Brasil BAR
(Map p57; ☎670 372 390; Avinguda de Gabriel Roca 27; ⏰8pm-4am Mon-Sat) The name is a little misleading, as here anything South American goes, from salsa to lambada. A good place to give your body a shakedown while sipping on Caribbean tipples such as *mojitos* and *caipirinhas*.

ES PORTITXOL, ES MOLINAR & CIUTAT JARDÍ

Kaskai BAR
(☎971 241 284; www.kaskai.com; Carrer del Vicari Joaquín Fuster 71; ⏰1pm-2am) This place sells itself as something of a mixed modern cuisine experience, with Asian and local dishes, but it works better as a chilled-out bar. The dominant black and blood-red decor and candlelit tables invite you to dally over a few drinks, which might well be accompanied by a DJ session from Thursday to Saturday.

☆ Entertainment

From live concerts to opera, from a good movie to a summer bullfight, from sailing regattas to a football match, there's plenty to do in Palma. You can book tickets to many events by phone or online through **Servicaixa** (☎902 332 211; www.servicaixa.com). You can also get tickets to many events at El Corte Inglés department store.

Nightclubs

The epicentre of Palma's clubbing scene remains around the Passeig Marítim (Avinguda de Gabriel Roca) and the Club de Mar, where you'll find the city's largest and most popular *discotecas*.

Although most clubs open around midnight or earlier, don't expect to find much action until at least 2am. Things will continue going strong until 5am, when glassy-eyed clubbers stumble outside. Some may head home, while others head to the 'afters', early-morning clubs (some around Plaça de Gomila) that keep the music going past the breakfast hour.

Admission prices range from €10 to €20, usually including your first drink, although if you're not dressed to impress you may be turned away no matter how much cash you're willing to spend.

Abraxa's CLUB
(☎971 455 908; www.abraxasmallorca.com; Passeig Marítim 42; ⏰10pm-6am Thu-Sat Sep-Jun, nightly Jul & Aug) Formerly known as Pacha (of the famous Ibiza line), this is Palma's most established club. Hordes of dancers of every nationality descend on Abraxa's two dance floors, spilling onto the terrace and grooving to the house music spun by Mallorca's top DJs.

GAY & LESBIAN PALMA

The bulk of gay life on the island happens in and around Palma. Left your sex toys at home? Head for **Lust Universe** (Map p44; www.lustuniverse.com; Carrer de les Caputxines 5D; ⌚11am-2pm & 5-8pm Mon-Fri, 11am-2pm Sat). The biggest concentration of gay bars is on Avinguda de Joan Miró, south of Plaça de Gomila. To get your night going, you could start with the following:

Dark (☎971 725 007; www.darkpalma.com; Carrer de Ticià 22; ⌚4.30pm-2.30am Sun-Thu, 4.30pm-10.30am Sat, Sun & holidays)

Aries Sauna Hotel Pub (☎971 737 899; www.ariesmallorca.com; Carrer de Porras 3; ⌚sauna 4pm-midnight, bar 10pm-6am)

Yuppii Club (www.yuppii.es; Carrer de Joan Miró 98; ⌚midnight-late Thu-Mon)

Useful websites for plugging into Palma's gay networks:

» www.mallorcagaymap.com (a paper version is available from some tourist offices)

» www.gay-mallorca.blogspot.com (in Spanish)

El Garito LIVE MUSIC, BAR

(☎971 736 912; www.garitocafe.com; Dàrsena de Can Barberà; ⌚7pm-4.30am) DJs and live performers, doing anything from nu jazz to disco classics and electro beats, heat up the scene from around 10pm. Admission is generally free, but you're expected to buy a drink.

Mar Salada BAR, CLUB

(☎971 702 709; www.marsalada.net; Moll de Pelaires; ⌚10pm-late) Famed as the favourite club of Spain's Prince Felipe – at least before he became a father of two – this laid-back venue in the Club de Mar draws a sophisticated crowd. The standard entry is around €15 but, to keep the pedigree, erm, royal, some punters might be charged more.

Tito's CLUB

(☎971 730 017; www.titosmallorca.com; Passeig Marítim 33; ⌚11.30pm-6am Jun-Sep, 11.30pm-6am Thu-Sun Oct-May) A classic club with occasional sexy floor shows to liven things up, it's only open Thursday to Sunday in the low season (October to May), but nightly throughout summer.

Salero BAR, CLUB

(☎971 000 000; www.saleroclub.com; Passeig Marítim 33; ⌚11pm-6am) Just beside Tito's, Salero is has nothing too challenging when it comes to music – Madonna, Shakira and the Black Eyed Peas all feature in its top 10. The club's salsa roots come to the fore on Tuesday and Thursday nights at 10pm when the line between dance classes and nightclub blur agreeably.

Cinemas

Palma has at least seven cinema complexes, each with several screens, but only one showing films that aren't dubbed into Spanish.

Renoir CINEMA

(☎971 205 408; www.cinesrenoir.com; Carrer d'Emperadriu Eugènia 6; tickets €6.50) This is your best chance if you want to see movies in their original language (with Spanish subtitles). It has four screens and generally runs sessions from about 4.30pm to 10.30pm.

Theatre

Auditòrium CLASSICAL MUSIC

(Map p57; ☎971 734 735; www.auditoriumpalma.es; Passeig Marítim 18; ⌚box office 10am-2pm & 4-9pm) This spacious, modern theatre is Palma's main stage for major concert performances (as well as congresses), ranging from opera to light rock. The Sala Mozart hosts part of the city's opera program (with the Teatre Principal), while the Orquestra Simfònica de Balears (Balearic Symphony Orchestra) are regulars from October to May.

Teatre Principal THEATRE

(Map p44; ☎971 219 696; www.teatreprincipaldepalma.cat; Carrer de Sa Riera 2; ⌚box office 5.30-8.30pm Tue-Sat) Built in 1854 and restored in 2007, this is the city's prestige theatre for drama, opera and big-name concerts. The renovation works re-created the theatre's heyday majesty of 1860 and combined it with the latest technology, resulting in great acoustics.

Teatre Municipal DANCE
(☎971 710 986; espectacles@sf.a-palma.es; Passeig de Mallorca 9; ⊙box office 1hr before show) Here you might see anything from contemporary dance to drama.

Live Music

Most of Palma's live acts perform on the stages of intimate bars around Sa Llotja, although in recent years neighbours' complaints have shortened the opening hours or even shut down some venues. Concerts begin between 10pm and midnight and wrap up no later than 2am. Check www.vamosmallorca365.com for concert details.

Jazz Voyeur Club MUSIC BAR
(Map p44; ☎971 905 292; www.jazzvoyeurfestival.com; Carrer dels Apuntadors 5; admission free; ⊙from 9.30pm daily-Oct, closed Sun & Mon Nov-Mar) A tiny club no bigger than most people's living rooms, Voyeur hosts live bands nightly for much of the year – jazz is the focus, but you'll also hear flamenco, blues, funk and the occasional jam session. Red candles burn on the tables and a few plush chairs are scattered about – get here early if you want to grab one. In autumn it hosts a fine jazz festival.

Blue Jazz Club BLUES, JAZZ
(Map p44; ☎971 727 240; www.bluejazz.es; 7th fl, Passeig de Mallorca 6; admission free; ⊙10pm-midnight Thu, 11pm-1am Fri & Sat, 8.30-10.30pm Mon) Located on the 7th floor of the Hotel Saratoga, this sophisticated club with high-altitude views over Palma offers after-dinner jazz and blues concerts from Thursday to Saturday, and a Monday evening jam session. Admission may be free but you're expected to buy a drink.

Bluesville BAR
(Map p44; bluesvillebar.com; Carrer de Ma d'es Moro 3; ⊙10.30pm-late Tue-Sat) As dark and smoky as a blues bar should be, this intimate spot a stone's throw from the busy Carrer dels Apuntadors hosts free blues concerts usually around midnight, mostly attracting a young hippie crowd.

Assaig LIVE MUSIC
(☎971 431 344; www.assaig.com; Carrer del Gremi Porgadors 16; admission free-€30) More than just a concert hall, this cultural centre in northern Palma is a place for up-and-coming artists to practise and promote their music. Free concerts are held on the cafe stage, while more-formal shows are put on at the larger concert hall, usually on Fridays and Saturdays from 10pm.

Sport

FOOTBALL

Palma's top division **RCD Mallorca** (☎971 739 941; www.rcdmallorca.es; Estadi Son Moix, Camí dels Reis) is one of the better sides battling it out in the Primera Liga. They have never finished as champions but usually wind up with a respectable spot about halfway down the ladder. The side has played at the **Estadi Son Moix** (Camí dels Reis), about 3km north of central Palma, since 1999. You can get tickets at the stadium or call the ticket booking number.

BULLFIGHTING

Bullfights take place about half a dozen times from mid-July to the end of August at the **Plaza de Toros** (☎971 751 634; Carrer del Arquitecte Gaspar Bennàzar 32). The fact that the season is so short is an indication that the activity is not that widely followed in Mallorca. Tickets can be obtained at the ring; the program usually begins around 6pm.

Shopping

Start your browsing in the chic boutiques around Passeig d'es Born. The Passeig itself is equal parts high street and highbrow, with chain stores like Massimo Dutti and Zara alongside elitist boutiques. In the maze of pedestrian streets west of the Passeig, you'll find some of Palma's most tempting (and expensive) stores. Another good shopping street is the pedestrianised Carrer de Sant Miquel.

If you're looking for Mallorcan-made glassworks, ceramics, baskets or other artisan goods, stroll around the **Passeig de la Artesania** (Crafts Walk; Plaça de l'Artesania & Carrer del Bosc), a well-marked route that includes more than a dozen shops and workshops.

Food & Drink

Colmado Manresa FOOD, DRINK
(Map p57; ☎971 731 631; Carrer de Sa Fàbrica 19; ⊙9.30am-1.30pm & 5-7.30pm Mon-Fri, 9.30am-1.30pm Sat) This old-timey grocer in Santa Catalina is where the locals head for typical island products like *sobrassada, ensaïmades,* brown bread, olive oil and marmalade.

Colmado Santo Domingo FOOD
(Map p44; ☎971 714 887; www.colmadosantodomingo.com; Carrer de Santo Domingo 1; ⊙10am-8pm

Mon-Sat) It's almost impossible to manouevre in this narrow little shop, so crowded are its shelves with local Mallorcan food products – cheeses, honey, olives, olive oil, pâté, fig bread, to name just a few – while *sobrassada* hangs from the ceiling.

Xocoa CHOCOLATE
(Map p52; ☎971 718 596; www.xocoa.es; Carrer de Josep Tous i Ferrer 4; ⏲10am-2pm & 5-8pm Mon-Sat) One of Spain's most celebrated purveyors of designer chocolates finds a home in Palma opposite the Mercat de l'Olivar. Exquisite packaging and presentation are part of the whole package.

Típika FOOD, HANDICRAFTS
(Map p44; ☎971 728 983; www.tipika.es; Carrer d'en Morei 1; ⏲10.30am-7pm Mon-Fri, 10.30am-4pm Sat) This small shop is dedicated to promoting the craftsmanship and gastronomy of Mallorca. Here you'll find wines, olive oils and a small but carefully chosen selection of other food products, as well as ceramics and other handicrafts from small family artisan businesses across the island.

Fashion & Furnishings

Camper SHOES
(Map p44; ☎971 714 635; www.camper.com; Avinguda de Jaume III 16; ⏲10am-8.30pm Mon-Sat) Best known of Mallorca's famed shoe brands, funky, eco-chic Campers are now incredibly popular worldwide.

B Connected Concept Store FASHION, HOMEWARES
(Map p57; ☎971 282 195; www.bconnected-conceptstore.com; Carrer de Dameto 6; ⏲10am-2.30pm & 5-8pm Mon-Fri, 10am-3pm Sat) This designer 'concept' store is very much at home in the new Santa Catalina. Apart from furnishings and a few fashion items (it has another shop devoted to vintage fashions a few blocks away), you'll find all sorts of knick-knacks that you never knew you needed but just have to have. The look is contemporary with the occasional retro touch.

Farrutx SHOES
(Map p44; ☎971 715 308; www.farrutx.com; Passeig d'es Born 16; ⏲10.30am-8.30pm Mon-Fri, 10.30am-2pm Sat) This Mallorca brand's exquisite leather shoes for women are guaranteed to make you drool.

Carmina SHOES, ACCESSORIES
(Map p44; ☎971 229 047; www.carminashoemaker.com; Carrer de l'Unió 4; ⏲10am-2pm & 5-8pm Mon-Fri, 10am-2pm Sat) Another classic of Mallorcan shoemaking, Carmina is the more traditional complement to Camper, making a virtue of dark tones, brogues and loafers.

Món CLOTHING
(Map p44; ☎971 724 020; Plaça del Rosari 2; ⏲10am-1.30pm & 4-8pm Mon-Fri, 10am-1.30pm Sat) You can find some great deals at this outlet, where flirty, feminine fashions from labels like Essentiel and Hoss hang on the racks. They're the still-desirable leftovers from the mother store, **Addaia** (Carrer de Sant Miquel 57).

Books & Maps

La Casa del Mapa BOOKS, MAPS
(Map p44; ☎971 225 945; casamapa@imi.a-palma.es; Carrer de Sant Domingo 11; ⏲9.30am-2pm Mon-Fri) You could come to this government-run shop for topographical maps and other hiking resources, but we like it just as much for facsmiles of some examples from Mallorca's ancient cartographicaphical heritage – the 1375 map of the known world by Abraham Cresques is a real find.

Trading Place BOOKS
(Map p57; ☎871 941 350; www.mallorca-books.com; Carrer del Pou 35; ⏲10am-1.30pm & 5-7.30pm Mon-Fri, 10am-1.30pm Sat) One of the largest dealers in secondhand books (mostly English, but some Spanish and German), it also sells furniture and serves as something of a meeting and information point for Palma's expat community.

Fine Books BOOKS
(Map p44; ☎971 723 797; nottinghillbooks@hotmail.com; Carrer de Morei 7; ⏲9.30am-8pm Mon-Sat, 9.30am-2pm Sun) This extraordinary collection of secondhand books, including some really valuable treasures, rambles over three floors. If you can't find what you're looking for, Rodney will try to track it down for you.

Dialog BOOKS
(Map p52; ☎971 228 129; www.dialog-palma.com; Carrer del Carme 14; ⏲9.30am-2pm & 4.30-8.30pm Mon-Fri, 10am-1.30pm Sat) The selection of German- and English-language books here is small but very carefully chosen, with especially good sections on languages and books about Mallorca.

Artisan & Local Specialities

Bordados Valldemossa HANDICRAFTS
(Map p52; ☎971 716 306; Carrer de Sant Miquel 26; ⏲10am-8pm Mon-Sat) Embroidered linens, many made on the island, fill this old-timey shop.

MARKET WATCH

Flea markets, speciality markets and artisan markets abound in Palma. For handicrafts, head to the artisan markets on **Plaça Major** (10am-2pm Mon & Sat Mar-Jul & Sep-Dec, daily Aug & Sep) or **Plaça des Meravelles Artisan Market** (8pm-midnight May-Oct). A sprawling **flea market** (10am-2pm) takes over the Avingudes west of the city centre (Avinguda de Gabriel Alomar and Avinguda de Villalonga) each Saturday. The Christmas market (p60) takes over the Plaça Major from 16 December to 5 January.

Quesada ARTS & CRAFTS

(Map p44; ☎971 715 111; Passeig d'es Born 12; ⏲10am-8pm Mon-Fri, 10am-2pm Sat) The typical Mallorcan two-toned patterned textiles called *roba de llengües* (striped cloths) have been sold here since 1890, as well as other exquisite pieces.

Rosario P ARTS & CRAFTS

(Map p52; ☎971 723 586; Carrer de Sant Jaume 20; ⏲10.30am-1pm & 5-8pm Mon-Fri, 10.30am-1.30pm Sat) Artisan boutiques such as this one dot central Palma. Here you'll find delicate hand-painted tops, dresses and shawls, all made with light-as-breath silk.

Vidrierias Gordiola ARTS & CRAFTS

(Map p44; ☎971 711 541; www.gordiola.com; Carrer de la Victoria 2; ⏲closed Sat afternoon) Mallorca's best-known glassmakers offer everything from traditional goblets and vases to decidedly modern works of art.

Information

Emergency

Ambulance (☎061) Emergency phone number, valid in Palma and across the island.

General EU Emergency Number (☎112) Catch-all emergency number.

Policía Local (☎092; Avinguda de Sant Ferran 42) Municipal Police station, northwest of the centre.

Policía Nacional (☎091; Carrer de Ruiz de Alda 8) National Police.

Red Cross (☎971 202 222) An alternative for calling ambulances.

Internet Resources

City of Palma Tourist Site (www.imtur.es) The city's main tourist portal.

Consell de Mallorca Tourist Site (www.infomallorca.net) Regional government's tourism website.

Asociación Hotelera de Palma de Mallorca (www.visit-palma.com) Has hotel and general information for Palma de Mallorca.

Media

For local news in English have a look at the *Daily Bulletin* (www.majorcadailybulletin.es). More substantial are the weekly German-language newspapers, Mallorca Magazin (www.mallorcamagazin.net) and *Mallorca Zeitung* (www.mallorcazeitung.es).

For an idea of what's on, try the fortnightly *Youthing* (www.youthing.es) and quarterly V&mos365 (www.vamosmallorca365.com). *Dígame* (www.digamemallorca.com) is a free monthly with islandwide events, but isn't that detailed. You'll find most of them in the tourist offices and distributed in bars.

There is a growing stable of glossy monthlies in English and German. The free *abcmallorca* (www.abc-mallorca.com) has articles on the city and island. Contemporary Balears (www.contemporarybalears.com) is published three times a year and has interesting articles and listings. Look out for it in hotels and some restaurants, bars and galleries. Anglo Info (www.angloinfo.com) has a forum, events listings and a directory of English-speaking businesses.

The annual *Mallorca Geht Aus!* (€9.50; also available in Germany, Austria and Switzerland) has more than 200 glossy pages packed with stories and reviews of anything from *fincas* (farmhouses) to clubs.

Medical Services

In the main newspapers (such as the *Diario de Mallorca*) you will find a list of pharmacies open from 9am to 10pm and others (a handful) from 10pm to 9am.

Hospital Son Dureta (☎971 175 000; Carrer de Andrea Doria 55) To get here from the centre, take bus 5 (from Passeig de Mallorca), 29 (from Passeig Marítim) or 46.

Farmácia Castañer-Buades (☎971 711 534; Plaça de Joan Carles I 3; ⏲9am-midnight) Pharmacy.

Farmácia Salvà Trobat (☎971 458 788; Carrer de Balanguera 3; ⏲24hr) Pharmacy.

Safe Travel

Palma is fairly safe. The main concern is petty theft – pickpockets and bag-snatchers. Some streets are best avoided at night, when the occasional dodgy character comes out to play; one such area is around Plaça de Sant Antoni and the nearby avenues, such as Avinguda de Villalonga and Avinguda d'Alexandre Rosselló.

Tourist Information

You can get lots of local city info by dialling 010, with luck even in English.

Airport tourist office (☎971 789 556; www.imtur.es; Aeroport de Palma; ⊙8am-8pm Mon-Sat, 8am-4pm Sun) Tourist information.

Consell de Mallorca tourist office (☎971 712 216; www.infomallorca.net; Plaça de la Reina 2; ⊙8am-8pm Mon-Fri, 9am-2pm Sat) Covers the whole island. For cultural and sporting events, consult *On Anar*, its free quarterly 'what's happening' guide with a version in English.

Main municipal tourist office (☎902 102 365; www.imtur.es; Casal Solleric, Passeig d'es Born 27; ⊙9am-8pm) Tourist office.

Municipal tourist office (☎902 102 365; Parc de les Estacions; ⊙9am-8pm) In one of the railway buildings off Plaça d'Espanya.

Municipal tourist office (Santa Catalina) (☎902 102 365; palmainfo@a-palma.es; cnr Passeig Marítim & Avinguda d'Argentina; ⊙9am-8pm) West of the centre.

Getting There & Away

AIR Palma's Son Sant Joan Airport lies 8km east of the city and receives an impressive level of traffic. A number of airlines (p207) service Mallorca.

BOAT Palma is also the island's main port. There are numerous boat services to/from Mallorca from mainland Spain and the other islands of the Balearics (p209).

BUS All island buses depart from (or near) the **bus station** (☎971 177 777; www.estaciondeautobuses.es/mallorca; Avinguda de Joan March 27). Services head in all directions, including Valldemossa (€1.50, 30 minutes), Sóller (€2.35, 30 minutes), Pollença (€4.90, 45 minutes) and Alcúdia (€4.80, 45 minutes). Other coastal and inland centres are served by less-frequent bus lines. A handful of areas are more easily reached by train.

TRAIN Two train lines run from Plaça d'Espanya. The **Palma–Sóller railway** is a popular panoramic run. The other line (☎971 177 777) is more prosaic, running northeast to Inca (€1.80) and then splitting into a branch to Sa Pobla (€2.40, 58 minutes) and another to Manacor (€2.40, 66 minutes). Services start at 5.44am and finish at 10.09pm on weekdays. Departure times on weekends (when both lines are all-stops trains) vary but the frequency remains about the same.

Getting Around

TO/FROM THE AIRPORT Bus 1 runs every 15 minutes from the airport to Plaça d'Espanya (on the train-station side) in central Palma (€2, 15 minutes) and on to the entrance of the ferry terminal. It makes several stops along the way, entering the heart of the city along Avinguda de Gabriel Alomar i Villalonga, skirting around the city centre and then running back to the coast along Passeig de Mallorca and Avinguda d'Argentina. It heads along Avinguda de Gabriel Roca (aka Passeig Marítim) to reach the Estació Marítima (ferry port) before turning around. Buy tickets from the driver.

Taxis are generally abundant (when not striking) and the ride from the airport to central Palma will cost around €16 to €21.

TO/FROM THE FERRY PORT Bus 1 (the airport bus) runs every 15 minutes from the ferry port (Estació Marítima) across town (via Plaça d'Espanya) and on to the airport. A taxi from/to the centre will cost around €7 to €10.

BICYCLE There are plenty of activities operators (p56) in Palma who rent out city and mountain bikes.

BUS There are 25 local bus services around Palma and its bay suburbs run by **EMT** (☎971 214 444; www.emtpalma.es). Single-trip tickets cost €1.25, or you can buy a 10-trip card for €8.

CAR & MOTORCYCLE Parking in the centre of town can be complicated. Some streets for pedestrians only and most of the remaining streets, including the ring roads (the *avingudes*, or *avenidas*) around the centre, are either no-parking zones or metered parking. Metered areas are marked in blue and generally you can park for up to two hours (€2.50), although time limits and prices can vary. The meters generally operate from 9am to 2pm and 4.30pm to 8pm Monday to Friday, and 9am to 2pm on Saturday.

METRO Of limited use to most travellers, a metro line operates from Plaça d'Espanya to the city's university. A single trip costs €0.75; return costs €1.40.

TAXI For a taxi call ☎971 728 081, 971 755 440, 971 401 414, 971 743 737 or 971 200 900. For special taxis for the disabled, call ☎971 703 529. Taxis are metered but for trips beyond the city fix the price in advance. A green light indicates a taxi is free to hail or you can head for one of the taxi stands in the centre of town, such as those on Passeig d'es Born. Flagfall is €2.25; thereafter you pay €1.02 per kilometre (more on weekends and holidays). There's a €0.70 supplement for every piece of luggage. Other extras include €2.70 for the airport or the port, and €0.60 for Castell de Bellver.

BADIA DE PALMA

The broad Badia de Palma stretches east and west away from the city centre. Some of the island's densest holiday development is to be found on both sides, but the beaches, especially to the west, are quite striking in spite of the dense cement backdrop.

East of Palma

Beyond the quiet beach of Ciutat Jardí and the Cala Gamba marina, you arrive in the mass beach-holiday area focused on Platja de Palma and S'Arenal. A couple of nearby escape hatches allow respite from the madding crowds.

CA'N PASTILLA TO S'ARENAL

In the shadow of the airport, heavily built-up **Ca'n Pastilla** is where Palma's eastern package-holiday coast begins. The **Platja de Ca'n Pastilla** marks the western and windier end of the 4.5km stretch of beach known as **Platja de Palma**; the windsurfing here can be good. Just west of Ca'n Pastilla is the pleasant **Cala Estancia**, a placid inlet whose beach is perfect for families. The waterfront, with a pedestrian walkway, is backed by low-rise developments with hotels, eateries, cafes and bars. Just a two-minute walk further west from Cala Estancia along the waterfront is the überlaid-back, sunset chill lounge, Puro Beach (p75). If you ever felt like having a business card that simply said 'The Dude', this is where you'd most likely flash it.

S'Arenal hosts produce and flea markets on Tuesdays and Thursdays.

Sights & Activities

Palma Aquarium AQUARIUM

(☎971 746 104; www.palmaaquarium.com; Carrer de Manuela de los Herreros i Sorà 21; adult/child under 18yr/under 3yr €20.50/16.50/free; ⏰10am-6pm; 👪) The Palma Aquarium is one of the best of its kind in the Mediterranean and one of few good reasons for visiting Platja de Palma. Five million litres of salt water fill the 55 tanks, home to sea critters from the Mediterranean (rays, sea horses, coral and more) and far-away oceans. The central tank, which you walk through via a transparent tunnel, is patrolled by 20 sleek sharks.

In total some 8000 specimens are found here ranging across a number of marine environments, with some stirring exhibits covering the threat to world tuna stocks. Yes, you'll see Nemo and there are good information panels in English, French, German and Spanish. You could easily spend half a day here.

Aqualand AMUSEMENT PARK

(☎971 440 000; www.aqualand.es; Ma6014; adult/child €24/16; ⏰10am-6pm Jul & Aug, 10am-5pm mid-May–Jun & Sep) Aqualand is a typical watery amusement park, with rides, aqua gym, and kids' amusements. It's just outside S'Arenal by the Cala Blava roundabout; take the Km15 exit on the Palma–S'Arenal motorway.

Attraction BOAT TRIPS

(☎971 746 101; www.attractioncatamarans.com; Carrer de Nanses; adult/child incl meal & drink €49/26.50) Attraction does five-hour catamaran trips around the Badia de Palma during the day, and hosts night trips that are basically party excursions.

Ciclos Quintana BICYCLE RENTAL

(☎971 442 925; www.ciclosquintana.com; Carrer de San Cristóbal 32; aluminium/carbon bikes per day €19/25, per week €90/120) You'll find plenty of rental outlets along S'Arenal's beachfront

WORTH A TRIP

CALA BLAVA

Nothing could be further removed from the beer gardens of Platja de Palma than residential **Cala Blava**, 2.5km southwest of S'Arenal. There are several rocky locations for a dip, and one sandy beach. After the fork in the Ma6014 road (to Cala Blava and Cala Pi), take the first right – it's a few hundred metres down to the beach (bus stop Carrer D'Ondategui 36). Look for the Pas a Sa Platja sign and stairs opposite Carrer de Mèxic.

The continuation south of Cala Blava is Bella Vista. Part of the coast is off-limits as a protected area, but you could slip down to the Calò des Cap d'Alt for a swim in crystal-clear waters. Hungry? Stop at **Restaurante Panorámica Playa** (p75).

On the west side of the Badia de Palma, you could head south of Magaluf to a couple of pretty inlets. Cala Vinyes has placid water, and the sand stretches inland among residential buildings. The next cove, Cala de Cap Falcó, is an emerald lick of an inlet surrounded by tree-covered rocky coast. The developers are getting closer and closer... Follow signs south for Sol de Mallorca and then the signs for each of these locations. Bus 107 from Palma reaches Cala Vinyes via Magaluf.

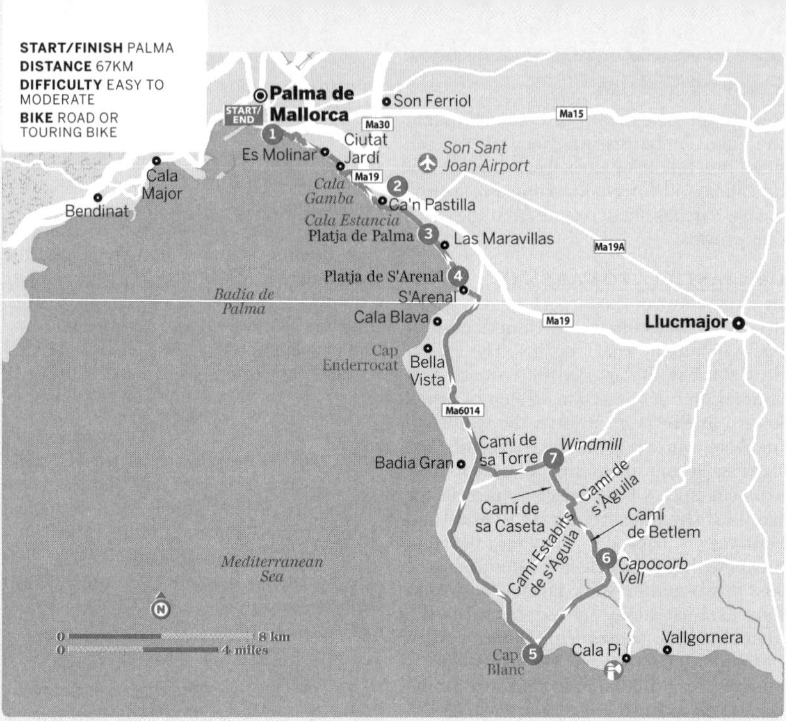

Cycling Tour

Palma to Capocorb Vell

Covering a huge swath of the Badia de Palma, this circular ride follows an easygoing seafront cycle path, then heads slightly inland towards Cap Blanc on the island's south coast. The return journey winds through peaceful country lanes, before a deserved downhill reverses the route back to town.

Pick up the waterfront bike path anywhere in 1 **Central Palma** and head southeast. Hugging the coast for most of the way, the path is a breezy sweep to 2 **Ca'n Pastilla**, from where you follow the seafront road to the end of the long sandy strip of 3 **Platja de Palma** and its extension 4 **S'Arenal**. From here, follow the wooden signs for 5 **Cap Blanc**. Although along a major road, the 23km ride cuts through pleasant enough countryside, and motorists are used to lycra-clad two-wheelers plying the route. The road rises to 150m but none of the ascents is too gruelling.

You're unable to reach the lighthouse at the cape, so scoot on round the bend to the left, rather than taking the signed road to the right. When you come to a junction (with signs right to Cala Pi), take a left for 6 **Capocorb Vell**, whose entrance is just on the left. There's a rustic bar at the ruins.

Exit the bar to the right and take the Camí de Betlem, a quiet country lane (also signed Carreró de Betlem). Follow this to the junction, and continue onto the Camí Estabits de s'Àguila, which rolls along surrounded by farmland. Turning sharp right, it becomes the Camí de s'Àguila. After 200m, a left turn will bring you onto the Camí de sa Caseta, beautifully shaded by overhanging trees and lined by dry-stone walls. The end of the lane is marked by a 7 **windmill** and, to the left, a church. Turn left here, where a wooden sign points you along the tranquil Camí de sa Torre and onwards to S'Arenal. Take a right when you hit the Ma6014 and follow the wooden signs to Platja de Palma. From here, you can easily retrace your tracks all the way back to the capital.

but if you're after a road bike try Ciclos Quintana, just up from the main drag.

Tours

Segway Tours TOURS

(☎605 666 365; www.segwaypalma.com; Carretera del Arenal 9; 1/2/3hr tours €35/60/75) See the city by Segway, with one-hour beach tours, two-hour tours to Es Portitxol and three-hour versions that go to the Catedral and back to Platja de Palma.

Eating

There's no shortage of places to eat in Platja de Palma and S'Arenal, anything from German sausages to mediocre paella; most people come here for the partying, not fine food. A predominantly German crowd pours in for endless drinking and deafening music, a phenomenon known as Ballermann (after the name of a famous beachside drink and dance local – Balneari 6). There are even Ballermann CDs.

Restaurante Panorámica Playa SEAFOOD

(☎971 740 211; Passeig de les Dames 29; mains €8-15; ⏲1-3.30pm & 7.30-11pm) Hungry? You can stop at Restaurante Panorámica Playa and tuck into some fish on the terrace, which has magnificent views of the Badia de Palma. Walk down the steps for a dip in the 'pool' – a platform from which to launch yourself into the sea.

Drinking & Entertainment

The core of the nightlife takes place in enormous beer gardens on or near Carrer del Pare Bartomeu Salvà, known to German revellers as Schinkenstrasse (Ham St) and about three-quarters of the way along the beach east towards S'Arenal (orientation points are Balneario 5 and 6 on the beach). You'll hear them before you see them, and there's very little to distinguish one from the other.

Puro Beach BAR

(☎971 744 744; www.purobeach.com; ⏲11am-2am Apr-Oct) This laid-back, sunset chill lounge carries more than a hint of Ibiza with a tapering outdoor promontory over the water and an all-white bar that's perfect for sunset cocktails, DJ sessions and fusion-food escapes. Blend in with the monochrome decor and wear white, emphasising your designer tan. It is just a two-minute walk east of Cala Estancia (itself just east of Ca'n Pastilla).

Getting There & Away

Bus 23 runs from Plaça d'Espanya to Ca'n Pastilla and parallel to Platja de Palma through S'Arenal and on past La Porciúncula to Aqualand (one hour). Buses run every half hour or so and once every two hours they continue on to Cala Blava (€1.25; one hour 50 minutes). Bus 15 runs from Plaça de la Reina and passes through Plaça d'Espanya on its way to S'Arenal every eight minutes. For the aquarium, get off at Balneari 14.

West of Palma

The Badia de Palma stretches to the southwest of central Palma in a series of little bays and beaches that are the nucleus of a series of heavily built-up resort areas. The beaches themselves are mostly very pretty and clean; the tourism is at its English-breakfast-and-binge-drinking worst in Magaluf. Beyond, the coast quietens considerably until rounding Cap de Cala Figuera.

CALA MAJOR

Cala Major, once a jet-set beach scene about 4km southwest of the city centre, is a pretty beach and the first you encounter on your way west of the city. Sandwiched in between the multistorey hotels and apartments right on the beach is a motley crew of bars, snack joints and dance spots. Even more than the beach, the main attraction here is the Fundació Pilar I Joan Miró (p75).

Take Bus 3 or 46 from the Palma city centre (Plaça d'Espanya) for Cala Major.

Fundació Pilar i Joan Miró GALLERY

(☎971 701 420; miro.palma.cat; Carrer de Saridakis 29; adult/child €6/free; ⏲10am-7pm Tue-Sat, 10am-3pm Sun; 🚌3 from Plaça Espanya, 6 from Plaça de la Reina) Inland from the waterfront is a major art stop, the Fundació Pilar i Joan Miró. Top Spanish architect Rafael Moneo designed the main building in 1992, next to the studio in which Miró had thrived for decades. With 2500 works by the artist (including 100 paintings), along with memorabilia, it's a major collection.

No doubt influenced by his Mallorquin wife and mother, Miró moved to Palma de Mallorca in 1956 and remained there until his death in 1983. His friend, the architect Josep Lluís Sert, designed the studio space for him above Cala Major.

A selection of his works hangs in the Sala Estrella, an angular, jagged part of Moneo's creation that is the architect's take on the artist's work. The rest of the building's exhibition space is used for temporary shows. Miró sculptures are scattered about outside. Beyond the studio is Son Boter, an 18th-century farmhouse Miró bought to increase his privacy. Inside, giant scribblings on the whitewashed walls served as plans for some of his bronze sculptures.

Take bus 3 or 46 from Plaça d'Espanya.

GÈNOVA & AROUND

Most travellers come up here, around 1km roughly north of the Fundació Pilar i Joan Miró in the satellite settlement of Gènova, to visit the closest caves to the capital. Locals know it more for the promise of hearty eating in one of several crowded restaurants.

From Palma or Cala Major, take bus 46 to Coves de Gènova. Alight at Camí dels Reis 19; from here it's about a 300m walk. If you have wheels, follow the signs to Na Burguesa off the main road from the centre of Gènova (a short way north of the Coves turn-off). About 1.5km of winding, poor road takes you past the walled-in pleasure domes of the rich to reach a rather ugly monument to the Virgin Mary, from where you have sweeping views over the city (this is about the only way to look *down* on the Castell Bellver) and bay.

Sights

Coves de Gènova CAVES

(☎971 402 387; Carrer d'es Barranc 45; adult/child under 10yr €8/4; ⏲10am-1.30pm & 4-6.30pm Tue-Sun) About 1km roughly north of the Fundació Pilar i Joan Miró, in the satellite settlement of Gènova, you can poke about the stalactites and stalagmites of the Coves de Gènova. Discovered in 1906, the caves are not as interesting as the Coves del Drac in the east of the island, but are a pleasant enough distraction. You reach a maximum depth of 36m and will be shown all sorts of fanciful, backlit shapes. The temperature is always around 20°C in the caves, and water has been dripping away for many millennia to create these natural 'sculptures'.

Eating

Mesón Ca'n Pedro SPANISH €€

(☎971 402 479; www.mesoncanpedro.com; Carrer del Rector Vives 4; mains €12-25; ⏲12.30-4.30pm & 7pm-12.30am Tue-Sun) Palma folk love escaping up here to eat in one of the hearty restaurants. One of the best here is Mesón Ca'n Pedro, famous for its snails. It has another place at Carrer del Rector Vives 14.

SES ILLETES & PORTALS NOUS

The islands *(illetes)* in question lie just off pine-backed beaches. This is altogether a much classier holiday-residential zone. The coast is high and drops quite abruptly to the turquoise coves, principally Platja de Ses Illetes and, a little less crowded, Platja de Sa Comtesa. Parking is a minor hassle.

Virtually a part of Ses Illetes is **Bendinat**, named after the private castle of the same name (a neo-Gothic reworking of the 13th-century original that can only be seen from the Ma1 motorway). The area is jammed with high-class hotels and villas that are not for the financially faint-hearted. Next up is **Portals Nous**, with its super-marina for the super-yachts of the super-rich at restaurant-lined **Puerto Portals**. The beach that stretches north of the marina is longer and broader than those in Ses Illetes.

Local Palma bus 3 reaches Ses Illetes from central Palma (€1.10); you can pick it up on Passeig de la Rambla or Avinguda de Jaume III). Buses 103, 104, 106 and 111 from Palma's bus station call in at Portals Nous (€1.45; 30 to 50 minutes).

Eating & Entertainment

Restaurante Es Parral MALLORCAN €€

(☎971 701 127; Paseo de Illetes 75; mains €11-18; ⏲1-3.30pm & 7-10.30pm Tue-Sat Apr-Oct) On the main road above the main beach, this intimate restaurant serves up tasty local dishes with a few Basque imports thrown in for good measure. Its '*menu mallorquín*' (€18) is a rare opportunity to sample local tastes in the area.

Virtual Club COCKTAIL BAR

(☎971 703 235; www.virtualclub.es; Passeig d'Illetes 60; ⏲10am-midnight Apr-Nov) This waterside pleasure dome with a serviceable list of cocktails, thatched huts and shades, wicker chairs and wicked DJ sounds is perfectly at home in this upscale area. There's also a kind of cavernous bar that fills with strange strobe lighting at night.

PALMANOVA & MAGALUF

About 2km southwest from Portals Nous elite yacht harbour and much-flaunted €500 notes is a whole other world. Palmanova and Magaluf have merged to form what is the epitome of the sea, sand, sangria and shagging (not necessarily in that order) holiday that has lent all of Mallorca an undeserved notoriety.

Sights & Activities

There is a reason for Palmanova's and Magaluf's popularity: the four main beaches between Palmanova and Magaluf are beautiful and immaculately maintained. The broad sweeps of fine white sand, in parts shaded by strategically planted pines and palms, are undeniably tempting and the development behind them could be considerably worse.

On Saturday morning in Magaluf, a fairly standard crafts and knick-knacks market sets up around Carrer Blanc (a good four blocks from the beach) for the area's few early risers.

Marineland AMUSEMENT PARK
(☎971 675 125; www.marineland.es; Carrer Garcilaso de la Vega, Costa d'En Blanes; adult/child €22.50/€16.50; ⏰9:30am-6pm mid-Apr–Oct) Marineland has dolphin shows, an aquarium, reptiles and so on. It's at the Puerto Portals roundabout between Portals Nous and Palmanova.

Western Water Park AMUSEMENT PARK
(☎971 131 203; www.westernpark.com; Carretera de Cala Figuera; adult/child €21/13; ⏰10am-6pm Jul & Aug, 10am-5pm Mon-Sat May, 10am-5pm Jun & Sep) At the southern end of Magaluf, this place has wave pools, sea lions, falcon shows and Wild West–themed eateries and shops.

Cruceros Costa de Calvià BOAT TRIPS
(☎971 131 211; www.cruceroscostadecalvia.com; adult/child €16/8; ⏰11am, 1pm & 3pm Mon-Fri, 11am & 3pm Sat & Sun May-Sep) This operator offers two-hour boat trips in a glass-bottomed boat with the chance of seeing dolphins. There are departures from the main beach in Magaluf, calling at Palmanova 15 minutes later.

Big Blue Diving DIVING, SNORKELLING
(☎971 681 686; www.bigbluediving-mallorca.net; Carrer de Martí Ros García 6; snorkelling per person €30, 1-/2-dive package €59/89; ⏰Apr-Oct) A well-run dive centre right on Palmanova beach.

Entertainment

While restless young Germans party at the Platja de Palma beer gardens east of the city, their British equivalents are letting themselves loose on the nightspots of Magaluf. This is big stag- and hen-night territory, and few holds are barred. The drinking antics of the Brits in Magaluf have long been legendary (for all the wrong reasons). The bulk of the action is concentrated around the north end of Carrer de Punta Ballena. Pubs and bars are piled on top of one another.

Information

Palmanova tourist office (☎971 682 365; Passeig de la Mar; ⏰9am-6pm Mon-Fri, 9am-3pm Sat)

Magaluf tourist office (☎971 131 126; Carrer de Pere Vacquer Ramis 1; ⏰9am-6pm Mon-Fri, 9am-3pm Sat)

Hotel Information (www.palmanova-magaluf.com) Run by the local hoteliers' association.

Getting There & Away

The most direct bus from Palma is the 105 (€2.75; 45 minutes), which runs 11 times a day. Bus 107 (seven times a day) takes five minutes longer as it stops at Marineland en route. The 106 (one hour) is the most frequent service.

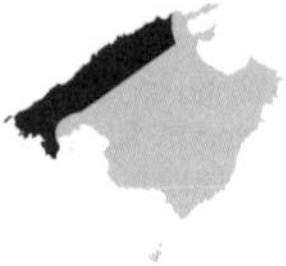

Western Mallorca

Includes »

Andratx 79
Port d'Andratx 79
Sant Elm 83
Valldemossa 87
Port de Valldemossa 90
Deià & Around 90
Sóller 92
Port de Sóller........95
Biniaraix 98
Fornalutx............98
Cala de Sa Calobra & Cala Tuent..........101
Monestir de Lluc & Around.............102

Best Places to Eat

- Son Tomás (p85)
- Es Racó d'es Teix (p91)
- Traffic (p101)
- Ca's Carreter (p95)
- Sebastian (p91)

Best Places to Stay

- Finca Son Palou (p169)
- Ca'l Bisbe (p168)
- Ca Madò Paula (p166)
- Hostal-Residencia Catalina Vera (p165)
- S'Hotel des Puig (p167)

Why Go?

Western Mallorca is one of the most beautiful corners of the Mediterranean.

All along the west coast, the Serra de Tramuntana surveys the Mediterranean from on high, jagged peaks of bare stone yielding to pine forests before plunging down to the water's edge like the ramparts of some epic island fortress. Clinging to its slopes are towns and villages such as Sóller, Valldemossa and Deià. Picturesque in both setting and architecture, they're equally famous for the artistic celebrities who have called them home over the years. By the water's edge, sheltered yacht harbours add the merest hint of glamour and beaches ensure that the west of the island doesn't miss out on Mallorca's summer call to the coast. And whether you explore it all by hiking, sailing or driving, it's definitely worth spending a few days exploring this lovely part of Mallorca.

When to Go?

Western Mallorca is at its best in spring and autumn – smaller crowds plus most hotels and restaurants are open; at this time of year, nights can be rather chilly. Summer can be extremely busy with the coast road overwhelmed by pelotons of cyclists and restaurants and hotels operating at close to capacity. Summer is also the time for the best weather, whether for a swim in the Mediterranean or clear-sky views along the coast, and Deià and Valldemossa have enticing musical concerts.

THE SOUTHWEST

Heavily and, for the most part, tastelessly developed, the southwest corner of the island holds a couple of pretty coastal surprises. It remains to be seen whether these last redoubts of natural beauty will resist human greed. Judging by the building scandals and phalanxes of cranes in and around Andratx, it might be an idea to get in quick before the cement-mixers do.

To Cap de Cala Figuera

The residences of the rich in the soulless suburban-style development of Sol de Mallorca, 2km south of Magaluf, look across the Punta de S'Estaca to three dreamlike inlets collectively known as **Portals Vells**. The view over the turquoise-emerald waters is enviable. Will the developers' grip stretch to the other side?

To reach Portals Vells, take the road from south Magaluf (the number 8 roundabout by Aqualand) in the direction of El Toro and, after 800m, the narrow road south through the golf course, rather than swinging right (west) for El Toro. About 2km through pine woods you reach a junction. To the left is signposted 'Playa Mago', which is two narrow inlets. The one on the right has a restaurant and is generally frequented by nudists, while the longer inlet with the narrow, shady beach to the right is prettier.

Nicer than either is **Cala Portals Vells**, another 1.8km south from the junction. Turquoise waters lap the beach, whose sands stretch back quite a distance beneath rows of straw umbrellas. To the south a walking trail leads to caves in the rock walls, one of them containing the rudiments of a chapel.

A few hundred metres back up from the beach, the road south to the **Cap de Cala Figuera** lighthouse is blocked off as private property.

Andratx

POP 5050 / ELEV 132M

Andratx is the largest town in the southwest. Typically for Mallorca, it lies well inland as a defensive measure against pirate attack, while its harbour, Port d'Andratx, lies 4km southwest. Andratx is pasted like crunchy peanut butter onto the flank of foothills of the Serra de Tramuntana. Its most important buildings stand tall on two rises. The 16th-century **Castell de Son Mas**, on the hill at the northern end of town, is an elegant defensive palace that now houses *ajuntament* (town hall). From it you can see the hulk of the **Església de Santa María d'Andratx**, built in the 18th century on the site of the original 1248 church.

Eating

Font i Caliu MALLORCAN €€
(☎971 137 070; Carrer de Juan Carlos I 2; mains €8-13; ⏰Sun-Fri; 🚭) For simple island fare in a time-warp atmosphere, Font i Caliu is a good choice. There's a courtyard out the back or you could take an inside table with ageing white linen beneath exposed beams for some *trampó* (a cold vegetable dish), followed by *arros brut* (dirty rice), a typical rice dish jammed with *sobrassada* (Mallorcan cured sausage), rabbit and other optional meats.

Information

Tourist office (☎971 628 019; Avinguda de la Curia; ⏰10am-2pm Mon-Fri) Housed in the town hall at the top end of town.

Port d'Andratx

POP 1205

Port d'Andratx surrounds a fine, long natural bay that attracts yachties from far and wide. It has an affluent air and is a pleasant place for an evening waterfront meal, although its appeal is partly skin-deep; it attracts a broad mix of visitors and the blight of development is rapidly eroding its charm.

Sights

The port is short on sights. Along Carrer d'Isaac Peral, you could easily slip past the tiny **Església de la Verge del Carme** without noticing it. Like any Mallorcan coastal resort, Port d'Andratx has a small number of operators offering diving, snorkelling and boat rental.

FREE **Museo Liedtke** GALLERY
(www.liedtke-museum.com; Carrer de l'Olivera 35; ⏰hours vary) The eccentric Museo Liedtke, 2km south of the port centre, was built between 1987 and 1993 into the cliffs near Cap de Sa Mola by German artist Dieter Walter Liedtke. Home to his art and temporary exhibitions, it's also a selling point for Liedtke's theories on life. It's often closed, but the coastal views warrant the detour.

Western Mallorca Highlights

1. Wander the steep and scented lanes of **Deià** (p90), one of Mallorca's prettiest towns
2. Drive the length of the coast from **Andratx** (p79) in the south to the monastic peace of **Monestir de Lluc** (p102) in the north
3. Lose yourself in the narrow lanes of **Valldemossa** (p87)
4. Walk through citrus, almond and olive groves to the villages of **Biniaraix** (p98) and **Fornalutx** (p98)
5. Discover the beauty and Modernista flair of the island's orange capital in **Sóller** (p92)
6. Feel your heart leap as you take the dramatic hairpin drive to **Sa Calobra** (p101)
7. Linger over *arroz bogavante* (lobster rice) in **Son Tómas** (p85) in **Banyalbufar** (p85)
8. Climb to the impregnable fortress ruins of **Castell d'Alaró** (p100)
9. Dive the transparent depths off the **Illa de Sa Dragonera** (p83)
10. Disappear into timeless **Orient** (p99) in Mallorca's quiet back country

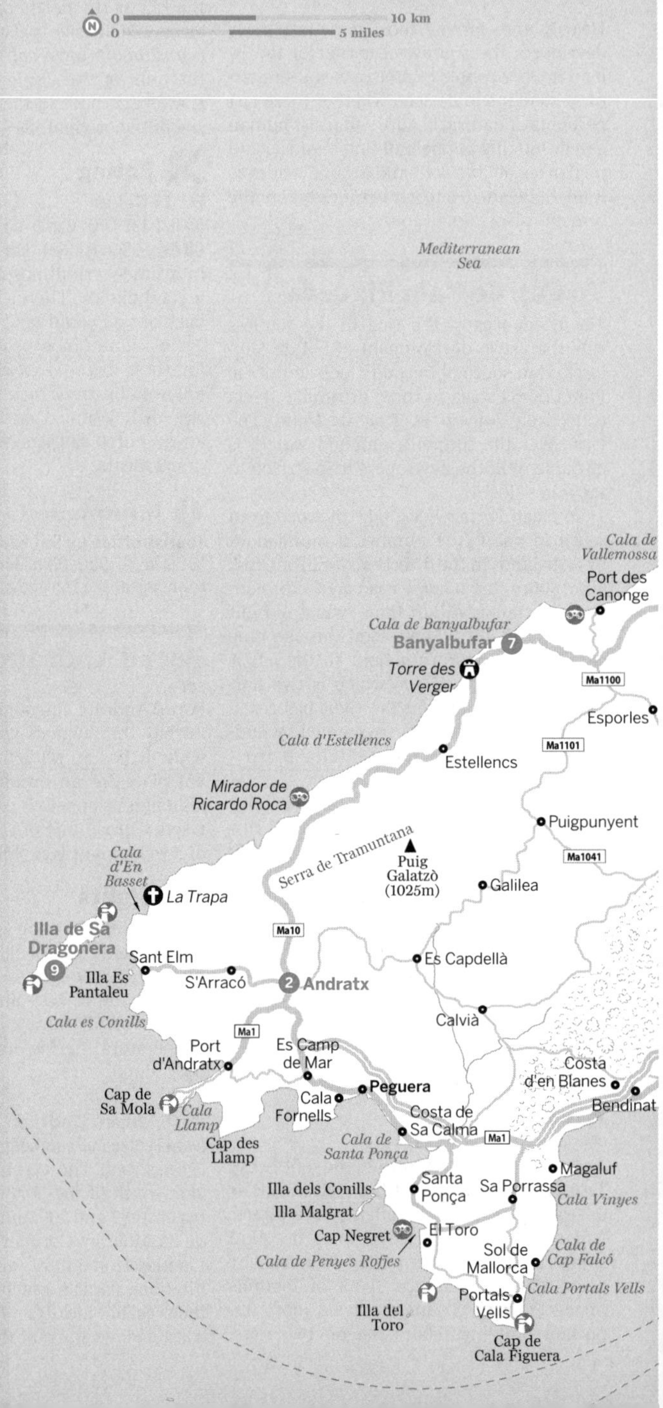

Serra de Tramuntana
Sa Calobra
6
Cala Tuent
Torre de Sa Calobra
Torrent de Pareis
Ermita de Sant Llorenç
Puig Roig (1002m)
Monestir de Lluc
2
Puig Tomir (1103m)
Escorca
Ma10
Ma2130
Puig Major (1445m)
Badia de Sóller
Cap Gros
Mirador de Ses Barques
Son Torella
Puig de Massanella (1365m)
Port de Sóller
Embassament de Cúber
4
Fornalutx
Refugi de Cúber
Binibona
Caimari
Campanet
Ma10
Sóller
5
4
Biniaraix
Puig de l'Ofre (1093m)
Selva
Moscari
Cala de Deià
Lluc Alcari
Son Marroig
Comasema
Mancor de la Vall
Ma13
1 Deià
Castell d'Alaró
Puig d'Alfàbia (1069m)
Puig de S'Alcadena (815m)
Miramar
Puig des Teix (1062m)
8
Puig de Santa Magdalena (307m)
Ma2100
10
Biniamar
Port de Valldemossa
Orient
Puig d'Alaró
Jardins d'Alfàbia
Lloseta
Inca
3 Valldemossa
Alaró
Bunyola
Binissalem
Ma1110
Raixa
Consell
Ma11
Costitx
S'Esgleieta
Santa Maria del Camí
Biniali
Sencelles
Ma1040
Ma13A
Ses Alqueries
Ma13
Establiments
Santa Eugènia
Son Sardina
Ma13
La Cabaneta
Ma13A
La Vileta
Palma de Mallorca
Ma20
Son Ferriol
Ma15
Gènova
Terreno
Algaida
Cala Major
Airport
Cala Gamba
Ca'n Pastilla
Cala Estancia
Randa
Las Maravillas
Badia de Palma
Puig de Randa (548m)
S'Arenal
Cala Blava
Ma19
Llucmajor
Cap Enderrocat
Ma19

CALA LLAMP

Southeast of town, Cala Llamp is a sandless bay with sparkling, bottle-green water that can be difficult to find due to the truly epic construction climbing up the hillside. If you have your own wheels, it's worth venturing along this rugged stretch of coast, if only for a dip in the bay or to relax over a drink at the Gran Folies Beach Club. To get to Cala Llamp, take the Ma1020 from the centre of Port d'Andratx and follow the signs over the ridge.

Activities

Aqua Mallorca Diving DIVE CENTRE
(Dragonera Diving; ☎971 674 376; www.aqua-mallorca-diving.com; Avinguda de l'Amirante Riera Alemany 23; 5-/10-dive package €140/270, 2hr snorkel adult/child €19.50/15; ⏲8.45-9.30am, noon-2.30pm & 5-6pm Apr-Oct) The main local dive shop, this place has an office along the waterfront southwest of the main restaurant strip.

Llaüts BOAT RENTAL
(☎971 672 094; www.llauts.com; Carrer de San Carlos 6A; per hr/half day/day €40/120/170; ⏲Apr-Oct) A good place for boat rentals, Llaüts has 4m crafts for those with no boat licence, with prices on request for more experienced boat users. Rates drop slightly outside July and August. You'll find it southwest of the main waterfront restaurant strip; opening hours are unreliable so ring ahead.

Eating

The waterfront is lined with restaurants, all with dining areas right on the water. Quality varies as always in such ports, but a few places stand out.

Ca'n Pep SPANISH, MALLORCAN €€
(☎971 671 648; www.canpepandratx.com; Avinguda de Mateu Bosch 30; mains €11-23; ⏲noon-midnight; ⓔ) Spanning the bridge between classy and casual, Ca'n Pep gets the important things right, with dishes such as cod croquettes, lobster paella, a seafood platter and wild-sea-bass fillets wrapped in asparagus and bacon, all served up on its breezy harbourside perch.

Restaurante La Gallega SEAFOOD, GALICIAN €€
(☎971 671 338; Carrer Isaac Peral 52; mains €13-25; ⏲1.30-11pm Tue-Sun, closed Nov) A couple of blocks inland from the waterfront, Restaurante La Gallega is a popular seafood restaurant with its inspiration coming from Galicia in Spain's northeast. The *mariscada Galicia* (Galician seafood platter) is well priced at €25 per person, but you'll need to order for two people or more.

Restaurante El Coche SEAFOOD €€
(☎971 671 976; www.restaurantes-andratx.com; Avinguda de Mateu Bosch 13; mains €12.90-19; ⏲1-3.30pm & 7-10.30pm Wed-Mon; ⓔ) A slightly classier option than most along the waterfront, El Coche has been going strong since 1977, outlasting most of the competition in the process. The dishes are Mallorcan seafood classics with the occasional unusual twist, such as the sea bream with garlic, vinegar and chili.

Drinking

Most of the harbourside restaurants morph into bars as the night wears on, but there are some reasonable choices at the southwestern end of the strip.

La Ronda Artcafé CAFE
(☎971 674 711; www.laronda-artcafe.com; Avinguda de l'Almirante Riera Alemany 8; ⏲11am-1am) A change of ownership has brought a touch of sophistication to Port d'Andratx's drinking scene. La Ronda's pluses include its fine collection of contemporary art, open fireplace, lovely back garden and roof terrace, all set in a waterside terrace. Staff here freshly bake cakes and bread and serve up everything from coffee and juices to wine and cocktails.

Gran Folies Beach Club BAR
(☎971 671 094; www.granfolies.net; Carrer de Congre 2, Cala Llamp; ⏲10am-2am) This restaurant-bar sits right above the rocky cove in Cala Llamp and offers use of a pool to cavort in between cocktails. It also does breakfast and full meals and runs occasional yoga classes.

Tim's BAR
(Avinguda de l'Almirante Riera Alemany 7; ⏲10.30am-late) Tim's is a busy bar that can stay open as late as 4am at the height of summer. It screens live football on the big screen (take note British visitors), and has live music on Friday and Saturday nights. Cocktails start from €7.50.

Information

Tourist office (☎971 671 300; Avinguda de Mateu Bosch; ⏲9am-4pm May-Sep, 9am-3pm Mon-Fri, 9am-2pm Sat Oct-Apr) Next to the bus stop.

Getting There & Away

Most of the 102 buses from Palma continue from Andratx to the port (€1.45, 10 minutes). Bus 100 runs seven or eight times a day between Andratx and Sant Elm, calling in at Port d'Andratx en route.

Sant Elm

POP 95

This tranquil beach haven in Mallorca's extreme southwest is one of our favourite corners of this often overdeveloped coast. To get here, the Ma1030 ducks and weaves up hill and down dale from S'Arracó, and there's a sense of having stumbled on a well-hidden secret.

Sights & Activities

Sant Elm's main town **beach** is a pleasant sandy strand (no shade) that faces the gently lapping Mediterranean to the south. Within swimming distance for the moderately fit is **Illa Es Pantaleu**, a rocky islet that marks one of the boundaries of a marine reserve. The reserve is dominated by the 4km-long **Illa de Sa Dragonera**, which looms like an aircraft carrier to the west. Constituted as a natural park, it can be reached by ferry (p84). The ferry lands at a protected natural harbour on the east side of the island, from where you can follow trails to the capes at either end or ascend the **Na Pòpia peak** (Puig des Far Vell, 349m). The ferry operators also do **glass-bottomed-boat tours** around the island. If you want to dive off the island, try Scuba Activa (p84).

To the south of Sant Elm's main beach is **Cala es Conills,** a sandless but pretty inlet (follow Carrer de Cala es Conills).

THE RUTA DE PEDRA EN SEC

A breathtaking walkers' week in Mallorca would see you traverse the entire mountainous northwest, from Cap de Formentor to Sant Elm. Old mule trails constitute the bulk of the (still incomplete) 150km GR221 walking route, aka the Ruta de Pedra en Sec (Dry Stone Route). The 'dry stone' refers to an age-old building method here and throughout the island. In the mountains you'll see paved ways, farming terraces, houses, walls and more built of stone without the aid of mortar.

The GR221 begins in **Pollença** near Can Diable and the Torrent d'en Marc stream, but you could start with a day's march from Cap de Formentor. A reasonably fit walker can accomplish the stretch from Pollença to Port d'Andratx in as little as four days, but with an extra few days you can include stops in some of the beautiful villages en route.

The first stretch is an easy walk of about four to five hours gradually curving southwest to the **Monestir de Lluc** (where you can stay overnight). You will ascend about 600m in the course of the day, before dropping back down a little to the monastery. The following day sees another fair climb to over 1000m, taking you past the Puig de Massanella (1365m), southwest to the Embassament de Cúber dam, past Puig de l'Ofre (1093m), which many like to bag, and down the Biniaraix ravine to Sóller to sleep. You might want to spend a couple of days here to explore the surrounding area.

To **Deià** you're looking at two to three hours' walking (from Sóller you could follow several trails, not just the GR221) and another two hours for **Valldemossa**. Those in a hurry could make it as far as **Estellencs** but, again, you might want to spread the walking over a couple of days. The last day would see you hiking from Estellencs to **Sant Elm** via **La Trapa**.

The walking requires a reasonable level of fitness but no special skills or equipment, other than good boots, sun protection, water bottle and so on. Good map-reading and compass skills are essential, as paths are not always well marked (one of the delays in completing the GR221 trail has been that 92% of the Serra de Tramuntana is private property and many rights of way are disputed). With various alternative routes, it is easy to become disoriented.

There are five refuges along the way, in Pollença, Monestir de Lluc, Escorca, Port de Sóller and Deià (to book a sleeping berth, call ahead on ☎971 137 700 from 9am to 2pm Monday to Friday, or visit www.conselldemallorca.net/refugis). There are plenty of other overnight options in the villages. For more information on the route, check out the Consell de Mallorca's web page, **Pedra en Sec i Senderisme** (www.conselldemallorca.net/mediambient/pedra).

A couple of nice walks head north from Plaça del Monsenyor Sebastià Grau, at the northeast end of town. One follows the GR221 long-distance route for about an hour to **La Trapa**, a ruined former monastery. A few hundred metres from the building is a wonderful lookout point. You can start on the same trail but branch off west about halfway (total walk of about 45 minutes) to reach **Cala d'En Basset**, a lovely bay with transparent water but not much of a beach.

Scuba Activa DIVING, SNORKELLING
(☎971 239 102; www.scuba-activa.com; Plaça del Monsenyor Sebastià Grau 7; dive incl equipment €32; ⏲Apr-Oct) This well-run dive centre can also arrange snorkelling.

Eating

El Pescador SEAFOOD €€
(☎971 239 198; Avinguda de Jaume I 48; mains €11-15; ⏲1-3.30pm & 7.30-10.30pm) El Pescador is perched off Plaça de Na Caragola, halfway into town (past the tourist office). Paella is a good midday option and meat mains are available, but the best bet is the fish of the day (sold by weight).

Information

Tourist office (☎971 239 205; Avinguda de Jaume 1 28B; ⏲9am-4pm May-Sep, 9am-3pm Mon-Fri & 9am-2pm Sat Oct-Apr) A short walk from the beach.

Getting There & Away

Seven or eight buses run from Andratx to Sant Elm (€1.45, 40 minutes) via Port d'Andratx and S'Arracó. You can also take the boat between Sant Elm and Port d'Andratx (€7.75, 20 minutes, daily February to November).

Ferry to Illa de Sa Dragonera (☎639 617 545) Ferries to Illa de Sa Dragonera (€13, 15 minutes, three to four daily February to November) operate from the small harbour north of Sant Elm's main beach.

SERRA DE TRAMUNTANA

Dominated by the rugged Serra de Tramuntana range, Mallorca's northwest coast and its hinterland form a spectacular contrast to the mass coastal tourism you leave behind around Palma. The vertiginous coastline is unforgiving, rocky (mostly limestone) and mostly inaccessible; the villages are largely built of local stone (as opposed to concrete), the agricultural terraces climbing up from the coast date back centuries, and the high, rugged interior is much loved by walkers for its beautiful landscapes of pine forests, olive groves and spring wild flowers. In 2011 the region's unique cultural and geographical features were recognised when Unesco inscribed the Cultural Landscape of the Serra de Tramuntana on its World Heritage List.

The range covers 1100 sq km and is 90km long, extending all the way north to the Cap de Formentor. The highest peaks are concentrated in the central mountain range. The highest, Puig Major de Son Torrella (1445m), is off-limits and home to a military communications base. It is followed by Puig de Massanella (1365m). The area is virtually bereft of surface watercourses, but rich in subterranean flows that feed the farming terraces of the coastal villages.

Andratx to Valldemossa

Welcome to the one of the Mediterranean's prettiest stretches of coastline, traversed by the Ma10 road that climbs away from Andratx into the wooded hills marking the beginning of the majestic Serra de Tramuntana range.

ESTELLENCS

POP 350 / ELEV 151M

Estellencs is a coquettish village of stone buildings scattered around the rolling hills below the **Puig Galatzò** (1025m); the views of the village are stunning, especially from the main road as you approach from the north, while the village is at its best as you climb down the hill away from the main road. A 1.5km road winds down through terraces of palm trees, citrus orchards, olives, almonds, cacti, pines and flowers to the local 'beach', **Cala d'Estellencs**, a rocky cove with crystal-clear water. To ascend Puig Galatzò, a walking trail starts near the Km97 milestone on the Ma10 road, about 2½km west of Estellencs. It's not easy going, so you'll need good maps and plenty of water and food. Reckon on a five- to six-hour round trip. An alternative but easily confused trail leads back down into Estellencs.

An **arts-and-crafts fair** is usually held in Estellencs on the 3rd weekend of April.

Eating

Montimar MALLORCAN €€
(☎971 618 576; Plaça de la Constitució 7; mains €30-40; ⏲1-3.30pm & 7-10.30pm Tue-Sun; 🚭) In

town, this bastion of traditional Mallorcan cooking, opposite the church, remains the best of the handful of eateries. Dishes range from grilled sardines to rice (minimum of two people), rabbit pâté or *sobrassada* (Mallorcan cured sausage) with honey, while Mallorcan cheeses are the pick of the desserts.

Cafeteria Vall-Hermos CAFE €
(☎971 618 610; www.vallhermos.com; Carrer de Eusebio Pascual 6; mains €8-12; ⏲10am-8pm Sun-Fri, 10am-11pm Sat Thu-Tue Feb-Nov; 🚭) This simple cafe on the main drag through town boasts some fine views. The food here is hearty if hardly cutting edge, but the variety (from *bocadillos* or tapas to more substantial offerings) should suit most budgets and appetites. Or you could simply stop by for a drink to admire the views; it stays open later in summer. There are also apartments for rent here.

Shopping

Estel@rt FOOD, HANDICRAFTS
(☎971 149 092; carmejover@estelart.net; Carrer de Sa Siquia; ⏲10am-2pm & 5-8pm Tue-Sat, 10am-2pm Sun) At the northern end of town, this engaging little place sells primarily Mallorcan and Menorcan clothes, jewellery, ceramics and food products; the selection is small but well chosen. There's a two-room art gallery downstairs, and coffee, wine and cakes are available.

BANYALBUFAR

POP 485 / ELEV 112M

Eight kilometres northeast of Estellencs, Banyalbufar is similarly positioned in a cleft in the Serra de Tramuntana's seaward wall, high above the coast. If anything it's an even tighter and steeper huddle and its quiet lanes winding down towards the sea beckon strollers. A steep 1km walk downhill brings you to a shingle cove, **Cala de Banyalbufar**, where you can swim; there's also a lovely waterfall nearby.

The village was founded by the Arabs in the 10th century; the name Banyalbufar means 'built next to the sea' in Arabic. All around the village are carved-out, centuries-old, stone-walled farming terraces, known as *ses marjades* and forming a series of steps down to the sea; they are kept moist by mountain well water that gurgles down open channels and is stored in cisterns. Just out of town is the Torre des Verger (p85), one of the most recognisable symbols of Mallorca.

Sights

Torre des Verger FORTRESS
(Torre de Ses Animes; Carretera de Banyalbufar-Andratx) One kilometre out of town on the road to Estellencs, the Torre des Verger is a 1579 *talayot* (watchtower), an image you'll see on postcards all over the island. It's one of the most crazily sited structures on the island – one step further and it would plunge into the Mediterranean far below.

Climb to the top, fighting off vertigo as you go, and scan the horizon for yachts where sentinels once warned of pirates.

Bodega Son Vives WINERY
(☎609 601 904; www.sonvives.com; Carretera de Banyalbufar-Andratx; ⏲11am-7pm Thu-Sun May-Oct) High on the hill at the southern entrance to the village, this small winery has cellar-door tastings and sales in summer. It offers a number of fusion wines, but its best drop comes from the locally grown Malvasia grape. Son Vives also produces olive oil.

Eating

Son Tomás SPANISH, MALLORCAN €€
(☎971 618 149; sontomas@yahoo.es; Carrer de Baronia 17; mains €13.50-23; ⏲12.30-4pm & 7.30-10pm Wed-Sun, 12.30-4pm Mon; 🚭) A classic spot, this place almost seems to lean over the main road at the southwest end of town. Although it draws cyclists seeking snacks to its streetside tables, the upstairs restaurant is first class. Crackling *lechona* (suckling pig), a chunky *suquet* (a seafood and potato hotpot) and one of the best renditions of rice with lobster we tasted on the island await the ravenous.

Restaurante Es Trast MEDITERRANEAN €€
(☎971 148 544; Carrer de Comte Sallent 10; mains €16.90-19.90; ⏲11am-4pm & 7-11pm Thu-Tue Feb–mid-Dec; 🚭) This stylish yet casual place covers all the options – tapas (from 12.30pm to 6.30pm), salads and pasta cater to those looking for a light meal, while heartier dishes (such as pork sirloin with Mediterranean vegetables, or the fish of the day) will suit those desiring for something more substantial. The tastes are fresh and Mediterranean, and washed down with local wines.

In addition to the main dining area, there's a streetside terrace and a lovely narrow, stone-walled terrace out the back.

Ca Madò Paula MEDITERRANEAN €€
(☎971 148 717; www.camadopaula.com; Carrer de la Constitució 11; mains €12.50-16.90; ⏲1-4pm & 7.30-10pm Wed-Mon; 🚭) The small dining room

here could be that of your Mallorcan grandmother, while the rear garden is perfect for quiet summer nights. The menu tips its hat to Italian cooking, but there are also dishes such as fresh salmon with seafood sauce.

Shopping

Malvasia de Banyalbufar WINE

(☎971 148 505; www.malvasiadebanyalbufar.com; Carrer de Comte Sallent 5; ⏲11am-2pm & 5-8pm Tue-Sat, 11am-2pm Sun Jun-Aug, 11am-5pm Sat, 11am-2pm Sun Sep-May) This shop run by a co-operative of local wineries was set up to promote the locally grown Malvasia grape. As such, it's the perfect place to pick up a bottle of wine for a picnic or to take back home.

ESPORLES & THE INLAND CIRCUIT

A few hundred metres beyond the Port des Canonge turn-off, the Ma1100 breaks off southward towards Esporles. After 1km you reach a road junction and La Granja.

From La Granja, those with wheels could make a circuit inland. Follow the Ma1101 south, which plunges through thick woods and slithers down a series of hairpin bends to reach **Puigpunyent**. This typical inland town offers few sights but the luxury, rose-hued hilltop **Gran Hotel Son Net** (p166) is reason enough to detour here if money is no object.

From Puigpunyent, make a dash for **Galilea**, a high mountain hamlet about four serpentine kilometres south. Climb to the town's church square for views across the valleys and a drink in the bar next door, or head even higher up this straggling place for a greater sense of altitude. **Scott's Galilea** (p166) has a series of luxury studio apartments here.

Back in Puigpunyent, take the Ma1101 to **Esporles**, in the Tramuntana foothills. This shady village, set beside a generally dry stream, has a Saturday market. The tree-lined Ma1040 serves as the main road, on which reside a pompous church and numerous bar-eateries. Of these, Es Brollador (p86) is the pick. Esporles can be animated at night, as many folk from Palma have opted to live here and commute to the capital.

Sights

La Granja HISTORIC BUILDING

(☎971 610 032; www.lagranja.net; Carretera de Esporles-Banyalbufar; adult/child €12.50/6; ⏲10am-7pm May-Oct, 10am-6pm Nov-Apr) This magnificent *possessió* has been turned into something of a kitsch Mallorca-land exhibit, with folk in traditional dress doing traditional things. The grand mansion is, however, well worth the visit, as are its extensive gardens; some elements of the property date to the 10th century. You could spend hours exploring the period-furnished rooms, olive and wine presses, grand dining room, stables, workshops and some medieval instruments of torture in the cellars. In the gardens a stout old yew is estimated to be around 2000 years old!

Eating

Es Brollador SPANISH €€

(☎971 610 539; Passeig del Rei 10; mains €11.50-21.50, set menus €14-30; ⏲10am-10pm; 🚭) With its tiled floors, high ceilings and rear courtyard, Es Brollador makes a pleasant stop for anything from a morning coffee to lunch or dinner. The pork sirloin with a *sobrassada* sauce is memorable, while the set menus are always worth considering; it also serves

THE SEA VIEW

Driving, walking, cycling...whichever way you choose to explore the dramatic coast of the Serra de Tramuntana you're in for some spectacular views. But there's also a different approach worth considering. Take a **sailing route** from **Port d'Andratx** in the southwest, around past **Sant Elm** and **Illa de Sa Dragonera** and northeast to **Port de Sóller**, a good, quiet port to overnight in. Places to stop during the day for a dip (they are no good for dropping anchor overnight) are Port des Canonge, Cala de Deià and Lluc Alcari. The inlets of Estellencs and Valldemossa are too shallow for most yachts. The next stage, tracking to Cap de Formentor and rounding it to find shelter in the Badia de Pollença, takes longer under equal conditions. Good daytime stops are Cala Tuent, Sa Calobra, Cala Sant Vicenç and Cala Figuera. The total trip is around 60 nautical miles.

One of the main factors to consider is weather. Wind is more of a rule than an exception, which means you can get your sails out. However, depending on conditions, it can also be uncomfortable. In winter it is often dangerous to sail along this coastline. It is possible to charter yachts in Port d'Andratx at Llaüts (p82), or ask at the tourist office.

lighter meals. The outdoor tables are perfect for people-watching.

Rose MEDITERRANEAN €€
(☎971 614 360; www.restaurant-the-rose.com; Carrer de la Ciutat 3; mains €16.50-24; ⏰7-11.30pm Wed, 12.30-3.15pm & 7-11.30pm Thu-Sun; 🚭) Sitting at the junction of the roads leading to Gran Hotel Son Net, Palma, Galilea and central Puigpunyent, this is a breezy roadside restaurant with an appetising mix of meat and fish mains, usually dressed up with a little imagination. Locals love it.

ℹ Getting There & Away

The Palma–Estellencs bus (€3.30, one hour 20 minutes, four to 11 times daily) passes through Esporles and Banyalbufar.

Valldemossa

POP 2037 / ELEV 425M

Valldemossa is one of the most beautiful towns on the island. Known as the 'town of the four valleys', it's a blend of tree-lined, cobbled lanes, stout stone houses and impressive villas. Yes, the place swarms with tourist-bus contingents and, yes, the bulk of the restaurants and bars serve average fare at inflated prices. But look beyond all of this and you'll discover that its popularity is well founded.

Sights

Around town you may notice that most houses bear a colourful tile depicting a nun and the words *'Santa Catalina Thomàs, pregau per nosaltres'* ('St Catherine Thomas, pray for us'). Yes, Valldemossa has its very own saint.

For an exquisite view taking in the terraces, orchards, gardens, cypresses, palms, the occasional ochre house through the mountains and the distant plains leading to Palma (not to mention a rather inconveniently placed telephone wire), walk down Carrer del Lledoners to **Miranda dels Lledoners**.

Real Cartuja de Valldemossa MONASTERY
(Cartoixa de Valldemossa; ☎971 612 106; Plaça Cartoixa; adult/child €8.50/free; ⏰9.30am-6.30pm Mon-Sat, 10am-1pm Sun Mar-Oct, 9.30am-4.30pm Mon-Sat, 10am-1pm Sun Nov-Feb) This grand old monastery and former royal residence has had a chequered history, formerly home to kings, monks and a pair of 19th-century celebrities (Frédéric Chopin and George Sand). The monastery is a beautiful building surrounded by gorgeous gardens and enjoying fine views.

The building's origins date back to 1310 when Jaume II built a palace on the site. After it was abandoned, the Carthusian order took over and converted it into a monastery, which, in 1399, was greatly expanded. It was turned into rental accommodation (mostly to summer holidaymakers from Palma) after its monks were expelled in 1835.

A series of cells now shows how the monks lived, bound by an oath of silence they could break only for half an hour per week in the library. Following the rules of the order, just 13 monks lived in this cavernous place. Various items related to Sand's and Chopin's time here, including Chopin's pianos, are also displayed. Entry includes piano recitals (eight times daily in summer) and Jaume II's 14th-century **Palau del Rei Sanxo**, a muddle of medieval rooms jammed with furniture and hundreds of years of mementos, gathered around a modest cloister.

Casa Natal de Santa Catalina Thomàs HISTORIC BUILDING
(Carrer de la Rectoria) The Casa Natal de Santa Catalina Thomàs, birthplace of St Catherine Thomas, is tucked off to the side of the parish church, the **Església de Sant Bartomeu**, at the east end of the town. It houses a simple chapel and a facsimile of Pope Pius VI's declaration beatifying the saint in 1792; she was canonised in 1930.

Born in 1531 she is said to have had visions of (and was tempted by) the devil from a precocious age. Apparently this was a good thing and she wound up in the Església de Santa Magdalena in Palma, where she died in 1574. Sor Tomasseta, as she is affectionately known, has been venerated by locals ever since. There are no fixed opening hours, but you'll rarely find the doors closed.

Costa Nord CULTURAL CENTRE
(☎971 612 425; www.costanord.es; Avinguda de Palma 6; adult/child €7.50/free; ⏰9am-5pm Mon-Fri, 9am-1.30pm Sat & Sun) The brainchild of part-time Valldemossa resident and Hollywood actor Michael Douglas, Costa Nord describes itself as a 'cultural centre' and begins well with a 15-minute portrayal of the history of Valldemossa, narrated by Douglas himself. The subsequent virtual trip aboard Nixe, the 19th-century yacht of Austrian Archduke Luis Salvador, who owned much of western Mallorca, will be of less interest to most.

Valldemossa

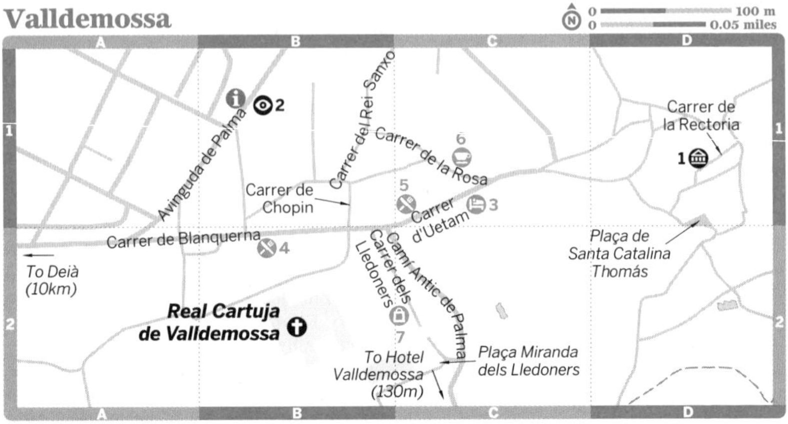

Valldemossa

Top Sights
Real Cartuja de Valldemossa............B2

Sights
1 Casa Natal de Santa Catalina Thomàs............D1
2 Costa Nord............B1

Sleeping
3 Es Petit Hotel............C1

Eating
4 Forn Ca'n Molinas............B2
5 Hostal Ca'n Mário............C1

Drinking
6 Aromas............C1

Shopping
7 Es Carreró............C2

Miramar HISTORIC BUILDING
(☎649 913 832, 971 616 073; www.sonmarroig.com; Carretera de Valldemossa-Deià; adult/child €5/free; ⏲9am-4.45pm) Miramar, 5km north of Valldemossa on the road to Deià, is one of Habsburg Archduke Luis Salvador's former residences, built on the site of a 13th-century monastery. The views from here are splendid.

The evangelist and patron saint of Catalan literature, Ramon Llull, founded the monastery, where he wrote many of his works and trained brethren for the task of proselytising among the Muslims. Walk out the back and enjoy the clifftop views.

Son Marroig HISTORIC BUILDING
(☎971 639 159, 649 913 832; www.sonmarroig.com; Carretera de Valldemossa-Deià; admission €4; ⏲9.30am-7.30pm Mon-Sat & holidays Apr-Sep, 9.30am-2pm & 3-5.30pm Mon-Sat & holidays Oct-Mar) Seven kilometres from Valldemossa is another of Hapsburg Archduke Ludwig Salvator's residences, Son Marroig. It's a delightful, rambling mansion jammed with furniture and period items, including many of the archduke's books. But above all, the views are the stuff of dreams.

Wander down to the Foradada, the strange hole-in-the-wall rock formation by the water. It's about a 3km walk, and a soothing swim in the lee of this odd formation is the reward.

Son Marroig hosts the **Festival Internacional de Deià**, a series of light-classical concerts on Thursday nights from June to September.

Festivals & Events

Sunday is market day in Valldemossa.

Festa de la Beata RELIGIOUS
(28 Jul) Valldemossa celebrates the life of Santa Catalina Thomàs; a six-year-old is chosen to represent the saintly child in the festivities.

Festival Chopin MUSIC
(www.festivalchopin.com; admission €15-25; Aug) Classical-music performances are held in Valldemossa's Real Cartuja throughout August; most of the works are by Chopin, although music by other composers also appears.

Eating

A sprinkling of cheerful eateries festoons the streets. Few are of culinary significance.

Hostal Ca'n Mário SPANISH, MALLORCAN €€
(☎971 612 122; hostalcanmario.iespana.es; Carrer d'Uetam 8; mains €8.50-12.50; ⊙1.30-3.30pm & 8-10pm Thu-Sun, 1.30-3.30pm Mon-Wed; ⊝) If you can grab a window table half the job is done, as you'll have views almost clear to Palma! Enjoy the simple local fare, with a selection of fish and meat dishes. It's a shame you can't rent a room here any more. It's the pick of the places in town and we recommend you try the stuffed eggplant, among other local specialities.

Forn Ca'n Molinas PASTRIES €
(☎971 612 247; Carrer de Blanquerna 15; coca de patata/ensaïmada €1.15/1.20; ⊙7.30am-8pm) This place along the main pedestrian drag has been baking up the local speciality of *coca de patata* and the island-favourite *ensaïmades* since 1920. It stays open later in the height of summer.

Hotel Valldemossa SPANISH, INTERNATIONAL €€€
(☎971 612 626; www.valldemossahotel.com; Camí Antic de Palma; mains €23-27; ⊙1-4pm & 7-11pm; ⊝) Easily the most luxurious dining option in town, this elegant hotel restaurant does everything from a sedate Sunday brunch (€28) to a Thursday set menu of Mallorcan specialities (€26) and a six-course *menú degustación* (€74 per person, minimum of two people). Otherwise à la carte options include lobster grilled with pumpkin risotto and lemongrass foam.

Ca'n Costa SPANISH €€
(☎971 612 263; Carretera de Valldemossa-Deià; mains €12-22; ⊙1-3.30pm & 7.30-10.30pm Wed-Mon; ⊝) The Ca'n Costa makes a great roadside rustic stop, with Mallorcan farmhouse decor. The restaurant has been here since 1975 and the building dates to the 13th century – the secret of its staying power is *porcelleta al forn* (suckling pig) and other perfectly cooked meats. The Valldemossa–Deià buses stop outside.

Drinking

Aromas CAFE
(☎971 616 185; aromasdevalldemossa@gmail.com; Carrer de la Rosa 25; ⊙11am-9pm; ⓦ) This engaging little cafe marches to a different beat from most places in town. For a start they have 48 different types of tea and 38 types of drinking chocolate to choose from. Then there are the revolving art exhibitions of some surprisingly well-known painters (Luis Bermejo was due not long after our visit). Out the back there's a fragrant garden. In sum – very cool!

Shopping

Es Carreró HANDICRAFTS
(☎971 616 348; vickyvalldemossa@hotmail.com; Carrer dels Lledoners 6B; ⊙11.30am-8.30pm Jun-Sep, shorter hours rest of year, closed Nov-Feb) Opened in April 2011, this fascinating boutique has designer homewares, jewellery and other items, most of which have been either handmade or recycled by the owner, Vicky Vidal. Her artistic eye rarely misses a beat, while there are also some lovely photographic images available. It's all a cut above your average mass-produced souvenirs on sale elsewhere in Valldemossa.

Information

Tourist office (☎971 612 019; Avinguda de Palma 7; ⊙9am-1.30pm & 3-5pm Mon-Fri, 10am-1pm Sat) On the main road running through town, about two minutes' walk from the main bus stop.

THE WINTER OF DISCONTENT

Valldemossa owes much of its fame to the fact that the ailing composer Frédéric Chopin and his domineering writer-lover George Sand spent their 'winter of discontent' here in 1838–39. Their stay in the town – at the grand **Real Cartuja de Valldemossa** (p87) no less – wasn't an entirely happy experience and Sand later wrote *Un Hiver à Mallorque* (Winter in Mallorca), which, if nothing else, made her perennially unpopular with Mallorquins. Chopin's poor health, constant rain and damp, and the not-always-warm welcome from the villagers, who found these foreigners rather too eccentric, turned a planned idyllic escape from the pressure cooker of social life in Paris into a nightmare. But time is a great healer and Valldemossa makes great mileage from its discontened former guests, with a music festival in Chopin's name and references to the couple visible all over town.

Getting There & Away

The 210 bus from Palma to Valldemossa (€1.50, 30 minutes) runs four to nine times a day. Three to four of these continue to Port de Sóller (€2.25, one hour) via Deià.

Port de Valldemossa

About 1.5km west from Valldemossa on the road to Banyalbufar, a spectacular mountain road (the Ma1113) clings to cliffs all the way 6km down to Port de Valldemossa. The giddying sea and cliff views are breathtaking and the descent is akin to traversing a precipice with a village glimpsed through the trees a very long way down below; drivers shouldn't take their eye off the road and there's only one place to pull over for photos. At journey's end, there's a shingle and algae 'beach' backed by low red cliffs and a cluster of a dozen or so houses, one of which is home to the justifiably popular Restaurant Es Port.

Eating

Restaurant Es Port SEAFOOD €€
(☎971 616 194; mains €12.80-23.50; ⏲10am-6pm Sep-May, 10am-10pm Jun-Aug) Seafood is the mainstay here, as you'd expect, and it all somehow tastes better out on the 1st-floor terrace on a midsummer's evening. Rice dishes steal the show, as does the mixed seafood platter (€23.50), while the *calamares al ajillo con patatas* (cuttlefish cooked with potato cubes and lightly spiced) is perfectly prepared.

Deià & Around

POP 773 / ELEV 222M

Deià is perhaps the most famous village on Mallorca. For a start, its setting is idyllic, with a cluster of stone buildings grafted on to a conical hill and snaking into the surrounding valleys, all set against the mountain backdrop of the **Puig des Teix** (1062m). The steep hillsides are terraced with vegetable gardens, citrus orchards, almond and olive trees and even the occasional vineyard. Deià was once a second home to an international colony of writers, actors and musicians, the best known of whom (to Anglo-Saxons at any rate) was the English poet Robert Graves.

Sights & Activities

The Ma10 passes though the town centre, where it becomes the main street and is lined with bars, restaurants and shops. Climbing up from the main road, the steep cobbled lanes, with their well-kept stone houses, overflowing bougainvillea and extraordinary views over the sea, farm terraces and mountains, make it easy to understand why artists and other bohemians have loved this place since Catalan artists 'discovered' it in the early 20th century. At the top of Es Puig, the hill at the heart of Deià, is the modest parish church, the **Església de Sant Joan Baptista** (whose **Museu Parroquial**, with a collection of local religious paraphernalia, rarely opens and certainly not to a regular timetable).

Opposite is the town **cemetery**. Here lies 'Robert Graves, Poeta, 24-4-1895 - 7-12-1985 E.P.D' (*en paz descanse,* meaning 'may he rest in peace'). His second wife, Beryl Pritchard (Beryl Graves), who died in 2003, is buried at the other end of the graveyard.

Casa Robert Graves HISTORIC BUILDING
(Ca N'Alluny; ☎971 636 185; www.lacasaderobertgraves.com; Carretera Deià-Sóller; adult/child €5/2.50; ⏲10am-4.20pm Mon-Fri, 10am-2.20pm Sat May-Oct, 9am-3.20pm Mon-Fri, 9am-1.20pm Sat Nov-Apr) A five-minute walk out along the road to Sóller, Casa Robert Graves is a fascinating tribute to the writer who moved to Deià in 1929 and had his house built here three years later. It's a fascinating and well-presented insight into his life; on show you'll find period furnishings, audiovisual displays and various items and books that belonged to Graves himself.

The three-storey stone house, Ca N'Alluny (House in the Distance), is a testament to his life and work. Graves left hurriedly in 1936 at the outbreak of civil war, entrusting the house to the care of a local. The Spanish authorities allowed him to return 10 years later and he found everything as he had left it. 'If I had felt so inclined, I could have sat down and...started work straight away', he later commented. And even now, the whole place is set up as if Graves had just stepped out for a stroll. His voice rings out through the rooms as his reading of his poem *The Face in the Mirror* is played in a loop of seemingly eternal playback; the effect is curiously powerful. In each room, informative text in Mallorquin, Spanish and English adds important context.

Famous for such works as *I, Claudius*, the novelised version of the Roman emperor's life, Robert Graves also wrote reams of verse and a book on his adopted homeland, *Mallorca Observed* (1965); the prologue to his

The Golden Fleece is set in Deià. A handful of his 146 works is available for sale at the ticket office, and ask there also for the 'Reading Suggestions' information sheet.

CALA DE DEIÀ

A 3km drive away (take the road out of town towards Sóller), or a slightly shorter walk, from the town is **Cala de Deià**, one of the most bewitching of the Serra de Tramuntana's coastal inlets and a real slice of rustic coastal paradise. Accessible only on foot, the enclosed arc of the bay is backed by a handful of houses and the small shingle beach gives onto crystal-clear water. Competition for a parking spot (€5 for the day) a few hundred metres back up the road can be intense; get here early. The beach is backed by a simple bar-eatery, Can Lluc, while on a rocky platform above the water, you can sit down for fresh fish at Ca's Patró March. Some fine walks criss-cross the area, such as the gentle **Deià Coastal Path** to the pleasant hamlet of Lluc Alcari. Three daily buses run from Deià (15-minute trip) from May to October.

LLUC ALCARI

Three kilometres northeast of Deià, this is a magical hamlet encrusted into the rocky mountainside. The village is largely consumed by its hotel, but the view from the main road of terracotta roofs and palm trees against the Mediterranean backdrop is one of the prettiest along this oh-so-pretty coast.

Eating

The main road through town is lined with restaurants, particularly at the village's eastern end. Quality varies, but there are some high-quality mainstays sprinkled among the others that come and go with the years.

Es Racó d'es Teix FUSION €€€
(☎971 639 501; www.esracodesteix.es, in German; Carrer de San Vinya Vella 6; mains from €35, 4-/6-course menú degustación €72/98; ⌚1-3pm & 7.30-10.30pm Wed-Sun Mar–mid-Nov; ⊜) Something of a legend on the island, Josef Sauerschell has one Michelin star and it's well deserved. He tends to concentrate on elaborate but hearty meat dishes – anything from deer in Armagnac sauce to loin of lamb with olive and pistachio crust. The cooking's not as outlandish as other places of this kind, but the results are every bit as rewarding.

Sebastian MEDITERRANEAN €€€
(☎971 639 417; Carrer de Felip Bauzà 2; mains €26-30; ⌚7.30-10.30pm Thu-Tue Mar–mid-Nov; ⊜) With its bare stone walls and crisp white linen, Sebastian offers a refined dining environment. The menu is short and subtle with three fish mains and three meat choices, each enhanced with a delicate sauce or purée. On offer when we were there was pan-fried breast of pigeon with rhubarb and aged balsamic, but the menu changes with the seasons.

El Barrigón Xelini SPANISH €
(☎971 639 139; www.xelini.com; Avinguda del Arxiduc Lluís Salvador 19; tapas from €3.75; ⌚12.30pm-1am Tue-Sun Sep-May, 5pm-1am daily Jun-Aug; ⊜) You never quite know what to expect here, but tapas – more than 50 kinds drawn from all over Spain – are at the core, with everything from dates wrapped in bacon to lamb tacos with oregano and mushrooms in garlic. On summer weekends, you might hear live jazz.

Ca's Patró March SPANISH €€
(☎971 639 137; Cala Deià; mains €9-18; ⌚10am-6pm Apr-Oct) This is probably the pick of the two places overlooking the water for its slightly elevated views, but it's a close-run thing. It has a wide range of grilled meat and fish dishes as well as lighter meals such as omelettes. It's run by the third generation of a local fishing family.

Restaurant Deià MALLORCAN €€
(☎971 639 265; info@restaurantdeia.com; Carrer de Felip Bauzà 1; mains €14-21; ⌚noon-4.30pm & 7-11pm; ⊜) This place, a few steps down off the main road at the eastern end of town, gets consistently good reviews from travellers. The dishes have a Mallorcan base with a few mainland detours: the rabbit with onions and wild mushrooms or duck *magret* with Mallorcan *sobrassada* and honey are pure island fare, the grilled salmon with caviar and vegetable risotto less so.

Can Lluc SEAFOOD €€
(☎649 198 618; Cala Deià; mains €10-16.50; ⌚10.30am-7pm Thu-Tue May-Oct) If you can't bear to drag yourself too far from your towel, this simple bar-eatery couldn't be more convenient. Cold drinks and grilled sardines on a lazy summer's afternoon – bliss.

Festivals & Events

Festival Internacional de Deià MUSIC
(☎971 639 178; www.dimf.com; admission €20; ⌚Thu Apr-Sep) Outside Deià on the Serra de Tramuntana coast, the Son Marroig mansion hosts the Festival Internacional de Deià, a series of light-classical concerts.

Getting There & Away

Deià is 15 minutes up the winding road from Valldemossa on the 210 bus route between Palma (€2.55, 45 to 60 minutes) and Port de Sóller (€1.35, 30 to 40 minutes).

Sóller

POP 9375 / ELEV 40M

As though cupped in celestial hands, the ochre town of Sóller lies in a valley surrounded by the grey-green hills of the Serra de Tramuntana – it's probably our favourite larger town on the island. The Arabs saw the potential of the valley, known as the Vall d'Or (Golden Valley), and accounts of orange and lemon groves, watered from sources in the hills, date to the 13th century.

Worth exploring in its own right, Sóller is a wonderful base for visiting nearby pretty villages such as Port de Sóller, Biniaraix and Fornalutx, and is the starting point for some stirring Serra de Tramuntana hikes. Sóller's train station is the terminus for the Palma–Sóller railway, one of Mallorca's most popular and spectacular excursions.

Sights

Simply wandering Sóller's peaceful, often cobbled, streets is a pleasure. In any direction, within a few minutes you exchange tight, winding lanes for country roads bordered by stone walls, behind which flourish orange and lemon groves.

Ca'n Prunera – Museu Modernista GALLERY, HISTORIC BUILDING

(971 638 973; www.canprunera.com; Carrer de Sa Lluna 86 & 90; adult/child €5/free; 10.30am-6.30pm Apr-Oct, closed Mon Nov-Mar) One of the most important museums to have opened in Mallorca in recent years, Ca'n Prunera occupies a landmark Modernista mansion, one of few such buildings in Sóller, and has a major collection of artworks. The list of luminaries on show here is astonishing – several works by Joan Miró, along with single drawings by Toulouse-Lautrec, Picasso, Gauguin, Klimt, Kandinsky, Klee, Man Ray and Cezanne.

Also part of the permanent collection is a gallery devoted to Juli Ramis (1909–90), a Sóller native and world-renowned painter who had his studio in the neighbouring village of Biniaraix, plus works by Miquel Barceló, Antoni Tapiès and Eduardo Chillida. There's also the strangely mesmerising *Movement* (2006) by Francesca Martí, a sculpture garden out the back, and a display of dolls from the early 20th century... All up, a rich and varied selection.

But this is so much more than a who's who of European masters and the building itself complements the eclectic collection. The mansion is a study in Modernista style, from the muted but intriguing stone and wrought-iron facade to the elaborate ceilings and early-20th-century furnishings.

FREE **Església de Sant Bartomeu** CHURCH

(Plaça de la Constitució; admission free; 11am-1.15pm & 3-5.15pm Mon-Thu, 11am-1.15pm Fri & Sat, noon-1pm Sun) A disciple of architect Antoni Gaudí, Joan Rubió got some big commissions in Sóller. The town didn't want to miss the wave of modernity and so Rubió set to work in 1904 on the renovation of the 16th-century Església de Sant Bartomeu. The largely baroque church (built 1688–1723) preserved elements of its earlier Gothic interior, but Rubió gave it a beautiful if unusual Modernista facade.

The interior is gilded yet sombre with dimly lit chapels offset by the ornate altarpiece. Our favourite perspective is to walk towards the altar, and then turn for a view of the chandelier, organ and luminous rose window. The church's candelabra-like summit is visible from all over town, set against the backdrop of the Serra de Tramuntana.

Banco de Sóller HISTORIC BUILDING

(Plaça de la Constitució) A student of Antoni Gaudí, Joan Rubió, is responsible for the strikingly Modernista frontage of the Banco de Sóller (nowadays Banco de Santander), right beside the Església de Sant Bartomeu. It's a daring effort, with two massive, circular galleries sticking out into the square and windows draped in lacy wrought-iron grilles.

Plaça de la Constitució PLAZA

(Town Centre) The main square, Plaça de la Constitució, is 100m downhill from the train station. Surrounded by bars and restaurants, filled with children playing in the evenings and home to the *ajuntament* (town hall), this is Sóller's heart and soul.

FREE **Sala Picasso & Sala Miró** GALLERY

(Plaça d'Espanya 6; 10am-6.30pm) Few train stations have such a rich artistic legacy. In two rooms at street level in Sóller's station, there are two intriguing art exhibitions, the Sala Picasso and Sala Miró. The former has more than 50 ceramics by Picasso from 1948

Sóller

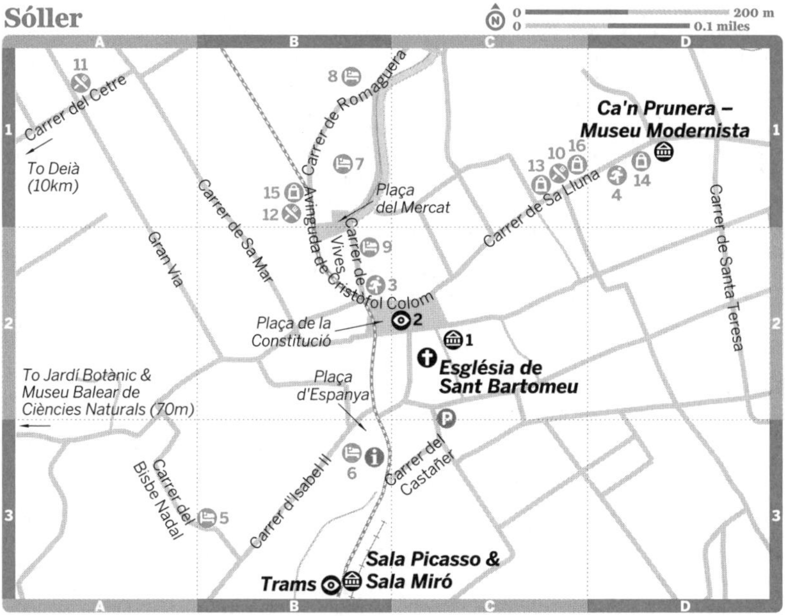

Sóller

Top Sights
- Ca'n Prunera – Museu Modernista D1
- Església de Sant Bartomeu C2
- Sala Picasso & Sala Miró B3
- Trams B3

Sights
- 1 Banco de Sóller C2
- 2 Plaça de la Constitució C2

Activities, Courses & Tours
- 3 Academia Sóller B2
- 4 Tramuntana Tours D1

Sleeping
- 5 Ca'l Bisbe B3
- 6 Ca'n Isabel B3
- 7 Gran Hotel Sóller B1
- 8 Hostal Nadal B1
- 9 Hotel S'Ardeviu B2

Eating
- 10 Ca'n Gata C1
- 11 Ca's Carreter A1
- 12 Sa Fàbrica de Gelats B1
- Sacova .... (see 3)

Shopping
- 13 Arte Artesanía C1
- 14 Ben Calçat D1
- 15 Fet a Sóller B1
- 16 Temps era Temps C1

to 1971, while the latter is home to a series of prints by the Catalan master; Miró's maternal grandfather was from Sóller.

Trams ANTIQUE TRAM
(Tranvías; one way €4; ⏲departures every 30 or 60 min 7am-9pm) Most visitors take a ride on one of Sóller's old-world, open-sided trams, which shuttle 2km down to Port de Sóller on the coast. They depart from outside the train station – pick up a timetable from the tourist office.

Jardí Botànic & Museu Balear de Ciències Naturals GARDENS, MUSEUM
(☎971 634 014; www.jardibotanicdesoller.org; Carretera Palma-Port de Sóller; adult/child €5/free; ⏲10am-6pm Tue-Sat, 10am-2pm Sun) A pleasant stroll (about 600m) west from the town centre brings you to the peaceful Jardí Botànic,

with collections of flowers and other plants native to the Balearic Islands, as well as samples from other Mediterranean areas. At one end of the gardens is the Museu Balear de Ciències Naturals, housed in a once-private mansion surrounded by lemon groves.

Activities

For planning walks around and beyond the Sóller basin, pick up the tourist office's pamphlet *Sóller Bon Dia Senderismo*. Lonely Planet's *Walking in Spain* describes three splendid day walks that set out from the village. For guided hikes, contact Tramuntana Tours (p94).

Tramuntana Tours GUIDED TOURS, BICYCLE RENTAL
(☎971 632 423; www.tramuntanatours.com; Carrer de Sa Lluna 72; bike rental per hr €3.50-5, per day €10-30; ⏲9am-1.30pm & 3-7.30pm Mon-Fri, 9am-1.30pm Sat) This experienced operator organises a range of activities-based guided excursions, including canyoning (€45), sea kayaking (€50), hiking (€25 to €45) and mountain biking (from €40) in the Serra de Tramuntana, as well as renting out as-new bikes. It also has a gear shop. If it's not open, try the sister shop in Port de Sóller, which has longer opening hours.

Courses

Academia Sóller LANGUAGE
(☎971 634 149; www.academiasoller.com; 2nd fl, Plaça de la Constitució 8; weekly intensive courses €240-450) This language school next door to Sacova restaurant runs Spanish-language courses.

Festivals & Events

Around the second weekend of May, Sóller is invaded by a motley crew of Muslim pirates. This conflict (involving about 1200 townsfolk) between *pagesos* (town and country folk) and Moros (Moors), known as **Es Firó**, is full of good-humoured drama and not a little drinking. It re-enacts an assault on the town that was repulsed on 11 May 1561. The centrepiece of this event is remembered as **Ses Valentes Dones** (Valiant Women). Two sisters, instead of cowering as corsairs barged into their house, took a heavy bar and proceeded to kill several of the pirates, thus contributing to the town's final victory.

Eating

Sa Fàbrica de Gelats ICE CREAM €
(☎971 631 708; www.gelatsoller.com; Plaça del Mercat; 1/2/3/4 scoops €1.40/2.50/3.60/4.20; ⏲10am-9pm Jul & Aug, shorter hours rest of year) This ice-cream 'factory' (the actual factory has moved just down the road) is a Mallorcan institution and you'll see its ice cream for sale all across the island. Among the 40 or so trays of locally made flavours, those concocted from fresh orange or lemon juice are outstanding. There's a small patio with a handful of tables so you can enjoy your ice cream alfresco.

Sacova SPANISH €€
(☎971 633 222; Plaça de la Constitució 7; mains €12-19.50; ⏲daily; 🚭) Of all the places on the main square, this one is definitely the best. The labyrinthine dining rooms are all about air-conditioned comfort, while the small crowded terrace is the place to enjoy the night air and the almost constant clatter of passing scooters. The paellas and other rice dishes (€13.50 to €15.80) are faultless, the *alioli* (garlic mayonnaise) superb and the grilled artichokes excellent.

REGIONAL SPECIALITIES

The products of Western Mallorca are famous throughout the island, particularly those from around Sóller. You'll see the red prawns from Port de Sóller bay on menus across Mallorca, but places to pick up other locally grown or produced foods, such as olive oil, wine and an almost endless array of other possibilities, include the following:

» **Sa Fàbrica de Gelats** (p94) Wonderful ice cream flavoured with Sòller's famous oranges

» **Fet a Sóller** (p95) All manner of oils, vinegars and Sóller products

» **Tramuntana Gourmet** (p98) More oils, figs and jams in Fornalutx

» **Malvasia de Banyalbufar** (p86) Serra de Tramuntana wines

» **Forn Ca'n Molinas** (p89) *Coca de patata* and *ensaïmades* from this Valldemossa pastry shop

Ca's Carreter MALLORCAN €€
(☎971 635 133; www.cascarreter.net; Carrer del Cetre 4; meals €30-35, mains €12.95-15.95; ⏲noon-4pm & 7.30-11pm Tue-Sat, noon-4pm Sun; ⊜) In an atmospheric former cart workshop, Ca's Carreter is a welcoming spot that serves unpretentious Mallorcan cooking, including fresh local fish and other mainly regional ingredients. The lamb casserole with honey, salmon with Sóller oranges, and zucchini stuffed with fish and spinach particularly caught our eye. It's a short pleasant walk northwest of the centre.

Béns d'Avall SEAFOOD €€€
(☎971 632 381; info@bensdavall.com; Urbanització Costa Deià, off Carretera Sóller-Deià; menú degustación €54-64; ⏲1-3.30pm & 7.30-10pm Wed-Sun Jul & Aug, shorter hours rest of year, closed mid-Dec–Feb; ⊜) Benet Vicens is one of the island's foremost chefs and his home kitchen is one of the epicentres of *nueva cocina balear* – nouvelle cuisine Balearic-style. Avoid complex decisions and opt for the tasting menu. The wine list is superlative, the service attentive if slightly fawning and the sunset to die for. To get here from Sóller, head 5km along the road to Deià. At about Km57, a sign points you 2km down a winding road to the restaurant, with its hopelessly romantic terrace overlooking the sea and surrounded by greenery.

Ca'n Gata MALLORCAN €
(☎971 638 634; Carrer de Sa Lluna 51; meals €15-20, set menus €9.75-12.50; ⏲9am-6pm Mon-Sat; ⊜) An agreeable place that extends all the way over a cobblestone floor to a pleasant back garden, Ca'n Gata works almost entirely with homemade dishes and local ingredients – the *ensalada de taronges de Sóller* (salad made from Sóller oranges) is typical. It also does tapas and serves fresh orange juice, and there's a resident cat as befits the name.

Shopping

Fet a Sóller FOOD
(☎971 638 839; www.fetasoller.com; Carrer de Romaguera 12; ⏲10am-6pm) Surrounded by Sóller's famous ice-cream shop Sa Fàbrica de Gelats, Fet a Sóller is an altogether different culinary experience. Mallorcan products, primarily those from around Sóller, line the shelves with olive oils, wines, almonds, jams, figs in cognac and balsamic vinegar made from Sóller oranges.

Arte Artesanía JEWELLERY
(☎971 631 732; www.arteartesania.com; Carrer de Sa Lluna 43; ⏲10.30am-1.30pm & 4.30-7.30pm Mon-Sat) A dynamic artistic space, Arte Artesania is at once classy and avant-garde, with its designer jewellery and small range of paintings and sculpture. They're the work of Spanish and international artisan-designers and exhibitions are often hosted here. It may have longer opening hours in the height of summer.

Temps era Temps HANDICRAFTS
(Carrer de Sa Lluna 67; ⏲10.30am-1.30pm & 5-7pm Mon-Fri, 10.30am-1.30pm Sat) Tastefully chosen artisan-made objects from around Mallorca and (not too far) further afield fill this artsy little boutique. Expect ceramics, soaps, jewellery, paintings and bags.

Ben Calçat SHOES
(☎971 632 874; www.bencalcat.es; Carrer de Sa Lluna 74; ⏲9.30am-8.30pm Mon-Fri, 9.30am-1.30pm Sat) This is the place to come for authentic Mallorcan handcrafted *porqueras*, shoes made from recycled car tyres. The bowling-shoe designs in some won't appeal to everyone, but this is very Mallorca. Prices start at €42.

Information

Tourist office (☎971 638 008; www.viu-soller.com; Plaça d'Espanya; ⏲9.45am-2pm & 3.15-5pm Mon-Fri, 9.15am-1pm Sat Mar-Oct, 9.30am-3pm Mon-Sat Nov-Feb) Sóller's tourist office is in an old train carriage beside the station.

Getting There & Away

BUS Bus 211 shoots up the Ma11 road from Palma to Sóller (€2.35, 30 minutes, up to five daily). Bus 210 takes the long way to/from Palma (€3.50) via Deià and Valldemossa (€1.85, 40 to 50 minutes). A local service connects Sóller with Fornalutx (€1.20, 15 minutes, two to four daily) via Biniaraix.

CAR & MOTORCYCLE When coming from Palma, you have the option of taking the tunnel (€4.55 toll per car and €1.80 per motorbike) or adding 7km to the trip and taking the switchbacks up to the pass with some great views back down towards Palma on the way.

TRAIN The Palma–Sóller train journey (p63) is a highlight.

Port de Sóller

Sóller's outlet to the sea is a quintessential Mallorcan fishing and yachting harbour, arrayed around an almost perfectly enclosed bay. In mid-2007, millions of euros were poured into sprucing up the port and some work continues. Even so, as with all such places, the atmosphere wavers between classy and crass. The architecture reflects French and even Puerto Rican influences, as these were the two main destination countries of many Mallorcan emigrants, some of whom returned with cash and imported tastes.

Sights

The bay is shaped something like a jellyfish and shadowed by a pleasant, pedestrianised and restaurant-lined esplanade. It makes for pleasant strolling, especially around the northern end where the heart of the original town is gathered together.

Museu de la Mar MUSEUM
(☎971 632 204; www.ajsoller.es/museudelamar; Carrer de Santa Caterina d'Alexandria 50; admission €3; ⏲10am-5pm Wed-Sat, 10am-2pm Sun Apr-Oct, 10am-1.30pm & 3-6pm Tue-Sat, 10am-2am Sun Nov-Mar) The Museu de la Mar tells the maritime history of Sóller. It's housed in a 13th-century chapel, the **Oratori de Santa Caterina d'Alexandria**, which stands imperiously on a high point overlooking the sea (stand four square to the wind and watch the Med crash against the cliffs). For us, the most interesting exhibits are the old photos of the port before tourism overwhelmed it.

Also inside the museum are displays of documents, models of boats and more, as well an imaginative audiovisual display. Lanes wind down to the port from the museum in a historic (and much renovated) area known as Santa Caterina.

Beaches

The beaches are OK, although hardly the island's best. The pick of the crop is **Platja d'en Repic** at the southern end of the bay, not least because it's nicely removed from the streams of passers-by. The same can't be said for **Platja d'es Port**, which is alongside the marina.

Activities

Barcos Azules BOAT TOURS
(☎971 630 170; www.barcosazules.com; off Passeig Es Travès; adult €14-23, child 6-12yr €7-12, under 6yr free) Tour boats do trips to Sa Calobra (up to four times daily Monday to Saturday) and Cala Tuent (once a day Monday to Friday from Easter to June and in September). Get tickets at a booth on the dock.

Octopus Dive Centre DIVE CENTRE
(☎971 633 133; www.octopus-mallorca.com; Carrer del Canonge Oliver 13; 1 dive with/without own equipment €36/49; ⏲9.30am-1pm & 2-6pm Mon-Sat, 11am-2pm May-Oct) Dive with Octopus Dive Centre, a five-star English-run PADI centre with good equipment. It operates boat dives at about 30 sites along the Serra de Tramuntana coast.

Escola d'Esports Nàutics Port de Sóller SAILING
(☎609 354 132; www.nauticsoller.com; Platja d'en Repic; 1-person sea kayak per hr/half day/day €10/25/40, 2-person €15/35/60) This place rents out sea kayaks and can also arrange boat rental and waterskiing (€110 per hour).

Tramuntana Tours GUIDED TOURS, BICYCLE RENTAL
(☎649 034 759, 971 632 799; www.tramuntanatours.com; Passeig Es Travès 12; bicycle rental per hr €3.50-5, per day €10-30, 3hr sea-kayaking excursion €50; ⏲9am-7.30pm Mar-Oct) This excellent gear shop and activity-tours operator right on the waterfront is the place to come for sea kayaking and bicycle hire. It can also arrange guided hikes into the Serra de Tramuntana, canyoning, mountain biking, boat charters and deep-sea fishing. There's another office in Sóller.

Eating

The Port de Sóller waterfront is lined with eateries.

Randemar SPANISH €€
(☎971 634 578; www.randemar.com; Passeig Es Travès 16; meals €25-35; ⏲12.15-4pm & 7-11.30pm mid-Mar–Nov; 🚭) You could almost feel like you're turning up to a Great Gatsby–style party in this pseudo-waterfront mansion, but most rarely make it that far, preferring to linger in the promenade-side terrace. There's a fair range of fish and meat dishes; our favourites include ham and cod croquettes or lobster *fideuà* (a paella-like noodle dish); the apple crumble is a great way to finish up.

Ca'n Miquelina SEAFOOD €€
(☎971 633 846; Carrer de Sant Ramon de Penyafort 25; mains €14-25; ⏲12.30pm-1am; 🚭) Much-loved by locals for its seafood *calderetas* (stews), Ca'n Miquelina is a cut above the average waterside restaurant. The stews range from lobster to monkfish to cuttlefish and you need a minimum of two to make up an order. It also does grilled sea bream and just about any other kind of fish imaginable – this being Spain, don't expect sauces.

START ANDRATX
FINISH MONESTIR DE LLUC
DISTANCE 140KM
DURATION SIX HOURS

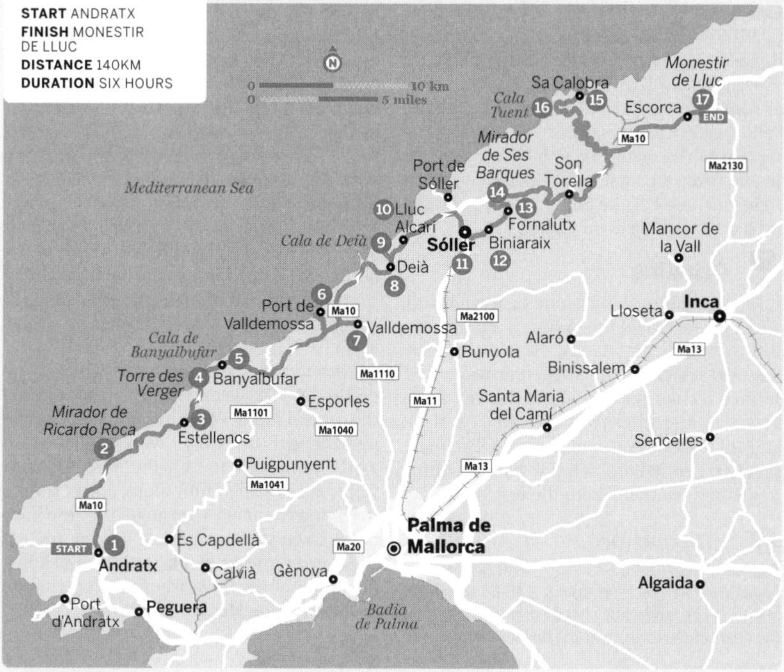

Driving Tour

Andratx to Monestir de Lluc

The villages and towns along the western Mallorca coast are places in which to linger, but to appreciate the sheer drama of this coastline, we recommend driving the 140km route from Andratx in the south to Monestir de Lluc in the north, making stops along the way. From 1 **Andratx**, the road climbs through pine forests to your first glimpse of the Mediterranean far below. Fourteen kilometres from Andratx, pull into the parking lot opposite Restaurant El Grau and climb up to the 2 **Mirador de Ricardo Roca** for some of the most extraordinary views anywhere along this coast. A further 4km on you pass through 3 **Estellencs**, before continuing on 5km to the 4 **Torre des Verger**, one of the Mediterranean's most dramatically sited watchtowers. The tower lies on the outskirts of 5 **Banyalbufar**, another charming coastal village, whereafter the road winds inland. At the road junction after 7km, take the narrow road north (left), which climbs through pine trees and boulders before crossing a high plateau. Take the turn-off west to 6 **Port de Valldemossa**, an exhilarating descent down to the water's edge, and then return back up again to the main road. By now, you're almost in 7 **Valldemossa**, which is always worth a pause, as is 8 **Deià**, which is nine spectacular kilometres beyond the Valldemossa turn-off along the Ma10. Don't miss the brief detour down off the main road to 9 **Cala de Deià**, one of Mallorca's prettiest coves, while the views of 10 **Lluc Alari** from the main road are exceptional. 11 **Sóller** has a fabulous location and is the gateway to 12 **Binaraix** and 13 **Fornalutx**, two of the loveliest villages on the island. From the latter, the Ma10 climbs up to the 14 **Mirador de Ses Barques**, before passing high-altitude lakes in the shadow of Mallorca's highest mountains. By the time you reach the turn-off to 15 **Sa Calobra**, the mountains are bare and otherworldly. Follow the hairpin bends down to Sa Calobra and detour to 16 **Cala Tuent**, before returning to the main road bound for 17 **Monestir de Lluc**.

Lua SPANISH, SEAFOOD €€
(☎971 634 745; luarestaurant@hotmail.com; Carrer de Santa Caterina d'Alexandria 1; mains €16.90-22; ⏰noon-4pm & 7-11pm Tue-Sun;) As narrow as some Amsterdam residences, this cheerful yellow eatery has a big heart. Grab one of the terrace tables or try for one by the window inside (over a couple of floors). Menu highlights include Port de Sóller prawns, and the grilled fish and seafood platter.

Drinking

Like any Mallorcan harbourside town where yacht masts crowd the skyline, summer evenings are long and happy – you could easily take up residence in a cafe-bar-restaurant terrace by the port or along Passeig de Sa Platja in the afternoon and find yourself still there in the wee small hours. There are plenty of lively bars, but few have anything to distinguish them from the rest.

Information

Tourist office (☎971 633 042; Carrer del Canonge Oliver 10; ⏰9.15am-1pm & 2.45-5pm Mon-Fri Mar-Oct) The moderately helpful tourist office is in the heart of the town, near the bus terminus.

Getting There & Away

Most buses to Sóller terminate in Port de Sóller. If driving, you must choose between going to the centre (take the tunnel) or the Platja d'en Repic side (follow the signs). The trams *(tranvías)* to Sóller runs along the waterfront. Several car-rental offices line Passeig Es Travès.

Biniaraix

From Sóller it's a pleasant 2km drive, pedal or stroll through narrow laneways to the timeless hamlet of Biniaraix. There's nothing much to see here and most people continue on to neighbouring Fornalutx. But there's something special about pausing, however briefly, in a place where most visitors arrive on foot, or along narrow country lanes lined with stone walls. The village started life as an Arab *alquería* or farmstead, and has a shady central square, Plaça de Sa Concepció.

The walking trail to Biniaraix is well signposted from the centre of Sóller.

Fornalutx

There are two ways to reach Fornalutx, one of Mallorca's loveliest stone-built villages in the shadow of high mountains. The first is along a narrow and scenic route from Biniaraix, passing through terraced groves crowded with orange and lemon trees en route. The other is the road that drops down off the Ma10, with lovely aerial views of the village's stone houses and terracotta roofs. Either way, Fornalutx is as pretty as a postcard, and the effect is heightened as you draw near, with green shuttered windows, colourful flower boxes, well-kept gardens and flourishing citrus groves. Many of the houses are owned by expats, but it's a far cry from the (comparative) bustle of Sóller. Like Biniaraix, Fornalutx probably has its origins as an Arab *alquería*.

Fornalutx rewards those who simply wander to get lost. Begin with the lanes around the central Plaça d'Espanya and pop into the **ajuntament** (town hall) with its cool courtyard dominated by a palm tree. Outside, water gurgles cheerfully along one of several irrigation channels. You can follow the course of the town stream east past fine houses and thick greenery, or climb the stairs heading north out of the town from the **Església de la Nativitat de Nostra Senyora**.

Eating

There are numerous restaurants and a handful of cafes in Fornalutx, most of which are located around the central Sa Plaça or occupy shady roadside terraces about half a kilometre out of the centre on the Ma2121 road leading northeast out of town.

Ca N'Antuna MALLORCAN €€
(☎971 633 068; Carrer de Arbona Colom 14; mains €10-15; ⏰12.30-4pm & 7.30-10.30pm Tue-Sat, 12.30-4pm Sun, closed mid-Nov–mid-Dec) This is a classic of Mallorcan cooking. It's locally famous for its oven-cooked lamb and other meats, but the calamari stuffed with meat is a great order. The hand juicer on the sill connecting the kitchen with the terrace is a nice touch – order up lots of local orange juice! The village and mountain views from the terrace are worth lingering over.

Shopping

Tramuntana Gourmet FOOD, WINE
(☎638 083 598; Carrer de Arbona Colom 4A; ⏰11am-8pm) Food products from the Serra de Tramuntana, with a few ring-ins from elsewhere on the island and the other Balearic Islands, are the staples at this fine little shop. There are free olive-oil tastings, as well as a range of jams, wines and unusual offerings, such as fig bread, available for purchase.

Getting There & Away

A local service connects Fornalutx with Sóller (€1.20, 15 minutes, two to four daily), via Biniaraix.

Road from Sóller to Alaró

A nice driving route suggests itself south of Sóller. To begin with, climb the valley into the hills (don't take the tunnel, which costs €4.55 and isn't as pretty) and enjoy the views to Palma as you follow the switchbacks on the other side.

Before entering Bunyola and the towns that lay beyond, it's worth pausing to visit two of Mallorca's prettiest and most imposing grand properties: Jardins d'Alfàbia and Raixa.

Sights

Jardins d'Alfàbia HISTORIC BUILDING, GARDENS

(☎971 613 123; www.jardinesdealfabia.com; Carretera de Sóller Km17; adult/child €5.50/free; ⏲9.30am-6.30pm Mon-Sat Apr-Oct, 9.30am-5.30pm Mon-Fri, 9.30am-1pm Sat Nov-Mar) After descending the hill from Sóller (or emerging from the tunnel), don't miss the enchanting Jardins d'Alfàbia, in the shadow of the Serra d'Alfàbia mountain range (maximum altitude 1069m) that stretches east. The endearingly crumbly *possessió* with a baroque facade (which looks like it was stripped from a Florentine basilica) is surrounded by gardens, citrus groves, palm trees and a handful of farmyard animals.

The murmur of water gurgling along narrow irrigation canals gives a hint of the place's past, for it began as the residence of an Arab Wāli (viceroy); in the Quran, paradise is considered to be a garden.

Little remains of the original Arab house, except for the extraordinary polychromatic, pyramidal *artesonado* (coffered ceiling), fashioned from pine and ilex, immediately inside the building's entrance. It is bordered by inscriptions in Arabic and is thought to have been made around 1170. From here you enter an inner courtyard. To the right is the *tafona* (large oil press) and construction in this part is a mix of Gothic, Renaissance and baroque styles. The rambling house is laden with period furniture and a 1200-volume library. Within the library is the original *Llibre de les Franqueses* (Book of Franchise), which was written by King Jaume I as the basis for all rights in Mallorca after the Christian conquest.

FREE **Raixa** HISTORIC BUILDING

(☎971 237 636; www.raixa.cat; off Carretera Palma-Sóller Km12.2; ⏲10am-2pm Sat & Sun, by appointment at other times) Recently restored and opened to the public, this formidable mansion is surrounded by expansive gardens and is also home to an informative interpretation centre for the Serra de Tramuntana. Apart from the gardens, it's worth exploring the cloisters, manor house, arcaded loggia, chapel and the unusual pavilions that climb the ridge behind the house.

The house once belonged to the Count of Roselló, Nunó Sanç, who fought alongside King Jaume I in the 1229 Christian conquest of the island. In the centuries that followed, it passed through the hands of various noble families before being abandoned and falling into disrepair. Now returned to its former glory, it's a splendid place to spend a couple of hours on a weekend.

BUNYOLA

About 2.5km south of the Jardins d'Alfàbia and just east of the highway to Palma lies this drowsy transport junction, known for olive oil and its *palo* (herbal liquor) distillery. There's not an awful lot to hold you here, except to observe a slice of Mallorcan village life in the central square, Sa Plaça, with its single bar. The square hosts a small Saturday morning market.

Sights

Església de Sant Mateu CHURCH

(Carrer de l'Església 2; ⏲mass) Next to the main square in the heart of town, the Església de Sant Mateu was built in 1230 but largely redone in 1756. You'll only be allowed to peek inside during mass.

Eating

Restaurant Es Carreró MALLORCAN, INTERNATIONAL €€

(☎971 615 440; Carrer Major 17; mains €9.50-19.50; ⏲1-4pm & 7-11pm Sat & Sun, 7-11pm Tue-Fri; 🚭) Restaurant Es Carreró is a few metres east of the square Sa Plaça. Take a seat on the romantic roof terrace and tuck into the fish of the day, or the *lechona asada crujiente con manzana y morcilla al horno* (crunchy roast lamb with apple and baked blood sausage).

ORIENT

A treat comes in the 9km road (the Ma2100) northeast from Bunyola to the hamlet of Orient. Nice enough by car, it is a favourite of cyclists (or at least, those in reasonable shape!). The first 5km is a promenade along a verdant valley that slowly rises to a bit of a plain and the Coll d'Honor (550m) before tumbling over the other side of a forested ridge. The next 2km of serried switchbacks flatten out on the run into Orient. All the way, the Serra d'Alfàbia is in sight to the north.

The reward at journey's end is Orient, one of the loveliest little villages on the island with its huddle of ochre houses clustered on a slight rise. A few houses seem to slide off as if they're an afterthought on the north side of the road.

Eating

Mandala FRENCH, ASIAN €€€
(971 615 285; Carrer Nou 1; mains €16.20-24.60; 1-3pm Tue-Thu & Sun, 8-10.30pm Fri & Sat mid-Sep–mid-Jun, 8-10.30pm Tue-Sun mid-Jun–Nov & mid-Jan–mid-Jun, closed Dec–mid-Jan;) You're assailed by the agreeable smells of the East as you enter this highly regarded French-run gourmet den of fusion cooking. There's a bit of everything here – Thai prawn curry, salmon in saffron, and duck *magret*. Bookings are essential, and if you can work out their opening hours, please let us know.

Ca'n Jaume SPANISH, INTERNATIONAL €€
(971 615 153; Carretera Alaró-Bunyola; mains €9.70-21.40; 1-4pm & 7.30-11pm Mon & Wed-Sat, 1-4pm Sun, closed Jul;) This knockabout place on the left as you enter town coming from Bunyola, with a dozen tables outside and the radio and TV both blaring in rowdy unison inside, is an antidote to the fusion cooking you'll find elsewhere in town. The traditional cooking includes partridge in a wild-mushroom sauce, and roast suckling lamb or kid.

ALARÓ

As the Ma2100 rises away from Orient, surrounded by cypresses and gardens, you could be forgiven for thinking you're in Tuscany. The road meanders about 4km northeast before taking a leisurely turn around the outriders of the mighty bluff that is **Puig d'Alaró** (821m). This rocky peak is matched to the east by **Puig de S'Alcadena** (815m). To the south you can make out the flat interior of Es Pla (The Plain).

Eight kilometres from Orient, you arrive in **Alaró**. Less immediately appealing than much-smaller Orient, it rewards those who explore a little. Head for Plaça de la Vila, flanked by the Casa de la Vila (town hall), parish church and a couple of cafes, and the busier junction of Carrer Petit and Carrer de Jaume Rosselló, with a couple of lively cafes. Plaça de la Villa hosts a lively Saturday morning market.

Sights

Castell d'Alaró CASTLE
(off Carretera Alaró-Bunyola) Perched at an improbable, Monty Python–esque angle, Castell d'Alaró is one of the most rewarding castle climbs on the island. The ruins are all that remain of the last redoubt of Christian warriors who could only be starved out by Muslim conquerors around 911, eight years after the latter had invaded the island. The views, from Palma to Badia de Alcúdia, are something special.

If the two-hour walk doesn't appeal, you can cover most of the climb by car. The first 4.2km to Bar-Restaurant Es Vergé are paved but have their fair share of potholes. The road deteriorates (but should be OK if it hasn't rained – ask at the restaurant for the current state of the road) for a further 1.2km beyond the restaurant to a parking area at

CANYONING THE SERRA DE TRAMUNTANA

For those with a taste for jumping into ravines and streams, canyoning could be the sport for you. The best places for this are concentrated in the central Serra de Tramuntana between Valldemossa and Sa Calobra. By far the most challenging (rated 5–6, for experts only) is the Gorg Blau-Sa Fosca canyon, descending north and then northeast from the dam of the same name. This 2.5km route (there and back) is tough. The drops and scrambling are accompanied constantly by freezing water and there is a 400m stretch in total darkness. Instead of turning back, you could continue north 3.3km along Torrent de Pareis, a much easier route surrounded by majestic rock walls. Either way, a local guide is essential. Two operators to contact include **Mallorca Canyoning** (691 230 291; www.mallorcacanyoning.com) and **Món d'Aventura** (606 879 514; www.mondaventura.com), while **Tramuntana Tours** (p96) in Port de Sóller also organises trips.

the base of a path that leads (in 15 minutes) to the ruins. Once there, you'll see several stone arched doors and parts of the walls of what was once clearly a major fortress.

Another minute's walk uphill brings you to the **Ermita de la Mare de Déu del Refugi**, a decrepit 17th-century chapel that locals still visit to give thanks for miraculous events.

If you can't bear to leave, try the **Refugi S'Hostatgeria** (p169).

Eating

Traffic MALLORCAN €€
(☎971 879 117; www.canxim.com; Plaça de la Vila 8; mains €13.25-25.50; ⏰12.30-4pm & 7.30pm-midnight Mon, Wed-Sun, 12.30-4pm Sun; 🚭) The pick of the places on Plaça de la Vila, this place run by Hotel Can Xim does Mallorcan specialities with a few innovative twists. We particularly enjoyed the leg of lamb stuffed with *sobrassada*, *butifarra*, dates and pine nuts. Meats are defintely the strong point, but you'll also find tasty fish dishes such as angler fish and aubergine pie with a prawn sauce on the menu.

Bar-Restaurant Es Vergé SPANISH €€
(☎971 182 126; Camí des Castell; mains €7.50-14; ⏰10am-10pm; 🚭) A simple place for hearty dishes (such as an especially tasty suckling pig), good views and the reassuring smell of wood smoke. The kitchen also whip ups salads, snails and *bocadillos* (filled rolls).

Getting There & Away

Buses and trains running between Palma and Sóller stop at Bunyola (the bus stop is at Sa Plaça, and the train station a short walk west of the centre). From there local bus 221 runs twice a day east to Orient (€1.20, 30 minutes). This is a microbus service and you need to book a seat in advance.

The Palma–Inca train calls at the Consell-Alaró train station (20 to 30 minutes), where it connects with local bus 320 for Alaró (15 minutes).

Cala de Sa Calobra & Cala Tuent

The Ma10 road from Sóller to the Monestir de Lluc is a beautiful drive. The first stop is the **Mirador de Ses Barques**, about 6km out of Sóller, with decent views all the way down to Port de Sóller; the cafe here serves freshly squeezed orange juice. The road unravels eastward to cross the Serra de Son Torrella range, and 16km out of Sóller a side road leads north up to the island's highest point, Puig Major (1445m). The peak is off-limits, however, as this is Air Force territory and topped by a communications base.

The Ma10 slithers past two artificial patches of liquid blue, the Cúber and Gorg Blau dams. Shortly after the latter, a 12km road branches north off Ma10 and down to the small port of **Sa Calobra**. Completed in 1935 with the sole aim of allowing tourists to reach the beach by land, this is one of Mallorca's most spectacular drives – the serpentine road has been carved through the weird mountainous rock formations, skirting narrow ridges before twisting down to the coast in an eternal series of hairpin bends.

If you come in summer you won't be alone. Divisions of buses and fleets of pleasure boats disgorge battalion after battalion of tireless tourists; it makes D-Day look like play lunch. Sa Calobra must be wonderful on a quiet, bright midwinter morning. From the northern end of the road a short trail leads around the coast to a river gorge, the **Torrent de Pareis**, and a small cove with fabulous (but usually crowded) swimming spots.

If you want to skip the crowd scenes, follow a turn-off west, some 2km before reaching Sa Calobra, to head to **Cala Tuent**, a tranquil emerald-green inlet in the shadow of Puig Major. The broad pebble beach is backed by a couple of houses and a great green bowl of vegetation that climbs up the mountain flanks. About 200m back from the beach, a turn-off leads 1.5km to Es Vergeret.

Eating

Es Vergeret MALLORCAN €€
(☎971 517 105; www.esvergeret.com; Camí de Sa Figuera Vial 21; mains €10-19; ⏰noon-6pm Feb-Oct) The shady terrace here looks from on high to the bay below, the ideal vantage point for enjoying paella, *tumbet* (vegetable stew) and other Mallorcan specialities. It's especially known for the grilled fish. Ring ahead if you want a table, especially in summer.

Getting There & Away

One bus a day (bus 355, Monday to Saturday, May to October) comes from Ca'n Picafort (9am) via Alcúdia, Cala Sant Vicenç, Pollença and the Monestir de Lluc. It returns at 3pm. The whole trip takes three hours and 50 minutes to Sa Calobra (with a one-hour stop at the Monestir de Lluc) and 2½ hours on the return leg. From Ca'n Picafort you pay €8.85 (€16 return). Boats make excursions to Sa Calobra and Cala Tuent from Port de Sóller.

Monestir de Lluc & Around

Back in the 13th century, a local shepherd claimed to have seen an image of the Virgin Mary in the sky. Later, a similar image appeared on a rock. Another story says that a statuette of the Virgin was found here and taken to the nearest hamlet, Escorca. The next day it was back where it had been found. Three times it was taken to Escorca and three times it returned. 'It's a miracle', everyone cried and a chapel was built near the site to commemorate it, possibly around 1268. The religious sanctuary came later. Since then thousands of pilgrims have come every year to pay homage to the 14th-century (and thus not the original) **statue of the Virgin of Lluc**, known as La Moreneta because of the statuette's dark complexion.

Sights

Monestir de Lluc MONASTERY, GARDENS
(☎971 871 525; www.lluc.net; Plaça dels Peregrins; monastery & gardens free, museum €4; ⊙8.30am-8pm, museum 10am-1.30pm & 2.30-5pm, gardens 10am-1pm & 3-6pm) The present monastery, the Monestir de Lluc, a huge austere complex, dates mostly from the 17th to 18th centuries. There's also a museum and modest gardens and, if you're lucky, you might hear the Els Escolanets (also known as Els Blauets, the Little Blues, because of the soutane they wear), the monastery's boarding school boys choir. This institution dates to the early 16th century.

Off the central courtyard is the entrance to the rather gloomy, late-Renaissance Basílica de la Mare de Déu (built in 1622–91 and bearing mostly baroque decoration), which contains a fine *retablo* (altarpiece) done by Jaume Blanquer in 1629, and the statuette of the Virgin Mary.

Outside, the Jardí Botànic (botanic garden) is worth a stroll, as is the climb up to the **Pujol dels Misteris**, a hill topped by a crucifix whose base is enveloped in barbed wire. Forget the cross and enjoy the lovely valley views behind it.

Activities

A couple of popular walking routes leave from the monastery. One is a four-hour circuit of **Puig de Massanella** (1365m), during the course of which the landowners will charge you €4. The other is the seven-hour **Puig Roig** (1002m) circuit, a long walk with plenty of ups and downs (but you don't ascend the peak). You can only do this on Sundays, when the landowners open the barriers. Ask for information at the monastery ticket office.

Eating

Several restaurants and cafeterias cater to your tummy's demands.

Ca s'Amitger MALLORCAN €€
(☎971 517 046; www.casamitger.es; Plaça dels Peregrins 6; mains €8-14; ⊙9am-11pm; 🚭) Meat dishes are the speciality here, with roast lamb or rabbit and local wines an especially fine combination.

Getting There & Away

BUS Up to two buses a day (May to October) run from Ca'n Picafort to the Monestir de Lluc (€5.50, 1¾ hours) on their way to Sóller and Port de Sóller. From Palma, two all-stops buses (bus 330) to Inca continue to Lluc via Caimari on weekends only (or take the train to Inca and change to bus 332).

Northern Mallorca

Includes »

Pollença............106
Cala Sant Vicenç....109
Port de Pollença.....110
Cap de Formentor... 112
Badia d'Alcúdia 112
Alcúdia.............112
Port d'Alcúdia.......114
Cap des Pinar.......115
Parc Natural de S'Albufera..........117
Son Serra de Marina 119
Colònia de Sant Pere 119

Best Places to Eat

» Restaurante Mirador de La Victòria (p117)

» Manzanas y Peras (p108)

» S'Arc (p114)

» Restaurante Jardín (p115)

» Cal Patró (p109)

Best Places to Stay

» Ermita de La Victòria (p171)

» Hotel Desbrull (p169)

» Petit Hotel Ca'n Simó (p170)

» Hostal Bahia (p170)

» Hostal Los Pinos (p170)

Why Go?

Mallorca's north has arguably the broadest appeal of any region on the island. The mountain chain of the Serra de Tramuntana is at its most spectacular where the range culminates on the Cap de Formentor, extending out into the Mediterranean with extraordinary and unrestrained drama. Northern Mallorca's geography also impresses on the pine-forested peninsula of Cap des Pinar, and in the pretty bays Badia de Pollença and Badia d'Alcúdia.

Significantly, humankind's impact upon the region has been more muted than is the case along the island's eastern and southern shorelines. Cala Sant Vicenç is one of Mallorca's loveliest coastal towns, while even the resorts along the two main bays have more charm than most. Inland, both Pollença and Alcúdia retain a medieval air and rank among Mallorca's most beguiling settlements.

When to Go

Some of the beach resorts barely have a pulse until May or after October (charming Cala Sant Vicenç is a case in point), and the best beach weather is from June to August. Yet, our favourite time to visit is spring and autumn – migrating birds flock to the Parc Natural de S'Albufera, the roads are quieter (especially out along the Cap de Formentor), Pollença's Good Friday celebration is not to be missed, and Alcúdia hosts one of Mallorca's best traditional markets in early October.

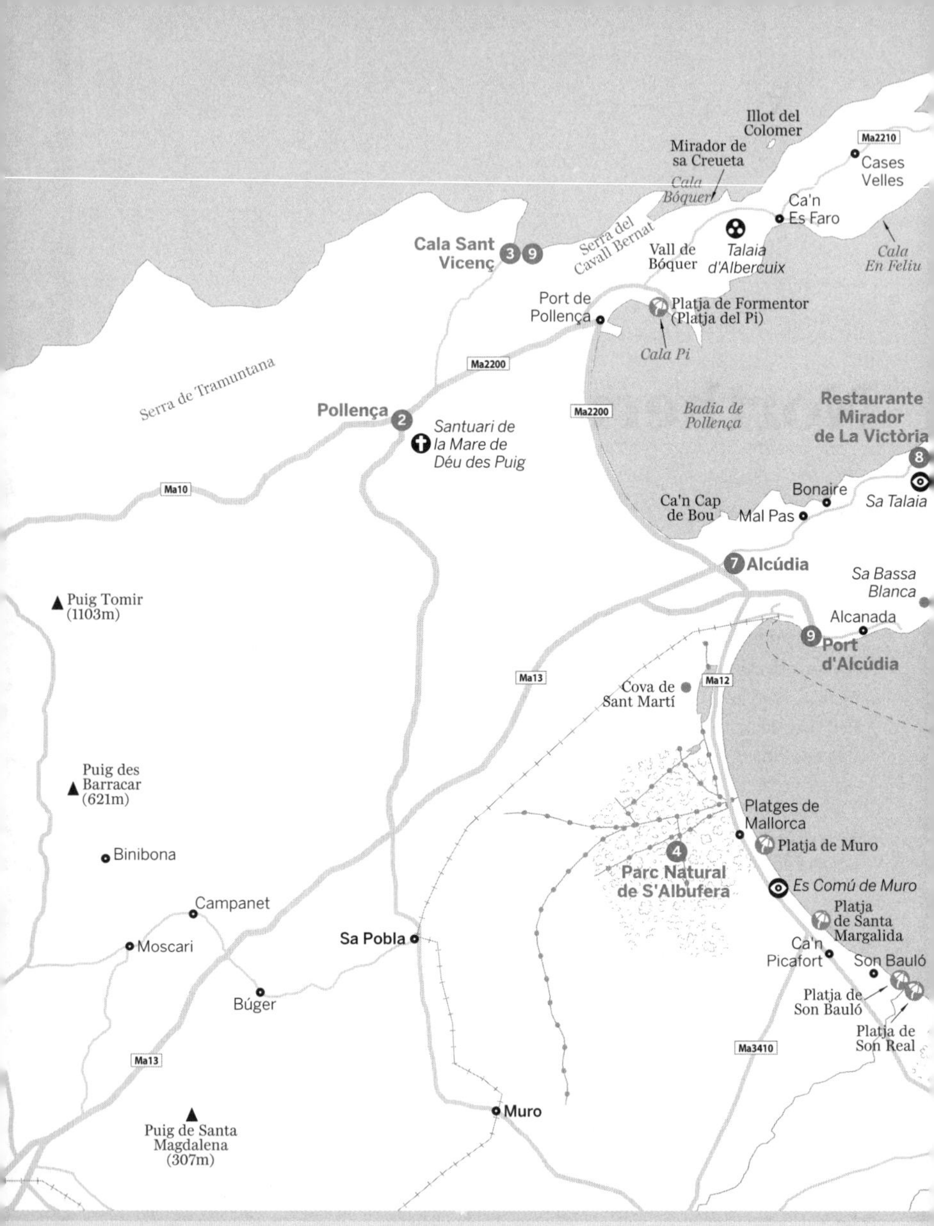

Northern Mallorca Highlights

1 Enjoy Mallorca's finest coastal scenery by driving or cycling the length of **Cap de Formentor** (p112)

2 Climb 365 steps and look down on pretty **Pollença** (p106)

3 Laze alongside turquoise waters, moving only to eat seafood in **Cala Sant Vicenç** (p109)

4 Seek out the rich birdlife amid the peace of **Parc Natural de S'Albufera** (p117)

5 Descend on foot to the remote **Platja des Coll Baix** (p117)

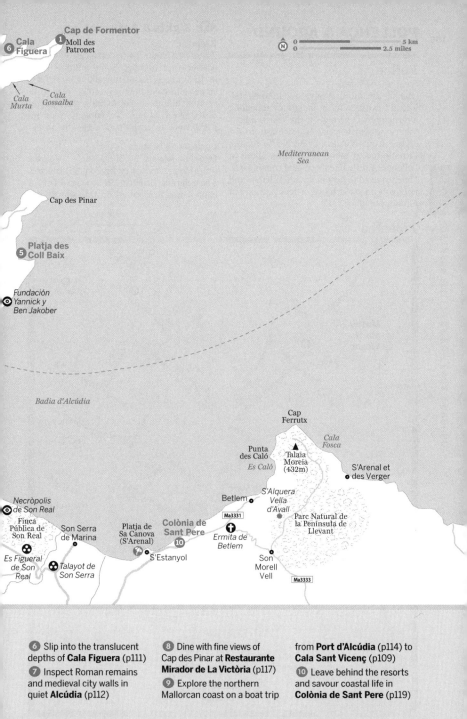

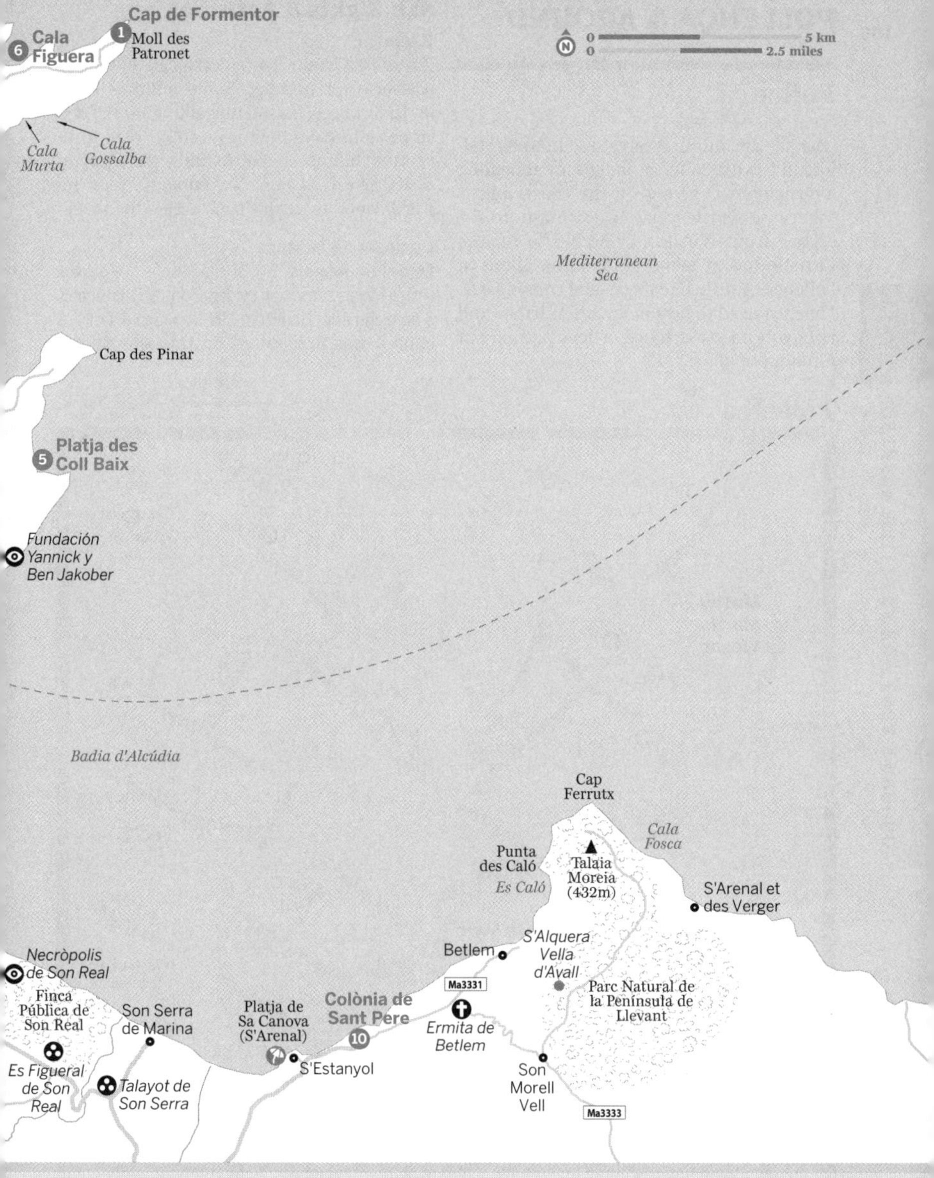

6 Slip into the translucent depths of **Cala Figuera** (p111)

7 Inspect Roman remains and medieval city walls in quiet **Alcúdia** (p112)

8 Dine with fine views of Cap des Pinar at **Restaurante Mirador de La Victòria** (p117)

9 Explore the northern Mallorcan coast on a boat trip from **Port d'Alcúdia** (p114) to **Cala Sant Vicenç** (p109)

10 Leave behind the resorts and savour coastal life in **Colònia de Sant Pere** (p119)

Pollença

POP 11,785 / ELEV 41M

One of the more interesting inland Mallorcan towns, Pollença makes an appealing alternative to staying on the coast, and is otherwise worth a day of exploration. Everyone from Winston Churchill to Agatha Christie has at some point hung about at Pollença. A little like its coastal cousin Deià, Pollença used to be a magnet for artists and is now home to a more or less permanent foreign populace.

Sights & Activities

Calvari RELIGIOUS SITE

(Carrer del Calvari) They don't call it Calvari (Calvary) for nothing. Some pilgrims do it on their knees, but plain walking up the 365 stone steps from the town centre to an 18th-century hilltop chapel (330m), the **Oratori del Calvari**, is penance enough. Your reward: views to savour back across the town.

Església de la Mare de Déu deis Àngels CHURCH

(Plaça Major; admission by donation; ⌚11am-1pm & 3-5pm Jun-Aug, 11am-1pm Mar-May, Sep & Oct) A church was first raised on this site shortly

Pollença

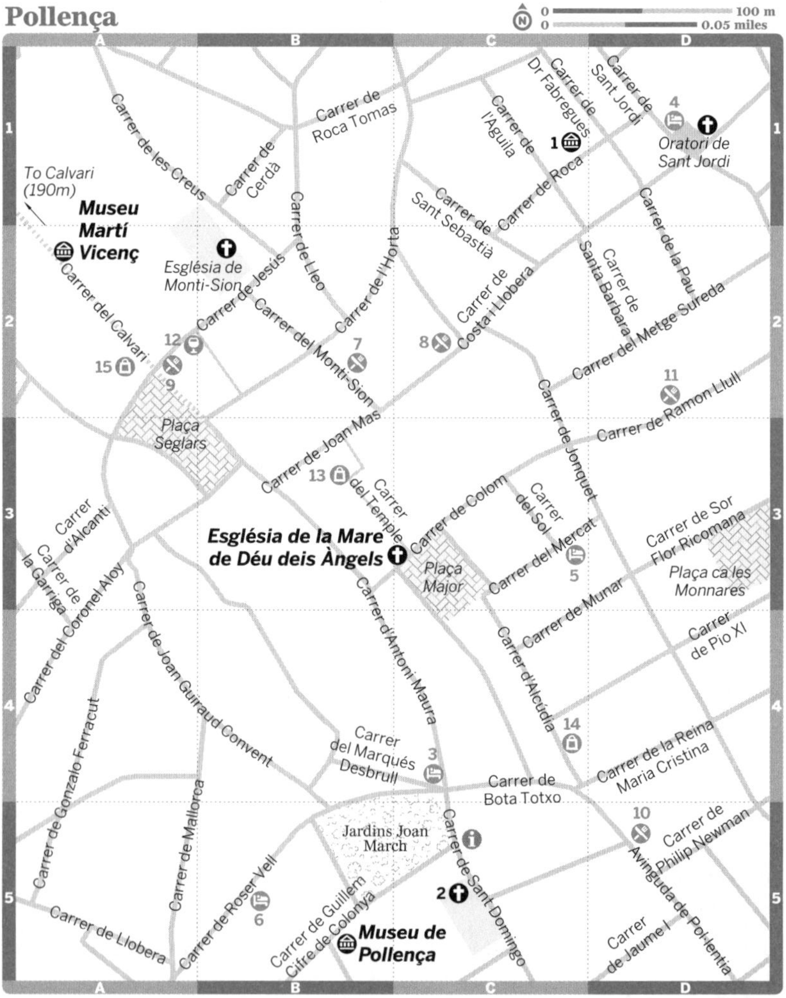

after the conquest in 1229. The present edifice dates to the 18th century. The unusually simple rough-sandstone facade is a lovely backdrop to the square, while within is an unusual barrel-vaulted ceiling and extravagant ceiling frescos; some of the latter have been restored with a heavy hand.

Museu de Pollença MUSEUM
(☎971 531 166; www.ajpollenca.net; Carrer de Guillem Cifre de Colonya; admission €1.50; ⏱10.30am-1pm Tue-Fri, 11am-1pm Sat & Sun) This museum's star attraction is the 17th-century baroque cloister of the Convent de Sant Domingo, in which it's housed, and a bright Buddhist Kalachakra mandala donated by the Dalai Lama in 1990. Other exhibits include archaeological finds from the area and some Gothic altarpieces.

Església de Santa Maria de Déu de Roser CHURCH
(town centre; ⏱mass) This convent church, adjacent to the Museu de Pollença, is a baroque job with barrel vault, gaudy retable and medallions in the ceiling. It's used for the Festival de Pollença.

Pollença

Top Sights

	Església de la Mare de Déu deis Àngels	C3
	Museu de Pollença	B5
	Museu Martí Vicenç	A2

Sights

1	Casa-Museu Dionís Bennàssar	C1
2	Església de Santa Maria de Déu de Roser	C5

Sleeping

3	Hotel Desbrull	C4
4	Hotel Son Sant Jordi	D1
5	L'Hostal	C3
6	Posada de Lluc	B5

Eating

7	La Font del Gall	B2
8	Latitud N	C2
9	Manzanas y Peras	A2
10	Restaurant Clivia	D5
11	Restaurant Trencadora	D2

Drinking

12	U Gallet	A2

Shopping

13	Artesania	B3
14	Enseñat	C4
15	Rocaia Complements	A2

FREE **Museu Martí Vicenç** MUSEUM
(☎971 532 867; www.martivicens.org; Carrer del Calvari 10; ⏱10.30am-2pm Mon-Fri, 10.30am-1pm Sat, 11am-1pm Sun) A short way up the Calvari steps is the Museu Martí Vicenç. The weaver and artist Martí Vicenç Alemany (born 1926) bought this property, once part of a giant Franciscan monastery that also included the nearby former Església de Monti-Sion, in the 1950s. His works, mostly canvases and textiles, are strewn around several rooms.

Casa-Museu Dionís Bennàssar MUSEUM
(☎971 530 997; www.museudionisbennassar.com; Carrer de Roca 14; admission €2; ⏱10.30am-1.30pm Tue-Sun Apr-Oct, by appointment Nov-Mar) Casa-Museu Dionís Bennàssar, the home of local artist Dionís Bennàssar (1904–67), hosts a permanent collection of his works. Downstairs are early etchings, aquarelles and oils, depicting mostly local scenes. Works on the other floors range from a series on fish that is strangely reminiscent of Miquel Barceló's efforts in Palma's cathedral to a series of nudes and portraits of dancing girls.

FREE **Santuari de la Mare de Déu des Puig** MONASTERY
(⏱10am-8pm) South of Pollença, off the Ma2200, one of Mallorca's most tortuous roads bucks and weaves up 1.5km of tight hairpin bends to this hilltop monastery (333m). The rambling residence was built in the 14th and 15th centuries and is worth the climb, not least for the splendid views over Pollença and Alcúdia bays.

The best views are those towards the jagged formations of the Formentor peninsula that look like giant waves about to break, while the Gothic chapel and refectory are highlights of the complex.

Festivals & Events

Davallament EASTER
(Good Fri) In the evening, the body of Christ is symbolically paraded down the steps of Calvari, in one of the island's most moving Easter celebrations.

Festes de la Patrona HISTORICAL
(late Jul-early Aug) This is the town's main event, with staged battles betwen Moors and Christians, culminating on 2 August.

Festival de Pollença TOWN FESTIVAL
(www.festivalpollenca.org; Jul & Aug) Various genres of music can be heard in concerts in the Sant Domingo cloister.

La Fira MARKET
(2nd Sun in Nov) A massive market held in the Convent de Sant Domingo and elsewhere around town.

Eating

Plaça Major is encircled by good-natured eateries and cafe-bars where you can receive sustenance morning, noon and night, but some of the better options lie ever-so-slightly further afield.

Manzanas y Peras €
(971 533 835; www.manzanasyperas.es; Carrer de Jesús 38; mains €3-7; 10am-4pm & 7-11pm Mon-Fri, 10am-4pm Sun) Tiny but brilliant. Two young Brits Paul and Caroline have created something of an oasis next to the Calvari steps. A long list of lunch specials includes the outstanding 'pork, apple and sage burger'. In the evening, it's all about tapas, from Thai fish cakes to bruschetta with melted goats cheese, blueberry jelly and walnuts.

Latitud N SPANISH, INTERNATIONAL €
(971 531 294; Carrer de Costa i Llobera 11; mains €20-25; 7-11pm Mon-Sat;) The rambling old building in which the poet Miquel Costa i Llobera was born, and which later housed the town's first cinema, is now the setting for atmospheric dinners amid a panoply of antiques. The menu consists of a very small selection of dishes, but each – such as the Chateaubriand – is perfectly prepared.

Restaurant Clivia MALLORCAN, SEAFOOD €€
(971 533 635; Avinguda de Pol·lentia 7; mains €12-23; 1-3pm & 7-10.30pm Thu-Tue) Set in what was once a private house, this spot offers fine food (especially the fish) prepared and presented with panache. The service is attentive and the ambience tranquil. Try the prawns from Sóller bay in Mallorca's west, or the house speciality of wild sea bass steamed in white wine.

La Font del Gall FUSION €€
(971 530 396; lafontdelgall@hotmail.com; Carrer del Monti-Sion 4; mains €8-15; 11.30am-3pm & 6.30-10pm Sun-Fri Mar-Oct) This Scottish-run place promises 'fresh contemporary cuisine with a Scottish twist', which means the menu ranges from brunch to haggis. The cooking is assured, and it has a range of set menus at lunch (from €9.95) and, unusually, dinner (from €15.95). Our favourite dish: the crisp, slow-roasted pork belly.

Restaurant Trencadora MEDITERRANEAN €€
(971 531 859; Carrer de Ramon Llull 17; mains €11-18; 12.30-3pm & 6.30-11pm daily Apr-Sep, closed Tue Oct & Mar, closed Nov-Feb) With its shady garden setting, this modern trattoria is worth the five-minute walk east of the centre. It serves up pizza, pasta, seafood and steaks.

Drinking

U Gallet BAR
(971 534 879; Carrer de Jesús 40; 10.30am-2.30pm & 7.30pm-3.30am Tue-Sun, 7.30pm-3.30am Mon) This is where the locals come for a drink, far from the madding (and largely foreign) crowd down on the central square. The narrow bar ends in a basic lounge area. If this or a barstool doesn't appeal, the timber tables in the street could be the go.

Shopping

Pollença is filled with engaging little boutiques and its Sunday market is one of the largest and liveliest in Mallorca.

Sunday Market MARKET
Although this market is held year-round, it really takes over the town in summer. Fruit and veg is usually concentrated in the Plaça Major, with handicrafts and other stalls taking over an ever-widening arc of surrounding streets.

MOORS & CHRISTIANS IN IMMORTAL COMBAT

August sees the staging in Pollença of one of the most colourful of Mallorca's festivals. This version of Moros i Cristians (Moors and Christians) celebrates a famous victory by townsfolk over a Moorish raiding party led by the infamous Turkish pirate Dragut (1500–65) in 1550. The 'battle' is the highpoint of the **Festes de la Patrona** (Feast of the Patron Saint, ie the Virgin Mary). Townsfolk dressed up as scimitar-waving Moorish pirates and pole-toting villagers engage in several mock engagements, to the thunder of drums and blunderbusses, around town on the afternoon of 2 August. The night before, the town centre is the scene of one almighty drinking spree, with folk thronging the bars and squares, and live concerts blaring through the night from 11pm. No wonder the following day's battles don't get started until 7pm!

Enseñat FOOD, WINE
(☎971 533 618; www.ensenyat.com; Carrer d'Alcúdia 5; ⏲8.30am-2pm & 4.30-8.30pm Mon-Sat, 8.30am-2pm Sun) This deli is the place to pick up gourmet groceries, Mallorcan wines, cheeses and meats, including homemade *sobrassada*. It's been in business since the 1940s.

Artesania ARTS & CRAFTS
(☎971 531 381; www.artesania-mallorca.com; Carrer del Temple 6; ⏲10.30am-2pm & 4-8.30pm May-Sep, shorter hours rest of year) Tucked behind the Església de la Mare de Déu deis Àngels, this appealing little shop sells high-quality handmade handicrafts by mostly small-scale Mallorcan artisans. There's glassware, soap, ceramics, paper products and wrought-iron work, and the the British owner, Lynn Hazelhurst, can explain more about the artist behind each piece.

Rocaia Complements CLOTHING, ACCESSORIES
(☎971 531 102; www.rocaia.com; Carrer del Calvari; ⏲10.30am-7pm Mon-Sat) This rambling yet stylish boutique almost at the foot of the Calvari steps ranges far and wide, from homewares and wind chimes to T-shirts, jewellery and black-and-white photos – it's almost impossible to leave without buying something. It also has two other branches around town, **Tao** and **Dada**.

Teixits Vicens TEXTILES
(☎971 530 450; www.teixitsvicens.com; Ronda Can Berenguer; ⏲10am-2pm & 5-8pm Mon-Fri, 10am-2pm Sat) Artisans have been making the striped Mallorcan fabrics known as *robes de llengües* here at this family-run business since 1854, and the contemporary fabrics they turn out are faithful to traditional designs. Some of their works are on display at the Museu Martí Vicenç.

Information

Pollensa Guide (www.thepollensaguide.com) This privately run website has useful information on Pollença, Port de Pollença and Cala Sant Vicenç.

Tourist office (☎971 535 077; www.pollensa.com; Carrer de Sant Domingo 17; ⏲8am-8pm Mon-Fri, 10am-1pm Sun May-Oct, 9am-4pm Mon-Fri & 10am-1pm Sun Nov-Apr)

Getting There & Away

BUS From Palma, bus 340 heads nonstop for Pollença (€4.90, 45 minutes, up to 12 daily). It heads on to Cala Sant Vicenç (€1.10, 20 minutes, six daily) and Port de Pollença (€1.10, 20 minutes, up to 30 daily).

CYCLING THE ECO-TRAILS

Cyclists should get their wheels out onto the **Ecovies** (Eco-Trails), a network of bike trails (about 45km in total) that stretches out between Pollença and Artà and the surrounding region. Information on the trails, a forerunner to a network of trails that will one day criss-cross the entire island, is available from the tourist offices in Pollença, Alcúdia, Port d'Alcúdia, Ca'n Picafort and Artà.

CAR & MOTORCYCLE From Palma, zip along the full length of the Ma13 motorway and follow the turn-off north as this becomes a normal dual-carriageway road. A much more picturesque approach would see you turn north from Inca up the Ma2130 road and then east along the Ma10.

Cala Sant Vicenç

POP 285

One of the loveliest little corners of the northern Mallorcan coast, Cala Sant Vicenç is arrayed around four jewel-like *cales* (coves) in a breach in the Serra de Tramuntana, with fine views across the turquoise waters northwest towards Cap de Formentor. The village is really only open for business from May to October.

Sights

The first of the beaches, **Cala Barques**, is sandy until you hit the water, when you have to pick your way over rocks to reach submersion depth. Pretty (well, they're all pretty) **Cala Clara** is similar. **Cala Molins** is the biggest of the four, with a deep sandy strand and easygoing access into the shimmering waters of this tranquil inlet. **Cala Carbó**, around the headland, is the smallest and least visited. It doesn't take more than 20 minutes to walk the entire distance between the four.

If you walk for 15 minutes along Carrer Temporal from behind Cala Clara and then down Carrer de Dionìs Bennàssar, you'll hit a rise with park benches and the **Coves de L'Alzineret**, seven funerary caves dug in pre-Talayotic times (c 1600 BC).

Eating

Cal Patró SEAFOOD, RICE €€
(☎971 533 899; Cala Barques; mains €13-25; ⏲12.30-3.30pm & 7.30-10.30pm Wed-Mon Easter-Jun, Sep, Oct, daily Jul & Aug) Locals in search of

fish head straight for the 'Captain's House' for the freshest catch of the day. The rices are well-regarded, while the cuttlefish Mallorcan-style (cooked in a rich sauce, casserole style) is tasty, if a little steep for a starter. The setting on the steps down to the beach is lovely, and service is friendly. It also does a good lobster stew.

Bar-Restaurant Cala Barques SEAFOOD **€€**
(☎971 530 691; Cala Barques; mains €14-25; ⌚12.30-3.30pm & 7.30-10.30pm Tue-Sun May-Oct) The location, overlooking the beach, couldn't be better. The menu features grilled fish and seafood with a barbecue in the evenings.

Information

Tourist office (☎971 533 264; Plaça de Cala Sant Vicenç; ⌚9am-2pm & 2.30-4pm Mon-Fri, 10am-1pm Sat May-Oct) Fifty metres inland from Cala Clara.

Getting There & Away

Cala Sant Vicenç is 6.5km northeast of Pollença, off the road towards Port de Pollença. The 340 Palma–Port de Pollença bus runs to Cala Sant Vicenç (€1.10, 20 minutes, up to six times a day) from Pollença and from Port de Pollença.

Port de Pollença

POP 6010

On the north shore of the Badia de Pollença, this resort is popular with British families soothed by fish and chips and pints of ale. Sailboards and yachts can be hired on the beaches, but this place is all about lazing by the beach for a couple of weeks.

Sights & Activities

The beaches immediately south of the main port area are broad, sandy and gentle. Tufts of beach are sprinkled all the way along the shady promenade stretching around the north end of town – these rank among Port de Pollença's prettiest corners. South along the bay towards Alcúdia, the beaches are a grey gravel mix and frequently awash with poseidon grass. At the tail end of this less than winsome stretch, **Ca'n Cap de Bou** and **Sa Marina** (just before entering Alcúdia) are popular with wind and kite surfers but otherwise are no great shakes.

Some of the island's best diving is in the Badia de Pollença. There's plenty of wall and cave action, some reasonable marine life (rays, octopuses, barracuda and more) along the southern flank of the Formentor peninsula, and more popular spots along the southern end of the bay leading to Cap des Pinar.

A weekly market is staged in town on Wednesdays. It's held on Plaça Miguel Capllonch, two blocks inland, northwest of the marina.

Boat Trips BOAT TRIPS
(☎971 864 014; Marina; adult/child to Platja de Formentor €10.50/5.25, to Cap de Formentor €21/10.50, to Cala Sant Vicenç €26/13; ⌚trips May-Sep) At the small ticket booth alongside the car park entrance at the marina, you'll find boat tickets to Platja de Formentor (up to five daily departures in summer), Cap de Formentor and Cala Sant Vicenç.

Scuba Mallorca DIVE CENTRE
(☎971 868 087; www.scubamallorca.com; Carrer d'El Cano 23; 2-dive package €80, equipment extra €10; ⌚9.30am-7.30pm Mon-Thu, 9.30am-6.30pm Fri & Sat, 9am-6pm Sun Jun-Sep, closed Sun Mar-May & Oct, closed Nov-Feb) Scuba Mallorca is a PADI five-star outfit and one of a couple of dive centres in town.

Sail & Surf Pollença SAILING, WINDSURFING
(☎971 865 346; www.sailsurf.eu; Passeig de Saralegui 134; courses €90-210; ⌚9am-6pm Mon-Sat Apr-Oct, 9.30am-2.30pm Mon-Sat Nov-Mar) Come here for two- to six-day courses in sailing and windsurfing. If you have experience, it also rents out equipment.

Kayak Mallorca KAYAKING
(☎648 111 618; www.kayakmallorca.com; La Gola; 3hr trip incl transport per person €40) On the beach south of the marina, Kayak Mallorca organises trips for any level all around the island.

POSEIDON'S GRASS

Beach-lovers in northern Mallorca are occasionally put off by beaches with great rafts of what many mistake for algae. This is sea grass (poseidon grass or *poseidonia*), vital for the hindering of erosion on the seabed. The oxygen it gives off helps clean the water, attracts abundant sealife and slows global warming by absorbing carbon dioxide. Thick layers on some beaches actually help keep them intact. It can give off an unpleasant odour, but its presence is nonetheless good for the maritime environment.

WALKING TRAILS ALONG THE CAP DE FORMENTOR

The peninsula has various trails that lead down to pebbly beaches and inlets. The walk from **Port de Pollença** to **Cala Bóquer** is signposted off a roundabout on the main road to Cap de Formentor. This valley walk, with the rocky Serra del Cavall Bernat walling off the western flank, is an easy 3km hike.

About 11km along the peninsula from Port de Pollença, separate trails lead off left and right from the road (there is some rough parking here) to **Cala Figuera** on the north flank and **Cala Murta** on the south. The former walk is down a bare gully to a narrow shingle beach, where the water's colours are mesmerising. The latter walk is through mostly wooded land to a stony beach. Each takes about 40 minutes down. Near Cala Murta but tougher to reach by land is **Cala Gossalba**. In all cases carry food and drink.

A couple of other small inlets to check out along the coast are **Cala des Caló** and **Cala En Feliu**. Walkers can also hike to or from the cape along the **Camí Vell del Cap**, a poorly defined track that criss-crosses and at times follows the main road. At Port de Pollença you can link with the GR221 trail that runs the length of the Serra de Tramuntana.

The Pollença and Port de Pollença tourist offices can give you booklets that contain approximate trail maps, which for these walks should be sufficient.

Rent March BICYCLE RENTAL
(☎971 864 784; www.rentmarch.com; Carrer de Joan XXIII 89; ⏱9am-1pm & 4-8pm Mon-Sat, 9am-12.30pm Sun) Rent March hires out all sorts of bikes, from simple no-gears jobs (€7 per day) and mountain bikes (€9) to Onix Obrea 27-gear cycles (€20 per day). Also has scooters and motorbikes.

Eating

Celler La Parra MALLORCAN €€
(☎971 865 041; www.cellerlaparra.com; Carrer de Joan XXIII 84; mains €10-16.50; ⏱1-3pm & 7.15-10.15pm) In business since the 1960s, this atmospheric, old-style Mallorcan restaurant is something of a rarity in these parts. It serves up genuine island fare, from fresh fish to *frito mallorquín* (sautéed lamb offal), *lechona* (roast lamb) and *tumbet* (Mallorcan ratatouille). Throw in a wood-fired oven, wine-cellar decor and not a pizza in sight, and you'll soon see why we like it.

Ca'n Cuarassa SPANISH, MALLORCAN €€
(☎971 864 266; www.cancuarassa.com; Carretera Port de Pollença-Alcúdia; mains €14.10-29.20; ⏱1-3.30pm & 7.30-11pm) This rambling place 3km south of central Port de Pollença offers a large garden dining space, kids play area, and a long menu of island and Spanish food. A good starter might be the octopus carpaccio, followed by fillet of turbot in a *cava* sauce. It's a little out on a limb, but worth it.

Stay SPANISH, INTERNATIONAL €€
(☎971 864 013; www.stayrestaurant.com; Moll Nou; mains €15-32; ⏱9am-11pm) The Gassó family, the same folk who operate Ca'n Cuarassa, have turned this place into a slick example of seaside chic, with an extensive outdoor dining area out on the pier. Yachties and their ilk hang here, savouring things such as assorted grilled seafood or lighter tapas. It's classy but casual, pricey but almost always worth it.

La Llonja & La Cantina SPANISH, INTERNATIONAL €€€
(☎971 868 430; www.restaurantllallonja.com; Carrer del Moll Vell; mains €13.60-67; ⏱La Llonja 1-3.30pm & 7.30-10.30pm Mon-Sat, La Cantina 8.30am-11pm) Upstairs overlooking the water, La Llonja does seriously good seafood and meat dishes with splashes of creativity (such as the lemonfish carpaccio), although the lobster stew (€67) is seriously overpriced. Downstairs, La Cantina is breezy and far easier on the pocket, serving breakfast, snacks and sandwiches.

Drinking

Port de Pollença doesn't exactly go off. You have to feel for those somewhat lost-looking adolescents wandering about late at night, dreaming of Ibiza clubs and wishing they hadn't been dragged here by their insensitive parents.

Information

Tourist office (☎971 865 467; www.puertopollensa.com; Passeig Saralegui; ⏱8am-8pm Mon-Fri, 10am-5pm Sat, 10am-1pm Sun May-Sep, 8am-3pm Mon-Fri Oct-Apr) The tourist office is on the waterfront in front of the marina.

Getting There & Away

The 340 bus from Palma to Pollença continues to Port de Pollença (20 minutes direct or 30 minutes via Cala Sant Vicenç). Bus 352 makes the run between Port de Pollença and Ca'n Picafort (€2.35, one hour), stopping at Alcúdia and Port d'Alcúdia along the way.

CAP DE FORMENTOR

Perhaps the most spectacular stretch of Mallorca's coast (and there's sturdy competition), Cap de Formentor is an otherworldly domain of vertiginous cliffs and jagged peaks jutting far out to sea; from a distance, it looks like an epic line of waves about to break.

The road onto the cape quickly climbs away from Port de Pollença, with splendid views of the bay. More breathtaking is the **Mirador de Sa Creueta** (232m), 3km northeast of Port de Pollença. From this lookout cliffs plunge into the depths on the peninsula's north coast. To the east, just off the coast, floats the **Illot del Colomer**, a rocky islet. From the same spot you can climb a couple of kilometres up a side road to the **Talaia d'Albercuix** watchtower (380m). It was built to warn of pirates and you can see why; the views extend far out to sea.

From here, the Ma2210 sinks down through the woods some 4km to **Platja de Formentor** (Platja del Pi). Parking costs €4 for the day. The road slithers another 11km from Hotel Formentor out to the cape and its **lighthouse**, where you'll find a snack joint, views to Cap Ferrutx to the south and a short walking track (the Camí del Moll del Patronet) south to another viewpoint.

Getting There & Away

The 18km stretch from Port de Pollença (via the Ma2210) is best done with your own vehicle, bicycle or two legs, although the 353 bus runs from Ca'n Picafort to Cap de Formentor (€3.10, one hour 20 minutes, twice daily May to October) and passes through Port d'Alcúdia, Alcúdia and Port de Pollença. Two extra services run between Port de Pollença and Cap de Formentor.

BADIA D'ALCÚDIA

Alcúdia

Just a few kilometres inland from the coast, Alcúdia is a place of quiet charm, containing all the character so lacking in many of Mallorca's coastal settlements. An engaging old town encircled by medieval walls and the remains of what was once the island's prime Roman settlement will provide the focal points of your visit. But the good hotels and restaurants ensure that you could do worse than make it your northern Mallorcan base.

Sights

Tuesday and Sunday are market days in Alcúdia, held on and around Passeig de la Victòria.

Pol·lentia ARCHAEOLOGICAL SITE
(☎971 897 102; www.pollentia.net; Avinguda dels Prínceps d'Espanya; adult/student & senior incl museum €3/2; ⏲9.30am-8.30pm Tue-Sat, 10am-3pm Sun May-Sep, 10am-3.30pm Tue-Fri, 10am-1.30pm Sat & Sun Oct-Apr) The ruins of the Roman town of Pol·lentia lie just outside Alcúdia's walls (the entrance is on Avinguda dels Prínceps d'Espanya). Founded around 70 BC, it was Rome's principal city in Mallorca and is the most important archaeological site on the island. The theatre in particular is worth the entrance fee.

Pol·lentia reached its apogee in the 1st and 2nd centuries AD and covered up to 20 hectares – its sheer geographical spread (most of it unexcavated) suggest it was a city of some size and substance.

In the northwest corner of the site is the Portella residential area – the most interesting of the houses is the **Casa dels Dos Tresors** (House of the Two Treasures), a typical Roman house centred on an atrium and which stood from the 1st to the 5th centuries AD. A short stroll away are the remnants of the **Forum**, which boasted three temples and rows of *tabernae* (shops). Finally, you walk another few hundred metres to reach the small but evocative 1st-century AD **Teatre Romà** (Roman Theatre), which seems to be returning into the rock from which it was hewn. The theatre is used for theatre performances in August.

Museu Monogràfic de Pol·lentia MUSEUM
(☎971 547 004; www.pollentia.net; Carrer de Sant Jaume 30; adult/child incl Pol·lentia €3/2; ⏲11am-2pm & 4-7pm Tue-Sun May-Sep, 10am-4pm Tue-Fri, 10am-2pm Sat & Sun Oct-Apr) This one-room museum has fragments of statues, coins, jewellery, household figurines of divinities, scale models of the Casa dels Dos Tresors and Theatre and other odds and ends dug up at the ruins of the Roman town of Pol·lentia. It's well presented but labels

ALCÚDIA'S HISTORIC MANSIONS

Alcúdia's old town is dotted with handsome mansions. Among the finest examples:

» **Ca'n Canta** (Carrer Major 18)

» **Ca'n Domènech** (Carrer dels Albellons 7)

» **Ca'n Fondo** (Carrer d'En Serra 13)

» **Ca'n Torró** (Carrer d'En Serra 15)

Sculptures by Ben Jakober and Yannick Vu, the British artist couple who live here some of the time, litter the garden. Follow the signs to Fundació and Bonaire. At the Bodega del Sol restaurant, turn right and keep on down the road, which turns into a potholed track. The foundation is on the right. The varying admission prices depend on how many parts of the complex you wish to visit.

Activities

Ask at the tourist office for its *10 Excursions* brochure, which details itineraries around the Alcúdia region that can be completed on foot or by bike.

Festivals & Events

Fira d'Alcúdia MARKET

(1st weekend Oct) The big annual market event is the Fira d'Alcúdia, which sees a produce market come together with traditional dances, music and parades.

Eating

S'Arc MEDITERRANEAN €€

(☎971 539 178; Carrer d'En Serra 22; mains €9-14; ⏲12.30-3.30pm & 6-11.30pm) Part of the Petit Hotel Ca'n Simó, this old-town charmer with internal courtyard and exposed stone walls offers Mediterranean flavours with some inventive twists, among them fish and seafood risotto with saffron-scented mushrooms.

Genestar INTERNATIONAL €€

(☎971 549 157; www.genestarestaurant.com; Plaça Porta de Mallorca 1; set menu €25, drinks extra; ⏲1-3.30pm & 8-11.30pm Mon, Tue, Thu-Sat, 8-11.30pm Sun) This modern, designer establishment lies just beyond the city walls; look for the bamboo trunks outside. With just eight tables, enthusiastic punters are served a five-course set meal (the menu changes weekly) that ranges broadly over Mediterranean and international themes. Book ahead.

Ca'n Pere MEDITERRANEAN €€

(☎971 545 243; www.hotelcanpere.com; Carrer d'En Serra 12; mains €9-15; ⏲12.30-3.30pm & 7-10.30pm) Another attractive stone-walled courtyard restaurant, Ca'n Pere, in the hotel of the same name, serves up fresh Mediterranean dishes such as black ravioli filled with prawns and salmon. Service can be slow when things are busy.

L'Arca d'en Peter MEDITERRANEAN €€

(☎971 539 178; www.larcadenpeter.com; Placeta de ses Verdures 1; mains €9-15; ⏲noon-3.30pm & 6-11.30pm; 🚭) Run by the same owners as Ca'n Pere, this place has a more modern look, appealing outdoor tables in the square, and faster service. The menu is almost identical.

Getting There & Away

The 351 bus from Palma to Platja de Muro calls at Alcúdia (€4.80, 45 minutes, up to 16 times daily). Bus 352 connects Ca'n Picafort (€1.60, 45 minutes) with Port de Pollença as often as every 15 minutes from May to October. Local service 356 connects Alcúdia with Port d'Alcúdia and the beach of Platja d'Alcúdia (€1.25, 15 minutes, every 15 minutes from May to October).

Port d'Alcúdia

POP 1895

Draped along the northeastern corner of the Alcúdia bay, Port d'Alcúdia is a busy beach-holiday centre with a more appealing waterfront, marina and fishing harbour than many along this coast. Further south, pleasant beaches, backed by less-pleasant concrete developments, are the name of the game.

Sights & Activities

Port d'Alcúdia is for doing more than seeing, with a wide range of activities on offer. You might also like to ask at the tourist office about the **Cova de Sant Martí**, about 1.6km southwest of the tourist office on Carretera d'Artà. It's an otherworldly religious shrine and grotto in a 15m-deep hollow, which dates back to the 13th century. It was closed when we visited due to safety concerns.

Transportes Marítimos Brisa BOAT TRIPS

(☎971 545 811; www.tmbrisa.com; adult €18-55, child €9-27.50; ⏲trips May-Oct) Transportes

Alcúdia

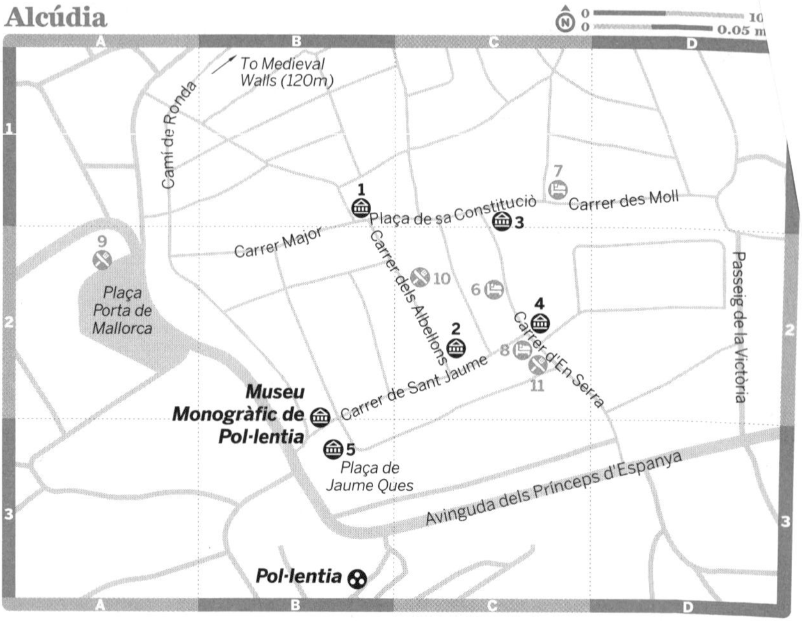

are only in Catalan, so ask for the 'English guidebook' pamphlet.

Museu de Sant Jaume MUSEUM
(☎971 548 665; Plaça de Jaume Ques; adult/child €1/free; ⏲10am-1pm Mon-Sat) This museum, housed in the eponymous church, will hold your attention only if you're into priestly vestments and other religious paraphernalia.

FREE **Medieval Walls** CITY WALLS
Although largely rebuilt, Alcúdia's city walls are impressive. Those on the north side are largely the medieval originals. Near the Porta Roja (Red Gate) are remnants of an 18th-century bridge. From the bridge, you can walk around 250m atop the walls, as far as Carrer del Progres, with fine views over the rooftops and towards the distant hills en route.

Beyond the bridge to the northeast, the Plaça de Toros (bullring) has been built into a Renaissance-era fortified bastion.

Fundación Yannick y Ben Jakober GALLERY, GARDEN
(Museo Sa Bassa Blanca; ☎971 549 880; www.fundacionjakober.org; Camí de Coll Baix; Tue & Thu free, by guided tour Wed, Fri & Sat €9-15; ⏲9.30am-12.30pm & 2.30-5.30pm Tue, 10am-noon Thu, guided tours 11am & 3pm Wed, Fri & Sat) Some 4.5km east of Alcúdia is the Fundació Yannick i Ben Jakober, an eclectic cultural institution that works on the restoration of artworks and concentrates on children's portraits from the 16th to 19th centuries. It also has exhibition space devoted to contemporary artists.

Alcúdia

Top Sights
- Museu Monogràfic de Pol·lentia B2
- Pol·lentia B3

Sights
- 1 Ca'n Canta B1
- 2 Ca'n Domènech C2
- 3 Ca'n Fondo C1
- 4 Ca'n Torró C2
- 5 Museu de Sant Jaume B3

Sleeping
- 6 Ca'n Pere C2
- 7 Fonda Llabres C1
- 8 Petit Hotel Ca'n Simó C2

Eating
- Ca'n Pere .... (see 6)
- 9 Genestar A2
- 10 L'Arca d'en Peter C2
- 11 S'Arc C2

Marítimos Brisa offers catamaran trips (adult/child €55/27.50, five hours), excursions to Platja de Formentor (€23/11.50, four hours) and Cala Sant Vicenç (€27/13.50, three hours), and trips in a glass-bottomed boat (€18/9, two hours).

5 Oceanos DIVE CENTRE
(☎971 549 957; www.5oceanos.com; Avinguda del Mal Pas 1; ⏰trips May-Oct) This dive centre, in one of the northern suburbs facing the bay, has trips out to the waters around Cap de Formentor.

Parapente Alfabia PARAGLIDING
(☎622 600 900; www.parapentealfabia.com) Parapente Alfabia offers the chance to go paragliding, with tandem flights for beginners.

Wind & Friends WATER SPORTS
(☎971 549 835, 627 086 950; www.windfriends.com; Carrer de Neptú; ⏰Apr-Oct) At Wind & Friends, next to the Hotel Sunwing on the waterfront, you can get organised for sailing, windsurfing and kite surfing. A four-day beginners' course in windsurfing will cost €190.

Hidropark AMUSEMENT PARK
(☎971 891 672; www.hidropark.com; Avinguda del Tucá; adult/child 3-11yr/under 3yr €20/10/free; ⏰10.30am-6pm May-Oct) About 600m inland from the beach, Hidropark is a typical water park with slides, wave pool and infants' splash-pool area.

Festivals & Events

Festival de Sant Pere CITY FESTIVAL, RELIGIOUS
(29 Jun) This festival celebrates the port's patron saint. The week leading up to this day is a time of concerts, kids shows and activities. On the big day a statue of Sant Pere is paraded on land and sea.

Eating

In general, the emphasis is on quantity rather than quality, but some places buck the trend and manage both.

Restaurante Jardín MEDITERRANEAN FUSION €€€
(☎971 892 391; www.restaurantejardin.com; Carrer dels Tritons; menú degustación €70; ⏰1.30-3.30pm & 8-11pm Fri & Sat, 1.30-3.30pm Sun mid-Mar–Dec) In a town with few stand-out options, this place is a real treasure. The cooking brings *nouvelle* twists to essential Med products and there are no à la carte choices – just sit back and enjoy the tasting menu.

Miramar SEAFOOD €€
(☎971 545 293; Passeig Marítim 2; mains €12.90-35; ⏰1-3.30pm & 7-11pm, closed Jan) Take up a spot on the ample terrace of this waterfront classic (since 1871) for one of a broad selection of paellas or *fideuà* (a paella-like noodle dish). Standard fish dishes (sole, bream etc) are well prepared, while the groaning seafood platter is epic in scale and price (€65 per person).

Steak House Carabela GRILLED MEATS, SEAFOOD €€
(☎971 547 704; Carretera d'Artà 14; mains €14-23; ⏰noon-midnight) Housed in an all-glass space a block back from the water just west of the main harbour, Carabela is a carnivore's fantasy. Although it also does seafood, it's really the meat that excels here; it is perfectly cooked to your specifications with just the right amount of charcoal grill flavour. Sauces are optional, while the T-bone steak (€22.30) is a truly gargantuan cut of meat.

Information

Main tourist office (☎971 547 257; www.alcudiamallorca.com; Passeig Marítim; ⏰9.30am-8.30pm Easter-Oct) In a booth behind the marina.

Tourist office (☎971 892 615; Carretera d'Artà 68; ⏰9.30am-3pm Mon-Fri Apr-Oct) Another branch south of the main harbour.

Getting There & Away

BUS There are bus services from Alcúdia.

BOAT Boats leave for Ciutadella on the island of Menorca from the ferry port.

Cap des Pinar

From Alcúdia and Port d'Alcúdia, Cap des Pinar thrusts eastward into the deep blue and, together with Cap de Formentor away to the north, encloses the Badia de Pollença within its embrace. Its northern neighbour may be more spectacular, but Cap des Pinar bristles with Aleppo pine woods at its eastern end as it rises to a series of precipitous cliffs. Unfortunately, the cape is military land and off-limits but the rest is well worth it.

Sights

From Alcúdia head northeast through residential Mal Pas and Bonaire to a scenic route that stretches to Cap des Pinar. After 1.5km of winding coastal road east of Bonaire you reach the beach and bar-restaurant

START/FINISH PORT D'ALCÚDIA
DISTANCE 32KM
DIFFICULTY EASY TO MODERATE
BIKE HYBRID OR MOUNTAIN BIKE

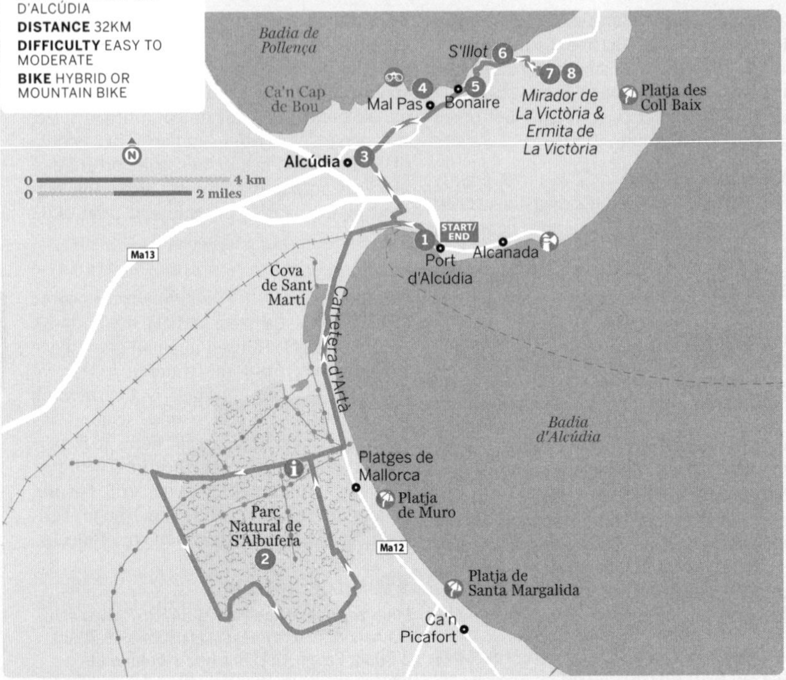

Cycling Tour
Port d'Alcúdia & Around

This ride is a pleasant dawdle through tranquil wetlands, followed by an old town turn and a ride around the bay.

Setting out from along the Passeig Marítim in 1 **Port d'Alcúdia**, head south towards C'an Picafort, signed left at the first roundabout you come to. Carretera d'Artà stretches rather uneventfully from here for 4.5km, before passing over a canal, at which point you should take an immediate right. A pitted road leads up to the 2 **Parc Natural de S'Albufera** and its information centre. From here, Rte 3 is the best option for cyclists, skirting the wetlands' edge and allowing leisurely pedalling. Despite the potholes, the peaceful surroundings and accompanying avian chorus make this a lovely ride.

Retrace your tracks to Port d'Alcúdia but follow the road (Carrer del Coral) round to the left instead of carrying along to the seafront. Continue until you hit a main road and take a left. After 2km you'll arrive at Plaça de Carles V in 3 **Alcúdia** and one of the town's sets of turreted gates. From Plaça de Carles V head down the road leading to Carrer de la Creu (signed) and take the next available right. At the main road, turn left, and after 2km the road begins to undulate as it passes through upmarket 4 **Mal Pas** and 5 **Bonaire** where yachts bob calmly in the harbour, before climbing higher around the bay along Cap des Pinar. You can pause to refuel at the beautifully sited but casual 6 **S'Illot**, with a terrace overlooking the bay. If you still have some energy left, follow the signs to the 7 **Mirador de La Victòria**, with the mountains rising to your right and a stunning view of the Badia de Pollença to your left.

You can take a well-earned break at the 8 **Ermita de La Victòria**, where there's a snack bar, restaurant and lodgings. Once you've got your breath back, breeze all the way back down to Alcúdia and folow the signs back to Port d'Alcúdia.

of S'Illot. A little further on, there are turn-offs to Albergue La Victòria and Ermita de La Victoria.

From Ermita de La Victòria, it's about a 40-minute uphill, signposted walk to **Sa Talaia**, a 16th-century lookout tower with views to the north, east and south. Back on the main road, walk about 1.5km east from the junction to where the road is blocked. It's worth the trip to continue savouring the changing views.

Platja des Coll Baix BEACH
A lovely, tranquil option on the peninsula is to head for the Platja des Coll Baix. A small flotilla of sailboats and the occasional tour boat can populate the bay, so early morning (sunrise!) is the best time to visit this lovely grey pebbly, sandy affair lapped by translucent waters.

From Alcúdia, it's about 8km to an open spot in the woods where you can leave your car or bike. Follow the directions for the Fundació Yannick i Ben Jakober and keep on for another 2km. From this spot, you could climb the south trail to Sa Talaia. Then follow the signs to Coll Baix, a fairly easy half-hour descent. The main trail will lead you to the rocks south of the beach, from where you have to scramble back around to reach it.

✖ Eating

There are a couple of particularly fine options (with views) for a meal on Cap des Pinar.

Restaurante Mirador de
La Victòria SPANISH, MALLORCAN €€
(☑971 547 173; Carretera Cap des Pinar; mains €11-23; ⊙1-3.45pm & 7-11pm May-Oct, closed Mon Nov & Feb-Apr, closed Dec & Jan) This is one of our favourite places for a meal in northern Mallorca, with well-regarded Mallorcan cooking and fine views out over the treetops towards Cap de Formentor. It's up the hill behind Ermita de La Victòria. Aside from local dishes such as eggplant stuffed with meat, and *pescado a la mallorquina* (roast fish, served with vegetables), it's deservedly proud of its rice dishes, and makes one of the best *aliolis* (garlic mayonnaises) on the island.

S'Illot SEAFOOD, RICE €€
(☑971 897 218; Carretera Cap des Pinar; mains €15-22; ⊙10am-11.30pm; ⊛) Right by the water's edge, adjacent to a pretty pebble beach and looking across the water to Cap des Formen-

tor, this rustic bar-restaurant has a lot going for it. It serves fine *fideuà* and rice dishes, but it's also the sort of place you might want to take up residence with a drink or two over a long summer's afternoon.

Parc Natural de S'Albufera

The 688-hectare Parc Natural de S'Albufera, west of the Ma12 between Port d'Alcúdia and Ca'n Picafort, is prime birdwatching territory, with 303 recorded species (more than 80% of recorded Balearic species), 64 of which breed within the park's boundaries; more than 10,000 birds overwinter here, among them both permanent residents and migrants.

These wetlands have been here for almost 100,000 years and the park's name derives from an old Arab toponym, Albuhayra (lagoon). In the 19th century especially, attempts were made (with differing degrees of success) to dry out the mix of salt and fresh water to create cultivable land and combat malaria. The so-called Gran Canal at the heart of the park was designed to channel the water out to sea. The five-arched **Pont de Sa Roca** bridge was built over it in the late 19th century to ease travel between Santa Margalida and Alcúdia. Many of the *marjales* (parcels of arable land won from the wetlands) date to the same period. The island government bought some of the land in 1985 and the park was born. The park is considered a Ramsar Wetland of National Importance and, in addition to the bird species, around 400 plant species have been catalogued here.

The park is well set up for visitors. Entrance to the park is free, but permits must

MALLORCAN WILD GOAT

If you're hiking anywhere along Cap des Pinar, keep an eye out for the Mallorcan wild goat (*Capra ageagrus hircus*), which survives only in the Serra de Tramuntana, around Artà and Cap des Pinar. Smaller than domestic goats, this Mallorcan species has red fur and a black back, and both males and females have horns. Although limited in their range, they're present in sufficient numbers to be legally hunted across Cap des Pinar from September to mid-July.

be obtained from the Centro de Recepción de Sa Roca (see below). From here, 14km of signposted trails fan out across the park. There are four marked itineraries through the park, from 725m (30 minutes) to 11.5km (3½ hours); two of these are possible by bike. Of the six *aguaits* (timber birdwatching observatories – come inside and watch in silence) some are better than others. You'll see lots of wading birds in action from the Bishop I and II *aguaits* on the north side of the Gran Canal. There are a further six observation decks. Holders of the Targeta Verda can use park bicycles and binoculars for free.

Facing the sea across from the park entrance is **Platja de Muro**. A 3km stretch of it is backed by **Es Comú de Muro**, a thick tangle of Aleppo pines and other dune flora that gives the beach a wilder feel than most around here, and is part of the Parc Natural.

Information

Tourist office (☎971 892 250; www.mallorcaweb.net/salbufera; ⏲visitor centre 9am-4pm, park 9am-6pm Apr-Sep, 9am-5pm Oct-Mar) The park's visitor centre, the Centro de Recepción de Sa Roca, is about 1km from the park entrance and can provide information on the park and its birdlife.

Getting There & Away

Buses between Ca'n Picafort and Alcúdia stop by a small car park near the park entrance.

SOUTH OF ALCÚDIA

Ca'n Picafort & Around

A smaller version of Port d'Alcúdia, Ca'n Picafort (7km further southeast around the bay) and its southern extension, **Son Bauló**, is a package-tour frontier town, somewhat raw and raggedy. But the beaches are pretty good and there are some interesting archaeological sites.

Sights & Activities

The bulk of the town is an uninspiring grid of streets backing on to **Platja de Santa Margalida**, a crowded shallow beach with turquoise water. To the northwest (walk along the beach from the heart of Ca'n Picafort) the beach of **Ses Casetes dels Capellans** (signposted off the Ma12 at the roundabout where you enter Ca'n Picafort from the north) is broad and backed by several beach restaurants and bars.

To the southwest, where the Son Bauló hotel and apartment belt ends, is **Platja de Son Bauló** and, beyond the trickle of water from the Torrent de Son Bauló, the wilder **Platja de Son Real**. This almost 5km stretch of coast, with snippets of sandy strands in among the rock points, is backed only by low dunes, scrub and bushland dense with Aleppo pines.

FREE Finca Pública de Son Real HISTORIC BUILDING
(☎971 185 363; sonreal@balears-sostenible.com; ⏲10am-7pm Apr-Sep, 10am-5pm Oct-Mar) Much of the area between the coast and the Ma12 highway has been converted into the Finca Pública de Son Real. Its main entrance is just south of the Km18 milestone on the Ma12, and the former farm buildings host an information office for those who wish to walk the property's several trails. There's also a multimedia display (adult/child €5/2.50) on traditional Mallorcan rural life.

Es Figueral de Son Real ARCHAEOLOGICAL SITE
From the Finca Pública de Son Real, one trail leads through a largely abandoned fig plantation to the overgrown Talayotic ruins of Es Figueral de Son Real. This settlement dates at least to 1000 BC and consists of several buildings that you'll need considerable imagination to decipher.

Necròpolis de Son Real ARCHAEOLOGICAL SITE
On the sea about 10 minutes' walk southeast of Platja de Son Bauló, this impressive necropolis appears to have been a Talayotic cemetery with 110 tombs (in which the remains of more than 300 people were found). The tombs have the shape of mini-*talayots* (ancient watchtowers) and date as far back as the 7th century BC. Some suggest this was a commoners graveyard.

Illot dels Porros ARCHAEOLOGICAL SITE
A few hundred metres further southeast from the Necròpolis de Son Real, the island called Illot dels Porros also contains remains of an ancient necropolis. It's a fairly easy swim for the moderately fit.

Eating

The waterfront and Avinguda de Josep Trias are lined with eateries, bars and pubs (all largely indistinguishable from one another).

WORTH A TRIP

BETLEM

Northeast along the coastal Ma3331, 3km from Colònia de Sant Pere, is the somnolent holiday settlement of **Betlem**. Not much goes on here – reason enough to visit. Along the coast, a 3km 4WD trail hugs the Aleppo-pine-fringed shoreline until it reaches a tiny protected bay called **Es Caló**, where a couple of sailboats occasionally find shelter and a handful of people stretch out on the stony strand and swim in the turquoise waters. Behind you, dramatic limestone hills rise sharply, some barely clothed in swaying grass. **Cap Ferrutx**, the windy cape north of Es Caló, is a tougher nut to crack as there are no trails. There are some hiking options in nearby Parc Natural de la Península de Llevant (p138).

If you don't feel like watching *Coronation Street* while scoffing Yorkshire pudding you'll have to head to the Ma12, where several locals places are scattered.

Information

Tourist office (☎971 850 310; Plaça de Gabriel Roca; ⏰9am-1pm & 5-7.30pm Mon-Fri Easter-Oct) At the southern end of Ca'n Picafort.

Getting There & Away

Bus 390 runs from Palma to Ca'n Picafort (€4.95, one hour 10 minutes, four to seven daily). Bus 352 is the main service between Ca'n Picafort and Port de Pollença (€2.35, one hour), via Port d'Alcúdia and Alcúdia.

Son Serra de Marina

This sprawling holiday residential development spreads 5km east along the coast from Son Bauló. Mallorquins and Germans alike flock to its southeast edge, for here starts the dune-backed **Platja de Sa Canova** (aka S'Arenal or Platja de Son Serra), a 2km stretch of virgin beach. Where the beach meets the settlement is where most people gather, among them windsurfing and kitesurfing enthusiasts.

Most people in town wander in to **El Sol Sunshine Bar** (☎971 854 029; www.sunshine-bar.net; Carrer de Joan Frontera; mains €8-18; ⏰noon-midnight; @) for breakfast, lunch, dinner or a cocktail. With its wicker chairs, internet point and laid-back feeling, it generates an almost Malibu vibe (only the accents are more like Munich). Friday is pizza day and Sunday's for brunch (10am to 3pm). It has live music on Fridays at 8pm, and sometimes also on Sundays.

Some buses on the Palma–Ca'n Picafort route continue to Son Serra de Marina.

Colònia de Sant Pere

Named after the patron saint of fishers (St Peter), this peaceful former farming village is an antidote to the tourist resorts to the west. The huddle of houses has expanded beyond the central square and church to accommodate a small populace that seems to be on permanent vacation. In the centre of town on the shady Passeig del Mar, some splash about in the water on the sandy, protected **Platja de la Colònia de Sant Pere**. Nearby is the small marina and fishing port. About 2.5km west, after the residential area of **S'Estanyol** (aka S'Estany des Bisbe), **Platja de Sa Canova** starts. From S'Estanyol the only way to Sa Canova is on foot.

Last in line as you head east along the town's waterfront you'll find **Sa Xarxa** (☎971 589 251; www.sa-xarxa.com; Passeig del Mar; mains €12-20; ⏰10am-11pm Tue-Sun mid-Feb–mid-Jan). You can order up all sorts of things, including Atlantic sole and an array of meat options, but come for the catch of the day done simply in a salty crust. Everything, such as the carpaccio with a hint of truffle oil, is done with a delicate touch.

The 481 bus (a taxi bus for a maximum of four people) runs between Artà and Colònia de Sant Pere (€1.90, 30 minutes, up to six times a day). You must call ☎650 233 957 by 7pm the day before to book the service.

The Interior

Includes »

Santa Maria del Camí & Around ... 121
Binissalem ... 121
Santa Eugènia ... 124
Inca ... 125
Sineu ... 128
Sa Pobla & Muro ... 129
Algaida ... 129
Petra ... 131
Manacor ... 131
Felanitx ... 133

Best Places to Eat

» Bacchus (p121)

» Celler Ca'n Amer (p126)

» Celler Es Grop (p128)

» Restaurante Sa Boveda (p128)

» Es Celler (p131)

Best Places to Stay

» Hotel León de Sineu (p172)

» Read's Hotel (p171)

» Petit Hotel Hostatgería San Salvador (p172)

» Es Castell (p171)

» Can Joan Capo Hotel (p172)

Why Go?

Mallorca's interior is a place of quiet charm, the alter ego to the island's more famous coastal attractions of sun, surf and seafood. Although the beaches are rarely more than hour away, the interior feels like it's a world away, a land of appealing wineries, hilltop monasteries, attractive stone villages, and rural homes converted into intimate retreats where you'll sleep in perfect tranquillity and eat dishes whose secrets have been passed down from one Mallorcan generation to the next. And therein lies one of Mallorca's most heartwarming tales: whereas tourism's impact upon the coast has too often been heavy-handed, here in the interior it has saved many traditions from disappearing altogether. As such, in places such as Sineu, Petra and Binibona you'll encounter a reassuringly time-stood-still view of Mallorca that survives nowhere else.

When to Go

Unlike the coast, inland Mallorca tends to remain open for business year-round: Palma folk like nothing better than escaping from city life in the depths of winter (such as it is) and finding a rural retreat for a heartwarming meal or a quiet night's sleep. The interior's festivals also rank among the most traditional on the island, from the Easter Sunday S'Encuentro of Montuïri to the 700-year-old livestock markets of Sineu in May or the yearly grape harvest in Binissalem in September.

THE CENTRAL CORRIDOR

Most travellers race quickly through the geographical heart of the island along the Ma13 motorway, although the older route (Ma13a) takes you through some interesting country. Sophisticated rural retreats and some of Mallorca's best vineyards are the main attractions, but charming villages such as Binibona in the Serra de Tramuntana foothills and Sineu further south are also compelling reasons to forsake the rush to the coast.

If you're heading west from here, the Ma2130 road north of Caimari is a spectacular route leading to the **Monestir de Lluc** (p102) and the Ma10 coast road heading south.

Santa Maria del Camí & Around

Just beyond Palma's expanding commuter belt, Santa Maria del Camí is a gateway to Mallorca's wine country and is home to one of the most celebrated hotel-restaurants on the island as well as a respected winery. The village itself doesn't really catch the eye, but it does have a couple of pretty squares.

Sights

If you're coming from Palma, the Ma13a widens to become the bar-lined Plaça dels Hostals as you roll into town. On its southern flank at No 30 rises the 17th-century **Antic Monestir de Nostra Senyora de Soledad**, aka Can Conrado. If the main doors happen to be swung open, you can peer into the magnificent front courtyard, while a glimpse of the rear gardens can be had around the corner from Carrer Llarg. That street leads to the original heart of the town, Plaça de la Vila, a quiet medieval square presided over by the 17th-century **Casa de la Vila** (Town Hall).

Bodegas Macià Batle WINERY
(☎971 140 014; www.maciabatle.com; Camí Coanegra; ⏲9am-7pm Mon-Fri) One of the island's biggest names in wine, Bodegas Macià Batle is based just outside of central Santa Maria. In addition to winery visits and tastings, you can admire their labels, all designed by renowned contemporary artists.

Festivals & Events

Festes de Santa Margalida TOWN FESTIVAL
(Jul) Held over three weeks in July, this festival involves concerts, traditional dances and communal meals. The key day is the 20th.

Eating

Bacchus SPANISH, INTERNATIONAL €€€
(Read's Hotel; ☎971 140 262; www.readshotel.com; mains €25-27) With one Michelin star and a celebrated reputation as one of the best places to eat on the island, Bacchus, in Read's Hotel, does fusion cooking at its best, served up in an elegant 16th-century dining hall. The restaurant is part of Marc Fosh's empire and, as such, one for a special occasion.

Getting There & Away

Santa Maria is around halfway along the Palma–Inca train line. Fares in either direction cost €1, and journey times range between 18 and 23 minutes.

Binissalem

POP 6200 / ELEV 131M

Binissalem stands in the heart of Mallorca's wine country, which is the main reason to visit. Like many towns in inland Mallorca, Binissalem has retained its Arabic name.

Sights

Most of Binissalem's buildings are made of a local white stone, and the central bulk of the striking **Església de Nostra Senyora de les Robines** is no exception.

A weekly **market** is staged on Fridays.

José Luis Ferrer WINERY
(☎971 511 050; www.vinosferrer.com; Carrer del Conquistador 103; guided tours €6; ⏲tours 11am & 4.30pm Mon-Fri, shop 9am-7pm Mon-Fri, 10am-2pm Sat) One of Mallorca's largest wineries, José Luis Ferrer, at the west end of the town, was launched in 1931. Ring ahead for guided tours.

Celler Tianna Negre WINERY
(☎971 886 826; www.tiannanegre.com; Camí d'es Mitjans; ⏲9am-4pm Mon-Fri, guided tours 10am & 2pm) This 20-hectare winery has architect-designed buildings (we love the cork fence) and an aim for sustainability in its wine-production processes. It produces a range of whites, reds and rosés.

FREE **Casa-Museu Llorenç Villalonga** MUSEUM
(☎971 886 014; www.cmvillalonga.org; Carrer de Bonaire 25; ⏲10am-2pm Mon & Fri, 10am-2pm & 4-8pm Tue & Thu, 10am-1pm Sat) From the mid-18th to the early 19th century, Binissalem's prosperity as a winemaking town was reflected in the construction of several notable

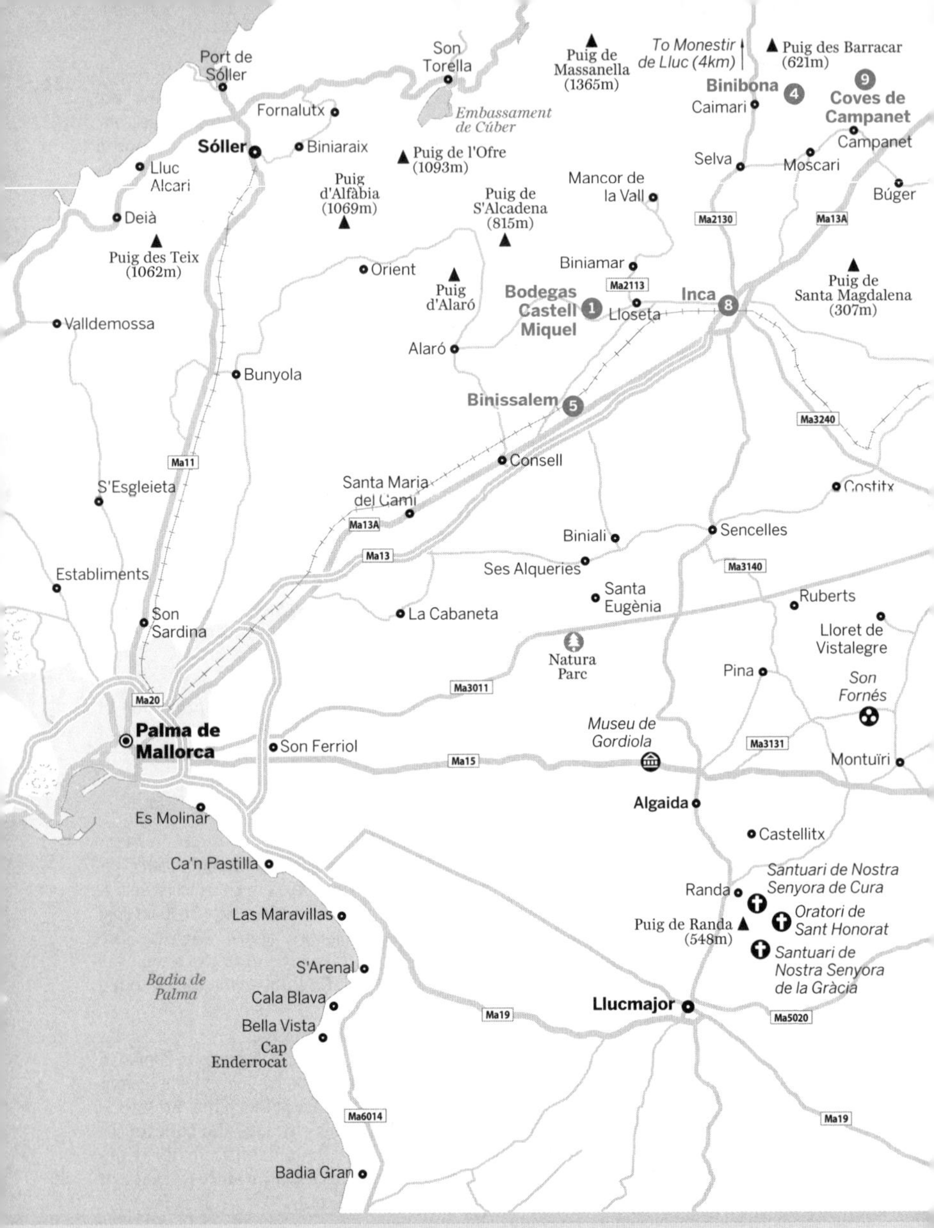

The Interior Highlights

1. Spend a few days sampling the wines of the region, starting with **Bodegas Castell Miquel** (p126)
2. Linger for longer than planned in the stone-built town of **Petra** (p131)
3. Immerse yourself in the markets and myriad charms of **Sineu** (p128)
4. Sleep in utter peace in a rural hotel in quieter-than-quiet **Binibona** (p127)
5. Revel in the late-September wine festivities at the Festes de la Verema in **Binissalem** (p121)
6. Take divine inspiration from the views at the **Santuari de Sant Salvador** (p133)

7 See how the rural señors lorded over the land at the mansion-museum of **Els Calderers** (p130)

8 Go on a leather-buying spree and feast traditionally in a *celler* in **Inca** (p125)

9 Venture underground and into another world at the **Coves de Campanet** (p127)

10 Hunt for pearls in the showrooms of **Manacor** (p131)

WINES OF THE INTERIOR

Wine has been produced on Mallorca since Roman times and the island's interior has two recognised wine-growing regions that have met the exacting standards of quality control known as DO (Denominación de Orígen).

The smaller of the two, Binissalem doesn't extend much beyond the village of the same name. The much larger Pla i Llevant DO region covers almost the entire eastern half of the island. Around half of the reds produced in these DO regions come from the local Manto Negro grape, while around two-thirds of the whites come from the Moll grape variety.

Numerous wineries across the two regions can be visited, including the following:

» **Bodegas Castell Miquel** (p126)

» **Bodegas Crestatx** (p129)

» **Bodegas Macià Batle** (p121)

» **Bodegas Miquel Oliver** (p131)

» **Celler Tianna Negre** (p121)

» **Jaume Mesquida Winery** (p130)

» **José Luis Ferrer** (p121)

» **Toni Gelabert** (p132)

mansions. One that has been well preserved is Can Sabater, a country residence for the writer Llorenç Villalonga and now the Casa-Museu Llorenç Villalonga.

Inside, note the 18th-century wine vats and room set aside for the crushing of grapes underfoot. Summer concerts are held in the garden.

Ca'n Novell WINERY
(☎971 511 310; Carrer de Bonaire 17; ⏰8am-1pm & 3-8pm Mon-Fri, 8.30am-2pm Sat) To step back in time, wander into Ca'n Novell, where locals fill their own bottles from huge, 18th-century vats. Made of olive wood and held together by sturdy rings of oak, these grand old barrels were a standard feature of cellars and mansions across much of this part of the island.

Festivals & Events

Festes de la Verema WINE FESTIVAL
(22-30 Sep) Also known as the Festa d'es Vermar, this festival celebrates the yearly grape harvest with folk dancing, craft markets, exhibitions and lots of local tipples. It culminates in a big public supper of *fideuà de vermar* – a noodle dish with rabbit, snails and *sobrassada* (Mallorcan cured sausage).

Eating

Singló SPANISH, INTERNATIONAL €€
(☎971 870 599; Plaça de l'Església 5; mains €8-15) You can eat well at Singló. Despite the cafeteria feel, it offers some enticing dishes, such as *porcella rostida* (roast suckling pig) or *bacallà a la mallorquina* (cod prepared with tomato and potato). It also has an extensive wine list.

Getting There & Away

Binissalem is on the train line between Inca and Palma (€1.35).

Santa Eugènia

Amid the quiet back roads south of Binissalem is the town of Santa Eugènia, home to a few picturesque windmills, and lovely views from the hilltop on which it's perched.

Kids will love the **Natura Parc** (☎971 144 078; www.naturaparc.net; Carretera de Sineu Km15.4; adult/child 3-12yr/under 3yr €9/6/free; ⏰10am-6pm), a nature theme park with everything from kangaroos to flamingos prancing around. It's a couple of kilometres southwest of Santa Eugènia on the Ma3011 to Palma.

Delightful French fare is on offer at **L'Escargot** (☎971 144 535; www.watoo.net/lescargot; Carrer Major 48; mains €9-17; ⏰7.30-11pm Wed-Mon), a Gallic oasis occupying a two-storey home with a garden, and serving up French cuts of beef such as *onglet*, and tangy fruit crumble to follow.

The 311 bus from Santa Maria del Camí runs to Santa Eugènia, but only three or four times a day (€0.90, 15 minutes).

Inca

POP 23,400 / ELEV 130M

There are two main reasons for coming to Inca – it has some of the finest traditional cellar restaurants on the island and it's at the heart of the island's leather industry: Spanish shoemakers Camper and Farrutx started here. Otherwise, it's not the most attractive of places.

Sights

The first impression upon arriving in town is one of heat and traffic and the new town sprawls without much charm. That said, a stroll down Carrer Major to Plaça de Santa Maria Major, dominated by the **church** of the same name and lively cafes, is pleasant. Also worth checking out is the baroque **Claustre de Sant Domingo**, on Plaça de Sant Domingo.

For extraordinary views, head east out of Inca for 2km and take the turn-off to the **Ermita de Santa Magdalena**. Then head south another 2.5km and continue up **Puig de Santa Magdalena** (307m) to reach the *ermita* (chapel) – a privileged position from where your gaze will sweep across the plains to the Serra de Tramuntana and the Alcúdia and Pollença bays.

Festivals & Events

Dijous Bo TOWN FESTIVAL
(Holy Thursday; 3rd Thu of Nov) This is the town's biggest shindig, with processions, livestock competitions, sporting events and concerts.

Eating

A peculiarity of Inca is its *cellers,* basement restaurants in some of central Inca's oldest buildings. As a rule, you'll find hearty Mallorcan cooking, to be washed down with local wines. The latter were once stored in the enormous 18th-century barrels that still line the *cellers*' walls.

Inca

Top Sights

Claustre de Sant Domingo A1

Eating

1 Celler Ca'n Amer B1
2 Celler Ca'n Ripoll A1
3 Celler Sa Travessa B2

Shopping

4 Ballco B3
5 Carmina D1
6 Lottusse Outlet D1
7 Munper D1

Inca

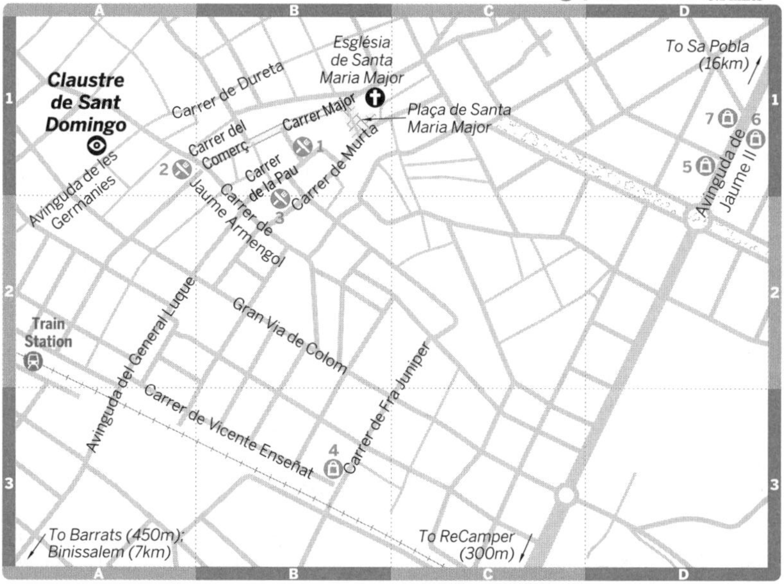

Celler Ca'n Amer SPANISH, MALLORCAN €€
(☎971 501 261; www.celler-canamer.com; Carrer de la Pau 139; mains €9-17; ⏲1-4pm & 7.30-11pm Mon-Sat, 1-4pm Sun) Typical Mallorcan cooking is the name of the game in this old house that seems out of place amid the more modern and impersonal buildings that surround it. The house specialty is lamb shoulder stuffed with eggplant and *sobrassada*.

Celler Ca'n Ripoll SPANISH, MALLORCAN €€
(☎971 507 639; www.cellercanripoll.com; Carrer de Jaume Armengol 4; mains €9.35-17.55; ⏲noon-4pm & 7.30-11.30pm Mon-Fri, noon-4pm & 8pm-midnight Sat & Sun) This enormous, cathedral-like 18th-century cellar features a high-beamed ceiling resting on a series of stone arches, and offers hearty meals with specialities such as roast suckling pig and fried eggs with *sobrassada* and chips. It's not quite valet parking but they can arrange a place to park your bike.

Celler Sa Travessa SPANISH, MALLORCAN €€
(☎971 500 049; Carrer de Murta 16; mains €9.50-19.50; ⏲1-4.30pm & 7-11.30pm Sat-Thu) In much the same category as Celler Ca'n Ripoll, house specialities here range from rabbit with onion to *llengua amb tàperes* (tongue with capers). Like most of Inca's cellar restaurants, it's big on atmosphere and a slice of Mallorca's inland past.

Shopping

Markets are staged in Inca on Thursdays, Fridays and Sundays, sprawling over a large part of the centre of town. The Thursday market is a major rural affair, and local leather is wheeled out in massive fashion. Leather goods, particularly shoes, are Inca's main shopping draw. Check out Gran Via de Colom, Avinguda de Jaume II and Avinguda del General Luque.

ReCamper SHOES
(☎902 364 598; www.camper.com; Polígon Industrial; ⏲10am-8pm Mon-Sat) Camper's factory outlet.

Lottusse Outlet SHOES, ACCESSORIES
(☎971 507 988; www.lottusse.com; Avinguda de Jaume II; ⏲10am-8.30pm Mon-Sat) Upmarket shoes and accessories.

Carmina SHOES
(☎971 880 938; www.carminashoemaker.com; Avinguda de Jaume II; ⏲10am-8pm Mon-Fri, 10am-2pm Sat) One of the biggest of Mallorca's shoe manufacturers.

Munper LEATHER GOODS
(☎971 881 000; www.munper.com; Avinguda de Jaume II; ⏲9.30am-7pm Mon-Fri, 9.30am-2pm Sat) Leather goods from a variety of brands.

Ballco SHOES
(☎971 500 810; www.ballco.com; Carrer de Vicente Enseñat 87; ⏲10am-8pm Mon-Fri, 10am-2pm Sat) Another long-standing shoe manufacturer.

Barrats SHOES
(☎971 500 803; www.barrats1890.com; Avinguda del General Luque 480; ⏲10am-8pm Mon-Fri, 10am-2pm Sat) Classics for men, brights for women.

Getting There & Away

If you're not driving down the Ma13 motorway from Palma, get the train along the same route, which runs frequently (€1.80, 35 to 40 minutes).

Around Inca

A scattering of towns and hamlets riding up into the foothills of the Serra de Tramuntana invites gentle touring.

LLOSETA & AROUND

Three kilometres west of Inca is **Lloseta**, another shoemaking town. In early June it stages a fair in Plaça d'Espanya with local shoe manufacturers. In Lloseta itself there's a fine place to stay, another to eat, and a good winery – what more could you need?

Sights

Bodegas Castell Miquel WINERY
(☎971 510 698; www.castellmiquel.com; Carretera Alaró-Lloseta Km8.7; ⏲4-8pm Mon-Fri) About 1.5km west of Lloseta on the road to Alaró is the German-owned, prize-winning Bodegas Castell Miquel. You can't miss the place – it looks like a little white castle. Along with wine, the German pharmaceutical professor who runs it, Dr Michael Popp, has developed a red-wine pill, Resveroxan, that supposedly contributes to a longer and healthier life.

Oli Caimari OLIVE OIL FACTORY
(☎971 873 577; www.aceites-olicaimari.com; Carretera Inca-Lluc Km6; ⏲9am-8pm Mon-Sat, 10am-2pm Sun) Caimari, north of Lloseta, is known for olive oil. Visit the factory and shop of Oli Caimari. The best time to visit is in November and December, when the oil is made.

Eating

Celler Ca'n Carrossa SPANISH, MALLORCAN €€
(☎971 514 023; Carrer Nou 28; mains €9-17; ⏲1-3.30pm & 7-11pm Tue-Sun) In Lloseta, here you

can sit inside by the exposed stone walls or opt for the garden. Despite residing inland, its fish dishes are especially regarded. Book ahead.

BINIBONA

A narrow lane northeast out of Caimari leads to the intriguing hamlet of Binibona. With its back to the Serra de Tramuntana, accessible only by quiet country byways and serenaded by sheep and cowbells, it has become a much-sought-out spot for those in search of tranquil but stylish rural getaways.

CAMPANET

Three kilometres south of Binibona is Moscari, from where you branch east for 2.5km to Campanet, the most engaging of all these villages. Encrusted onto a sharp ridge, the town's central square, Plaça Major, is dominated by a gaunt Gothic church, but the surrounding cafes are busier than the ill-attended Mass.

Almost 3km north of Campanet, set in a beautiful stretch of little-visited countryside, there's a small country chapel, the bricked-up **Oratori de Sant Miquel**. Just beyond are the Coves de Campanet.

Sights

Coves de Campanet CAVES
(971 516 130; www.covesdecampanet.com; Camí de ses Coves; adult/child over 10yr €11/5; 10am-7pm Apr-Sep, 10am-6pm Oct-Mar) Just over 3km from Campanet, these caves aren't as impressive as the Coves del Drac in Porto Cristo, but they're still wonderful, with stalactites and stalagmites in abundance. There are guided tours every 45 minutes and visits last just under an hour. Scientists find these caves especially interesting as they're home to a local species of blind, flesh-eating beetle.

Posada de Biniatró GALLERY
(971 509 530; Carrer de Miquel 20; 10am-1pm & 7.30-9.30pm Tue, 10am-1pm Wed-Fri, 7.30-9.30pm Sat) Just downhill from Campanet's Plaça Major, the Posada de Biniatró is a three-storey town house exhibiting works by a battery of island artists born from 1950 on, among them Miquel Barceló.

Eating

Can Calco MALLORCAN €€€
(971 515 260; www.cancalco.com; Carrer Campanet 1; set menus €26-32; 1-3.30pm & 7-10.30pm Tue-Sat) In the hotel of the same name, this poolside restaurant serves up thoughtfully presented dishes – the emphasis is on seafood (although there are some meat dishes) and all dishes are prepared according to Mallorcan traditions. It has its own boat in Badia d'Alcúdia, so the catch couldn't be fresher.

SOUTH OF INCA

A brief loop immediately south of Inca has the town of Sineu as its main objective. Follow the Ma3440 southeast for 8km and you hit upon **Llubí**. It is especially worth the effort for the **Festa del Siurell** on the Saturday before the Tuesday of Carnaval. This singular bit of fun involves townsfolk dressing up as *siurells*, the traditional Mallorcan whistles. That night, a big *siurell* is burned in effigy in Plaça de l'Església, which is dominated by the outsized parish church, the **Església de Sant Feliu**.

FINE POSSESSIONS

In rural Mallorca, the most powerful families owned grand farmsteads. Their Arab predecessors had been known as *alqueries*, but to the Christians who took over the island after 1229, they came to be called *possessions*. The oldest, dating to the 14th and even 13th centuries, had a marked defensive character, with watchtowers and forbidding walls that opened onto a *clastra* (courtyard). Over the following centuries these farmsteads became more complex. In the main building, the (often absentee) señors (lords) of the property would have their residence. In the surrounding outbuildings – *ses cases* (the houses) – would be located the dwelling of the *amo* (the main resident farmer and local boss), along with the *tafona* (olive press), *celler* (cellar), mill and other farm buildings. With the rapid decline in agriculture in Mallorca since the 1960s, many *possessions* were abandoned, but curiously the phenomenon that helped rob them of their purpose – tourism – might save them from destruction. A growing number are being converted into rural lodgings for tourists or places to visit. Three of our favourites for passing an afternoon:

» **Raixa** (p99)

» **La Granja** (p86)

» **Els Calderers** (p130)

Sineu

POP 2785 / ELEV 151M

Seven kilometres southeast of Inca along the Ma3240, the dense, ochre mass of Sineu rises on the horizon, draped across a ridgeback. This is without a doubt one of the most engaging of Mallorca's inland rural towns. It's also one of the oldest – a local legend traces the town's origins back to Roman Sinium, while the link to the Islamic settlement of Sixneu is less tenuous.

Sights

At Sineu's heart is Sa Plaça, a busy square fronted by several bars and the crumbling sandstone, late-Gothic facade of the 16th-century **Església de Santa Maria**; some local historians claim that the church's origins date to the 13th century. Other historic buildings are scattered around town.

On Plaça des Fossar, a **statue** honours Francisco Alomar, a Sineu-born professional cyclist who died in 1955; it has something of cult status among visiting cyclists.

Sineu is famous throughout Mallorca for its markets. Downhill on the southeast flank of the town, Plaça des Fossar is where the town's big market days are held; the weekly Wednesday market also takes over Sa Plaça up in the old town.

Convent dels Mínims HISTORIC BUILDING
(Ajuntament; Carrer de Sant Francesc) North of Sa Plaça, the town hall is housed in this 17th-century baroque convent. You can generally wander in any time to admire the somewhat neglected cloister. One block west is a beautiful example of a waymarking cross, the 1585 **Creu dels Morts** (Cross of the Dead).

Convent de la Concepció HISTORIC BUILDING
(Carrer del Palau 17) This 17th-century convent, an adaptation of the prior Muslim *al-qasr* (castle) and a two-minute stroll southwest of Sa Plaça, has a *torno,* a small revolving door through which you can receive pastries made by the nuns in return for a few euros. It was in the convent where King Jaume II had his inland residence built, making Sineu the de facto capital of rural Mallorca.

S'Estació Contemporary Art Museum MUSEUM
(☎971 520 750; www.sineuestacio.com; Carrer de S'Estació 2; ⏲9.30am-2pm & 4-7pm Mon-Fri, 10am-1pm Sat) One hundred metres east of Plaça des Fossar is this whimsical, German-run museum, where local and foreign-resident contemporary artists display work on three floors.

Festivals & Events

Sineu's Easter processions are also some of the largest on Mallorca.

Sa Fira LIVESTOCK MARKET
(Plaça des Fossar; 1st Sun May) Sineu's annual Sa Fira is a major produce market held on the first Sunday of May and dating to 1318.

Fira de Sant Tomás TOWN FESTIVAL
(2nd Sun Dec) In the depths of winter, the Fira de Sant Tomás features the annual *matanza* (pig slaughter). It's not for the faint-hearted.

Eating

Celler Es Grop MALLORCAN €€
(☎971 520 187; Carrer Major 18; mains €7.80-18.60; ⏲9.30am-4pm & 7-11pm Tue-Thu, 11am-4pm & 7pm-midnight Fri-Sun) Watch your step as you descend into this cheerful old whitewashed cellar with huge, old wine vats. The roast spring lamb vies with the rice dishes for our favourite order. It's around 100m northeast of Sa Plaça.

Restaurante Sa Boveda SPANISH, MEDITERRANEAN €€
(☎971 520 211; www.hotel-leondesineu.com; Carrer dels Bous 129; mains €8.50-16; ⏲1-3.30pm & 7-10.30pm) The basement restaurant of Hotel León de Sineu combines a lovely basement setting with innovative cooking. Unusually,

GIVING MURANO A RUN FOR ITS MONEY

It's believed the Phoenicians introduced glassmaking to Mallorca in the 2nd century BC, although by the Middle Ages, the supreme European glassmakers were those of Murano, in Venice. The story goes that one such artisan, Domenico Barrovier, sought refuge in Mallorca and passed on his know-how. By the 17th century, Mallorcan glass was competing on European markets. In 1719, the Gordiola family got involved in the business and after decades of difficulties, Gordiola's glass began to achieve recognition, and the family has almost single-handedly maintained the island's glass tradition to this day.

it also has set evening menus, which are terrific value for €16.90.

Celler Ca'n Font SPANISH, MALLORCAN €€
(☎971 520 313; www.canfont.com; Sa Plaça 18; mains €11.50-19.90; ⏲8.30am-3pm & 7.30-11pm Wed, 11am-4pm & 7.30-11pm Fri-Tue) Occupying one of Mallorca's oldest wine cellars, Ca'n Font serves up typical Mallorcan cooking such as *frito mallorquín* (fried lamb offal), stuffed eggplant and roast suckling lamb and pig. You eat surrounded by ancient oak barrels.

Soultapas TAPAS €
(☎971 520 508; Carrer Creu 2; tapas €2.50-14.50, 5 tapas €19.90; ⏲6pm-midnight Tue & Thu-Sat, 9am-3pm & 6pm-midnight Wed, 2pm-midnight Sun) This vaguely hip tapas bar serves up creative alternatives to the cellar cooking elsewhere in bright modern surroundings – the *pa amb oli entrecote de Argentina* (local bread, tomato and a fine cut of Argentine steak; €14.50) is a meal in itself.

Getting There & Away

Trains on the Palma–Manacor line run here (from Palma €1.75, 50 minutes). The station is about 100m from Plaça des Fossar.

Sa Pobla & Muro

Sa Pobla, a grid-street rural centre and the end of the (railway) line from Palma, is in Mallorca's agricultural heartland. Five kilometres south across the potato flats from Sa Pobla, Muro boasts the sandstone Església de Sant Joan Baptista, a brooding Gothic creation reminiscent of Sineu's main church.

Sights & Activities

Sa Pobla hosts a lively Sunday market.

Bodegas Crestatx WINERY
(☎971 540 741; www.bodegascrestatx.com; Carrer de Joan Sindic ; ⏲9am-1pm) One of the longest-standing winemakers on the island, Bodegas Crestatx is well worth a visit.

FREE **Can Planes** MUSEUM
(☎971 542 389; www.ajsapobla.net; Carrer d'Antoni Maura 6; ⏲10am-2pm & 4-8pm Tue-Sat, 10am-2pm Sun & holidays) Can Planes houses the **Museu d'Art Contemporani**, a changing display of works by Mallorquin and foreign artists residing on the island. Upstairs, the **Museu de Sa Jugueta Antiga** is a touching collection of old toys, some with a bullfighting theme.

Festivals & Events

Mallorca Jazz Festival MUSIC
(www.jazzinmallorca.com; Aug) Jazz comes to Sa Pobla for the annual Mallorca Jazz Festival.

Festes de Sant Antoni Abat TOWN FESTIVAL
(16-17 Jan) This festival has a little bit of everything with processions, fireworks, folk music, dancing and blessings for work animals. The night of the 16th is the most lively time.

Getting There & Away

Sa Pobla is an hour by train from Palma (€2.40, 57 minutes) via Inca. The station, where buses also terminate, is about 1km southeast of central Plaça de la Constitució. Muro is on the same line.

THE SOUTHEAST

Small hamlets lie scattered across this region of Mallorca. While few warrant more than a passing glance, they sit alongside numerous wineries and sometimes in the shadow of former monasteries high on the hilltops. Apart from wine, local products to track down here include pearls, woodwork and glasswork. The two main towns of the region, Manacor and Felanitx, are useful for orienting yourself but otherwise have little to offer.

Algaida

POP 3775 / ELEV 201M

Centred on a Gothic church, the **Església de Sant Pere i Sant Pau**, this quiet farming community kicks up its heels for the **Festes de Sant Honorat** (16 January) and the **Festa de Sant Jaume** (25 July). On both occasions, *cossiers* dance for an appreciative local audience. The origins of the *cossiers* and their dances are disputed. A group of dancers (six men and one woman), accompanied by a devil, perform various pieces that end in defeat for the demon.

Sights

FREE **Museu de Gordiola** GLASSWORKS FACTORY, MUSEUM
(☎971 665 046; www.gordiola.com; Carretera Palma-Manacor Km19; ⏲9am-7pm Mon-Sat, 9.30am-1.30pm Sun) Algaida's main attraction lies 2.5km west on the Ma15. The Gordiola glassworks, set in a mock-Gothic palace, has a factory area on the ground floor where you can observe the glassmakers working and

WORTH A TRIP

SANTUARI DE NOSTRA SENYORA DE CURA

Southwest of Algaida rises the 548m hill of Puig de Randa, atop which stands this gracious monastery, the **Santuari de Nostra Senyora de Cura**. As with most such monasteries, it was built partly for defence purposes. Ramon Llull lived here as a hermit, praying in a cave (now closed to visitors). In the 16th century, the Estudi General (university) in Palma created the Col·legi de Gramàtica here, and for centuries thereafter live-in students grappled with the complexities of Latin grammar, rhetoric and other classical disciplines.

There's a decent bar-restaurant within the monastery grounds.

The Santuari, which is variously signposted as 'Santuari de Cura' or simply 'Cura', is 5km beyond the small village of Randa.

sweating. Upstairs, the museum has a curious collection of glass items from around the world. The on-site shop contains some lovely pieces amid the tack.

Eating

Can Mateu MALLORCAN €€
(☎971 665 036; www.can-mateu.com; Carretera Vella de Manacor Km21; mains €10.50-19.50; ⏲1-4.30pm & 7-11.30pm Wed-Mon Mar-Jan) Around 1km from Algaida along the Ma3131 towards Pina, this sprawling roadside restaurant offers Mallorcan classics, like *frit Mallorquín* (fried lamb innards), *cargols* (snails), *arros brut* (dirty rice, a traditional dish) and *conejo con cebolla y gambas* (rabbit with onions and prawns).

Getting There & Away

Various buses heading from Palma to the east coast stop here (€1.85, 20 to 25 minutes). The most regular service is the 490 Palma–Felanitx run (five to nine services daily).

Montuïri & Around

Montuïri, on a sharp ridge 8km northeast of Randa on the Ma5017, is known for its apricots. That very colour infuses the place with a soft glow in the early morning. The sandstone **Església de Sant Bartomeu** dominates Plaça Major, through which runs Carrer Major, graced by the occasional mansion and bar.

A few kilometres south is **Porreres**, a typical inland Mallorcan town that has always been a reasonably prosperous agricultural centre, sustained by wheat, fig, carob and wine crops. The local winery is the main reason to pass through.

Pina lies 5.5km northwest of Montuïri. Stop for a look at **Sa Font**, one of the few reminders of the Arab presence on the island. This complex *qanawat* (well and water distribution structure) is difficult to date but was taken over by the Muslims' Christian successors after 1229. It lies 50m south of the **Església de Sants Cosme i Damià**, on the road to Lloret de Vistalegre.

Sights

Museu Arqueològic de Son Fornés ARCHAEOLOGICAL MUSEUM
(☎971 644 169; www.sonfornes.mallorca.museum; Carrer d'Emili Pou; adult/student €3/1.80; ⏲10am-2pm & 4-8pm Tue-Sun Mar-Oct, 10am-2pm Tue-Sun Nov-Feb) On the eastern exit of town heading for Lloret de Vistalegre (the Ma3220), this museum is housed in a cactus-fronted former mill and explains the history of the Son Fornés *talayot* (watchtower), which was inhabited from around 900 BC to the 4th century AD.

The *talayot* is one of the most important on the island and easy enough to visit. Head 2.5km northwest out of Montuïri on the Ma3200 towards Pina and you'll see it to the right (east) of the road.

Jaume Mesquida Winery WINERY
(☎971 647 106; www.jaumemesquida.com; Carrer de la Vileta 7; ⏲by appointment) With a range of whites, reds and rosés, and a commitment to sustainable production, this relative newcomer on Mallorca's winemaking scene is worth visiting – it arranges tastings, bike rides and even meals with wines as the centrepiece.

Els Calderers HISTORIC BUILDING, MUSEUM
(☎971 526 069; www.elscalderers.com; adult/child €8/4; ⏲10am-6pm Apr-Sep, 10am-5pm Oct-Mar) About 4km southeast of Sant Joan, on a pretty country back road, this stout rural mansion has been converted into a period museum. Els Calderers was built around

1750, although the estate has been occupied since the 13th century. The mansion may lack the grandeur and elegant decay of other such Mallorcan estates, but is nonetheless well worth the detour.

On the ground floor of the main building, around a leafy courtyard, are the main salons and guest rooms, along with the family chapel and wine cellar (every decent *finca* had one of each). You can sample a little house red. As a letter from 1895 (on display) notes, the Els Calderers wine was *muy flojito* (very average). This doesn't seem to have changed.

🎉 Festivals & Events

Festa de Sant Bartomeu TOWN FESTIVAL
(24 Aug) The main event of this celebration in honour of Montuïri's patron saint is traditional dancing by the *cossiers* (both on the eve and the 24th).

S'Encuentro RELIGIOUS
(Easter Sun) On Easter Sunday, a figure of Christ resurrected is met in a parade by a figure of the Virgin Mary, who does some excited hops to show her joy at the resurrection of her son.

Petra

POP 2010 / ELEV 120M

The charms of Petra aren't immediately apparent, but stay even a little while and its long, straight and narrow streets and stone houses will quickly grow on you. With an in-town winery, a couple of terrific places to eat and an interesting little museum, it's the sort of place where you'll most likely stay longer than you planned, and be very happy you did so.

◎ Sights

Petra's principal claim to historical fame is its favourite son, Juníper Serra, born here in 1713. A Franciscan missionary and one of the founders of what is now the US state of California, he could have had no inkling of his destiny as he grew up in this rural centre. The street on which the museum dedicated to his life is located is one of the prettiest in Mallorca.

Ermita de la Mare de Déu de Bonany MONASTERY
Four kilometres southwest of Petra on a wooded hill stands this hermitage where Juníper Serra gave his last sermon in Mallorca before heading for the New World. Elements of the present church date to the 18th

century but the place was overhauled in 1925. The views over the plains are magnificent.

Museu Fra Juníper Serra MUSEUM
(☑971 561 028; www.frayjuniperoserra.org; Carrer des Barracar Alt 6; ☺by appointment) The Museu Fra Juníper Serra contains mementos of Juníper Serra's missionary life. Next door at No 4 is the house in which he was born. Walk to Carrer des Barracar Baix 2 and ring the bell. If you get lucky, you'll get admission to the house and museum. All over the streets in this part of town are ceramic depictions of his eventful life.

Bodegas Miquel Oliver WINERY
(☑971 561 117; www.miqueloliver.com; Carrer de Sa Font 26; ☺10am-2pm & 3.30-6.30pm Mon-Fri) Bodegas Miquel Oliver is one of the island's most respected winemakers.

🍴 Eating

Es Celler MALLORCAN €
(☑971 561 056; escellerdepetra.blogspot.com; Carrer de l'Hospital 46; mains €7.40-12.75; ☺noon-midnight Tue-Sun) Step down off the street and into this wonderfully cavernous cellar restaurant with soaring ceilings and old wine barrels. The specialities are barbecued meats, roast lamb and roast suckling pig, and it's hugely popular with locals and tourists alike.

Ca N'Oms SPANISH, MALLORCAN €€
(☑971 561 920; www.canoms.com; Carrer de Caparrot de Ca N'Oms 7; mains €6.50-12; ☺8am-1am) This is a lovely place to eat fine variations on *pa amb oli*, including with cuttlefish, but it's also a wonderful chillout space with a designer touch and occasional live music in the evenings. The shady garden is perfect on a warm summer's evening.

ℹ Getting There & Away

Petra is one stop short of Manacor (nine minutes) on the Palma–Manacor train line and gets at least one service a day in both directions. From Palma the trip takes just under an hour and costs €2.25.

Manacor

POP 32,200 / ELEV 128M

Manacor, the island's second-largest city, is perhaps best known as the birthplace of tennis great Rafael Nadal and as a centre of furniture manufacturing. That we mention such things should speak volumes for its tourist appeal. That said, it does have a strik-

Manacor

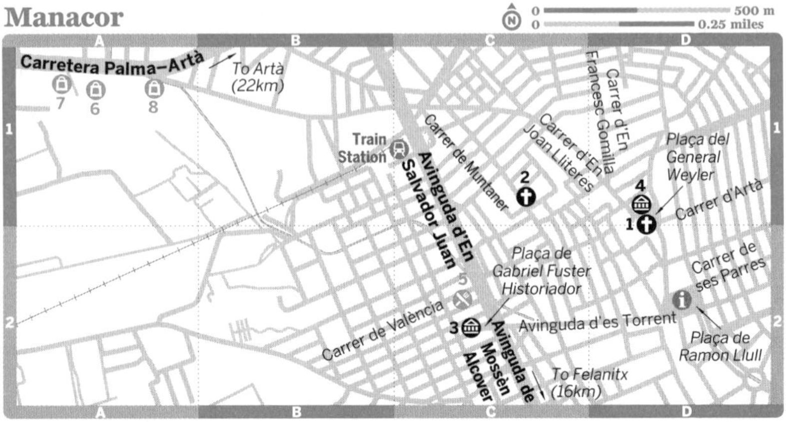

Manacor

Sights

1 Església de Nostra Senyora Verge dels Dolors D1
2 Església de Sant Vicenç Ferrer C1
3 Torre de Ses Puntes C2
4 Torre del Palau D1

Eating

5 Ca'n March C2

Shopping

6 Majorica Showroom A1
7 Oliv-Art A1
8 Orquidea A1

ing church at its centre, and there's some fine shopping to be had in the vicinity – from wineries to Mallorca's world-famous pearls, all on the city's outskirts.

Sights

FREE Església de Nostra Senyora Verge dels Dolors CHURCH
(☎971 554 348; Plaça del General Weyler; ⏰8.30am-12.45pm & 5.30-7.30pm) The massive Església de Nostra Senyora Verge dels Dolors lords it impressively over the Manacor skyline. It was raised on the site of the town's former mosque and has a hybrid Gothic/neo-Gothic style, which reflects the fact that construction began in the 14th century and wasn't completed until the 19th century.

Torre del Palau HISTORIC BUILDING
(off Plaça del General Weyler) A short distance north of the main church, in the courtyard of an apartment block, is the dishevelled Torre del Palau, all that remains of a royal residence that Jaume II began in the late 13th century.

FREE Església de Sant Vicenç Ferrer CHURCH, CLOISTER
(Carrer de Muntaner; ⏰8am-2pm & 5-8pm Mon-Fri) On the corner of Carrer de Muntaner is the baroque Església de Sant Vicenç Ferrer, which first opened for worship in 1617. It's attached to a fetching 18th-century cloister, now home to government offices.

FREE Torre de Ses Puntes GALLERY, HISTORIC BUILDING
(☎971 844 741; Plaça de Gabriel Fuster Historiador; ⏰6.30pm-8.30pm) Once part of the city's defences, this 14th-century tower is now used for exhibitions.

Toni Gelabert WINERY
(☎971 552 409; www.vinstonigelabert.com; Camí dels Horts de Llodrà Km1.3; ⏰by appointment) The family-run winery of Toni Gelabert does some superb whites. Take the Ma14 south out of Manacor; after 2km is a small sign on the right to the vineyard.

Eating

Ca'n March SEAFOOD, MALLORCAN €€
(☎971 550 002; www.canmarch.com; Carrer de València 7; mains €9-14; ⏰1-3.30pm & 8.30-11pm Fri & Sat, 1-3.30pm Sun & Tue-Thu; 🚭📝) Fish is the house strong point here, prepared with a minimum of fuss using salt from Es Trenc and island olive oil. Other dishes have a more adventurous touch, such as lamb in a date sauce, and lightly spiced Asian dishes. It's a block north of the Torre de Ses Puntes.

DON'T MISS

SANTUARI DE SANT SALVADOR

One of the most spectacular viewpoints in inland Mallorca, **Santuari de Sant Salvador** is a hilltop hermitage 5km southeast of Felanitx. The hermitage was originally built in 1348, the year of one of the most disastrous waves of plague in Europe. Perhaps here, far from ports and towns, the hermits were safe. It has undergone several refits since then. The main **church** (8am to 11pm) is a strange mix with gaudy columns and an elaborate cave nativity scene offset by a pleasantly unadorned barrel-vaulted ceiling and delicately carved stone altarpiece. Apart from the monastery, there's a prominent cross (built in 1957) on a neighbouring peak, while the car park is crowned by an enormous statue of Christ the King. At every turn, the views are heavenly.

In addition to the sleeping quarters, there's a small **cafe** (8am-7pm) and **restaurant** (6.30-9pm).

Shopping

Most visitors come to Manacor for the manufactured pearls, but you'll also find some fine woodwork on sale. There's a **craft market** on Plaça Sa Bassa on Saturday mornings.

Majorica Showroom PEARLS
(971 550 900; www.majorica.com; Carretera Palma-Artà Km47; 9am-8pm Mon-Fri, 9am-7pm Sat & Sun) Majorica is the best-known Manacor pearl manufacturer. The company was founded by Eduard Heusch, a German, in 1902 and now has its two-storey showroom on the edge of town on the road to Palma. Upstairs you can see a handful of people working on the creation of pearls, but the real factory is elsewhere and not open to visits.

Orquidea PEARLS
(971 644 144; www.perlasorquidea.com; Carretera Palma-Artà Km47; 9am-7pm Mon-Fri, 9am-1pm Sat & Sun) Orquidea, a two-minute walk closer to the centre of town than its competition, Majorica, is another purveyor of Mallorcan pearls.

Oliv-Art WOODWORK
(971 847 232; Carretera Palma-Artà Km47; 9am-7pm Mon-Fri, 9am-6pm Sat & Sun) Products made from olive wood fill this large warehouse-style shop, with some stunning woodwork mixed in among the tourist kitsch. From Monday to Friday, you can watch the woodworkers at work through the window. It's on the Palma approach to town, next to Majorica.

Information

Tourist office (971 847 241; www.visitmanacor.com; Plaça de Ramon Llull; 9.30am-2pm Mon, 9.30am-1.30pm Tue-Fri) In the town centre.

Getting There & Away

The train from Palma runs once an hour (€2.40, one hour). Various buses on cross-island routes also call in, terminating in front of the train station, a 10-minute walk from Plaça del General Weyler.

Felanitx

Felanitx is an important regional centre with a reputation for ceramics, white wine and capers (of the culinary variety). It makes an interesting stop in its own right, and as a gateway to two interesting hilltop monuments nearby – the Castell de Santueri and the Santuari de Sant Salvador.

Sights

Castell de Santueri CASTLE
Around 7km south of Felanitx, the proud walls of this castle turn a craggy peak into a defensive bastion. The castle was built by the Muslims, and not taken until 1231, two years after the rest of the island had fallen.

To get here, take the Ma14 for 2km, then follow the signs to the left (east). The road winds 5km to the base of the castle's white walls. You can scramble up to the (closed) entrance, from where views extend southeast far out to sea.

Església de Sant Miquel CHURCH
(Plaça de Sa Font de Santa Margalida) Lording it over the heart of town, this church has a baroque facade and acquired its current form in 1762. Above the Renaissance portal stands a relief of St Michael, sticking it to a discomfited-looking devil underfoot. Across the road, a flight of steps leads down to the Font, once the main town well.

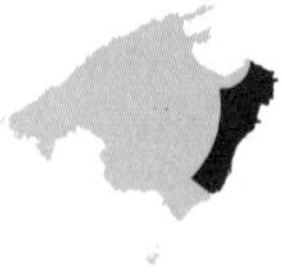

Eastern Mallorca

Includes »

Artà 136
Parc Natural de la Península de Llevant 138
Capdepera 139
Cala Ratjada........140
Coves d'Artà & Platja de Canyamel........143
Cala Millor & Around.............144
Porto Cristo 145
Portocolom.........147

Best Places to Eat

» Porxada de Sa Torre (p144)

» Bar Parisien (p138)

» Ca'n Pere (p141)

» Restaurant Sa Sinia (p149)

» Mar de Vins (p138)

Best Places to Stay

» Cases de Son Barbassa (p173)

» Hostal Porto Colom (p173)

» Agroturisme S'Horta (p173)

» Hotel Casal d'Artà (p172)

» Residence - The Sea Club (p173)

Why Go?

There's a reason that tourists arrive in Eastern Mallorca in their hundreds of thousands on their annual sun pilgrimage: this is one of the prettiests coasts on an island of many. Yes, there are stretches of coastline that can seem like a poster child for all that's abhorrent about Mediterranean coastal tourism. But Mallorca's rocky eastern walls conceal perfectly formed caves, coves and inlets, some of which are accessible only on foot – among these are Mallorca's most beautiful, with turquoise waters and with nary a hotel in sight. There are even resorts that are actually rather handsome, most notably Cala Ratjada with its picturesque harbour and wild coastal beaches nearby. Also here is medieval Artà, one of the island's better-preserved inland towns.

When to Go

You could be forgiven for thinking that Eastern Mallorca hibernates throughout the winter, rumbling into life only from April to October. There's an element of truth in this: many restaurants, hotels and other businesses only open in these months (sometimes waiting until May to dust off the cobwebs). That said, winters are relatively mild and the beauty of Eastern Mallorca's coastal inlets have an alluring charm without the crowds, as long as you don't wish to swim. Plus most towns and villages celebrate Sant Antoni with great gusto in mid-January.

Eastern Mallorca Highlights

1 Hike the wooded hills of the **Parc Natural de la Península de Llevant** (p138) to reach unspoilt coves

2 Soak up the rays at Cala Ratjada's **Platja de Cala Agulla** (p140)

3 Eat well down in town, then climb to the summit of **Artà** (p136)

4 Delve into the centre of the earth at the **Coves del Drac** (p145), Mallorca's most spectacular caves

5 Eat traditional Mallorcan cooking at **Porxada de Sa Torre** (p144)

6 Explore Mallorca's ancient history at **Ses Païsses** (p137), accompanied by birdsong

7 Walk from one beautiful cove to the next ending at sublime **Cala Magraner** (p146)

8 Search for princesses at the **Castell de Capdepera** (p139)

9 Savour the luxury of Mallorcan rural estates at **Cases de Son Barbassa** (p173)

10 Discover a whole new world beneath the Mediterranean's surface at **Portocolom** (p147)

ARTÀ & AROUND

Boasting the poetic distinction of being the first place in Mallorca to receive the morning sunlight, the island's northeastern corner is a refreshingly low-key area where rounded hills stubbled with green radiate out in every direction, and calm, pine-lined beaches (a number of which are accessible only by foot, horseback or boat) dot the coastline. Fascinating historic monuments, good hiking territory and one of the best beach resorts on the east coast all provide convincing excuses for a visit.

Artà

POP 6845

The antithesis of the buzzing resort culture found just a few kilometres away, the quiet inland town of Artà beckons with its maze of narrow streets, appealing cafes and medieval architecture, which culminates in an impressive 14th-century hilltop fortress that dominates the town centre.

Sights

Begin on Carrer de la Ciutat, the prettiest street in town, which is lined with shops, restaurants and squares rimmed with cafes.

Artà

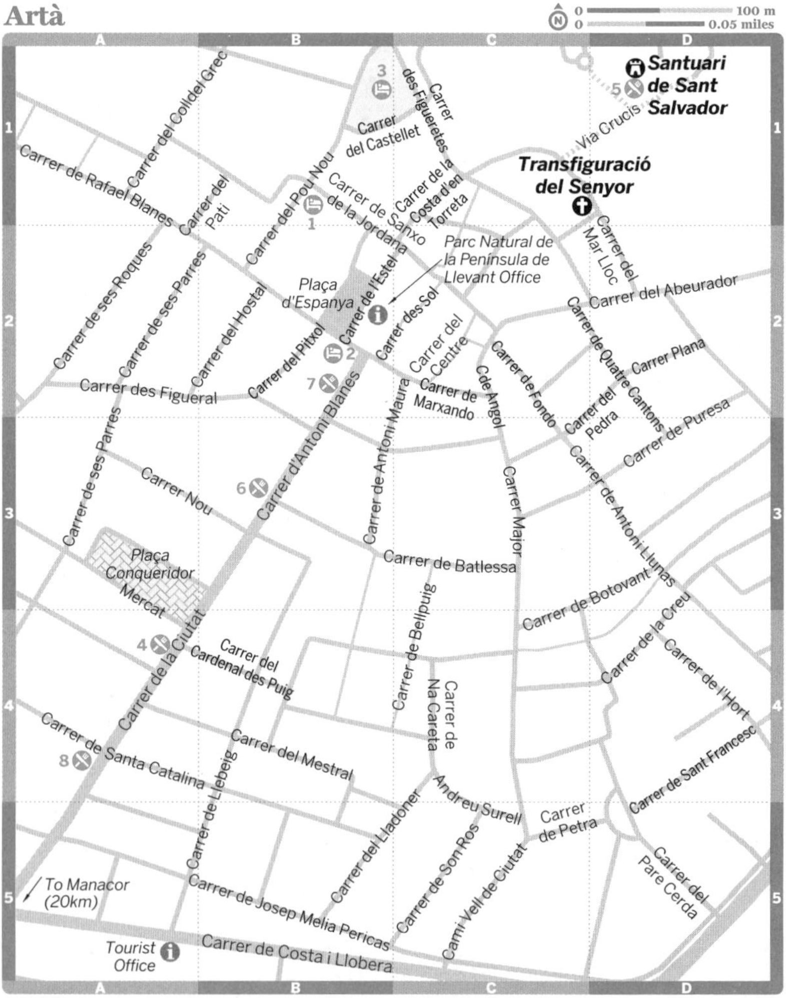

Head uphill to reach the historic centre – at its heart is the shaded Plaça d'Espanya, home to the pretty Ajuntament (town hall) building. On Tuesdays, a market sets up on Plaça Conqueridor.

Santuari de Sant Salvador CASTLE, CHURCH
(Via Crucis; ⏲8am-8pm Apr-Oct, 8am-6pm Nov-Mar) Atop the hill overlooking Artà, this walled fortress, built atop an earlier Moorish enclave and enclosing a small church, is a fascinating perch from which to survey the lay of the land.

A much-restored 4000-sq-metre complex, it boasts all the elements of a medieval fortress, down to the stone turrets ringing the top and the metre-thick walls. The views from here sweep over the rooftops of town, those of stone farmhouses and beyond to the bald, bumpy peaks of the Serra de Llevant.

The walls were built in the 14th century to protect the town from pirates or invaders. Now you'll find walkways, a simple cafeteria and an unremarkable salmon-coloured neoclassical church, which was built in 1832 after the modest chapel that pre-dated it was purposely burnt to the ground following a cholera epidemic.

From the Transfiguració del Senyor parish church, 180 steps lead up here along the grand, cypress-lined Via Crucis (Way of the Cross). You can also reach Sant Salvador by road.

Transfiguració del Senyor CHURCH, MUSEUM
(Carrer del Mar Lloc; admission €2; ⏲10am-2pm & 3-6pm Mon-Sat) This church, built atop the foundations of a Moorish mosque at the foot of the climb to the Santuari de Sant Salvador, was begun soon after the Christian reconquest, although the facade dates to the 16th century. Inside, note the large rose window, an ornately carved wooden pulpit, and an altar painting depicting Christ on Mount Tabor.

Artà

Top Sights

Santuari de Sant Salvador	D1
Transfiguració del Senyor	C1

Sleeping

1	Can Moragues	B1
2	Hotel Casal d'Artà	B2
3	Hotel Sant Salvador	B1

Eating

4	Bar Parisien	A4
5	Cafeteria Sant Salvador	D1
6	Mar de Vins	B3
7	Pedra i Flor	B2
8	Salvad'or	A4

DON'T MISS

EASTERN MALLORCA'S BEST BEACHES

- » **Cala Magraner**
- » **Cala Sa Nau**
- » **Cala Mitjana**
- » **Cala Marçal**
- » **Platja de Cala Agulla**
- » **Cala Matzoc**

Ses Païsses ARCHAEOLOGICAL SITE
(☎619 070 010; off Carretera Artà-Capdepera; admission €2; ⏲10am-5pm Mon-Fri, 10am-2pm Sat) Just beyond Artà proper lie the remains of a 3000-year-old settlement, the largest and most important Talayotic site on Mallorca's eastern flank. The site's looming stone gateway is an impressive transition into the world of prehistoric Mallorca, a world still shrouded in mystery.

We know little about the inhabitants' social or religious lives, but security was clearly an issue: they lived behind a double ring of stone walls, built between 650 BC and 540 BC. Within them, small stone houses were built in a circular pattern around a central *talayot,* or watchtower. This was a centre of some size – the walls' perimeter extends 320m. The site was abandoned after the Roman arrival in the 2nd century BC.

You could easily spend an hour or two wandering around the site, shaded by trees and serenaded by birdsong. To get the most out of your visit, buy the guidebook for sale at the site.

It's easy to get here from Artà. From the large roundabout east of the tourist office, follow the signs towards Ses Païsses; if you're walking or cycling, it's less than a kilometre from the main road.

Activities

The tourist office gives out an excellent brochure called *Bike Tours* that includes a dozen route maps and descriptions through the area that you can complete on foot or by bike. Particularly recommended is the demanding route (about 7km) from Artà to the Ermita de Betlem hermitage.

Artà Move TOURS, BICYCLE RENTAL
(☎654 399 262; www.artamove.com; bicycle hire half/full day from €12/20) This local activities company rents out bikes, as well as offering guided hiking and mountain-biking through the Parc Natural de la Península de Llevant.

Festivals & Events

Festes de Sant Antoni Abat TOWN FESTIVAL
(16-17 Jan) During this curious festival, everyone dresses in traditional costume and heads to the Santuari de Sant Salvador for dancing, music and a downright odd display of backward-facing equestrians swinging long sticks.

Eating

The gastronomy in Artà is top rate, with a string of charming eateries (many with terraces or sidewalk seating) running along Carrer de la Ciutat and other finds scattered around town.

Bar Parisien SPANISH, MEDITERRANEAN €€
(☎971 835 440; cafeparisien@hotmail.com; Carrer de la Ciutat 18; mains €11-19; 10am-midnight Mon-Sat) An appealing mix of old and new draws a sophisticated crowd to this stylish restaurant, famed for its fresh market cuisine. The white-wicker-chair look and modern art on the walls give it a casual but classy feel and the food is excellent – try the *cordero con ciruelas* (lamb with plums), *tumbet* (Mallorcan ratatouille) or fresh fish on display as you enter. The kitchen serves food from noon to 4pm and between 7pm and 10pm.

Mar de Vins SPANISH €
(☎662 030 460; lamardevins@hotmail.com; Carrer d'Antoni Blanes 34; mains €6-11; 10am-midnight Mon-Sat) The classics of Spanish home cooking are the staples here as Carlos, the engaging owner, writes his own menu daily, depending on what takes his fancy in the market. The *tortilla de patatas* (Spanish potato omelette) and *bacalao con alioli* (cod with garlic mayonnaise) are always present. There's contemporary art on the walls inside and a shady garden out back.

Salvad'or MEDITERRANEAN FUSION €
(☎971 829 275; Carrer de la Ciutat 22; mains €11-15; 1-3.30pm & 7-10.30pm Mon-Sat) The cooking here is assured, with fresh ingredients, a Mediterranean focus and a fusion take on it all – try the home-made ravioli with prawns and wild asparagus ragout or the goats cheese cannelloni. It's all served in a refined atmosphere.

Pedra i Flor CAFE €
(☎971 829 536; Carrer d'Antoni Blanes 4; snacks from €5; 10am-1pm & 5-8pm Mon-Fri, 5-8pm Sat) This delightful flower-shop-cum-cafe serves coffee, tea, wine and sandwiches on a few small sidewalk tables.

Cafeteria Sant Salvador CAFE €
(☎971 836 136; Carrer Costa Sant Salvador; mains €6-12; 8am-8pm Tue-Sun Apr-Oct, 8am-5.30pm Nov-Mar) Up beside the Santuari, this simple cafeteria serves sandwiches, a few mixed plates (meat, vegies and salad served together) and some home-made desserts. We like it more as a pit stop after the climb than your main meal of the day.

Information

Tourist office (☎971 836 981; Carrer de Costa i Llobera; 10am-2pm Mon-Fri) In the old train station, although it was moved temporarily for renovations when we visited.

Parc Natural de la Península de Llevant office (☎971 836 828; Carrer de l'Estel 2; 9am-2pm Mon-Fri) The park office (virtually on Plaça d'Espanya) can help with itinerary maps and organises guided walks, generally in Catalan and Spanish.

Getting There & Away

Bus services to/from Carrer de Costa i Llobera include Bus 411 to Palma (€9, one hour 20 minutes, three to five daily) via Manacor (€2.55, 25 minutes) and Bus 446 to Alcúdia (€5.10, 50 minutes, six daily Monday to Saturday) and Port de Pollença (€6, one hour).

The train station was being restored at the time of research as part of the planned extension of the Palma–Manacor train line to Artà.

Parc Natural de la Península de Llevant

This beautiful protected area, which begins about 5km north of Artà, is one of the most rewarding corners of the island's east. It's a mountainous park, dominated by the Serra de Llevant mountain range and culminating in the **Cap Ferrutx**, one of a number of dramatic fingers of land that jut out into the Mediterranean and along the northern and eastern coasts. Although parts of the park are accessible by car, it's hugely popular with hikers, cyclists and birdwatchers; the latter are drawn particularly by the prevalence of cormorants and Audouin's gulls.

Sights & Activities

Hiking

Hikers love this corner of Mallorca, not least because it offers the hiker plenty of options in a fairly small space.

A classic walk takes you through the heart of the park from **S'Alquera Vella d'Avall** (where you can park – take the Ma3333 north of Artà in the direction of the Ermita de Betlem and follow the signposted turn-off right at Km4.7, from where it's a further 600m to the car park) to the coast and a little beach at **S'Arenal et des Verger**. Reckon on two hours' walking time. To reach the same point from the east along the coast, you could start at **Cala Estreta** (where it's also possible to park). This walk follows the coast to **Cala Matzoc**, on past the medieval watchtower **Torre d'Albarca** and west. It takes another hour to reach S'Arenal et des Verger. Beyond that, the coast becomes harder to negotiate. At the main car park, close to S'Arenal et des Verger, a map highlights nine trails totalling 25km through the park. There's also a small information office that's rarely open.

Driving & Cycling

A narrow paved road (the Ma3333) begins in Artà, meandering for around 5km through pine woodland and fields before climbing steeply to reach the top of the ridge at around 7km. The views from here are splendid, especially as the road climbs down away from the summit to the north. The road then drops 2km down to the 19th-century **Ermita de Betlem**, still home to hermits who live a life of seclusion and self-sufficiency. The hermitage has a small church with irregular opening hours – its lovely stone-built exterior stands in contrast to the modern whitewashed interior and cave nativity scene, complete with stalactites and stalagmites. Strolling up the neighbouring hilltops brings some fine vistas into play.

Information

There's a park office (p138) in Artà.

Capdepera

POP 11,200

Eight kilometres due east of Artà, this small, dusty village is crowned by a stirring medieval fortress. The remainder of the village that tumbles down the hill is a bit run-down and has little to detain you.

Sights

Castell de Capdepera CASTLE

(☎971 818 746; www.castellcapdepera.com; adult/child €3/free, audioguide €2; ⏲9am-8pm) Most people who visit Capdepera head straight to the top of the village, where the early-14th-century Castell de Capdepera stands guard. A walled castle complex built on the ruins of a Moorish fortress, the Castell is one of the best preserved on the island.

The castle was constructed under the orders of Jaume II (son of the conquering Jaume I), who envisioned it as the boundary of a protected town. Within the walls, the church, a simple stone affair, contains a valuable wooden crucifix dating to the 14th century but is otherwise fairly nondescript. The watchtower, called **Torre Miquel Nunis**, predates the rest of the castle and is probably Moorish. In the 1800s a taller, round tower was built inside the original rectangular one.

Eating

Cases de Son Barbassa MEDITERRANEAN €€

(☎971 565 776; www.sonbarbassa.com; Camí de Son Barbassa; mains €13-24; ⏲Feb-Nov) This restaurant in the rural hotel of the same name is outstanding, with dishes such as turbot fillet in champagne with clam shells and

GOLF IN NORTHEASTERN MALLORCA

A handful of golf courses are within easy reach of Artà, Capdepera, Cala Ratjada and Cala Millor. Find well-maintained greens and great views at the following places:

» **Pula Golf** (☎971 817 034; www.pulagolf.com; Carretera Son Servera-Capdepera Km3; 9/18 holes €45/80; ⏲8am-7pm)

» **Canyamel Golf** (☎971 841 313; www.canyamelgolf.com; Avinguda d'es Cap Vermell; 9/18 holes €54/88; ⏲8am-8pm)

» **Capdepera Golf** (☎971 818 500; www.golfcapdepera.com; Carretera Artá-Capdepera Km3.5; 18 holes €49.50-79; ⏲8am-7pm)

oyster sauce, or lamb fillet with honey and rosemary. The service is excellent and the setting superb.

Festivals & Events

Festes de Sant Antoni RELIGIOUS
(St Anthony's Feast Day; 17 Jan) A traditional animal-blessing ceremony.

Mercat Medieval MARKET
(3rd weekend May) Medieval costumes and food stalls.

Festa de Sant Bartomeu TOWN FESTIVAL
(18-25 Aug) A week of exhibitions, concerts, parades and fireworks.

Information

Tourist office (971 556 479; informacio@ajcapdepera.net; Carrer de la Ciutat 22; 10am-1pm & 4-7pm Mon-Fri) In the town centre.

Getting There & Away

Bus 411 links Capdepera to Palma (€9.50, 1½ hours, up to five daily), via Artà (€1.15, 10 minutes) and Manacor (€3.45, 35 minutes). Bus 441 runs along the east coast, stopping at all the major resorts, including Porto Cristo (€2.90, 55 minutes, up to 10 daily) and Cala d'Or (€8.15, one hour 25 minutes).

Cala Ratjada

POP 6100

In the blinking lights of an early summer's evening, the pretty harbour of Cala Ratjada feels for all the world like an Italian fishing village and is a much more intimate experience than almost all other east coast resorts. With at least three good beaches, a lovely and long waterfront promenade following the contours of the coast, good restaurants and a host of water-borne activities to choose from, Cala Ratjada is close to our ideal Mallorcan coastal resort. German tourists discovered this fact long ago – you're more likely to hear German spoken here than Spanish.

Sights

Platja de Cala Agulla BEACH
(Cala Agulla) At the northern edge of town this fine beach wraps around a calm bay bathed by turquoise waters and hemmed in by hills blanketed in pine trees. There's precious little development to be seen from the sand, but the beach itself is packed with umbrellas for rent. If you're driving to the quieter western end of the beach, parking costs €4 per day.

Just north of Cala Agulla is the quieter Platja de ses Covasses, where the lack of a wide beach keeps visitors at bay.

Sa Torre Cega GALLERY, HISTORIC BUILDING
(971 563 033; www.fundacionbmarch.es; off Carrer de Elionor Servera; adult/child €3.60/free; tours 9.30am, 11am & 12.30pm Wed-Fri, 9.30am, 11am, 12.30pm, 4.30pm & 6pm Sat) On a hilltop west of the harbour, this estate was named for the 15th-century 'blind tower' (ie windowless tower) that sits at its centre. The beautiful Mediterranean garden is home to some 70 sculptures by greats such as Eduardo Chillida, Josep Maria Sert, Henry Moore and Auguste Rodin. All guided visits must be booked in advance through the tourist office.

Far de Capdepera LIGHTHOUSE
This lighthouse on Mallorca's easternmost tip is the endpoint of a lovely drive, walk or cycle through pine forests; it's around 1.5km east of Sa Torre Cega. The lighthouse, which sits 76m above the sea, began operating in 1861, and the views from here (all the way to Menorca on a clear day) are wonderful.

Font de Sa Cala BEACH
(Font de Sa Cala) South of Cala Ratjada is Font de Sa Cala, a beach suburb accessible via the tourist train, where the crystalline waters are perfect for snorkelling. The serene beach is surrounded by a harshly beautiful rocky coast.

Cala Gat BEACH
(Cala Gat) East of the harbour, beyond Sa Torre Cega, this fine little cove has a pretty beach backed by pine forests and receives far fewer visitors than other in town.

Platja de Son Moll BEACH
Cala Ratjada's most accessible beach is the busy Platja de Son Moll, just in front of Passeig Marítim in the centre of town.

Tourist Train TOURIST TRAIN
(adult/child €3.90/1.90; Apr-Oct) This cutesy train-on-wheels trundles around town, including Platja de Cala Agulla, Platja de Son Moll and Font de Sa Cala up to seven times daily.

Activities

Boat Trips

Illa Balear BOAT TOUR
(971 810 600; www.illabalear.com; adult one way/return from €15/20, child €8; Apr-Oct) Round-

trip excursions in glass-bottom boats to Porto Cristo, Sa Coma, Cala Millor and Cala Bona, with up to two daily departures from Sunday to Friday from April to October.

Hiking

Ask at the tourist office for the brochure entitled *Walking Guide*, which details 21 walks in the surrounding region. To beat the crowds, take the **walking trail** that leaves from the far northern end of Cala Agulla (aka Cala Nau) and head through the pines of a protected natural area toward the pristine **Cala Mesquida**, a beach backed with dunes. The round trip is 10km. Along the way, a smaller trail veers off to the right at the signpost for the 'torre', the **Talaia de Son Jaume II** watchtower. The trail (7km round trip from Cala Agulla) is marked with red dots, and the reward at the end is a spectacular panoramic view.

Cycling

The tourist office brochure *Bike Tours* has route descriptions and maps for 18 itineraries in the region, ranging from 9km to 56km.

Alquiler Cristobal BICYCLE RENTAL, MOTORBIKE RENTAL
(☎971 819 661; Carrer de Nereides; bike rental per day €8-20, per week €42-112, motorcycle 50cc/125cc per day from €25/30; ⏰9am-noon & 5-7pm Apr-Oct) A well-run place for bicycle and motorcycle hire.

M Bike BICYCLE RENTAL, CYCLE TOURS
(☎639 417 796; www.m-bike.com; Carrer de L'Agulla 95; bike rental per day €10-32, per week €60-119, 1/3/5 days of cycle tours €53/149/225; ⏰9am-12.30pm & 4-6pm Mon-Fri, 9-11am & 6pm for returns only Sat, 10-11am & 5-6pm Sun) Mountain bikes are the specialty here. It also runs daily cycle tours along coastal trails and to the Ermita de Betlem; all tours start at 10am.

Horse Riding

Rancho Bonanza HORSE RIDING
(☎619 680 688; www.ranchobonanza.com; Carrer de Ca'n Patilla; 1hr/2hr rides €15/25, 2-day riding excursion per person €150; ⏰8am-8pm Mon-Sat, 8am-1pm Sun) Runs four to five excursions daily with pony rides available for kids six years and under, as well as riding lessons. It helps if you speak German.

Eddi's Reitstall HORSE RIDING
(☎630 150 551; hipicocalaratjada.oyla.de; Carrer de Ca'n Patilla; 1hr/2hr/5hr rides €16/27/60; ⏰11am-1pm & 4-7pm Mon-Sat) One of the recommended German-run outfits to check in for a trail ride, Eddi's also has pony rides for kids (€8 per half hour) and two-hour night rides (€40).

Scuba Diving

Mero Diving DIVE CENTRE
(☎971 565 467; www.mero-diving.com; Carrer de Na Lliteres; introductory dive €79, 5-dive package €179, open-water PADI course €599; ⏰9am-6pm May-Oct) Divers can get their scuba fix at Mero Diving on lovely Cala Lliteres.

Dive & Fun DIVE CENTRE
(☎971 818 036; www.mallorcadiving.de; Font de Sa Cala; 1st dive €38; ⏰9am-6pm Apr-Nov) A dive centre located in the Beach Club Hotel in Font de Sa Cala.

Festivals & Events

Festes del Carme RELIGIOUS
(15-16 Jul) Cala Ratjada's main festival celebrates the Verge del Carme, the holy patroness of fishers. It includes an elaborate maritime procession, fireworks and a host of cultural events.

Feste de Sant Roc RELIGIOUS
(16 Aug) A feast honours the town's patron, Sant Roc, with fireworks and concerts.

Eating

Ca'n Pere SEAFOOD €€
(☎971 563 005; Avinguda América 34; mains €9-29; ⏰11am-1am Apr-Oct) One of our favourite places to eat along the waterfront, Ca'n Pere does a fine seafood grill and other tasty fish dishes; the best are those grilled and without sauce. It also does a fine grilled goats cheese with garlic, parsley, balsamic vinegar and honey. The atmosphere, whether inside or perched out over the water, is memorable.

Ca'n Maya SEAFOOD €
(☎971 564 035; www.canmaya.com; Carrer de Elionor Servera 80; mains €9-20; ⏰noon-4pm & 7pm-midnight Tue-Sun Feb-Dec) Savour shellfish and seafood – such as fried squid, grilled salmon, swordfish and *arròs de Granca* (spider-crab rice) – on the rustic-feeling glassed-in terrace by the harbour. It's probably the pick of Cala Ratjada's seafood restaurants.

La Bodeguita SPANISH, INTERNATIONAL €€
(☎971 819 062; www.labodeguita.es; Avinguda América 14; mains €8.50-21.50; ⏰9am-midnight) A modern classy look distinguishes La Bodeguita from other more rustic choices along this stretch of the waterfront. Its five tapas for €8.50 is a fabulous order but it also does

Cala Ratjada

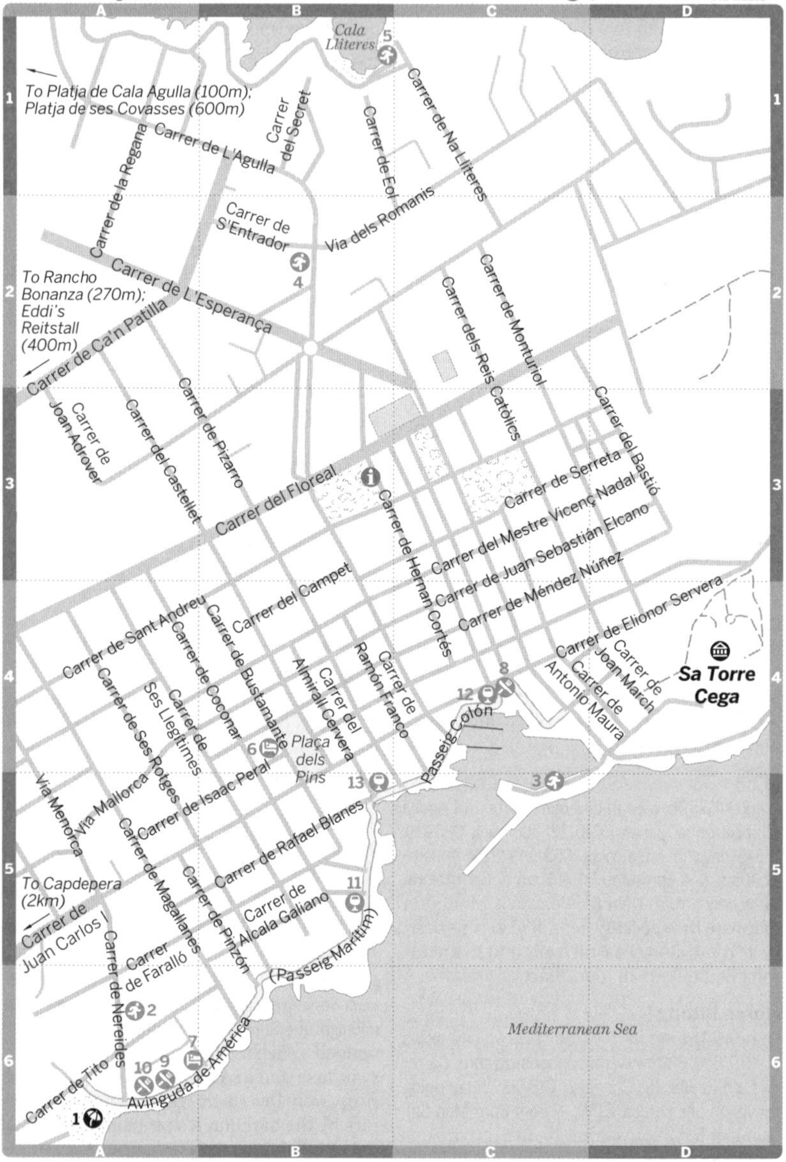

other fine dishes such as Argentine entrecôte atop spinach with feta and potato gratin.

Sa Cova SPANISH, INTERNATIONAL **€**

(☎660 462 627; www.sa-cova.es; Cala Lliteres; mains €9.80-16.50; ⏲9am-1am) This charming, casual little corner of a lovely rocky cove, Sa Cova has an agreeably bohemian air and is ideal for everything from a lazy breakfast to live music on Monday evenings. The mains are fairly standard with steaks and seafood, but it also does sandwiches, *bocadillos* (filled rolls), salads and cocktails.

Cala Ratjada

Top Sights
Sa Torre Cega D4

Sights
1 Platja de Son Moll A6

Activities, Courses & Tours
2 Alquiler Cristobal A6
3 Illa Balear C5
4 M Bike B2
5 Mero Diving B1

Sleeping
6 Hostal Gami B4
7 Residence – The Sea Club A6

Eating
8 Ca'n Maya C4
9 Ca'n Pere A6
10 La Bodeguita A6
Sa Cova ..... (see 5)

Drinking
11 Café Noah's B5
12 Sa Fonda 74 ..... C4
13 Sinai Café B5

Drinking

Sa Fonda 74 BAR, CAFE
(☎971 818 222; www.safonda74.es; Carrer de Elionor Servera 74; ⊙9.30am-1am) The location here overlooking the narrow end of the harbour is one of the best in town, with a classy outdoor terrace and an even classier indoor area. As if that weren't enough, there's live music (jazz, swing, soul) at 9pm on Saturdays.

Café Noah's BAR, CAFE
(☎971 818 125; www.cafenoahs.com; Avinguda América 2; cocktails €4.50-7.50; ⊙9.30am-late) A sophisticated bar-cafe with a trailing list of well-priced cocktails, Café Noah's is perfect for people-watching, straddling as it does the waterfront promenade. Inside there are comfy leather sofas for a more intimate evening. DJs get the crowd on their feet every night in summer.

Sinai Café LOUNGE, BAR
(☎971 566 117; Passeig Colón 10; cocktails €5-8, water pipes €8; ⊙8pm-4am) Slick and smooth, Sinai Café is under new management and promises everything from DJs and live music to the occasional high-class strip show. It draws a young, well-heeled professional crowd, and is known for its high-end cocktails, whiskeys and gins.

Information

Tourist office (☎971 819 467; www.ajcapdepera.net; Carrer de Hernan Cortés; ⊙10am-1pm & 4-8pm Mon-Fri) Located in the white town hall building; free wi-fi in the plaza out front.

Getting There & Away

Bus 411 links Palma de Mallorca and Cala Ratjada, via Artá, with up to five runs daily in each direction (€10.15 return, two hours).

From the port, there's a daily hydrofoil to Ciutadella (Menorca).

Coves d'Artà & Platja de Canyamel

The quiet beach resort of Canyamel is a fine alternative to far busier resorts along the eastern seaboard. Apart from the pleasant beach **Platja de Canyamel**, there's a fine medieval tower, restaurant and a majestic cave complex, which is under far less strain from tourism than other east coast cave complexes.

Sights

Coves d'Artà CAVES
(☎971 841 293; www.cuevasdearta.com; admission €11; ⊙10am-7pm) This series of natural caves burrows into the coast 1km north of Canyamel. Although Porto Cristo's Coves del Drac are more spectacular, these caves aren't far behind – the exit from the cave and views out over the Med are something special. Guided tours of the caves leave every 30 minutes. Once inside, you'll quickly discover that this is a seriously beautiful work of nature.

The guided visits, which last around 40 minutes and are offered in English, German, Spanish and French, lead visitors through an unassuming fissure in the rock wall that buffers the coast.

Soon you'll find yourself in a soaring vestibule, walking along a raised footpath past the 22-metre-tall 'Queen of Columns' and through several other rooms, including the 'Chamber of Purgatory' and 'Chamber of Hell'.

Even the walk to get here is spectacular – the caves are halfway up a sheer cliff face and once served as a refuge for the local inhabitants in times of war and invasion.

TRANQUIL COVES AROUND CALA RATJADA

Heading north from Cala Ratjada, you'll find a wonderfully undeveloped stretch of coastline flecked with beaches. Long-time favourites of nudists, these out-of-the-way coves are no secret, but their lack of development has kept them calm and pristine.

Cala Mesquida, surrounded by sand dunes and a small housing development, is the most accessible, with free parking and a regular bus service (bus 471) from Cala Ratjada (25 minutes, up to 15 daily).

It requires more determination to access the undeveloped coves due west. **Cala Torta**, **Cala Mitjana** and the beachless **Cala Estreta** are all found at the end of a narrow road that ventures through the hills from Artà, yet a more interesting way to arrive is via the one-hour walking path from Cala Mesquida. On the road down to Cala Torta, a branch road climbs to **Bar-Restaurante Sa Duaia** (☎651 826 416; www.saduaia.com; ⌚1-3.30pm & 7-10pm Tue-Sun), which rustles up serves of decent Mallorcan cooking to go with the pretty views and accommodation options.

Further west, and following a 20-minute trek along the coast from Cala Estreta, **Cala Matzoc** comes into view. The spacious sandy beach backs onto a hill where you'll find the ruins of a *talayot* (watchtower) still stands, once used to guard the coast from pirates.

Torre de Canyamel CASTLE
(☎971 841 134; Carretera Artà-Canyamel; admission €3; ⌚10am-3pm & 5-8pm Tue-Sat, 10am-2pm Sun) Just 3km inland from the beach and signposted off the main coast road, the famed Torre de Canyamel – a 23m-high, 13th-century defence tower of Muslim origin – is a rewarding detour.

Claper des Gegant RUIN
(admission €2; ⌚9am-6pm Mon-Sat, 9am-noon Sun) On a little dirt path near Canyamel Golf, is the ancient settlement of Claper des Gegant, featuring a circular *talayot*, defensive walls and several rooms in ruined outline.

Eating

Porxada de Sa Torre MALLORCAN €€
(☎971 841 310; www.restauranteporxadadesatorre.com; Carretera Artà-Canyamel Km5; mains €8.40-17; ⌚1-3.30pm & 7-11pm Tue-Sun, closed mid-Dec–Jan) This restaurant, located in the grounds of the Torre de Canyamel, is one of the best places to eat on the island. It's a beacon of Mallorcan cooking, with a range of traditional dishes available, including perfectly prepared *tumbet* (Mallorcan ratatouille), roast lamb, stuffed eggplant, steaks and *sobrassada* (cured Mallorcan sausage); you're welcome to visit the kitchen to see how the dishes are prepared. The stone-and-wood architecture, old farming implements, ancient olive press and friendly service round out a terrific package.

CALA MILLOR TO PORTOCOLOM

For the millions of tourists who descend every year on its sandy beaches, splash in its gentle waves and stay in all-inclusive resorts, the coast from Cala Millor to Portocolom is paradise. But for those who mourn the loss of Mallorca's once-pristine coastline, the overdevelopment is nothing short of an abhorrence.

If, however, you're seeking a quieter, more Mallorquin style of holiday, don't despair. This stretch of coastline is popular for a reason – it's undeniably beautiful. And the crowd-weary don't have to shy away. Stay in one of the cosy rural hotels and drive, cycle or hike to off-the-beaten-path beaches such as Cala Romántica or Cala Varques.

Cala Millor & Around

Along the waterfront at Cala Millor at twilight, when the sun turns the sky violet and the water a soft shade of aquamarine, you can almost imagine that the concrete jungle inland was just a mirage... The saving grace of Cala Millor is that its nearly 2km-long beach, backed by a promenade, is large enough to absorb masses of sun worshippers on all but the busiest summer days. To escape the crowds, set off for a challenging seaside hike to the **Castell de n'Amer**, which overlooks the sea.

Sights

Safari-Zoo ZOO
(☎971 810 909; www.safari-zoo.com; Carretera Portocristo-Son Servera Km5; adult/child 12yr & under €17/11; ⏰9.15am-6.15pm) Beyond the resort sprawl is the Safari-Zoo, where you see wild animals (including rhinos, hippos, zebras, giraffes, baboons, wildebeest and numerous antelope species) from the comfort of your car or an open-sided tourist train. The animals here have plenty of space to roam, unlike those in the depressing enclosures in the more traditional zoo that makes up the rest of the park.

Information

Tourist office (☎971 585 864; www.visitcalamillor.com; Passeig Marítim; ⏰9am-5pm Mon-Fri, 9am-4pm Sat) Occupies a kiosk right on the promenade.

Getting There & Away

Bus lines 441, 446, 447 and others run up and down the east coast, linking Cala Millor with resorts such as Cala d'Or (€7.30, 1¼ hours). Bus 412 heads to Palma (€9.10, 1½ hours, up to 15 daily).

Porto Cristo

POP 6700

Home to Mallorca's grandest caves, Porto Cristo is above all a day-trip destination and attracts would-be spelunkers in their droves to its vast underground caverns. It's true that as a resort it lacks some of the bang of glitzier destinations elsewhere on the coast, but that's no bad thing, and what Porto Cristo is missing in glamour it makes up for in unassuming charm.

Sights

Most of the activity crowds alongside the **Passeig de la Sirena** and the harbour, where a small crowded beach provides the perfect place to observe the comings and goings of fishing boats and yachts in the marina. Alongside the beach you'll find the modest **Coves Blanques**, a handful of small caves that were inhabited during the Talayotic period and were later used by fishers for shelter.

A sprawling market selling produce, artisan goods and various tacky souvenirs takes over the Passeig de la Sirena on Sunday mornings.

Coves del Drac CAVES
(Dragon's Caves; ☎971 820 753; www.cuevasdeldrach.com; Carretera de Cuevas; adult/child €11.50/free; ⏰10am-5pm) Mallorca has some wonderful cave complexes, but the Coves del Drac, on the southern side of town, are undoubtedly the most spectacular. A 1.2km shuffle with the inevitable crowd, accompanied by a multilingual commentary, leads to a vast amphitheatre and lake, where you'll enjoy a brief classical music recital. One-hour tours of the caves leave on the hour.

It's difficult to truly convey the magic of this place – at times it's akin to wandering through a vast underground cathedral complete with organ pipes, at others it's like having an aerial view of a petrified forest. The breathtakingly beautiful (and cleverly exploited) chambers, theatrically lit in bright colours, are adorned with impressive stalactites and stalagmites. The tour delves into the most beautiful parts of the 2km-long limestone tunnel and a short boat ride on the lake is possible after the concert.

Coves dels Hams CAVES
(☎971 820 988; www.cuevas-hams.com; Carretera Manacor-Portocristo Km11; adult/child 4-12yr/under 4yr €19/9.50/free; ⏰10am-5pm) On the northern side of town on the road to Manacor, this underground labyrinth is not as impressive as the Coves del Drac, but it does have some fine formations. The first 30 minutes of the visit involves a video presentation on Jules Verne (who died on 2 March 1905, the same day the caves were discovered) and clever AV projections.

At the end of the tour, Mozart music is piped through the underground chamber next to the lake. Apart from the generally smaller crowds, the Coves dels Hams has the advantage over its rival in that you're allowed to take photos inside (no flash), although the protective fences will spoil most shots. And you also get a free *moscatel* (a soft drink for kids). Even so, we reckon it's overpriced.

And one final thing: the massive signs all over town to the 'Caves' are slightly misleading – they lead here, so study the signs carefully if your desired destination is the Coves del Drac.

SOUTH OF PORTO CRISTO

The coast running south of Porto Cristo is textured with a series of beautiful, unspoilt coves, many of them signposted from the Ma4014 highway linking Porto Cristo and

Porto Cristo

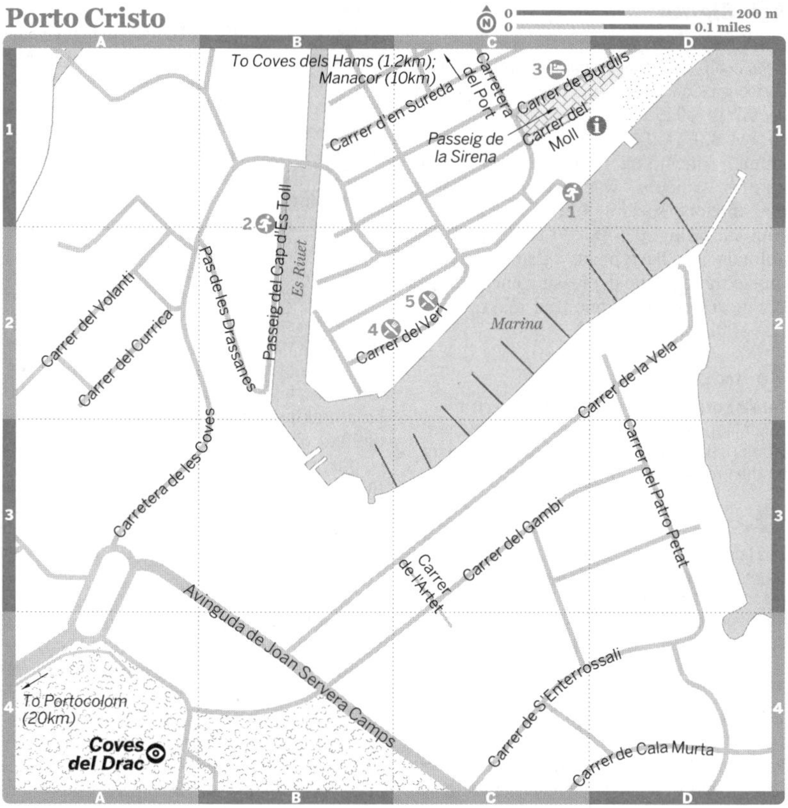

Porto Cristo

Top Sights
Coves del Drac A4

Activities, Courses & Tours
1 Illa Balear C1
2 Skualo Adventure Sports & Dive Centre B1

Sleeping
3 Felip Hotel C1

Eating
4 Sa Pedra B2
5 Siroco C2

Portocolom. The largest and most developed of the bunch is **Cala Romántica**, where a few hotels form one of the island's more serene resorts and a rough promenade has been hewn out of the rock face by the sea.

Beyond Cala Romántica you can seek out coves and caves such as **Cala Varques** (known for the cave on the cliff above the cove), **Cala Sequer**, **Cova del Pilar** or **Cala Magraner**. None has direct car access; plan on walking at least the last few minutes.

Activities

Skualo Adventure Sports & Dive Centre DIVE CENTRE
(☎971 815 094; www.mallorcadiving.com; Passeig del Cap d'Es Toll 11; 1st dive €39, plus equipment €10; ⏲9am-6pm Mon-Sat) This dive centre is the best in town. It also offers snorkelling and sea-kayaking.

Illa Balear BOAT TOURS
(☎971 810 600; www.illabalear.com; per person €18-24, one way to Cala Ratjada €15) Boat excursions (most in glass-bottomed catamarans) between Porto Cristo and other east coast resorts such as Cala Ratjada, Cala Romántica

and Cala Millor up to four times daily in summer.

Festivals & Events

Festes de Sant Antoni RELIGIOUS
(16-17 Jan) Porto Cristo goes all out with a bonfire and 'dance of the devils' for the eve of Sant Antoni (16 and 17 January), the traditional blessing of animals.

Verge del Carme RELIGIOUS
(16 Jul) The feast day of the patroness of fisherfolk is celebrated with great cheer along the coast.

Eating

Siroco SEAFOOD €€
(☎971 822 444; Carrer del Verí; mains €13.90-23.50; ⊙1-3.30pm & 7-10.30pm May-Oct) For inventive seafood dishes and Mallorcan specialities, this waterfront restaurant is a great option. It's especially proud of the seafood rice with lobster, the drier lobster paella, or lobster *fideuà* (a paella-like noodle dish), and with good reason.

Sa Pedra SEAFOOD €€
(☎971 820 932; Carrer del Verí; mains €14-21; ⊙1-3.30pm & 7-10.30pm May-Oct) The varied menu at this upscale eatery is dominated by thoughtfully presented fish dishes such as monkfish in a parsley sauce, while the mixed seafood grill (€38.50) is paradise for lovers of seafood.

Information

Tourist office (☎971 815 103; Carrer del Moll; ⊙9am-4pm Mon-Fri) At the end of the wharf.

Getting There & Away

A dozen bus lines serve Porto Cristo, among them lines 412 and 414 to Palma (one way/return €7.70/12, 1½ hours, two to seven daily) via Manacor (€1.70); lines 441, 442 and 443 connect to the east coast resorts (varied prices, scores of buses). You'll also find services to Cala Ratjada (€3.90, 30 minutes, three to 11 daily) and a Wednesday service to Sineu (€5, 40 minutes).

Portocolom

POP 3875

A sleepy place as far as east coast holiday resorts go, Portocolom has resisted the tourist onslaught with dignity. It cradles a natural harbour (one of the few on the island) and attracts German, British and Spanish families in equal numbers. Fishing boats, sailing boats and the odd luxury yacht bob in the calm waters of the horseshoe-shaped bay. The bay here is large and lacks the intimacy of those towns arrayed around small coves, although some of the shady streets are lined with big villas.

Sights

Within reach of town are some fine beaches, such as the immaculate little cove of **Cala Marçal** and, on the northern end of town, **Cala s'Arenal**, the locals' preferred beach. On the eastern headland at the mouth of the bay, there's a lighthouse, **Far de sa Punta de ses Crestes** with good views back towards the town.

Activities

Walkers and cyclists have plenty of options nearby. South of town, starting from Cala Marçal, an 8km walking trail links half a dozen coves, many of which are accessible only by foot or boat, eventually reaching Cala Ferrera. The tourist office can provide a map and route description for this and other excursions in their brochure *Excursions round Felanitx Municipality*. Included in the brochure are treks inland to the Castell de Santueri (p133) and to some of Eastern Mallorca's prettiest beaches; these include **Cala Sa Nau** (halfway to Cala Ferrera), a gorgeous long inlet with turquoise waters and a white-sand beach, and the similar **Cala Mitjana**.

Ask at the tourist office for information on glass-bottom boats (€19 to €27, two to six hours) to Cala d'Or and elsewhere along the coast.

Bahia Azul Dive Center DIVE CENTRE
(☎971 825 280; www.bahia-azul.de; Ronda de Creuer Balear 78; single dive €27-39; ⊙Apr-Oct) This dive centre in the Hostal Bahia Azul offers courses, try dives and equipment rental.

Skualo Adventure Sports Centre DIVE CENTRE, KAYAKING
(☎971 834 197; www.mallorcadiving.com; Carrer de Llampuga; single dive €39; ⊙Apr-Oct) Another well-respected dive centre, with snorkelling (€30 to €38) and sea kayaking (two- to three-hour excursion €38).

Moto Sprint BICYCLE RENTAL
(☎667 735 414, 971 824 858; Avinguda de Cala Marçal; per day from €12; ⊙8.30am-1pm & 4-9pm Apr-Oct) Opposite the tourist office.

START/FINISH FINCA CAN ROIG
DISTANCE 13KM
DURATION 2½ HOURS

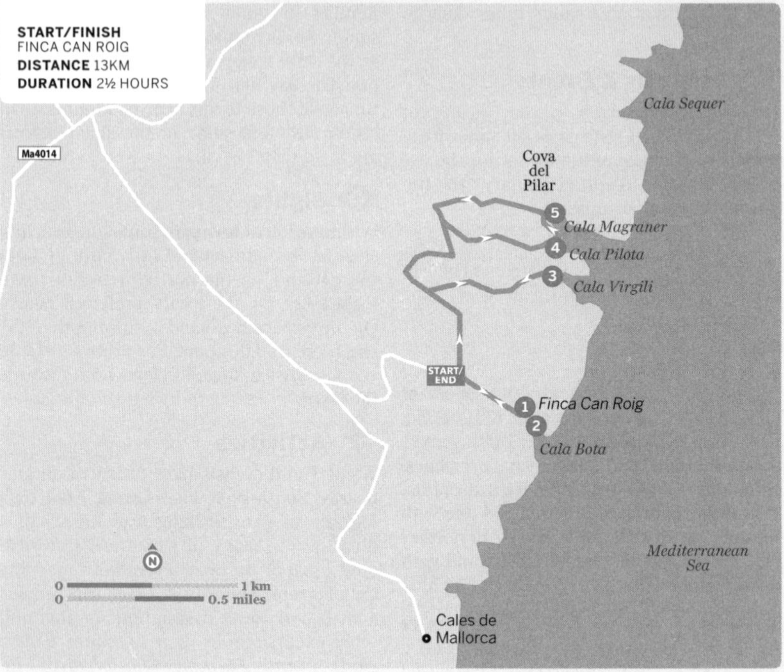

Walking Tour
Four Coves

Just north of Cales de Mallorca the chaos of the resorts falls away and, at last, nature takes over. Over the 6km between Cales de Mallorca and Cala Romántica, there's only pine-specked rocky coves, pitted cliff faces and the aquamarine of the Mediterranean. The walk begins at 1 **Finca Can Roig**, a rural estate near Cales de Mallorca. To get there, take the Carretera Porto Cristo–Portocolom (Ma4014) and at Km6 turn east toward Cales de Mallorca. Continue 2.2km and veer left; after 200m you'll reach the entrance to Can Roig.

Leave your car here and strike out along the wide, rocky track that parallels the coast. After about 15 minutes, a slightly narrower path turns off to the right. Follow it alongside a small gully and through patches of trees to reach 2 **Cala Bota**, a sheltered cove with a small sandy beach. A steep trail meanders around and above the cove, giving a bird's-eye view of its beauty.

From Cala Bota, backtrack on the trail you came in on, and turn right toward the next cove, 3 **Cala Virgili**. The track brings you to a smaller trail that heads off right down to this narrow cove, where a small shelter houses a dinghy. (The walk down takes about 10 minutes.)

Return to the main trail and continue to your right. You'll pass a small trail on your right, but keep straight until you come upon a second path. Take it towards the third cove, 4 **Cala Pilota**, backed by vertigo-inducing cliffs.

Head back to the main trail and walk just a couple of minutes before coming to a fork. Take the left-hand path, which rolls down to the final cove, 5 **Cala Magraner**, the grandest of the bunch both in size and beauty. The trail is wide at first but stops in a clearing; another, narrower trail leads you the last few minutes. After splashing in the crystalline waters, exploring the small caves that dot the rock, turn back and walk the full length of the main trail back to Finca Can Roig.

Eating

Restaurant Sa Sinia SEAFOOD €€
(☎971 824 323; cellersasinia@gmail.com; Carrer dels Pescadors 25; mains €15-25; ⏲1-3.30pm & 7.30-10.30pm Tue-Sun Feb-Oct) With menus designed by artist Miquel Barceló and chairs marked with plaques bearing the name of famous people who have sat there, this classic maritime eatery is the most respected place in town. Fresh fish of all kinds, lobster stew and homemade desserts are the house specialities, as is warm, old-fashioned service.

Restaurant Sa Llotja SPANISH €€
(☎971 825 165; www.restaurantsallotjaportocolom.com; Carrer dels Pescadors; mains €14.50-30.90; ⏲1-3.30pm & 7-10pm Tue-Sun Feb-Oct) A sleek eatery with a wonderful terrace overlooking the harbour, Sa Llotja tempts with dishes like monkfish, lobster stew, herb-encrusted lamb and the odd intriguing combination such as the red prawn carpaccio with tomato, coriander and citrus sorbet. It also serves a lunchtime set menu (€34), as well as cheaper snacks (such as sandwiches and grilled foie gras) at lunchtime.

Restaurante HPC SPANISH, MEDITERRANEAN €€
(☎971 825 323; www.hostalportocolom.com; Carrer de Cristòfol Colom 5; mains €10-23; ⏲1-3.30pm & 7-11pm) The stylish, high-ceilinged restaurant below the Hostal Portocolom offers a bit of everything, from homemade pizzas to paella, grilled fish, Mallorcan suckling pig, and duck magret. The atmosphere's classy but never stuffy, especially at the outdoor tables. Our main complaint is being served a designer *aperitivo* we didn't order and then being charged for it.

Information

Tourist office (☎971 826 084; turisme@felanitx.org; Avinguda de Cala Marçal 15; ⏲9am-2pm Mon-Fri Apr-Oct) At the southern end of town, on the road to Cala Marçal.

Getting There & Away

Ten bus lines service Portocolom, including the coastal routes 441, 442 and 443 (varied prices, dozens daily). Up to seven buses link with Palma (€5.50, 1½ hours).

Southern Mallorca

Includes »

Cala Pi & Around....152
Sa Ràpita & Around..152
Colònia de Sant Jordi..........153
Platja des Trenc.....155
Ses Salines.........155
Santanyí & Around..157
Cala Figuera........159
Parc Natural de Mondragó..........159
Portopetro..........159
Cala d'Or...........160

Best Places to Eat

» Port Petit (p160)
» Varadero (p160)
» Restaurante Petite Iglesia (p159)
» Bodega Barahona (p156)
» Restaurante-Bar Pep Serra (p154)

Best Places to Stay

» Blau PortoPetro (p174)
» Can Canals (p174)
» Hotel Cala Santanyí (p174)
» Hotel Ca'n Bonico (p174)
» Ca'n Bessol (p174)

Why Go?

The fortresslike coastal geography between the Badia de Palma (Bay of Palma) and Colònia de Sant Jordi has preserved this area as one of the least-developed of the island. Much of the coast is buffered by tall, nearly impenetrable cliffs splashed with the sapphire blue waters of the Mediterranean. They may not always be very accessible, but their untamed, raw beauty is hypnotising.

Beyond the cliffs are intimate coves and long beaches, true marvels of nature. Whether enclosed tightly by fjord-like cliffs, or silky sweeps of sand backed by pines and junipers, these are some of Mallorca's best beaches. And best of all, the existence of parks and natural areas, and the proliferation of working farms and rural estates has, for the most part, kept this part of the island free from the worst excesses of overdevelopment. In other words, this is how all of Mallorca's coast once looked.

When to Go

Mallorca's southern reaches live for the summer, to the extent that you won't find much going on if you arrive before Easter or after October. That's not to say you can't visit at other times: if you do you're likely to have the place to yourself, including some eerily quiet resort towns with just a handful of restaurants, hotels and shops open. But summer is undoubtedly the best time and you'll enjoy it most if you seek out southern Mallorca's resort-free stretches of coastline.

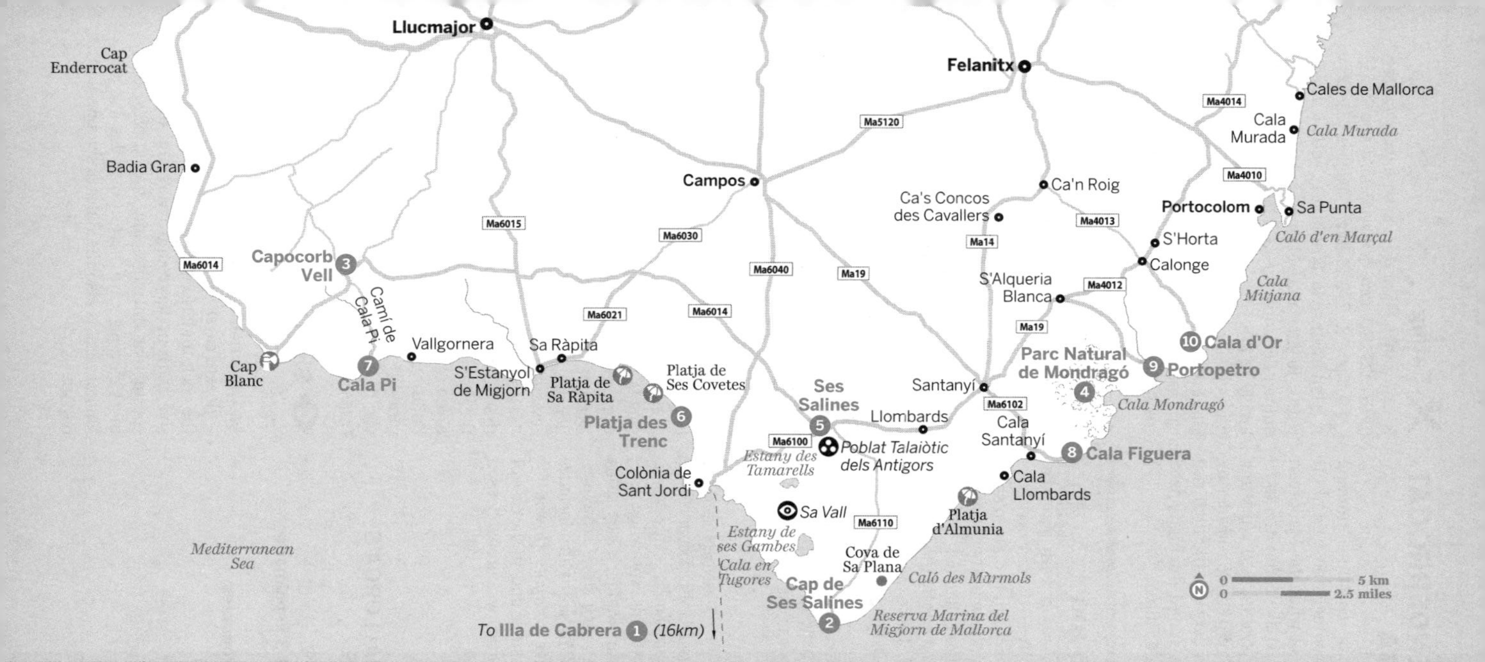

Southern Mallorca Highlights

1. Take a day trip to the **Illa de Cabrera** (p154), home to Mallorca's only national park
2. Hike to the tiny coves that dot the coast surrounding the **Cap de Ses Salines** (p155)
3. Step across the thresholds of centuries-old houses at **Capocorb Vell** (p152)
4. Log some new bird species at the lovely **Parc Natural de Mondragó** (p159)
5. Get into the groove of newly cool **Ses Salines** (p155)
6. Discover Mallorca as it once was by lazing on the sands of **Platja des Trenc** (p155)
7. Learn that not all resorts are the same at quietly pretty **Cala Pi** (p152)
8. Promenade along the elevated walkway of **Cala Figuera** (p159)
9. Catch the spirit of the Mediterranean summer at Portopetro's **Varadero** (p160)
10. Dine in one of the sophisticated restaurants in Port Petit in **Cala d'Or** (p160)

FROM CAP ENDERROCAT TO SA RÀPITA

The lonely stretch of coastline running along the island's southernmost flank is unspoilt, a reminder of what the Mallorcan coast must have looked like before the tourist onsalught. Its survival in such a pristine state is all the more refreshing considering its location, squeezed between the high-rise hotels on the east coast and the high-speed activity of the Badia de Palma.

Cala Pi & Around

An agreeably low-key resort with a reputation for attracting retirees, Cala Pi overlooks a gorgeous beach. Reached via a steep staircase, the beach is only 50m wide but stretches more than 100m inland, flanked on either side by craggy cliffs that ensure the inlet stays as still as bath water. There are no facilities at beach level so bring any provisions you're likely to need.

On the coast, a circular 17th-century defence tower pays homage to the Mallorca of ages past, when pirate threats were constant.

Sights

Capocorb Vell ARCHAEOLOGICAL SITE
(☎971 180 155; www.talaiotscapocorbvell.com; Carretera Arenal-Cap Blanc Km23; admission €2; ⏲10am-5pm Fri-Wed) At this sprawling prehistoric village, you can wander along stony pathways and beside rough stone structures that date to 1000 BC. The site, which includes 28 dwellings and five *talayots* (tower-like structures made with stone and, in the case of Capocorb Vell, no mortar) was probably used through Roman times.

DON'T MISS

SOUTHERN MALLORCA'S TOP BEACHES

- » Platja des Trenc
- » Sa Plageta and S'Espalmador (Illa de Cabrera)
- » Platja de Ses Roquetes
- » Cala Mondragó
- » Cala Esmerelda
- » Cala Pi
- » Cala Santanyí
- » Cala Llombards

Eating

Restaurante Miquel SPANISH, MALLORCAN €€
(☎971 123 000; Torre de Cala Pi 13; mains €9-26; ⏲1-3.30pm & 7.30-10.30pm Tue-Sun Mar-Oct) A Mallorcan-style farmhouse with a huge patio, Restaurante Miquel is warmly recommended, and has a fabulous fixed-price lunch (€15) with specialities like paella, mussels in marinara sauce or grouper with lemon sauce. It also has a long list of Mallorcan specialties (including rabbit with mushrooms), most of which go for under €10.

Getting There & Away

Bus 520 links Cala Pi and Palma once in the morning and once in the evening (€5.10, 1½ hours).

Sa Ràpita & Around

Coming from the west, the rural Ma6014 highway parallels the coast, rolling past the gnarled olive trees of old Mallorcan estates and the crumbling rock walls that define their borders. The main settlement along this stretch of coast, Sa Ràpita is a sleepy seaside village whose rocky shoreline, harangued by waves, provides a scenic diversion from the rest of the shabby town. Neighbouring **Vallgornera** has the longest cave on the island.

Past Sa Ràpita and off the Ma6030 highway is the ramshackle hamlet of **Ses Covetes**. A €5 parking fee (which includes a free post-beach shower) allows you to wander among a handful of informal bars and restaurants and down to the long and silky **Platja de Ses Covetes**. This unspoilt (although not uncrowded) beach forms part of the **Reserva Marina del Migjorn de Mallorca** (a protected marine reserve), and no buildings mar its backdrop of dunes and pines. If you walk east along the shorefront, you'll soon come upon **Platja des Trenc** (p155).

Sights

FREE **Cova des Pas de Vallgornera** CAVES
In Vallgornera (3km east of Cala Pi), half a dozen caves burrow their way through the rock underfoot. Some are truly impressive, with underground rivers and lakes or spectacular stalactites and stalagmites. The most famous cave here, Cova des Pas de Vallgornera, is also the Balearics' longest, at 6435m.

WORTH A TRIP

CAP BLANC

If you're travelling the coast road from Palma to Capocorb Vell and Cala Pi, there's a wonderfully secluded spot that warrants a detour en route. Take the Ma6014 highway south from S'Arenal and turn right at the sign pointing to 'Cap Blanc'. You'll soon come across a lighthouse and desolate-seeming military compound. Park beside the fence.

You can't reach the lighthouse, but a trail setting off from the fence leads you on a five-minute walk through scrubby bushes and over the pitted rocks to a sheer cliff. The views of the Mediterranean are nothing short of majestic with ruddy-coloured cliffs running up the coast and fishing birds circling overhead. Breezy and sunny, this is a fabulous picnic spot, but be careful with kids or dogs; there is no fence and the drop is abrupt.

Most caves can be visited but you should go with a guide or local expert, such as **Jose Antonio Encinas** (☎609 372 888).

Eating

Restaurant Ca'n Pep SEAFOOD €€
(☎971 640 102; canpep2larapita@hotmail.com; Avinguda Miramar 30; mains €9-24; ⏲11am-11pm Tue-Sun Dec-Oct) One of numerous seafood eateries in Sa Ràpita, this local institution is rightfully famous for its seafood and rice dishes. The decor is predictably maritime and the menu has a helpful visual listing of all fish served, although some, like the local *cap roig* (red head) are so ugly that you might prefer not to know what you're eating!

Getting There & Away

Bus 515 runs to and from Palma (€5.15, one hour, up to five times daily).

COLÒNIA DE SANT JORDI & AROUND

More than any other resort area in Mallorca, the southeastern tip of the island celebrates its natural beauty. West of the family resort, Colònia de Sant Jordi stretches the 7km of the unspoilt Platja des Trenc, while to the southeast a vast nature reserve protects a long swathe of rocky coastline softened by pristine beaches. Offshore sits the Balearics' only national park, the Parc Nacional Marítim-Terrestre de l'Arxipèlag de Cabrera (usually simplified to 'Illa de Cabrera'), while inland a smattering of preserved *talayotic* sites interrupt a serene, pastoral landscape.

Colònia de Sant Jordi

POP 2410

The biggest beach resort of the southern coast, Colònia de Sant Jordi has long been the summertime spot of choice for Palma residents. A prim town whose well-laid-out streets form a chequerboard across the hilly landscape, the Colònia is a family-friendly place surrounded by some of the best and least-developed beaches on Mallorca. But we like it best as the jumping off point for the offshore Illa de Cabrera. A pedestrian promenade follows the rocky coast all the way around the Colònia.

Sights

Colònia de Sant Jordi's main attractions are its wonderful beaches, both in town and beyond its borders. Best known is the Platja des Trenc, a 20-minute walk from the northwestern end of town.

FREE **Centro de Visitantes Ses Salines** AQUARIUM
(☎971 656 282; cnr Carrer de Gabriel Roca & Plaça del Dolç; ⏲9.30am-2.30pm & 3.30-6pm) At the northeastern end of town, a block back from the Platja Es Port, this wonderful place is part aquarium and part interpretation centre for the offshore marine environs of the Parc Nacional Marítim-Terrestre de l'Arxipèlag de Cabrera. The visit ends with a climb up a spiral ramp that wraps around an extraordinary mural by Miguel Mansanet, based on 16th-century Mallorcan maps of the Mediterranean.

It opened in 2008 and is still waiting on the interpretative panels that will accompany the tanks, but otherwise it's an exceptional place.

VISITING ILLA DE CABRERA

Nineteen uninhabited islands and islets make up the only national park in the Balearic Islands, the **Parc Nacional Marítim-Terrestre de l'Arxipèlag de Cabrera** (☎971 725 010; reddeparquesnacionales.mma.es/parques/cabrera; ⊙Easter-Oct), an archipelago whose dry, hilly islands are known for their birdlife, rich marine environment and abundant lizard populations. The **Illa de Cabrera**, the largest island of the archipelago and the only one you can visit, sits just 16km off the coast of Colònia de Sant Jordi. Other islands are used for wildlife research. Only 200 people per day (300 in August) are allowed to visit this highly protected natural area, so reserve your place at least a day ahead. Although private boats can come to Cabrera if they've requested navigation and anchoring permits in advance from the park administration, nearly all visitors arrive on the organised cruises. **Excursions a Cabrera** (☎971 649 034; www.excursionsacabrera.es; Carrer de l'Explanada del Port; adult/child €38/25; ⊙normal boat 10am-5.30pm, speedboat noon-2.30pm Easter-Oct) runs both slow boats and speedboats from Colònia de Sant Jordi; **Mar Cabrera** (☎971 656 403; www.marcabrera.com; Carrer de l'Explanada del Port; adult/child from €38/30; ⊙9am-7pm Easter-Oct) operates a speedboat service.

On the longer trips, after sailing past a few small islands swarming with birds, you'll be dropped off on Cabrera, where there's a tiny information office, public restrooms, a canteen and a covered eating area. Although Excursions a Cabrera offers a lunch for €8, you're better off bringing a picnic.

During the day you're pretty much on your own. Many people simply enjoy the wonderfully calm beaches, **Sa Plageta** and **S'Espalmador**. At times, the park can seem over-protected – there are few hiking trails open to the public, and for most of them you'll either need to tag along with a guide or request permission from the park office – but this is an extremely fragile ecosystem.

Activities

Team Double J BICYCLE RENTAL

(☎971 655 765; www.teamdoublej.com; Avinguda de la Primavera 9; per day from €7.50-15, per week €35-95; ⊙9.30am-1pm & 3-6pm Feb-Oct) Rent bikes here – the team can also give you information on area routes.

Piraguas Mix KAYAKING

(☎971 652 474; www.piraguasmixkayaks.com; S'Alqueria Rotje; sea kayaks from €30 per day, guided excursions per person €30; ⊙10am-1pm & 4-7pm Apr-Oct) One of the most respected sea-kayaking outfits on the island.

Eating

Restaurante-Bar Pep Serra SEAFOOD €€

(☎971 655 399; Carrer de l'Enginier Gabriel Roca 87; mains €14.50-26.50; ⊙1-3.30pm & 7.30-10.30pm Tue-Sun Jul-Sep, shorter hours rest of year) Famous for its paella and grilled seafood (it has its own fishing boat), this appealingly unsophisticated yet still pricey waterfront eatery has a few sidewalk tables and a laid-back air. As always with paella and rice dishes, you'll need a minimum of two to make an order.

Heladería Colonial ICE CREAM €

(☎971 655 256; Carrer de l'Enginier Gabriel Roca 9; ice creams from €3.50; ⊙11am-10pm Mar-Nov) Ice-cream lovers from across the island know this wonderful family-run ice-cream shop in the heart of town. It also has a bar-restaurant if you manage to resist the street-side ice-cream display and make it inside.

Marisol SPANISH, INTERNATIONAL €

(☎971 655 070; Carrer de l'Enginier Gabriel Roca; mains €8.50-20; ⊙1-3.30pm & 7-11pm Thu-Tue Feb-Oct) Enjoy Marisol's pasta dishes and pizzas, fish and shellfish, rice dishes and stews at a table on the spacious covered terrace by the water. The food is fairly standard portside fare, but the setting is pleasant enough.

Information

Tourist office (☎971 656 073; www.mallorcainfo.com; Carrer del Doctor Barraquer 5; ⊙10am-2pm Mon-Fri) On the waterfront at the southwestern end of the port.

Getting There & Away

Bus 502 links the town to Palma (€6.15, up to eight times a day, 1¼ hours).

The best-known walking route heads up to a restored 14th-century castle, a fortress once used to keep pirates off the island. It was later converted into a prison for French soldiers, more than 5000 of whom died after being abandoned in 1809 towards the end of the Peninsular War. The 30-minute walk to the castle meanders along the northern side of the island before taking you to the 80m-high bluff where the castle looms.

Guides also sometimes lead the 20-minute walk to Es Celler, a farmhouse owned by the Feliu family, who owned the entire island in the early 20th century. It's now a small museum with history and culture exhibits. Nearby stands a monument to the French prisoners who died on Cabrera.

Other possible routes lead to the N'Ensiola lighthouse (four hours, permission required), the southern sierra of Serra de Ses Figueres (2½ hours, permission required), or the highest point of the island, the 172m Picamosques (three hours, permission required).

The island is a wonderful place for snorkelling. While you need special permission to dive here, you can snorkel off the beach. Or, in July and August, sign up for the guided snorkelling excursions offered by park rangers.

This is prime territory for birdwatching: marine birds, birds of prey and migrating birds all call Cabrera home at least part of the year. Common species include the fisher eagle, the endangered Balearic shearwater, Audouin's gull, Cory's shearwater, shags, ospreys, Eleonora's falcon and peregrine falcons, as well as 130 or so migrating birds.

Wildlife is also abundant. The Balearic lizard is the best-known species on Cabrera. This small lizard has few enemies on the archipelago and 80% of the species population lives on the island.

On the cruise back to Colònia de Sant Jordi, the boat stops in **Sa Cova Blava** (Blue Cave), a gorgeous cave with crystalline waters where passengers can take a dip. Speedboats also stop here.

Platja des Trenc

Platja des Trenc, the largest undeveloped beach on Mallorca, runs 3km northwest from the southern edge of Colònia de Sant Jordi. With long stretches of blindingly white sand and an idyllic setting among pine trees and rolling dunes, des Trenc proves just how pretty the Mallorcan coast was before development got out of hand.

Indeed, it's thanks to the out-of-control building sprees elsewhere on the island that this strip of sand has remained so pristine. Locals outraged by the concrete jungles of places like S'Arenal and Cales de Mallorca fought long and hard to save des Trenc from a similar fate, digging their heels in and eventually freezing plans in the 1980s to convert this area into a sprawling golf and beach resort; the anti-development graffiti on some of the half-finished villas speaks volumes. Des Trenc is now considered a 'natural area of special interest'. Officially a nudist beach, it draws a mixed clothed and unclothed crowd.

To reach the parking lot (per vehicle €6), take the signed turn-off west off Ma6040. The narrow, paved road passes mounds of yellowed salt at the Salines de Llevant salt fields then winds its way alongside fields sprinkled with wildflowers to reach the low-lying marsh area near the beach.

Ses Salines

Used as a source of salt since the days of the Romans, Ses Salines (the Salt Fields) is an unassuming agricultural centre that's rapidly garnering a reputation as one of southern Mallorca's most agreeable inland towns. With cool bar-restaurants, a historic hotel and shops selling the cleverly marketed local salt, it has transformed itself from a waystation en route to somewhere else to a destination in its own right. It also stands on the cusp of some lovely country – replete with walking and cycling trails, this is above all a rural area where nature reigns supreme.

Sights

The town's attractions are fairly far-flung and you'll need a car to reach them.

Cap de Ses Salines LIGHTHOUSE
(Carretera de Cap de Ses Salines) Follow the Ma6110 highway 9km south of Llombards

TIME 'MARCHES' ON: THE STORY OF JOAN MARCH

The March family owns nearly 3% of Mallorcan territory, not to mention a hefty portion of the island's grandest manor houses, its weightiest art collections and its biggest bank. The family patriarch, Joan March Ordinas, was the world's seventh-richest person when he died in 1962, leaving his family extensive land holdings and a string of rumours about the questionable sources of his money. Revered and reviled in Mallorca, Joan March was an astute businessman who founded the successful Banca March and invested heavily in Mallorca.

These days the family runs ambitious cultural foundations that dabble in everything from art and archaeology to theatre and music. March's descendants still own more than 100 sq km of land on the island and no matter what their critics say, they've proven to be excellent stewards of it, preserving the vast majority as forest and farmland. The largest *possessió*, or estate, is Sa Vall, an unspoilt natural paradise near Ses Salines.

For more on the family and its cultural foundations, check out www.march.es and www.fundacionbmarch.es.

to reach the Cap de Ses Salines, a beautiful bluff on Mallorca's southernmost tip with a lighthouse dating back to 1863. There's not much here at the cape, but stretching out along either side of it are wonderfully unspoilt beaches protected by the **Reserva Marina del Migjorn de Mallorca**.

The eastern beaches are hewn out of the coastal cliffs that run up towards exquisitely beautiful coves like **Caló des Màrmols**, beaches like the **Platja d'Almunia** and caves like **Cova de Sa Plana**. A rugged coastal path links them all in an 8km trail.

Botanicactus GARDENS

(☎971 649 494; www.botanicactus.com; Carretera Ses Salines-Santanyí; adult/child €8/4.20; ⏰9am-6.30pm) Just outside town is the sprawling Botanicactus, which claims to be the largest botanical garden in Europe. Come to wander among its 1000-plus species of Mediterranean, exotic and wetland plants.

Poblat Talaiòtic dels Antigors ARCHAEOLOGICAL SITE

One kilometre out of Ses Salines, heading towards Colònia de Sant Jordi, follow the signs for this neglected archaeological site. There's no visitors centre, the gate is always open, and only rusted and virtually illegible plaques remain, so use your imagination to see how these low stone walls would have once constituted a prehistoric settlement.

Activities

Artestruz Mallorca OSTRICH FARM

(☎971 650 562; www.artestruzmallorca.com; Ma6014; adult/child €3/2; ⏰10am-8pm) Signposted off the Ma6014, 3km northwest of Ses Salines, this ostrich farm is certainly different. The main attraction is the chance to ride one of the ostriches, which kids will love. Meals (featuring ostrich meat, ostrich eggs and Mallorcan wine) are available with advance notice, and there's also a shop onsite, selling ostrich-leather products such as bags and even computer cleaners made from ostrich feathers.

Eating

Bodega Barahona SEAFOOD €€

(☎971 649 130; www.bodegabarahona.com; Plaça Sant Bartomeu 2; mains €8-16; ⏰1-4pm & 7.30-11pm Tue-Sun) This perennially popular corner bar has been going strong since 1945. The secret to its staying power is the rice, seafood and fish dishes – no fusion cooking here, just recipes that haven't changed in decades. Its specialties are lobster stew and *arròs notari*, a rice dish overflowing with seafood and a rich squid-ink sauce. The bar is on the main road through town, next to the church.

Cassai Grand Café & Restaurant TAPAS, INTERNATIONAL €

(☎971 649 721; www.cassai.es; Carrer de Sitjar 5; mains & tapas €4.50-14.50; ⏰11am-midnight Tue-Sun) A beguiling yet understated designer space both indoors and out, Cassai has the ambience of an Ibiza chill-out cafe for grown-ups. It also runs a designer homewares store elsewhere in town and it shows in its rustic-sophisticated decor. Dishes include fish croquettes, pork tenderloin skewers with brie, and a well-priced *plat du jour* (€8.50).

Asador Es Teatre GRILLED MEATS €€
(☎971 649 540; www.asadoresteatre.com; Plaça Sant Bartomeu 4; mains €11.90-21.80; ⊙11am-11pm Thu-Tue) Run by the same people as the adjacent Bodega Barahona, Asador Es Teatre is utterly different, specialising in roast lamb, T-bone steaks and other fine cuts of meat. The building dates to the 19th century, but the outdoor terrace is the place to be.

Drinking

Bodega Llum de Sal BAR, CAFE
(☎971 649 773; www.llumdesal.es; Carrer Burguera Mut 14; ⊙9am-midnight) One of the loveliest bars in this part of the island, this achingly hip split-level place on the main road through town is our sort of place: you can get everything from your morning coffee to an evening cocktail. It also sells gourmet food products, including the local salt in a number of ready-made herb combinations for fish, meats and even wok cooking.

Shopping

In addition to Cassai Gourmet, Bodega Llum de Sal sells some wonderful salt varieties.

Cassai Gourmet FOOD & WINE
(☎971 642 861; Plaça Sant Bartomeu 9; ⊙10am-1.15pm & 4.30-8pm) The official sales point for Flor de Sal d'Es Trenc, the salt you'll see for sale all over Mallorca, this shops sells the natural variety, as well as those scented with Mediterranean, hibiscus and black olive herbs among others. It also sells wines, olive oils and other local food products.

Getting There & Away

The easiest way to arrive here is with your own wheels, not least because you'll need them to explore the surrounding attractions. Infrequent buses run to/from Campos and Santanyí.

SANTANYÍ TO CALA D'OR

The resorts that cling to the island's eastern flank have grown into a more or less continuous stream of hotels, seafood restaurants and umbrella-packed beaches. The only merciful exception to the sprawl in the busiest part of southern Mallorca is the Parc Natural de Mondragó, a bit of fresh air in the form of immaculate beaches rimmed with ruddy cliffs and junipers.

Santanyí & Around

The busy inland town of Santanyí differs from most of the settlements nearby in that tourism is a mere side effect of its charm. A historic town, it's now the social and commercial meeting place for those living along the coast and in the countryside nearby. Market days (Wednesdays and Saturdays) are the busiest times, but any fine afternoon will see a crowd enjoying the terrace bars of the main square.

Sights

Cala Santanyí BEACH
Santanyí's only real beach access, Cala Santanyí is popular although not overdeveloped. The spacious beach is the star in a scenic show that also includes a gorgeous, cliff-lined cove and impossibly cobalt-coloured waters. The beach sits at the bottom of a ravine of sorts where there is a sandy car park (walking or cycling back to town or to the resort centre requires some substantial leg strength).

A small path leads away from Cala Santanyí and along the coast, where the natural rock arch **El Pontàs** rises out of the surf. This is a popular spot to snorkel.

Cala Llombards BEACH
A petite cove defined by rough rock walls topped with pines, Cala Llombards is a truly beautiful place. A small informal beach-hut bar and rows of sun loungers shaded by palm-leaf umbrellas constitute the extent of human intervention. The main thing that's on offer is the soul-satisfying view – turquoise waters, a sandy beach and the reddish rocks of the cliffs that lead like a promenade towards the sea.

To reach Cala Llombards, follow the sign off the Ma6102 down a stone-walled road bordered by meadows of grazing sheep.

Eating

Es Coc MALLORCAN FUSION €€
(☎971 641 631; www.restaurantescoc.com; Carrer de Aljub 37; mains €16.50-24.50, menú degustación €39.50; ⊙1-3.30pm & 7.30-10.30pm Mon-Sat) All decked out in wood and exposed stone, Es Coc blends local traditions with some innovative detours en route to your table. Try dishes like the *lubina, tumbet y espuma de tumbet* (sea bass, Mallorcan ratatouille and ratatouille foam).

START CAP DE SES SALINES
FINISH COLÒNIA DE SANT JORDI
DISTANCE 9KM
DURATION THREE HOURS

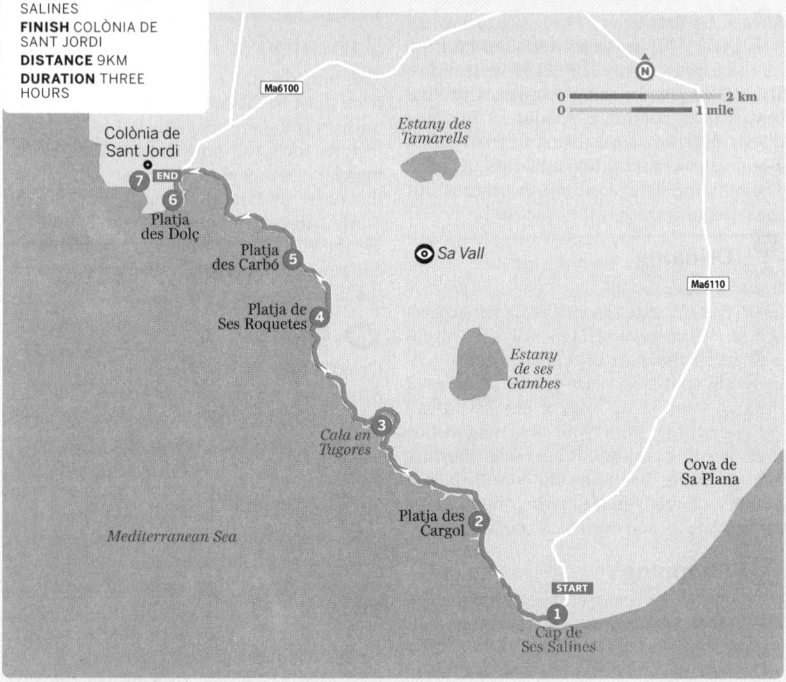

Walking Tour

Cap de Ses Salines to Colònia de Sant Jordi

Pristine coastline can be hard to come by in Mallorca, but this walk has it in abundance. A coastal trail between Cap de Ses Salines and Colònia de Sant Jordi, it's a flat but rocky trek across battered coastal rock outcroppings and forgotten sandy beaches perfect for swimming. Be sure to take plenty of water; there are no fresh water sources and very little shade along the way. Plants you'll see along the trail include wild asparagus and leafy *azucena de mar* (sea purslane), whose fragrant white flowers appear in July and August.

Leave your car on the shoulder of the road at 1 **Cap de Ses Salines**, which is signposted from the main highway. From here, head towards the sea and turn right (west). You'll see the Mediterranean glistening in a thousand shades of blue to your left, the Illa de Cabrera in the distance and the extensive Sa Vall estate, owned by the March family, bordering the walk on your right. This private estate is an endless expanse of scrubby Mediterranean vegetation and is home to two important wetland areas.

After 30 minutes of a fairly flat walk over the ruddy-coloured calcareous rocks that dominate the coast here (the same ones as those used in Palma's Catedral), you'll come upon the first 'virgin' beach of the walk, 2 **Platja des Cargol**, which is protected by a natural rock pier. In summer this place can get quite crowded on land and at sea.

Continue along the coast to reach other coves and beaches, like 3 **Cala en Tugores** (one hour further on), 4 **Platja de Ses Roquetes**, 5 **Platja des Carbó** (after 2¼ hours) and finally 6 **Platja des Dolç** (after three hours). The beaches, with their fine-as-flour sand and gentle waves the colour of turquoise, are simply gorgeous. Even with summer crowds, the idyllic setting amid juniper trees and squawking seagulls ensures that it always feels like an escape.

When you get to the town of 7 **Colònia de Sant Jordi**, you've reached the end of the walk.

Information

Parc Natural de Mondragò office (☎971 642 067; Carrer de Can Llaneres 8; ⏱10am-4pm Mon-Fri) Information on visiting this coastal protected area.

Getting There & Away

Up to six buses head to Palma (€6.35, 1½ hours) daily.

Cala Figuera

If you could see Cala Figuera from the air, it would look like a snake with its jaws open wide, biting into the pine trees and low buildings of the resort. Although the town itself is rather dumpy and offers little in the way of entertainment, the romantic, restaurant-lined port is one of the prettiest on the east coast. A few yachts and pleasure cruisers line up beside the painted fishing boats, but Cala Figuera retains its air of old-world authenticity. Local fishers really still fish here, threading their way down the winding inlet before dawn and returning to the port to mend their nets.

Eating

Restaurante Petite Iglesia FRENCH €
(☎971 645 009; www.la-petite-iglesia.com; Carrer de la Marina 11; mains €13.50-17.50; ⏱7-11pm) It may not have sea views at this place two blocks up the hill from the water, but it's nonetheless close to being the loveliest setting in town. Inhabiting the shell of a small stone church with outdoor tables under the trees, this place serves up French home cooking with wild boar cooked in its own juices and Provençal beef stew.

Mistral Restaurante MALLORCAN, INTERNATIONAL €
(☎971 645 118; www.mistral-restaurante.com; Carrer de la Verge del Carme 42; mains €14.50-18; ⏱6-11pm mid-Apr–Oct) Choose between tasty, typical tapas or more elaborate dishes such as grilled sole fish with fresh parsley paste, or *tumbet* (Mallorcan ratatouille) with meat or fish at this stylish spot just up from the port.

L'Arcada MALLORCAN, INTERNATIONAL €
(Carrer de la Verge del Carme 80; mains €12-18.50; ⏱1-3.30pm & 7.30-10.30pm Apr-Oct) Come here for Mallorcan treats such as rabbit with onions, and courgettes stuffed with fish and seafood. The ubiquitous pizza is also on offer here if you must. There's a decent elevated view of the port.

Drinking

Bon Bar BAR, CAFE
(☎971 645 206; Carrer de la Verge del Carme 27; ⏱10.30am-midnight) Views – that's what this place is all about. High above the main body of the inlet and with uninterrupted views, this is the place to nurse a drink, although it also sells pizzas and ice creams.

Getting There & Away

Bus 502 makes the trip from Palma (€6, 1½ hours) via Colònia de Sant Jordi and Santanyí no more than three times a day, Monday through Saturday.

Parc Natural de Mondragó

A natural park encompassing beaches, dunes, wetlands, coastal cliffs and inland agricultural land, the 766-hectare Parc Natural de Mondragó is a beautiful area for swimming or hiking, but is best known as a birdwatching destination. Most people who head this way come to take a dip in the lovely **Cala Mondragó**, one of the most attractive coves on the east coast. Sheltered by large rocky outcrops and fringed by pine trees, it's formed by a string of three protected sandy beaches connected by rocky footpaths.

Birdwatchers have a ball with the varied species found in the area, which include falcons and turtledoves. Among those species that nest here are Peregrine falcons and Audouin's gulls. Taking one of the walking trails that crisscross the park will give you plenty of birdwatching opportunities. Also keep an eye out for Algerian hedgehogs, Hermann's tortoise and the Balearic toad.

Cala Mondragó is 2km south of Portopetro. Bus 507 links Mondragó with Cala d'Or (€1.40, 30 minutes, seven times daily Monday through Friday) and a few other seaside resorts.

Information

Park office (☎971 181 022, 971 642 067; Carretera de Cala Mondragó; ⏱9am-4pm) The small park office is by the car park. There's another branch in Santanyí.

Portopetro

There's something in the air in Portopetro. This intimate fishing port's slower pace and laid-back style is immediately apparent as you stroll its steep, shady streets and look out over the protected natural inlet that originally made this town such a hit with fishers. Centred on a boat-lined inlet and surrounded by residential estates, Portopetro is really just a cluster of harbourside bars and restaurants, with a couple of small beaches nearby.

Eating

Restaurant Celler

Ca'n Xina SPANISH, MALLORCAN €€
(☑971 658 559; Passeig del Port 52; mains €11.95-21.30; ⊙noon-3.30pm & 7.30-10.30pm Thu-Tue May-Oct) This friendly eatery boasts a shady terrace by the port, and serves delicious Mallorcan specialities like *trampó* (summer salad made with tomatoes and peppers), paella, stuffed eggplant and grilled catch of the day.

La Caracola MALLORCAN, INTERNATIONAL €
(☑971 657 013; Avinguda del Port 40; mains €9-12; ⊙1-3.30pm & 7.30-10.30pm) In addition to the usual suspects of paella and pasta, this enduringly popular place has been pleasing diners with plates of stuffed squid *(calamares rellenos)*, homemade soups and *tumbet* (Mallorcan ratatouille) for 20 years. Not the flashiest place in town, though it's usually the most crowded.

Varadero FUSION €€
(☑971 657 428; www.varadero-portopetro.com; Passeig de la Aduana 5; mains €14-26; ⊙11am-11pm Mar-Nov; ☑) This chic place hasn't taken long to become a fixture with young sophisticates. With a frisky international menu (including Mediterranean and Indonesian flavours alongside standards such as grilled lobster) and postdinner chill-out lounge, when low music infuses the teak-furnished waterside terrace with a tropical feel; the water almost laps at your toes. The terraced interior, plush with sofas, is ideal for a cocktail.

❶ Getting There & Away

Up to five buses a day head from Portopetro to Palma (€6.75, 1½ hours) and Cala d'Or (€1.40, 10 minutes).

Cala d'Or

POP 3775

Although the pretty cove beaches and calm, azure waters are still here, they can be hard to find amid this flashy, overgrown resort. Each *cala* has its own main drag, where pubs, restaurants and souvenir shops flourish, making it very difficult to get a handle on the place.

◉ Sights

The main *calas* from west to east are Cala Egos, where there's a tiny, overcrowded beach; Cala Llonga (Port Petit), home to the marina; Cala d'Or (Cala Petita), with its tree-lined shores; Cala Gran (Big Cove), with the widest beach of the lot; Cala Esmeralda, considered the prettiest cove; and Cala Ferrera, a busy, long beach backed by hotels.

Cala d'Or's real claim to fame is its yacht marina, Port Petit, one of the most glamorous on Mallorca and the main reason why this corner of Cala d'Or is earning a reputation as a stylish, live-large kind of place.

⭐ Activities

Xplore Mallorca CANOEING, KAYAKING
(☑971 659 007; www.xploremallorca.com; Carrer de Alga; day trips €15-50; ⊙May-Oct) Mountainbiking (€18), hiking (€15), cycling (€19), and sea-kayaking (€18) excursions of varying duration. Children pay half price.

Sea Riders BOAT TOURS
(☑615 998 732; www.searidersweb.com; Cala Llonga; tours adult/child from €22/16; ⊙Apr-Oct) Sea Riders, in Cala Llonga, offers a kid-friendly boat ride as well as a faster 'adrenaline' ride (€37) with up to three departures daily in July and August.

Moto Sprint BICYCLE RENTAL, MOTORBIKE RENTAL
(☑971 659 007; www.moto-sprint.com; Carrer d'en Perico Pomar 5; bike rental per day €7.50-16, motorbike rental €29-93; ⊙8am-1pm & 4.30-8pm) Rent a bike and cycling equipment, or a scooter.

✖ Eating

There are loads of bog-standard resort-style restaurants and predictably bad pizzerias in Cala d'Or. Port Petit is a great place to go for high-quality seafood and atmospheric dining.

Cala d'Or

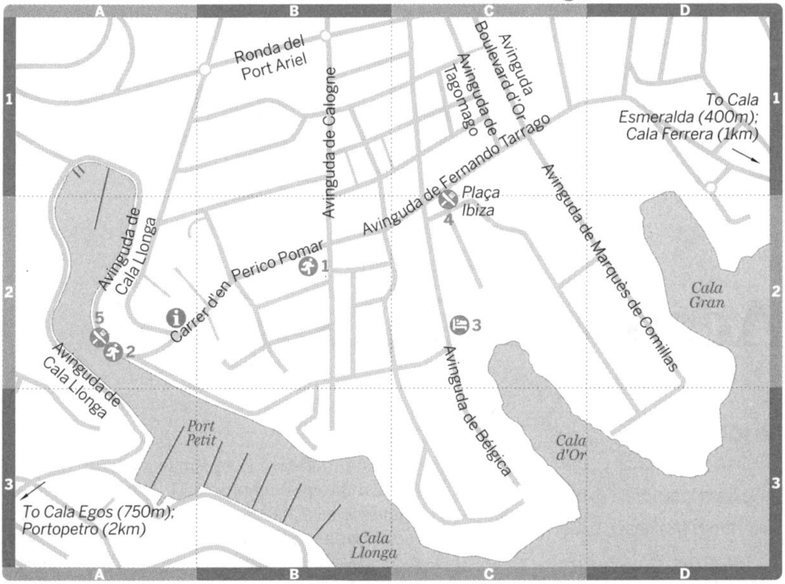

Port Petit SPANISH €€€
(☎971 643 039; www.portpetit.com; Avinguda de Cala Llonga; lunch menú €21.50, mains €23-29, dinner menú €37.50-65; ⏲1-3.30pm & 7-11pm Wed-Mon Apr-Oct) One of Mallorca's top tables, the high-end Port Petit offers innovative spins on classic Mallorcan seafood and produce, served on its sleek, covered upstairs terrace looking down over the yacht port. Service is attentive and the cooking assured, with dishes like the guinea fowl in aromatic herbs catching our eye.

Fernando Café INTERNATIONAL €
(☎971 657 011; Plaça Ibiza 31; mains €6.50-16.70; ⏲noon-midnight) Amid the cookie-cutter bars and Tex-Mex restaurants, this sophisticated place is a real find. The food – pizza, pasta and fish dishes – isn't wildly different from standard resort fare, but the prices are reasonable and the romantic atmosphere created by white tablecloths, candles and a garden setting make it stand out.

Cala d'Or

Activities, Courses & Tours
1 Moto Sprint ... B2
2 Sea Riders ... A2

Sleeping
3 Hotel Cala D'Or ... C2

Eating
4 Fernando Café ... C2
5 Port Petit ... A2

Information

Tourist office (☎971 826 084; Avinguda de Cala Llonga; ⏲8.30am-2pm Mon-Fri, 9am-1pm Sat) On the road from the town centre down to Port Petit.

Getting There & Away

Bus 501 heads to Portopetro (€1.40, 10 minutes, five times a day), then on to Palma (€7.80, one hour 20 minutes, up to six times a day). Bus 441 runs along the eastern coast, stopping at all the major resorts.

Accommodation

Includes »

Palma de Mallorca... 164
Western Mallorca.... 165
Northern Mallorca... 169
The Interior..........171
Eastern Mallorca 172
Southern Mallorca... 174

Best Places to Stay

» La Posada del Marqués (p166)

» Puro Oasis Urbano (p165)

» Es Petit Hotel (p166)

» S'Alquería Blanca (p169)

Best Rural Hotels

» S'Alquería Blanca (p169)

» Finca Son Palou (p169)

» Cases de Son Barbassa (p173)

Best Budget Options

» Hostal-Residencia Catalina Vera (p165)

» Hostal-Restaurante C'an Jordi (p174)

» Hostal Porto Colom (p173)

Where to Stay

The quality of accommodation is generally higher in the Mallorcan interior and the coastal hinterland – with no sea views, places in the interior have had to work harder, with the result that accommodation inland is often filled with character and individual style. This is less of an issue in Western Mallorca, where you'll find fantastic accommodation choices from Estellencs to Sóller – anywhere along the Ma10 that shadows the western coastline is a good base for exploring the island's west. Palma de Mallorca is another good option – giving easy access to the rest of the island, as well as Palma's sights, restaurants and watering holes. You will find some outstanding accommodation choices around the northern, eastern and southern coasts, although large-scale resorts are more dominant there.

Outside the peak season of May to early September, you can usually find a place in Palma and most key locations without booking. In the high season, booking becomes much more important.

Out of season (especially November to Easter) many places on the coast (except Palma) close. Increasingly, Palma is becoming a weekend short-break destination, which means that even in low season it can be an idea to at least call ahead. Prices can skyrocket in high season (usually May to October), while there are usually fantastic deals to be had out of season.

Pricing

Throughout this guidebook, the order of accommodation listings is by author preference, and each place to stay is accompanied by one of the following symbols (the price relates to a double room with private bathroom):

CATEGORY	COST
€ budget	< €75
€€ midrange	€75-175
€€€ top end	> €175

Camping & Youth Hostels

There are no official camping grounds on the island (the last of them closed in 2006), although it is possible to pitch a tent at the Monestir de Lluc. There are two youth hostels (*albergues juveniles* in Spanish, *albergs socials* in Catalan): one in Platja de Palma, near the capital, and the other in Cap des Pinar in the north. For more information, check out www.reaj.com, the official website for Spain's network of youth hostels.

Hotels & Hostales

Officially, places to stay are classified into *hoteles* (hotels, one to five stars) and *hostales* (one to two and, very rarely, three stars).

A *hostal* (sometimes called a *pensión*) is basically a small private hotel, often a family business. The better ones can be bright and spotless with rooms boasting full en suite bathroom.

Hoteles cover the full range of quality from straightforward places through to charming boutique hotels and super-luxury hotels.

At the budget end, prices will vary according to whether the room has only a *lavabo* (washbasin), *ducha* (shower) or *baño completo* (full bathroom, that is, bath/shower, basin and loo). At the top end you may pay more for a room on the *exterior* (outside) of the building or with a *balcón* (balcony), and you will often have the option of a suite. Seaside views usually attract higher rates. Checkout time is generally noon.

Useful resources for booking hotels and *hostales* online include:

» **Federación Hotelera de Mallorca** (www.mallorcahotelguide.com) Hotel-booking engine run by the island's main hoteliers' association.

» **Asociación Hotelera de Palma** (☎971 283 625; www.visit-palma.com) A hotel guide to the capital.

» **Reis de Mallorca** (www.reisdemallorca.com) For hotels with character.

» **First Sun Mallorca** (www.firstsunmallorca.com) Hotels around Cala Ratjada and Canyamel.

Refugis

Simple hikers' huts *(refugis)*, mostly but not exclusively scattered about the Serra de Tramuntana, are a cheap alternative to hotels when hiking. Some are strategically placed on popular hiking routes. Many are run by the **Consell de Mallorca's environment department** (☎971 173 700; www.conselldemallorca.net/refugis), while others are run by the **Institut Balear de la Naturalesa** (Ibanat; ☎971 517 070; ⊙book 10am-2pm Mon-Fri). Dorm beds generally cost around €12 in each; some also have a couple of double rooms and meal service. Call ahead, as more often than not you'll find them closed if you just turn up.

Rural Properties

Numerous rural properties, mountain houses and traditional villas around the island operate as upmarket B&Bs and they're undoubtedly Mallorca's most atmospheric places to stay. Many of the properties are historic and often stylish country estates offering outstanding facilities, including swimming pools, tennis courts, and organised activities and excursions. The local tourism authorities subdivide them into three categories: *agroturisme* (accommodation on working farms, where sometimes the income from the lodgings allows the farms to keep working), *turisme de interior* (mansions converted into boutique hotels in country towns) and *hotel rural* (usually a country estate or *possessiò* converted into a luxury hotel).

Useful resources for booking rural properties online include the following:

» **Agroturismo Balear** (☎971 717 122; www.fincasinmallorca.com)

» **Associació Agroturisme Balear** (☎971 721 508; www.topfincas.com)

» **Finca Mallorca** (www.fincamallorca.de, in German)

» **Fincas 4 You** (www.fincas4you.com)

» **Guías Casas Rurales** (www.guiascasasrurales.com, in Spanish)

» **Las Islas Reisen** (☎ in Germany 05069-34870; www.las-islas-reisen.de)

» **Mallorca Farmhouses** (☎ in UK 0845 800 8080; www.mfh.co.uk)

» **Rustic Rent** (☎971 768 040; www.rusticrent.com)

» **Secret Places** (www.secretplaces.com)

» **Top Rural** (www.toprural.com)

» **Traum Ferienwohnungen** (www.traum-ferienwohnungen.de, in German)

BOOK YOUR STAY ONLINE

For more accommodation reviews by Lonely Planet authors, check out hotels.lonelyplanet.com/Mallorca. You'll find independent reviews, as well as recommendations on the best places to stay. Best of all, you can book online.

GET THEE TO A MONASTERY

For a more meditative retreat from the daily grind, you could opt for one of a handful of monasteries (technically hermitages, as their inmates were hermits and not monks) that offer rooms on the island. In most cases, the hermits left long ago and their former cells have been converted into simple but comfortable accommodation, often with spectacular views. The best options:

» **Hospedería del Santuari de Lluc** (p169)
» **Santuari de la Mare de Déu des Puig** (p169)
» **Petit Hotel Hostatgería Sant Salvador** (p172)
» **Santuari de Monti-Sion** (p172)
» **Hospedería Santuario de Cura** (p172)

PALMA DE MALLORCA

Where you stay depends on what you want to get out of your visit. The intimate boutique hotels of the city centre (especially those near the Passeig d'es Born or around the Plaça Major) place you in the thick of the capital's shopping, restaurant and nightlife districts. For views, head to the Passeig Marítim or Passeig de Mallorca.

OLD PALMA

TOP CHOICE **Hotel Santa Clara** BOUTIQUE HOTEL €€€
(Map p44; ☑971 729 231; www.santaclarahotel.es; Carrer de Sant Alonso 16; s/d from €136/187; ❀❄@❛) Boutique meets antique in this historic mansion, converted with respect, where subdued greys, steely silvers and cream blend harmoniously with the warm stone walls, ample spaces and high ceilings of the original structure.

Hostal Brondo HOSTAL €
(Map p44; ☑971 719 043; www.hostalbrondo.com; Carrer de Ca'n Brondo 1; d €65, s/d/tr without bathroom €40/55/65; ❀❛; ❏3, 15) Climb the courtyard stairs to arrive in a cosy sitting room overlooking the narrow lane. Six of the 10 high-ceilinged rooms (room 6 has a pair of glassed-in balconies) have private bathrooms and all are furnished individually in varying styles, from Mallorcan to vaguely Moroccan. It was closed for renovations at time of research, but should be better than ever once it reopens.

Hotel Palacio Ca Sa Galesa HISTORIC HOTEL €€€
(Map p44; ☑971 715 400; www.palaciocasagalesa.com; Carrer del Miramar 8; s/d from €202/256; ❄@❛❄; ❏2) Welcome to one of the classiest acts in town. Rooms in this enchanting 16th-century mansion are arranged around a cool patio garden. A genteel air wafts through the elegant bedrooms, each named after a famous composer and furnished with antiques, artwork and silk bed throws. There are free bicycles for guest use.

Hotel Dalt Murada HISTORIC HOTEL €€
(Map p44; ☑971 425 300; www.daltmurada.com; Carrer de l'Almudaina 6A; r €95-200; ❄❛; ❏2) Gathered around a medieval courtyard, this carefully restored old town house, dating from 1500, has 14 rooms and is a gorgeous option, with antique furnishings (think chandeliers and canopied beds) and art work, much of which belongs to the friendly family who still own and run the place. The decidedly 21st-century penthouse suite has incomparable views of the cathedral.

PLAÇA MAJOR & AROUND

Misión de San Miguel BOUTIQUE HOTEL €€
(Map p52; ☑971 214 848; youarehotels.com; Carrer de Can Maçanet 1; r €85-150; ❀❄@❛) This 32-room boutique hotel is an astounding deal with excellent prices and stylish designer rooms; it does the little things well with firm mattresses and rain showers, although some rooms open onto public areas and can be a little noisy. In a mark of distinction, its restaurant has become part of the Fosh group. Service is friendly and professional.

Hotel Born HISTORIC HOTEL €€
(Map p44; ☑971 712 942; www.hotelborn.com; Carrer de Sant Jaume 3; s €52-68, d €76-97, ste €108; ❀❄@❛; ❏1, 3, 15) Stepping into this 16th-century Ca'n Maroto manor house is like stepping back in time. From the palatial reception area, take the spiral staircase to a red-carpeted hallway where carved wooden doors creak open to reveal simply furnished rooms, whose high ceilings dwarf antique, slightly careworn furniture.

Convent de la Missió BOUTIQUE HOTEL €€€
(Map p52; ☎971 227 347; www.conventdelamissio.com; Carrer de la Missió 7; r incl breakfast €225-390; P⊖❄☎; 🚌3, 7, 15, 50) A functioning convent from the 1600s until 2003, this intimate boutique hotel has just 14 rooms and a Zen-like calm created by all-white rooms with wispy curtains and airy spaces. Though there's no pool, couples will enjoy the romantic Arab-style hot tub and sauna located in the stone-walled underground cellar.

ES PUIG DE SANT PERE

Puro Oasis Urbano BOUTIQUE HOTEL €€
(Map p44; ☎971 425 450; www.purohotel.com; Carrer del Mont Negre 12; s/d/ste from €119/128/170; ⊖❄@☎≋) Achingly chic with a decor that crosses Ibiza-style minimalism with Marrakesh flair, this 14th-century palace-turned-26-room boutique hotel has positioned itself as the place to be and be seen. By day, lounge on the canopied day beds of the patio or take a dip in the plunge pool; by night join a fashionable crowd for cocktails in the bar. As a guest here, you can also access the Puro Beach club.

Hotel San Lorenzo HISTORIC HOTEL €€€
(Map p44; ☎971 728 200; www.hotelsanlorenzo.com; Carrer de Sant Llorenç 14; s €145-185, d €155-195, ste from €235; ⊖❄☎≋) Tucked away inside the old quarter, this hotel is in a beautifully restored 17th-century building. It has a fragrant Mallorcan courtyard, its own bar, a rooftop terrace with cathedral views and a lovely small garden with swimming pool. Rooms come in a range of styles, from antique wooden furniture and tiled bathrooms to bright blue rooms with Mallorcan fabrics.

Hotel Tres BOUTIQUE HOTEL €€€
(Map p44; ☎971 717 333; www.hoteltres.com; Carrer dels Apuntadors 3; s/d from €160/170; ⊖❄@☎≋) With complimentary slippers and robes in each room, king-sized beds and in-room DVD players, there's no doubt about Hotel Tres' upscale boutique credentials. The decor mixes urbane and eco-chic, with slate-walled showers, cowhide benches and bamboo plants in the bathrooms. If you want a terrace, request Room 101, 201 or 206. Wi-fi in all rooms and young, friendly staff only add to the cool factor.

Hostal Apuntadores HOSTAL €
(Map p44; ☎971 713 491; www.palma-hostales.com; Carrer dels Apuntadors 8; s/d €55/68, without bathroom €35/55; ⊖❄@☎) Just off the main drag (bring earplugs), this unfussy spot makes up for its smallish rooms and lumpy beds with balconies in some rooms overlooking Plaça de la Reina, lots of sunlight and a rooftop terrace that overlooks a cathedral and serves drinks.

Hotel Palau Sa Font HOTEL €€€
(Map p44; ☎971 712 277; www.palausafont.com; Carrer dels Apuntadors 38; s €95, d €155-203, ste €220; ⊖❄@☎≋; 🚌1, 6, 15) Tucked away on a quiet side street, this former 16th-century palace offers 19 rooms decorated in a sparse, minimalist style. Wrought-iron beds, exposed-stone columns and a few splashes of colour in the form of a pale green headboard or a simple red chair give the rooms a feeling of almost monastic calm wedded to contemporary Mediterranean style.

PASSEIG MARÍTIM & WESTERN PALMA

Hotel Mirador HOTEL €€
(Map p57; ☎971 732 046; www.hotelmirador.es; Avinguda de Gabriel Roca 10; s/d €90/108, with sea view €114/156; P⊖❄@☎≋) The Mirador bills itself as a 'classic' hotel. No Nordic minimalism here; rooms are decorated with overstuffed chairs, sensible lamps and yellow bedspreads. The road outside can be pretty busy, so the double-glazing is a plus. However, you'd probably need to have a sea-facing room to justify being this far (a 20-minute walk) from the centre.

ES PORTITXOL, ES MOLINAR & CIUTAT JARDÍ

Hotel Portixol BOUTIQUE HOTEL €€€
(☎971 271 800; www.portixol.com; Carrer de la Sirena 27; s €145, s/d with port view from €225/240, with sea view from €275/290; ⊖❄@☎≋) Two kilometres south of Palma's centre is the jewel of this fishing-village-turned-resort – the hip Hotel Portixol. With a soothing fusion of cool Mediterranean and Scandinavian styles, this harbour-front hotel has been making guests happy for more than 50 years.

WESTERN MALLORCA

PORT D'ANDRATX

Hostal-Residencia Catalina Vera HOSTAL €
(☎971 671 918; www.hostalcatalinavera.es; Carrer Isaac Peral 63; s/d €39/59, s without bathroom €29, apt from €100; P⊖☎) Sitting a block back from the water, this is one of the nicest places to stay in this part of Mallorca. The rooms are simple but impeccable, with occasional antique furnishings; best of all, they're

located in a leafy garden – a haven of peace in this busy summer port. Pablo and his family are welcoming hosts.

ESTELLENCS

Petit Hotel Sa Plana HOTEL €€

(971 618 666; www.saplana.com; Carrer de Eusebi Pascual; r €90-110; mid-Jan–Nov;) Each of the five rooms at this lovely old stone house is named after a Mediterranean wind and has its own style, but all are tastefully turned out with terracotta-tiled floors and wood furnishings. The tousled garden and warm, family-run atmosphere are further bonuses. It's at the western entrance to town, nicely secluded above the main road.

Hotel Nord BOUTIQUE HOTEL €€

(971 149 006; www.hotelruralnord.com; Plaça Triquet 4; s €77-107, d €98-130; Feb-Oct;) This charming hotel just down the hill from the main road in an old stone building offers rooms in wood, stone and terracotta with modern wood beams and stone feature walls. Some have four-poster beds and all are well-sized; the most expensive come with a balcony and good views. Highly recommended.

Finca S'Olivar RURAL HOTEL €€

(971 618 593, 629 266 035; www.fincaolivar.org; Carretera C-710 Km93.5; r €84-138, d/tr from €109/195; P@) About 1km east of town, this series of renovated stone hermitages scattered over a sprawling valley property (with olive terraces) is perfect for those in search of total tranquillity. Rooms are simple, but it's all about location here. The swimming pool seems to hang at the edge of nothing.

BANYALBUFAR

Ca Madò Paula HISTORIC HOTEL €€

(971 148 717; www.camadopaula.com; Carrer de la Constitució 11; s/d from €80/100; @) Partway down the road to the village cove, the four guest rooms of pretty stone Ca Madò Paula are decorated simply with a few antique touches and a couple have sea views. It's a tranquil and well-kept place with a family-run feel. There's a three-night minimum stay policy; prices drop the longer you stay.

Son Borguny HISTORIC HOTEL €€

(971 148 706; www.sonborguny.com; Carrer de Borguny 1; s/d/ste €75/95/120;) A charming small hotel a block up from the main road, Son Borguny occupies a 15th-century home. The attractive rooms are never overdone and feature occasional stone walls and wooden beams, plus some have partial sea views. It's a lovely quiet place to spend a week, taking advantage of its 'stay seven nights, get one night free' policy.

Hotel Sa Baronia HOTEL €

(971 618 146; www.hbaronia.com; Carrer de Baronia 16; s/d/tr €55/72/95, half-board €65/94/135; Easter-Oct;) A rambling building with an old-world feel, family-run Baronia is built in the ruins of a Muslim-era fort (part of the central tower remains). The rooms are modern and simple with tired-looking decor – the style is more Spanish grandmother circa 1950s than baronial – but the views from most of the balconies are exceptional; some face the sea, others the village. There's a cliff-side swimming pool, and the courtyard hosts jazz concerts in summer.

ESPORLES & THE INLAND CIRCUIT

Scott's Galilea HOTEL €€

(971 870 100; www.scottsgalilea.com; Sa Costa d'En Mandons 3; s/d studio apt from €110/140, villas from €200; Feb-Oct; P@) The views here are some of the best in the Serra de Tramuntana, and the place is run with an admirable attention to detail; the beds are supremely comfortable. Rooms are large and lovingly kept. Highly recommended.

La Posada del Marqués HISTORIC HOTEL €€€

(971 611 230; www.posada-marques.com; Es Verger; d €204-225, ste €270-310; P@) Deep in the mountains around Esporles, the spectacularly located La Posada del Marqués is a luxurious retreat from the clamour of the modern world. The views sweep down the valleys to the distant plains, while the 16th-century stone manor conceals rooms with grand baroque interiors. It's not all about the past – there are plasma TVs, DVD players and internet access.

Gran Hotel Son Net HOTEL €€€

(971 147 000; www.sonnet.es; Carrer del Castell de Son Net; r from €415; P@) Pampering is the order of the day here. This award-winning 17th-century mansion is home to a considerable art collection, a renowned restaurant in a grand stone-walled hall, and has plush, spacious rooms and suites. A four-night minimum is required from May to October.

VALLDEMOSSA

Es Petit Hotel BOUTIQUE HOTEL €€

(Map p88; 971 612 479; www.espetithotel-valldemossa.com; Carrer d'Uetam 1; r €127-172 Mar-Nov, €102-138 Dec-Feb; @) This friendly family home (the owners still live here) has been converted into an enticing boutique hotel. In the shady garden and on the terrace with a countryside view, you could be an island away from the flow of Cartuja visitors that streams by the front door.

Hotel Valldemossa HISTORIC HOTEL **€€€**
(☎971 612 626; www.valldemossahotel.com; Camí Antic de Palma; s/d/ste €256/380/500 Apr-Oct, €216/326/419 Nov-Mar;) Composed of two 19th-century stone houses that once belonged to the monastery, this hotel has 12 immaculate rooms. Luxury is the name of the game here, with a blend of antique furnishings and artwork, plus modern comforts. There are four-poster beds, indoor and outdoor pools and the service is as impeccable as the gardens are immaculately manicured.

Cases de Ca's Garriguer RURAL HOTEL **€€**
(☎971 612 300; www.vistamarhotel.es; off Carretera Valldemossa-Banyalbufar; s €90-110, d €115-150; Apr-Oct;) This lovely stone-built property on an elevated plateau 3km west of Valldemossa is one of the better-priced such places in Mallorca. Rooms are large, supremely comfortable and the more expensive ones come with private terraces. Seek out some good deals on offer combining accommodation with car hire.

DEIÀ & AROUND

S'Hotel des Puig HISTORIC HOTEL **€€€**
(☎971 639 409; www.hoteldespuig.com; Carrer des Puig 4; s €78-92, d €125-140, d with terrace €134-160, ste €199-222; Feb-Nov;) The eight rooms of this gem in the middle of the old town reflect a muted modern taste within ancient stone walls. Out the back are secrets impossible to divine from the street, such as the pool and lovely terrace. The 'House on the Hill' has appeared in a number of books about Mallorca, and even in a Robert Graves short story.

Hostal Villaverde HOSTAL **€**
(☎971 639 037; www.hostalvillaverde.com; Carrer de Ramon Llull 19; s/d €46/74, d with terrace €88;) This charming *hostal* in the heart of the hilly village (on its southern flank) offers homey rooms and splendid views from the sunny but leafy terrace. A small number of the doubles have their own terraces and superlative views.

Sa Pedrissa HISTORIC HOTEL **€€€**
(☎971 639 111; www.sapedrissa.com; Carretera de Valldemossa-Deià; s €180-350, d €190-380, ste €250-650; Feb-Nov;) Sublime. From a high rocky bluff looking down along the coast and inland to Deià, this stunning mansion (which once lorded it over an olive oil farm and may date back to the 17th century) is a luxurious choice. The service is faultless, the views from the pool terrace and some rooms are glorious, and the rooms exude class and sophistication.

Hostal Miramar HOSTAL **€€**
(☎971 639 084; www.pensionmiramar.com; Carrer de Ca'n Oliver; s/d €75/95, s without bathroom €39; Mar–mid-Nov;) Hidden within the lush vegetation above the main road and with views across to Deià's hillside church and the sea beyond, this 19th-century stone house with gardens is a shady retreat with nine rooms. Various artists (you can scarcely see the breakfast room walls for canvases) have stayed here over the years. The rooms with shared bathrooms have the best views; others look onto the garden.

La Residencia HOTEL **€€€**
(☎971 639 011; www.hotel-laresidencia.com; Son Canals; s/d from €316/519;) 'The Res' to its habitués, this is the place to rub shoulders with the rich and famous. A short stroll from the village centre, this former 16th-century manor house is a luxurious resort hotel set in 12 hectares of manicured lawns and gardens. A minimum stay of two to three nights is required from June to September.

LLUC ALCARI

Hotel Costa d'Or HOTEL **€€**
(☎971 639 025; www.hoposa.com; Lluc Alcari; s/d incl breakfast from €99/171; Apr-Oct;) This secluded spot offers designer rooms in a stone building that backs on to woods high above the Mediterranean. Rooms with sea views cost considerably more, but you get the same views from the restaurant, terrace and pool. A 15-minute walk through pine forest takes you down to a little pebbly beach with crystal-clear water.

SÓLLER

Ca'n Isabel HOTEL **€€**
(Map p93; ☎971 638 097; www.canisabel.com; Carrer de d'Isabel II 13; s €99.50-131.50, d €124.50-156.50; mid-Feb–mid-Nov;) With just six rooms, this 19th-century house is a gracefully decorated hideaway, with a fine garden out the back. The decor won't be to everyone's taste, but the owners have retained the period style impeccably; the 'Romantic Room' has a gorgeous free-standing antique bathtub. The best (and dearest) of the rooms come with their own delightful terrace.

Ca'l Bisbe HOTEL €€

(Map p93; ☎971 631 228; www.hotelcalbisbe.com; Carrer del Bisbe Nadal 10; s €75-110, d without balcony €105-115, with balcony €127-137, ste €142-170; ⏲Mar-Oct; P) The bishop who once lived here would no doubt appreciate the addition of the pool in this nicely restored parish residence. The room decor is largely modern, but some grand details (such as the stone arches and fireplaces) remain intact in the public areas and the rooms are nice and spacious.

Ca N'Aí HOTEL €€€

(☎971 632 494; www.canai.com; Camí de Son Sales 50; s ste €150, d ste €237-275; P) An impossibly romantic Mallorcan *possessió* ensconced among generous orange groves (more than 5000 trees, we're told), this place is a fragment of heaven on earth with spacious suites, each with its own private terrace and a true sense of rural bliss. Rooms are classy if understated, and the restaurant has a good reputation. It's around 1km northwest of the town centre.

Hotel S'Ardeviu HOTEL €€

(Map p93; ☎971 638 326; www.sollernet.com/sardeviu; Carrer de Vives 14; s €85-95, d €100-120; ⏲Feb-Oct;) Hidden down a lane in a mid-19th-century town house in the centuries-old heart of the town, the seven rooms spread out over this cool stone house vary, some with bare stonework and others whitewashed. One room has a balcony with lovely Sóller views, three look onto the garden, with the rest overlooking the quiet lane.

Ca's Curial BOUTIQUE HOTEL €€

(☎971 633 332; www.cascurial.com; Carrer de La Villalonga 23; d €130-183, ste €160-225; P@) Barely out of the centre, this idyllically set hotel offers eight rooms, including three suites. Loll around in the grounds to the scent of the oranges or have a dip in the pool. It's hard to leave this sturdy stone *finca* (farmhouse) to go visit anything!

Gran Hotel Sóller HOTEL €€€

(Map p93; ☎971 638 686; www.granhotelsoller.com; Carrer de Romaguera 18; s €135-170, d €225-500, ste €500-1350; P@) As the name suggests, this is the big one: a five-star luxury getaway set in a late-19th-century mansion. The rooms are nicely luxurious without being spectacular. The great bonus is all the extras, from the gourmet restaurant and fitness centre to the neat ideas sometimes on offer, such as Chinese massages on the roof.

Hostal Nadal HOSTAL €

(Map p93; ☎971 631 180; Carrer de Romaguera 20; s/d/tr €24/37/48, without bathroom €20/29/39;) It may be simple, but it's home, and about as cheap as it gets on the island. Rooms are no-frills basic but clean and there's a courtyard out the back to flop in after a day's hiking.

PORT DE SÓLLER

TOP CHOICE **Hotel Citric Sóller** HOTEL €

(☎971 631 352; www.citrichotels.com; Camí del Far 15; s/d with mountain view €30/37, with sea view €34/42; @) Wake up to watch the rising sun flood across the bay into your grandstand room. Not bad for a newly renovated budget hotel (formerly Hostal Brisas), right on the waterfront at the quieter, southern end of the bay. The simple whitewashed rooms come with lime-green splashes of colour and it's worth paying (not much) extra for one with a sea-facing balcony. From here it's a short wander to Platja d'en Repic.

Muleta de Ca S'Hereu HOTEL €€

(☎971 186 018; www.muletadecashereu.es; Camp de Sa Mar; s/d/ste €90/140/165; P@) Your car will hate you for the 1.8km track of switchbacks, but this lordly country mansion, dating to 1672, will enchant. Eight sprawling rooms and a handful of apartments, some with distant sea glimpses from this mountainside position, are filled with charm and antiques, but the light colour schemes ensure that the old-world look never overwhelms. Wander the olive groves or relax on the terraces. You may be woken by donkey braying.

Espléndido Hotel HOTEL €€

(☎971 631 850; www.esplendidohotel.com; Passeig Es Travès 5; s/d with garden view from €135/160, r with sea view from €195; @) Run by the snappy Hotel Portixol folks in Palma, this marvellous 1954 carcass has been transformed into cutting-edge four-star waterfront luxury digs. Espléndido's best rooms have terraces that open up straight to the sea, and facilities include a spa and gym.

FORNALUTX

Fornalutx Petit Hotel BOUTIQUE HOTEL €€

(☎971 631 997; www.fornalutxpetithotel.com; Carrer de l'Alba 22; s €70-110, d €100-165, ste €180-240; ⏲mid-Feb–mid-Nov; @) This tastefully converted former convent just below the main square is as much art gallery as boutique hotel. Each of the eight rooms is named after a contemporary Mallorcan painter and displays their canvases. There's a free guest sauna and hot tub and a wonderful terrace with views over the fertile valley.

Ca'n Reus HISTORIC HOTEL €€
(☎971 631 174; www.canreushotel.com; Carrer de l'Alba 26; s €100, d €120-150, ste €170; P⊖❄@📶🏊) This place is tempting for a romantic escape. The British-owned country mansion was built by a certain Mr Reus, who got rich on the orange trade with France. The eight rooms are all quite different and all have views; each is stunning and has restrained antique furnishings and exposed stonework, with plenty of light throughout. Children under five are not welcome.

ROAD FROM SÓLLER TO ALARÓ

S'Alqueria Blanca RURAL HOTEL €€
(☎971 148 400; www.alqueria-blanca.com; off Carretera Palma-Sóller Km13.6, Bunyola; r €130-180, ste from €200; ⊙Jan-Nov; P❄🏊) S'Alqueria Blanca is a majestic country residence in sprawling grounds about 2km west of Bunyola, with six rooms (three doubles and three suites). The oldest buildings (where the rooms are) formed the Arab *alquería* (Muslim-era farmstead). A whimsical Modernista building was added in 1906. If travelling north from Palma, the turn-off west is at Km13.6; head 700m further down the trail.

Finca Son Palou RURAL HOTEL €€
(☎971 148 282; www.sonpalou.com; Plaça de l'Església, Orient; r €120-155, with terrace €165-211, ste €185-230; ⊙closed mid-Dec–mid-Jan; P⊖❄@📶🏊) Climb up Carrer de Sant Jordi to the church of the same name and this quiet village mansion, a typically superb rural property on 100 hectares. Rooms have a rustic simplicity, with terracotta floor tiles, timber furnishings and, in some cases, exposed beams.

Hotel Can Xim HOTEL €€
(☎971 518 680; www.canxim.com; Plaça de la Vila 8, Alaró; s €60-80, d €80-100; P❄@📶🏊) This family-run place has an ideal location overlooking the square. Rooms are spacious and light-filled with modern wooden beams, if ever-so-slightly soulless. It's well-priced by Mallorcan standards.

Refugi S'Hostatgeria REFUGIO €
(☎971 182 112; Alaró, per person €12; ⊙May-Sep) The Refugi S'Hostatgeria has finally opened for those who wish to sleep overnight, close to the Castell d'Alaró. Much of the building material was lifted by helicopter – how on earth did medieval Mallorquins build the great stone fortress? There's a snack bar, and three rooms with four beds each (bring your sleeping bag). You can get sandwiches and drinks in the bar, open from 9am to 11pm.

MONESTIR DE LLUC & AROUND

Hospedería del Santuari de Lluc MONASTERY €
(☎971 871 525; www.lluc.net; Plaça dels Peregrins; d/apt from €41/58.50; ⊖) The monastery's accommodation section has 81 rooms and 39 apartments. They vary in size and facilities (some have kitchen access); some look over the courtyard, but those with mountain views are best, while the downstairs rooms are dark and best avoided. The rooms are popular with school groups, walkers and pilgrims.

NORTHERN MALLORCA

POLLENÇA

Hotel Desbrull BOUTIQUE HOTEL €€
(Map p106; ☎971 535 055; www.desbrull.com; Carrer del Marqués Desbrull 7; s €65-80, d €70-90; ⊖❄📶) The best deal in town, with six pleasantly fresh if coquettishly small doubles in a modernised stone house. White dominates the decor in rooms and bathrooms, offset with strong splashes of colour, and if you like the contemporary art on the walls, you can buy it. Run by a friendly brother-sister combination.

Posada de Lluc BOUTIQUE HOTEL €€
(Map p106; ☎971 535 220; www.posadadelluc.com; Carrer del Roser Vell 11; s €110-134, d €115-170, with terrace €144-210; P⊖❄@📶🏊) This 15th-century, two-storey town house in central Pollença was handed over to the brethren of the Monestir de Lluc as a resting place for pilgrims. It's now a fetching inn with a variety of rooms. The most straightforward are the doubles on the 1st floor facing the street. Those overlooking the pool and with their own terrace have more of a wow factor.

Santuari de la Mare de Déu des Puig MONASTERY €
(☎971 184 132; per person €22) Stay in the former monks' cells of this monastery for an ascetic, tranquil experience.

L'Hostal HOTEL €€
(Map p106; ☎971 535 282; www.hostalpollensa.com; Carrer del Mercat 18; s €65-104, d €86-120; ⊖❄@📶) Here you'll find simple rooms with clean lines and exposed stone walls, white tiled floors, a splash of primal colour in the decor and modern art on the walls. It's a comfortable, well-priced option in the heart of town.

Hotel Son Sant Jordi HOTEL €€
(Map p106; ☎971 530 389; www.hotelsonsantjordi.com; Carrer de Sant Jordi 29; s €62-125, d €86-155, ste €120-192; P) Occupying a fine old house and sharing a bit of square with the 16th-century Oratori de Sant Jordi chapel, this hotel has rooms with high ceilings, terracotta floors (with varying styles), canopied beds and plenty of light. Out back, a surprisingly expansive garden frames a curvaceous pool.

CALA DE SANT VINCENÇ

Hostal Los Pinos HOSTAL €
(☎971 531 210; www.hostal-lospinos.com; Urbanització Can Botana; s €39-49, d €66-86; May–mid-Oct;) Set back from the road between Cala Molins and Cala Carbó, Hostal Los Pinos comprises two gleaming white villas sitting on a leafy hillside. Superior doubles have partial sea views and are wonderfully large with separate sleeping and lounge areas and balconies. The smaller singles have old-style Mallorcan decor.

PORT DE POLLENÇA

Hostal Bahia HOTEL €€
(☎971 866 562; www.hoposa.com; Passeig Voramar; s/d from €50/62; Apr-Oct; @) A 19th-century villa converted into a hotel, the Bahia occupies a waterfront spot along a shady pedestrian esplanade. The rooms are simple with parquet floors, but they're elevated above the ordinary if you can get one with a balcony facing the sea. Room prices vary almost daily. The location – close to the action but a little removed from the clamour – is perfect.

Hotel Sis Pins HOTEL €€
(☎971 867 050; www.hotelsispins.com; Passeig d'Anglada Camarasa 77; s €33-66, d €56-110, d with sea view €70-144; Feb-Oct; @) Going strong since 1952, this monument to the early days of Spain's coastal tourism boom has a certain old-style graciousness. The rooms are fairly standard, but well-priced and those facing the sea are the best.

CAP DE FORMENTOR

Hotel Formentor HISTORIC HOTEL €€€
(☎971 899 100; www.barceloformentor.com; Platja de Formentor 3; d €145-419; Apr-Oct; P@) This hotel is a jewel of pre-WWII days and a Mallorca classic. From 1929 the ritzy hotel digs have played host to the likes of Grace Kelly, Winston Churchill, Mikhail Gorbachev, John Wayne and the Dalai Lama. Rooms are pleasing without being the latest in grand luxury. The singles are a little small, but the seaside doubles and suites are a taste of paradise.

ALCÚDIA

Petit Hotel Ca'n Simó BOUTIQUE HOTEL €€
(Map p113; ☎971 549 260; www.cansimo.com; Carrer de Sant Jaume 1; s €75-80, d €98-128; @) This stylish hotel, in the heart of the old quarter, inhabits a renovated 19th-century town house, and has seven double rooms. All the usual elements of rural Mallorcan decoration are here – exposed stone walls and wrought-iron furnishings. And it's wondrous how they managed to squeeze in a little indoor pool, spa bath and fitness room.

Ca'n Pere BOUTIQUE HOTEL €€
(Map p113; ☎971 545 243; www.hotelcanpere.com; Carrer d'en Serra 12; s €70-75, d €90-105, d with spa bath & terrace €110-120;) A fine boutique option hidden in the old town, Ca'n Pere has all-stone walls and all-white furnishings; some rooms also have the modern equivalent of four-poster beds. Those with the spa bath and private balcony rank among northern Mallorca's best bargains.

Fonda Llabres HOTEL €
(Map p113; ☎971 545 000; www.fondallabres.com; Plaça de sa Constitució 6; s/d €32/38, without bathroom €22/32;) Fonda Llabres, occupying the old telephone exchange, offers cheap yet comfortable beds in the centre of town. The rooms are simple and smallish but well-kept and fine budget value. Reception is in the downstairs bar.

PORT D'ALCÚDIA

Botel Alcúdia Mar RESORT €€€
(☎971 897 215; www.botelalcudiamar.es; Passeig Marítim 1; s €103-193, d €142-266; Mar-Oct; P@) It's not often that we feature resort-style accommodation – there's a sameness to so many places here – but this place rises above the crowd with its privileged location away from the crowds yet in the centre of town, and for the quiet sophsitication of its installations. Great atmosphere.

Hostal Vista Alegre HOSTAL €
(☎971 547 347; www.hvista-alegre.com; Passeig Marítim 10; s €15-20, d €30-40, tr €45-55; @) It's somehow reassuring to find a good-old-fashioned Spanish *hostal* amid all the resorts. No frills here, just bargain prices and basic but clean rooms. The 17 doubles face inland and have air-con, while three large triples face the port and have a small balcony: no air-con here, but the sea breeze should suffice.

CAP DES PINAR

Ermita de La Victòria
MONASTERY €

(Hostatgeria Ermita de la Victoria; ☑971 549 912; www.lavictoriahotel.com; Carretera Cap des Pinar; s/d €45/68, breakfast €8; ☺) About 600m east of S'Illot, a road winds up high to a magnificent viewpoint and this early 15th-century hermitage. The 12 renovated rooms have a crisp feel, all white walls and cream linen with timber window shutters and beams. The massive stone walls and terracotta floors lend it Mediterranean grace and the position is perfect.

Albergue La Victòria
HOSTEL €

(☑971 545 395; www.reaj.com; Carretera Cap des Pinar Km4.9; dm/full board €16/28, towels €1.75; ☺Mar-Nov; ☺) This place, reached after 1.5km of winding road east of Bonaire, sums up Mallorcan coastal development: a concrete eyesore in a stunning location. It's basic but good value if you don't mind bunking down in dorms. Like most such places it does have a strong institutional feel, but the surroundings more than compensate.

COLÒNIA DE SANT PERE

Hotel Rocamar
HOTEL €€

(☑971 828 503; www.hotelrocamar.net; Carrer de Sant Mateu 9; s €60-70, d €90-105; ☺✲@☎✉) This renovated hotel is a breath from the central square and beach. Creams, beiges and browns dominate the decor and the spacious, light rooms have parquet floors and pleasantly neutral, white furniture. From the roof terrace, where you can plonk into the Jacuzzi, you can see the deep blue sea. If the resorts to the west drive you crazy, this could be your antidote.

THE INTERIOR

SANTA MARIA DEL CAMÍ

Read's Hotel
HOTEL €€€

(☑971 140 26; www.readshotel.com; Ca'n Moragues; d from €395, ste €470-790; P☺✲@☎✉) Northeast of central Santa Maria is one of the island's most exquisite country-manor getaways. Set in immaculate gardens with thick palm trees, this warm stone mansion offers 23 rooms. The better ones have their own terraces and no expense has been spared with the fittings – expect Bang & Olufsen TVs. There are indoor and outdoor pools and a spa. From Plaça dels Hostals, follow the signs down country lanes for about 2km.

SOUTH OF BINISSALEM

Sa Torre
RURAL HOTEL, APARTMENTS €€

(☑971 144 011; www.sa-torre.com; Carrer de les Alqueries 70; apt €135; P☺✲@✉) Located about 1km west of Biniali, this wonderful haven rests on the edge of the tiny hamlet Ses Alqueries (now home mostly to Palma commuters). This grand *finca* has been in the same family since 1560 and offers five spacious, self-catering apartments.

NORTH OF INCA

TOP CHOICE Es Castell
RURAL HOTEL €€

(☑971 875 154; www.fincaescastell.com; Carrer de Binibona; s €100-120, d €130-170, ste €170-190; P☺✲@☎✉) If you've come to Binibona for peace and quiet, go a little further beyond the town for utter tranquillity. The Es Castell is an 11th-century farm estate, set out on a ledge by itself in the shadow of the mountains, that encompasses a muddle of sturdy stone houses and 300 hectares dominated by olive trees, and makes the perfect rural escape.

Agroturisme Monnàber Vell
RURAL HOTEL €€

(☑971 516 131; www.monnabervell.com; s €99-128, d €116-152, ste €123-194; ☺closed mid-Dec–mid-Feb; P☺✲@☎✉) Agroturisme Monnàber Vell is a few hundred metres south of the Oratori de Sant Miquel and is found at the end of a track that winds through the fields and woods. The standard double rooms are comfortable if a trifle bland, but the suites have plenty of character.

Hotel Can Furiós
RURAL HOTEL €€€

(☑971 515 751; www.can-furios.com; Camí Vell de Binibona 11; d €170-225, ste €195-310; ☺✲☎✉) A renovated 16th-century stone mansion with a handful of rooms and suites. It gets consistently good reviews from travellers and it occupies the most beautiful old stone building in a village of many. The rooms blend tradition with modern comforts, warm colour schemes and soft lighting. There's a fine restaurant as well, ensuring you'll rarely have cause to stray too far.

Finca Ets Abellons
GUESTHOUSE €€€

(☑971 875 069; www.albellons.es; Caimari; s €120, d €160-200, ste €220-240; ☺✲@☎✉) This stone farmhouse is another fine escape, set in the hills 1km north of Binibona. The 12 rooms (half with own terrace) have terracotta floors, timber ceilings and graceful, rural antique furnishings. The owners have another property, **Hotel Binibona** (www.binibona.es), in the village itself with similar rooms and facilities.

SINEU

TOP CHOICE Hotel León de Sineu HOTEL €€
(☎971 520 211; www.hotel-leondesineu.com; Carrer dels Bous 129; s/d/ste €81/108/126;) Set in a 15th-century house that was long used as a wine cellar, León de Sineu retains much of its traditional look; the uneven tiled floors add to the appeal. Out the back, the gardens fall away down several levels, stuffed with fountains, palms and huge sunflowers, leading to the pool. Friendly service and a thoughtfully presented breakfast round out a great package.

Can Joan Capo Hotel BOUTIQUE HOTEL €€€
(☎971 855 075; www.canjoancapo.com; Carrer de Degà Joan Rotger 4; r €160-220;) Sineu's slickest hotel has seven rooms, each with its own style – furnishings range between wood-heavy decor to light wrought-iron frames, while beamed ceilings are a recurring theme. The public areas are a study in converting an old stone building into an intimate designer space, with strategically placed antique farm tools, soothing little alcoves and pleasing archways.

Hotel Celler de Ca'n Font HOTEL €
(☎971 520 295; www.canfont.com; Sa Plaça 18; s/d €40/52;) Sitting atop a well-regarded cellar restaurant of the same name and right on the main square, Ca'n Font is the only budget option in town. It has no-frills hostal-style rooms that are clean, functional and worth every euro.

SANTUARI DE NOSTRA SENYORA DE CURA

Hospedería Santuario de Cura MONASTERY €
(☎971 120 260; Santuario de Cura; s/d €38/54; P) Located inside the monastery grounds, the two-star *hospedería* has 31 doubles and four junior suites that are simple but spick-and-span. They're lovely and quiet once the day-trippers have returned down the mountain, and the bar-restaurant serves Mallorcan specialties.

PETRA

Hotel Sa Plaça HOTEL €€
(☎971 561 646; Plaça de Ramón Llull 4; s/d €90/110; closed Nov;) The only overnight option in Petra is, thankfully, a good one. The nights are quiet here in an 1840s stone town house, with just three rooms and a popular restaurant, overlooking a pleasing square with a fountain.

PALMA TO FELANITX

Petit Hotel Hostatgería Sant Salvador MONASTERY €
(☎971 581 952; www.santsalvadorhotel.com; Santuari de Sant Salvador; s/d €45/68, 6-bed apt €112-140; Feb-Oct;) High above the plains in the fortresslike monastery of Sant Salvador, the monks have long since gone, but their former cells have been converted into simple, spruce rooms, each with an outstanding panoramic view and private bathroom. As with most such places, you'll really enjoy being here once the crowds have left or early in the morning.

Santuari de Monti-Sion MONASTERY €
(☎971 647 185; off Carretera Felanitx-Portocolom; by donation;) The Santuari de Monti-Sion, a former monastery, was first erected in the 14th century and is especially curious because of its pentagonal cloister. The views all around Es Pla (The Plain) are inspiring and the monks' cells have been modernised to rent out to guests, although all sorts of permit issues mean that it can't charge hotel rates – ask in the bar for the going donation rate.

EASTERN MALLORCA

ARTÀ

Hotel Sant Salvador BOUTIQUE HOTEL €€
(Map p136; ☎971 829 555; www.santsalvador.com; Carrer del Castellet 7; s €105-175, d €120-190; P) The eight rooms of this luxurious boutique hotel echo the dignified character of this restored manor house, with canopied beds and antique furnishings, plus you'll find contemporary art in other rooms. Surrounded by a lush garden, the hotel also runs a stylish bar and two restaurants.

Hotel Casal d'Artà HOTEL €€
(Map p136; ☎971 829 163; www.casaldarta.de; Carrer de Rafael Blanes 19; s/d €55/91;) Hotel Casal d'Artà is a wonderful old mansion in the heart of town. The decor may be quaint, but a sense of light and space pervades this place. You'll find fresh fruit in your room on arrival and fresh flowers on your breakfast table. There's a flower-filled roof terrace, with a bubbling fountain and incomparable views over the village. Ask for room 4 or 8; both have sybaritic baths sunken into a tiny alcove.

Can Moragues HOTEL €€
(Map p136; ☎971 829 509; www.canmoragues.com; Carrer del Pou Nou 12; s/d €87/127, s/d ste €106/160; P) A cheery yellow country-house-turned-hotel, Can Moragues offers cosy, im-

peccably clean rooms that respect the house's original architecture, with touches like exposed stone walls and wood-beam ceilings, and a mixed contemporary-antique look. Prices drop by 10% from November to March.

AROUND ARTÀ

Cases de Son Barbassa BOUTIQUE HOTEL €€€
(☑971 565 776; www.sonbarbassa.com; Camí de Son Barbassa; s €115-193, d €154-250, s/d ste €144/246; ⊙Feb-Nov; P⊜❋@夝⊛) This stunning rural estate, dotted with olive and almond trees, is presided over by a 16th-century stone tower. The hotel itself has 12 rooms, all individually decorated in a rustic-chic style that preserves the original architectural elements of the house. In short, it's one of the better rural properties on an island full of high-quality places and the restaurant is outstanding. The hotel is located just off the road to Cala Mesquida, and signposted off the main Artà–Cala Ratjada road.

CALA RATJADA

TOP CHOICE Residence – The Sea Club HOTEL, GUESTHOUSE €€
(Map p142; ☑971 563 310; www.theseaclub.es; Avinguda de América 27; s €60-150, d €100-250; ⊙Apr-Oct; ⊜❋@) This British-run place is a real treat along the waterfront promenade. The rooms in this old colonial home have been lovingly renovated, and have crisp linen and soothing colour schemes; prices soar in July and August, but are exceptional value at other times. It's the sort of place that allows you to have a beach holiday without the depersonalised service of some resorts.

Agroturisme S'Horta RURAL HOTEL €€
(☑600 232 627; www.agroturisme-shorta.com; Camí na Ferrera; r €74-130; ⊙Mar-Oct; ⊜夝⊛) The old stone walls, terracotta floors and wood furniture make for a fine combination at this quiet rural home just beyond the outskirts of Cala Ratjada. Family-run and surrounded by trees, it's a terrific chance to sample the tranquillity of rural Mallorcan life without the usual price tag. Accommodation comes in a range of studios or apartments suitable for up to four people.

Hotel Cala Gat HOTEL €€
(☑971 563 166; www.hotelcalagat.com; Carretera del Faro; s €49-72, d €78-114; ⊙Apr-Oct; ⊜❋@) Set amid dense woodlands on the road to the lighthouse and thus removed from the clamour of downtown, Hotel Cala Gat has a lovely small beach almost to itself and pleas-

ant if uninspiring modern rooms. Overall it's a terrific package for its mix of peace and comfort. Of all the beach hotels, this is probably the one we'd choose.

Hostal Gami HOSTAL €
(Map p142; ☑971 563 605; www.hostalgami.com; Carrer de Bustamante 19; s €16-29, d €23-44; ⊙Apr-Nov; ⊜夝) Outstanding value for a one-star option, this simple well-run *hostal* in the heart of town is probably the pick of the budget places. Most balconies overlook the square and you're a short walk from the beach.

PORTO CRISTO

Felip Hotel HOTEL €€
(Map p146; ☑971 820 750; www.thbhotels.com; Carrer de Burdils 41; s €42-92, d €49-133; ⊜❋@⊛) Since 1890 this once-stately hotel has dominated Porto Cristo. While no longer the grande dame it once was, the Felip still retains an old-world elegance. Rooms are on the small side but artfully placed mirrors make the most of the space. Dark wood, bronze lamps, marbled bathrooms and bullfight-themed art on the walls reveal its old-fashioned soul.

SOUTH OF PORTO CRISTO

Es Picot HOTEL €€
(☑667 735 276; www.espicot.com; Camí de Sa Mola Km3; €85-115; P⊜❋@夝⊛) You can stay at the charming rural hotel Es Picot, 5km from Cala Varques. Six simply decorated rooms with terraces and amazing views comprise this intimate hotel, whose restaurant featuring 'authentic Mallorcan cuisine' is a real treat. It's around 5km northwest of Cales de Mallorca off the PM401.

PORTOCOLOM

Hostal Porto Colom HOSTAL €
(☑971 825 323; www.hostalportocolom.com; Carrer d'en Cristòfol Colom 5; s €35-55, d €50-90; ❋) Right on the waterfront, Hostal Porto Colom has breezy rooms decked out in bright yellows and blues (which might get to you after a while), with parquet floors and big beds. Downstairs, there's a cool restaurant and lounge bar.

Hostal Bahia Azul HOSTAL €
(☑971 825 280; www.bahia-azul.de; Ronda del Creuer Balear 78; s/d €45/65; ⊙Apr-Oct; ⊜❋夝⊛) Run by a Mallorquin-German couple, this 15-room hotel offers breezy Mediterranean-themed rooms (ask for one with a sea view) and services geared toward divers and cyclists. Extras include a leave-one-take-one library, a sauna, and an intimate patio with sun lounges.

SOUTHERN MALLORCA

CALA PI

Sa Bassa Plana RURAL HOTEL €€

(☎971 123 003; www.sabassaplana.com; Carretera Cap Blanc Km25.4; s €58-74, d €71-98, ste €106-135; P) Set on a working farm, Sa Bassa Plana has 10 double rooms and 12 suites (with kitchenette). They're not luxurious, but they are large and comfortable; some are outfitted with antique furniture, evoking an old-world elegance. Half-board is available and 90% of the food here is grown on the premises.

SA RAPITA & AROUND

Can Canals RURAL HOTEL €€

(☎971 640 757; www.cancanals.es; Carretera Campos-Sa Ràpita Km7; s €80-105, d €120-163; Feb-Dec; P) A stunning rustic guesthouse near Ses Covetes, Can Canals has 12 well-appointed rooms, which are located inside a lovely farmhouse and simply ooze with rural Mallorcan charm. There's a spa and wellness centre on site, as well as salt- and freshwater pools.

COLÒNIA DE SANT JORDI

Hostal Restaurante Playa HOSTAL €

(☎971 655 256; www.restauranteplaya.com; Carrer Major 25; s €30-38, d €48-62;) Traditional Mallorcan fabrics, rustic wooden furniture and a cheerful Mediterranean air make this unfussy hotel by the water an excellent option. Four of the seven rooms have ocean views and catch a lovely sea breeze. Downstairs the seaside restaurant serves island specialities.

SES SALINES

Hotel Ca'n Bonico HISTORIC HOTEL €€€

(☎971 649 022; www.hotelcanbonico.com; Plaça Sant Bartomeu 2; s €124-139, d €168-198; Feb-Oct; @) This fine old town house dates back to the 13th century, with many original features remaining, among them the defence tower (now a library) and a former jail; the family who runs it, too, descends from the original owners. The rooms are modern with a light colour scheme to offset the history that weighs heavily upon the public areas.

SANTANYÍ & AROUND

Hotel Cala Santanyí HOTEL €€

(☎971 165 505; www.hotelcalasantanyi.com; Carrer de Sa Costa dels Etics; s €95-110, d €130-160, ste €154-204, apt €106-201; mid-Apr–early Nov; @) From the outside, this place seems like so many other coastal Mallorcan hotels, but there's much to recommend it. For a start, it's a family-run place, something which shows in the warmth of the welcome and the attention to detail.

CALA FIGUERA

Hotel Villa Sirena HOTEL €€

(☎971 645 303; www.hotelvillasirena.com; Carrer de la Verge del Carme 37; s €49-60, d €68-78, 2-person apt €61-81, 4-person apt €102-130; hotel Apr-Oct, apt year-round;) Perched on a bluff at the edge of the resort, this pleasant two-star hotel has enviable views of the sea. Rooms aren't fancy, but extras like a breezy seaside terrace make this a great choice.

Hostal-Restaurant Ca'n Jordi HOSTAL €

(☎971 645 035; www.hostalcanjordi.webs.com; Carrer de la Verge del Carme 58; s/d €31/43, studio €45-57, apt €58-83;) The simple, spacious rooms with balconies offer splendid views over the inlet. The owners also rent out a few apartments and villas. There's nothing too fancy here, and some of the *hostal* rooms are small, but they're clean and the location's good.

PORTOPETRO

Blau PortoPetro HOTEL €€€

(☎971 648 282; www.blau-hotels.com; Avinguda des Far 12; s €150-200, d €200-250; Mar-Nov; P@) The only five-star hotel in the vicinity, the Blau made a real splash when it opened in 2005. A chic spa and hotel with all the amenities, this is no intimate boutique hotel, but its 300-plus rooms offer the ultimate in style and comfort. It's probably the pick of such places along Mallorca's southern coast.

CALA D'OR

TOP CHOICE **Hotel Cala D'Or** HOTEL €€

(Map p161; ☎971 657 249; www.hotelcalador.com; Avinguda de Bélgica 48; s with garden view €51-90, with sea view €81-130, d with garden view €82-135, with sea view €102-160; Apr-Oct; @) Built in 1932 and later used as a military barracks, the four-star D'Or has returned to life as a 95-room hotel overlooking the rocky Cala d'Or. The tidy rooms have balconies and garden or sea views.

Ca'n Bessol RURAL HOTEL €€

(☎639 694 910; www.canbessol.com; Carrer de la Sisena Volta 287; s €80-92, d €94-112; Mar-Nov; P@) Just off the highway linking S'Horta with Cala Ferrera, on the outskirts of Cala d'Or, lies this sprawling family-run rural hotel, a fantastic alternative to the towers found closer to the resort. Four romantic rooms with antique furnishings overlook a lush garden and pool area.

Understand Mallorca

MALLORCA TODAY 176

After decades of tourism, Mallorquins are responding to uncertain times by seeking to reclaim their roots.

HISTORY 178

Join us on a journey through the great ebbs and flows of Mediterranean history.

LANDSCAPE & WILDLIFE 188

Rugged natural ramparts, quietly beautiful cliff-encircled coves and birdlife in abundance – we introduce you to Mallorca's natural wonders.

MALLORCAN ARCHITECTURE 192

Learn all about Mallorca's architectural story, from prehistoric watchtowers to Palma's iconic cathedral, Modernista masterpieces and palaces with patios.

ARTS & CRAFTS 195

We give you a taster of Mallorca's impressive portfolio of literature, painting, music and traditional crafts.

population per sq km

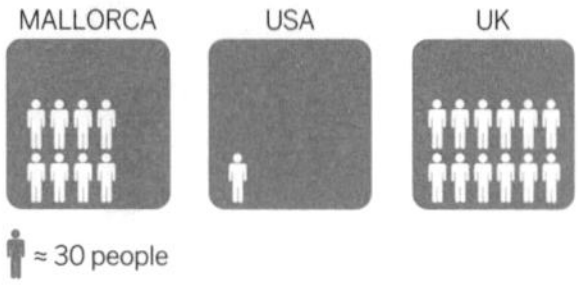

Mallorca Today

Struggle for the Soul of Mallorca

Mallorca stands at a crossroads. On one level, this is an island eternally grateful for the economic windfall that comes from being the favourite summer escape for many travellers from northern Europe: were it not for tourism, Mallorca would most likely be an impoverished provincial backwater. As it is, a staggering three out of every four Mallorquins rely on tourism for their livelihood, and this shift away from a largely agricultural society has radically transformed Mallorquin life in every way.

But therein also lies the problem: tourism since the mid-1950s and the accompanying massive development have turned the island's values on their head. In a process known as *balearización,* great swaths of the coast have been scarred by thoughtless construction and all too often builders and the authorities have cheerfully ignored regulations limiting construction. Furthermore, the massive arrival of mainland Spaniards and Europeans, buying up property across Mallorca (20% of Mallorca's inhabitants are foreigners), has pushed housing prices beyond the reach of many locals and unleashed debate on island identity. Some fear that local culture and language are being swept aside. How to hold on what remains of the past has become the central question in modern Mallorquin life.

A Question of Language

One way in which Mallorquins have asserted their fidelity to their roots is through language: Mallorquin, a dialect of Catalan that has evolved since the conquest in 1229. Their tongue was edged out of the public realm under Franco, but it has returned as a badge of pride for many Mallorquins. You're not expected to speak it, but you'll hear it spoken everywhere.

Top Reads

» *Mañana Mañana* (Peter Kerr) The pick of the books about trying to live like a Mallorquin.

» *Bread and Oil: Majorcan Culture's Last Stand* (Tomás Graves) Food-dominated book centred on traditional Mallorca's greatest passions.

» *British Travellers in Mallorca in the Nineteenth Century* (eds Brian J Dendle and Shelby Thacker) An intriguing anthology of Mallorcan travellers' tales.

» *Die Balearen* (Ludwig Salvator) Classic German-language study of the islands.

Top Films

» *Woman of Straw* (1963) Stars Sean Connery with Artà as the backdrop.

» *The Magus* (1968) Features Anthony Quinn, Michael Caine and Candice Bergen with Mallorca standing in for a Greek island.

belief systems
(% of population)

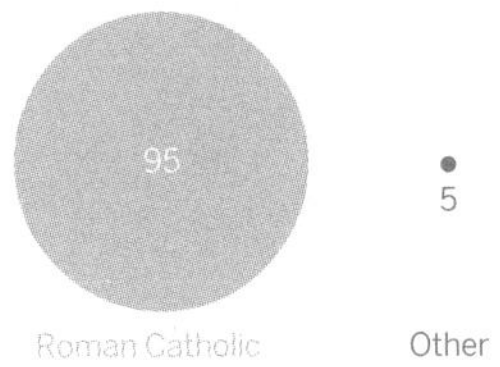

if Mallorca were 100 people

78 would be Mallorquin
10 would be Other
9 would be from mainland Spain
3 would be German

But there's a sharper edge to the issue. Many Mallorquins see the preservation of their language as a means of asserting their cultural independence from the mainland, in the process thumbing their noses at Spanish nationalists in Madrid and Catalan nationalists in Barcelona alike. The latters' campaign to reclaim, protect and promote Catalan identity through the Catalan language – the idea of *Els Països Catalans* (The Catalan Lands) and the insistence by some Catalan nationalists that 'standard Catalan' be the sole vehicle of communication in this largely fictitious entity – has particularly angered many Mallorquins.

Tourism's Other Face

Tourism's takeover of the island may have come at a cost of significant cultural alienation, but a solution of sorts may have been found. Even better, it's one that revives long-abandoned agricultural lands and puts them at the service of a very different kind of tourism: the new wave in *agroturisme* (agrotourism). A world away from the all-you-can-eat buffets and all-inclusive packages of many coastal resorts, these rural estates privilege traditional architecture, traditional island cooking and a closeness to nature that many islanders feared had been lost in the unseemly rush to milk the tourist cash cow.

Environmentalists fighting a constant battle to turn the tide of thought and brake development have also scored some successes, including the creation and improvement of several natural parks. Some tourist developments – such as those around Platja des Trenc – have also been halted. This debate, and the shift away from quantity to quality as the focus of island tourism, was a long time coming, but it has arrived just in time to save the last vestiges of Mallorca's stunning natural beauty, the very beauty that drew the tourists in the first place.

» Population: 869,067

» GDP per head (Spain): €22,511

» GDP per head (Balearic Islands): €21,070

» Unemployment rate (Balearic Islands): 21%

» Number of passengers through Mallorca's airport (2010): 21,117,417

» *A Winter in Mallorca* (1969) Relives Chopin and George Sand's ill-fated stay on the island.

» *Presence of Mind* (*El Celo*, 2000) Stars Sadie Frost, Harvey Keitel and Lauren Bacall; a private tutor comes to the island to educate two orphaned children.

Mallorca Playlist

» *Chopin in Mallorca* (2001)

» *Terra Secreta*, Maria del Mar Bonet (2008)

» *Mi Niña Lola*, Concha Buika (2007)

» *Cool Vibes Vol 1*, Daniel Vulic (2007)

» *Nada es Igual*, Chenoa (2005)

Talking Points

» **Tourism** We're worried that we may have sold our soul

* **Identity** We're Spanish when it comes to football but otherwise keep our distance

» **Overdevelopment** Let's save the island's last wilderness areas

History

Mallorca's position in the heart of Europe's most fought-over sea has placed it in the path of the great sweeps of Mediterranean history and these events have radically transformed the island time and again. And yet, for all its experience of invasion, war, prosperity and hunger, Mallorca has rarely been at the heart of great European affairs.

Mallorca's story begins with a series of unsolved mysteries, with a culture whose *talayots* (watchtowers) rank among the few signposts to their presence on the island; these stone towers continue to intrigue archaeologists. Famed as warriors, the Talayotic people served as the feared mercenaries of the great Phoenician armies of antiquity, and their fierce reputation ensured that they had the island to themselves until the arrival of the Romans in the 2nd century BC. Roman Mallorca was a strategically important outpost of empire and remained largely peaceful until the Vandals swept all before them in AD 426, before yielding to the Byzantines a century later. But it was the Muslim armies who brought the gifts of prosperity and religious coexistence to the island, ruling for over 300 years from the early ninth century. Together with mainland Spain (with which it has shared its history since the Middle Ages) Mallorca is one of the few parts of Europe to have experienced a long and prosperous period of Muslim rule.

For a comprehensive history of the ancient, pre-Roman world in Mallorca, Spanish readers should look no further than *Guía Arqueológica de Mallorca*, by Javier Arambau, Carlos Garrido and Vicenç Sastre.

In 1229 Jaume I seized the island and it has been in Christian (and, most often, Catalan) hands ever since, although that hasn't necessarily guaranteed peace. The triumphant victory of Jaume I soon descended into unseemly squabbles among his heirs. Over the centuries that followed, life was often pretty grim for Mallorca's rural poor, living at the whim of absentee landlords, subject to poverty and plague, and rising up in brave yet futile rebellions whenever the grinding poverty became too much. Through no fault of its own, Mallorca also found itself buffeted by the winds of change blowing from the Spanish mainland, from the

TIMELINE

7200 BC

Archaeologists date the first human settlements in Mallorca to around 7200 BC, based on carbon-dated findings in the southwest of the island in Cova de Canet, a cave near Esplores.

c 1200 BC

Warrior tribes invade Mallorca, Menorca, Corsica and Sardinia. Those in Mallorca and Menorca are known today as the Talayotic people because of the stone towers they built.

c 500 BC

Phoenician traders install themselves around the coast, extending their influence across Mallorca. Balearic warriors serve as mercenaries in Carthaginian armies.

grand questions of royal succession to the devastating Spanish Civil War in the 1930s.

In the years that followed the Civil War, particularly from the 1960s, Mallorca was transformed beyond recognition by the mass tourism which has yanked the island from centuries of provincial doldrums and propelled it to newfound wealth and somewhat forced cosmopolitanism.

The Talayotic Period

The Balearic Islands were separated from the Spanish continent a mere eight million years ago. They were inhabited by a variety of animal life that carried on in splendid isolation until around 9000 to 10,000 years ago, until the first groups of Epipaleolithic people set out from the Spanish coast in rudimentary vessels and bumped into Mallorca.

The earliest signs of human presence on the island date to around 7200 BC. In the following 6000 years the population, made up of disparate groups or tribes, largely lived in caves or other natural shelters as hunter-gatherers. About 2000 BC they started building megalithic funerary monuments, but the island was certainly not at the epicentre of advanced ancient civilisation. In Egypt they were creating the pyramids at this time.

Things were shaken up with the arrival of warrior tribes in Mallorca and Menorca around 1200 BC, probably from Asia Minor, which overwhelmed the local populace. They are known today as the Talayotic people, because of the buildings and villages they left behind. The *talayots* are their call sign to posterity. The circular (and sometimes square-based or ship's hull-shaped) stone edifices are testimony to an organised and hierarchical society. The most common were the circular *talayots,* which could reach a height of 6m and had two floors. Their purpose is a matter of conjecture. Were they symbolic of the power of local chieftains, or burial places for them? Were they used for storage or defence? Were they religious sites? There were at least 200 Talayotic villages across the island. Simple ceramics, along with artefacts in bronze (swords, axes, necklaces), have been found on these sites.

The ancients knew Mallorca and Menorca as the Gymnesias Islands, from a word meaning 'naked' (it appears that at least some of the islanders got about with a minimum of covering). Talayotic society seems to have been divided into a ruling elite, a broad subsistence farming underclass and slaves. It is not known if they had awritten language.

Contact with the outside world came through Greek and Phoenician traders. The Carthaginians attempted to establish a foothold in Mallorca but failed. They did, however, enrol Mallorquins as mercenaries. Balearic men were gifted with slingshots (which it is said they learned to use with deadly accuracy as children). These Mallorquin and Menorcan slingshot

Mallorca's Talayotic Sites

- Ses Païsses
- Capocorb Vell
- Necròpolis de Son Real
- Museu Arqueològic de Son Fornés
- Es Figueral de Son Real
- Illot dels Porros

123 BC

On the pretext of ending Balearic piracy, the Roman general Quintus Cecilius Metelus, later dubbed Balearicus, storms ashore and in a short time takes control of Mallorca and Menorca.

AD 426

Raids on Mallorca by the Vandals, central European barbarian tribes that had pillaged their way across Europe to North Africa, lead to the destruction of the Roman city of Pol·lentia.

534

Belisarius takes control of the Balearic Islands in the name of Byzantine Emperor Justinian, who until his death in 565 attempted to re-establish the Roman Empire across the Mediterranean.

707

Muslim Arabs in North Africa raid Mallorca for the first time. Four years later they would begin the conquest of the Spanish mainland.

warriors (*foners* in Catalan) called themselves Balears (possibly derived from an ancient Greek word meaning 'to throw'), and so their island homes also came to be known as the Balearics. These men weren't averse to payment and developed a reputation as slings for hire. In Carthaginian armies, they would launch salvos of 4cm to 6cm oval-shaped projectiles on the enemy before the infantry went in. They also carried daggers or short swords for hand-to-hand combat but wore virtually no protection. They were present in the Carthaginian victory over the Greeks in Sicily in the 5th century BC and again in the Punic Wars against Rome.

Jewish cartographers, led by the Cresques family, achieved the height of fame for their extraordinary maps, which were used by adventurers from all over Europe. Abraham Cresques (c 1325–87) and his son Jafuda (c 1350–1410) created one of the best-known such maps in 1375 (now in the national library in Paris).

Romans, Vandals & Byzantines

When the Roman Consul Quintus Cecilius Metelus approached the shores of Mallorca in 123 BC, possibly around Platja des Trenc in the south, he did not come unprepared. Knowing that the island warriors were capable of slinging heavy stones at his ships' waterline and sinking them, he had come up with a novel idea. Using heavy skins and leather, he effectively invented the first armoured vessels. Stunned by their incapacity to inflict serious damage, the Mallorquin warriors fled inland before the advance of Metelus' men. Within two years the island had been pacified.

Metelus had 3000 settlers brought over from mainland Iberia and founded two military camps in the usual Roman style (with the intersecting main streets of the *decumanus* and *cardus maximus*). Known as Palmeria or Palma and Pol·lentia, they soon developed into Mallorca's main towns. Pol·lentia, neatly situated between the two northeast bays of Pollença and Alcúdia, was the senior of the two.

At the same time as Pol·lentia was embellished with fine buildings, temples, a theatre and more (Pol·lentia has Mallorca's most extensive Roman remains), some Roman citizens opted for the rural life and built grand country villas. Nothing remains today but it is tempting to see them as the precursor to the Arab *alqueries* (farmsteads) and Mallorcan *possessions* (country estates).

The indigenous population slowly adopted the Roman language and customs but continued to live in its own villages. Plinius the Elder reported that Mallorcan wine was as good as in Italy, and the island's wheat and snails were also appreciated.

Archaeological evidence, such as the remains of the 5th-century early Christian basilica at Son Peretó, shows that Christianity had arrived in the island by the 4th century AD. By then storm clouds were gathering, and in the 5th century they broke as barbarian tribes launched assaults on the Roman Empire. The Balearic Islands felt the scourge of the Vandals (an East Germanic tribe that plundered their way into Roman territory) in 426. Forty years later, having crashed across Spain to establish their base in North Africa, they returned to take the islands.

869

Norman raiders sack Mallorca's population centres, just 21 years after an Arab raid from Muslim Spain, which Mallorca's leaders had agreed to in return for being left in peace.

SIMON GREENWOOD/LONELY PLANET IMAGES ©

» Norman re-enactment

903

Muslim forces take control of Mallorca in the name of the Caliph of Córdoba in Spain. Local Christian warriors resist another eight years in redoubts across the island.

1075

Mallorca becomes an independent *taifo* (small kingdom) in the wake of the civil conflicts that shattered the Caliphate of Córdoba into a series of *taifas* across Spain.

The Vandals got their comeuppance when Byzantine Emperor Justinian decided to try to rebuild the Roman Empire. His tireless general, Belisarius, vanquished the Vandals in North Africa in 533 and the following year took the Balearic Islands. After Justinian's death in 565, Byzantine control over territories in the western Mediterranean quickly waned. By the time the Muslims swept across North Africa in the first years of the 8th century, the Balearic Islands were an independent Christian enclave.

The Islamic Centuries

An Arab noble from Al-Andalus (Muslim Spain), Isam al-Jaulani, was forced by bad weather to take shelter in the port of Palma in 902. During his stay he became convinced that the town could and should be taken, along with Mallorca and the rest of the Balearic Islands, and incorporated into the Caliphate of Córdoba. On his return to Cordoba the Caliph Abdallah entrusted him with the task and Al-Jaulani returned with a landing party in 902 or 903.

The port town fell easily but Al-Jaulani, who was made Wāli (governor) of what the Arabs dubbed the Eastern Islands of Al-Andalus, remained engaged in guerrilla-style warfare against pockets of Christian resistance on the islands for eight years. By the time he died in 913, the islands had been pacified and he had begun work to expand and improve the archipelago's only city, now called Medina Mayurka (City of Mallorca).

The Muslims divided the island into 12 districts and in the ensuing century Mallorca thrived. They brought advanced irrigation methods and the *alqueries,* the farms they established, flourished. Medina Mayurka became one of Europe's most cosmopolitan cities. By the end of the 12th century, the city had a population of 35,000, putting it on a par with Barcelona and London. The *al-qasr*, or castle-palace (Palau de l'Almudaina), was built over a Roman fort and the grand mosque was built where Palma Catedral now stands. With the raising of walls around the new Rabad al-Jadid quarter (roughly Es Puig de Sant Pere), the city reached the extents it would maintain until the late 19th century. It was a typical medieval Muslim city, a medina like Marrakech or Fez. Few of those narrow streets that made up its labyrinth, now called *estrets* (narrows), remain. Medina Mayurka enjoyed close relations with the rest of the Muslim world in the western Mediterranean, although by 1075 the Emirs (princes) of the Eastern Islands were independent of mainland jurisdiction.

Al-Jaulani's successors dedicated considerable energy to piracy, which by the opening of the 12th century was the islands' principal source of revenue, although such activities aroused the wrath of Christian

PLAGUE

Mallorca's connection to the seafaring trade routes of the Mediterranean ensured that it was particularly vulnerable to the ravages of the plague, which hit the island repeatedly, decimating the population in the process.

1114–15

A Catalan–Pisan crusading force lands in Mallorca to end the piracy damaging Mediterranean trade. They take Medina Mayurka (Palma) in 1115 and free 30,000 Christian slaves before leaving the island.

1148

Mallorca signs a trade agreement with the Italian cities of Genoa and Pisa, opening Mallorcan markets to the Italians and reducing the threat of further Christian assaults on the island.

1185

The Muslim governor of the island, Wāli Ishaq, dies ending a period of unprecedented prosperity. His rule represents the highpoint of Almoravid control over Mallorca.

1203

The Almohads in peninsular Spain defeat the Almoravid regime in Medina Mayurka and take control of the island, although life continues largely unchanged for most of Mallorca's inhabitants.

merchant powers. In 1114, 500 vessels carrying a reported 65,000 Pisan and Catalan troops landed on Mallorca and launched a bloody campaign. In April the following year they entered Medina Mayurka. Exhausted after 10 months' fighting, they left Mallorca laden with booty, prisoners and freed Christian slaves when news came that a Muslim relief fleet was on the way from North Africa.

In 1116 a new era dawned in Mallorca, as the Almoravids (a Berber tribe from Morocco) from mainland Spain took control. The Balearics reached new heights in prosperity, particularly under the Wāli Ishaq, who ruled from 1152 to 1185. In 1203 Mallorca fell under the sway of the Almohads who had taken control of Al-Andalus.

THE JEWS IN MALLORCA

The first Jews appear to have arrived in Mallorca in AD 70, the same year the Romans largely destroyed Jerusalem and its temple. Under Muslim rule, a small Jewish minority thrived in Medina Mayurka (the name the Moors gave to Mallorca). Christian Mallorca, after the 1229 conquest, was not so kind.

Although barred from most professions and public office, Mallorca's Jews were esteemed for their learning and business sense. Jewish doctors, astronomers, bankers and traders, generally fluent in Catalan and/or Spanish, Latin, Hebrew and Arabic, often played key roles.

By the end of the century, there were perhaps 2000 to 3000 Jews in Ciutat (Palma). They were evicted from the area around the Palau de l'Almudaina and moved to the Call (Catalan equivalent of a ghetto) in the eastern part of Sa Calatrava, in the streets around Carrer de Monti-Sion. They were locked in at night and obliged to wear a red and yellow circular patch during the day. In 1315 their synagogue was converted into the Església de Monti-Sion and they would not have another until 1373. In 1391, rioting farmers killed some 300 Jews in an anti-Semitic pogrom.

In 1435 the bulk of the island's Jews were forced to convert to Christianity and their synagogues were converted into churches. At the beginning of the 16th century they were forced to move from the Call Major to the Call Menor, centred on Carrer de Colom. They were now Christians but were under suspicion of secretly practising Jewish rites; they were a particular target for the Inquisition and the last auto-da-fé (trial by fire) of such so-called *judaizantes* took place in 1691, when three citizens were burned at the stake.

Known as *xuetes* (from *xua*, a derogatory term referring to pork meat), they were shunned by the rest of the Christian populace much as they had been before and it was not until the 19th century that they were finally able to breathe easier. A veritable flurry of 19th-century writers and poets came from *xueta* families. Today the descendants of these families (who even in the mid-20th century were shunned by many other Mallorquins) are estimated to number between 15,000 and 20,000.

September 1229

Under Jaume I, king of the Crown of Aragón, Catalan troops land at Santa Ponça in Mallorca, defeat the Muslims and camp before the walls of Medina Mayurka.

December 1229

Jaume I enters the city, which his troops sack, leaving it in such a state that a plague the following Easter kills many of the inhabitants and invading soldiers.

1267

Mallorquin icon and would-be saint, Ramon Llull, has a series of visions that will ultimately transform him into one of the most important Catalan cultural figures in history.

1276

Jaume I dies, almost 50 years after bringing Christian rule to Mallorca. The territories under his rule are divided between his two sons, prompting decades of internecine conflict.

No doubt all this internecine strife between Muslim factions had not gone unnoticed in Christian Spain, where the Reconquista (the reconquest of Muslim-held territory by the Christian kingdoms) had taken on new impetus after the rout of Almohad armies in the Battle of Las Navas de Tolosa in 1212. By 1250 the Christians would take Valencia, Extremadura, Córdoba and Seville, and the last Muslims would be expelled from Portugal. In such a context it is hardly surprising that a plan should be hatched to take the Balearic Islands too, especially as Mallorca continued to be a major source of piracy that seriously hindered Christian sea trade.

Jaume I El Conqueridor

On 5 September 1229, 155 vessels bearing 1500 knights on horseback and 15,000 infantry weighed anchor in the Catalan ports of Barcelona, Tarragona and Salou and set sail for Mallorca. Jaume I (1208–76), the energetic 21-year-old king of Aragón and Catalonia, vowed to take the Balearic Islands and end Muslim piracy in the process. Jaume I (later dubbed The Conqueror) landed at Santa Ponça and, after two swift skirmishes, marched on Medina Mayurka, to which he laid siege. Finally, on 31 December, Christian troops breached the defences and poured into the city, pillaging mercilessly. In the following months, Jaume I pursued enemy troops across the island but resistance was feeble.

With the conquest of Mallorca complete, Jaume I proceeded to divide it up among his lieutenants and allies. The Arab *alqueries*, *rafals* (hamlets) and villages were handed over to their new *senyors* (masters). Many changed name but a good number retained their Arab nomenclature. Places beginning with Bini (Sons of) are Arab hangovers. Many took on the names of their new lord, preceded by the possessive particle *son* or *sa* (loosely translated as 'that which is of...'). Jaume I codified this division of the spoils in his *Llibre del Repartiment.*

Among Jaume's early priorities was a rapid program of church-building, Christianisation of the local populace and the sending of settlers from Catalonia (mostly from around the city of Girona). For the first century after the conquest, Ciutat (the city) held the bulk of the island's population. The Part Forana ('Part Outside' Ciutat) was divided into 14 districts but all power in Mallorca was concentrated in Ciutat. Beneath the king, day-to-day government was carried out by six *jurats,* or 'magistrates'.

The Christian Catalan settlers basically imposed their religion, tongue and customs on the island and the bulk of the Muslim population was reduced to slavery. Those that did not flee or accept this destiny had only one real choice: to renounce Islam. The Jewish population would also have a roller-coaster time of it.

DEITIES

Some historians claim the funny white, green and red clay figurine-whistles known as *siurells* were introduced to Mallorca by the Phoenicians and may have represented ancient deities. Classic figures include bulls, horse-riders and dog-headed men.

1343

Pere III of the Crown of Aragón invades Mallorca and seizes the crown from Jaume III, who would die six years later in the Battle of Llucmajor trying to get it back.

1382

Sac i Sort (Bag and Luck) is introduced whereby the names of six candidates to be named *jurats* (magistrates) for the following 12 months were pulled out of four bags.

1391

Hundreds of Jews die in a pogrom as farmers and labourers sack the Jewish quarter of Palma. Months later, those involved are released without sentence for fear of causing greater unrest.

1488

The Inquisition, which had operated from the mainland, is formally established in Mallorca. In the following decades hundreds would die, burned at the stake as heretics.

THE EVANGELISING CATALAN SHAKESPEARE

Born in Ciutat (ie Palma) de Mallorca, the mystic, theologian and all-round Renaissance man before his time, Ramon Llull (1232–1316), started off on a worldly trajectory. After entering Jaume I's court as a page, Ramon was elevated to major-domo of Jaume II, the future king of Mallorca. Ramon lived it up, writing love ditties and enjoying (apparently) a wild sex life.

Then, in 1267, he saw five visions of Christ crucified and everything changed. His next years were consumed with profound theological, moral and linguistic training (in Arabic and Hebrew). He founded a monastery (with Jaume II's backing) at Miramar for the teaching of theology and Eastern languages to future evangelists. His burning desire was the conversion of Jews and Muslims and he began to travel throughout Europe, the Near East and North Africa to preach. At the same time he wrote countless tracts in Catalan and Arabic and is considered the father of Catalan as a literary language. In 1295 he joined the Franciscans and in 1307 risked the ire of Muslims by preaching outside North African mosques. Some say he was lynched in Tunisia by an angry mob while others affirm he died while en route to his native Mallorca in 1316. He is buried in the Basílica de Sant Francesc in Palma. His beatification was confirmed by Pope John Paul II and the long, uncertain process of canonisation began in 2007.

In the Part Forana the farmsteads came to be known as *possessions* and were the focal point of the agricultural economy upon which the island would largely come to depend. The *possessions* were run by local managers faithful to their (frequently absentee) noble overlords and were often well-off farmers themselves. They employed *missatges* (permanent farm labour) and *jornalers* (day wage labourers), both of whom generally lived on the edge of misery. Small farm holders frequently failed to make ends meet, ceded their holdings to the more important *possessions* and became *jornalers*.

One of the most beautiful descriptions written of the island was the Catalan painter Santiago Rusiñol's *Mallorca, L'Illa de la Calma* (Mallorca, the Island of Calm, 1922), in which he takes a critical look at the rough rural life of many Mallorquins.

On Jaume I's death in 1276, his territories were divided between his two sons, Jaume II and Pere II; in the years that followed Mallorca was tossed between the two, a process continued under their heirs. By 1349, the previously independent kingdom of Mallorca was tied into the Crown of Aragón, although it retained a high degree of autonomy.

The fortunes of Mallorca, and in particular Palma, closely followed those of Barcelona, the Catalan headquarters of the Crown of Aragón and merchant trading hub. In the middle of the 15th century, both cities (despite setbacks such as outbreaks of the plague) were among the most prosperous in the Mediterranean. Palma had some 35 consulates and trade representatives sprinkled around the Med. The city's trade community had a merchant fleet of 400 vessels and the medieval Bourse, Sa Llotja, was an animated focal point of business.

1521

Armed workers and farm labourers rise up in the beginning of the Germania revolt against the nobles. In October 1522, Carlos V sends troops to Alcúdia to quell the revolt.

1706

The Austrian pretender to the Spanish throne in the War of the Spanish Succession (1702–15) takes control of Mallorca. Nine years later, Mallorca is defeated by Felipe V.

1773

King Carlos III orders that the Jews of Palma be allowed to live wherever they wish and that all forms of discrimination and mistreatment of the Jewish population be punished.

1809

Thousands of French troops captured in battle in mainland Spain are sent to Illa de Cabrera, where they live in appalling conditions. The survivors would not be released until 1814.

Not all was rosy. In the Part Forana farm labourers lived on the edge of starvation and crops failed to such an extent in 1374 that people were dropping dead in the streets. Frequent localised revolts, such as that of 1391 (the same year that furious workers sacked the Call in Ciutat), were stamped out mercilessly by the army. A much greater shock to the ruling classes was the 1521 Germania revolt, an urban working-class uprising provoked largely by crushing taxes extracted from the lower classes. They forced the viceroy (by now Mallorca was part of a united Spain under Emperor Carlos V) to flee. In October 1522 Carlos V sent in the army, which only re-established control the following March.

By then Mallorca's commercial star had declined and the coast was constant prey to the attacks of North African pirates. The building of *talayots* around the island (many still stand) is eloquent historical testimony to the problem. Some of Mallorca's most colourful traditional festivals, such as Moros i Cristians in Pollença and Es Firó in Sóller date to these times. As Spain's fortunes also declined from the 17th century, Mallorca slid into provincial obscurity. Backing the Habsburgs in the War of the Spanish Succession (1703–15) didn't endear Mallorca to the finally victorious Bourbon monarch, Felipe V, who in 1716 abolished all the island's privileges and autonomy.

Between the 16th and 18th of March 1938, Italian air force bombers based in Mallorca launched 17 raids on Barcelona, killing about 1300 people. Apparently Mussolini ordered the raids, without the knowledge of the Spanish Nationalist high command.

RAIDS

Mallorca in the Civil War

The 1931 nationwide elections brought unprecedented results: the Republicans and Socialists together won an absolute majority in Palma, in line with the results in Madrid. The Confederatión Espanola de Derechas Autónomous (Spanish Confederation of the Autonomous Right) won the national elections in 1933 and all the left-wing mayors in Mallorca were sacked by early 1934. They were back again in a euphoric mood after the dramatic elections of 1936 again gave a landslide victory to the left.

For many generals this was the last straw. Their ringleader, General Francisco Franco, launched an uprising against the central Republican government in July 1936. In Mallorca the insurrection found little resistance. On 19 July rebel soldiers and right-wing Falange militants burst into Cort (the town hall) and arrested the left-wing mayor, Emili Darder (he and other politicians would be executed in February 1937). They quickly occupied strategic points across Palma with barely a shot fired. More resistance came from towns in the Part Forana, but was soon bloodily squashed.

By mid-August battalions of Italian troops and warplanes sent by Franco's ally, the dictator Benito Mussolini, were pouring into Mallorca. The island became the main base for Italian air operations and it was from here that raids were carried out against Barcelona with increasing intensity as the Civil War wore on.

1837

A passenger steamer between Barcelona and Palma begins service, creating a regular link to the mainland. Among its first passengers were George Sand and Frédéric Chopin, in 1838.

KRZYSZTOF DYDYNSKI/LONELY PLANET IMAGES ©

» Statue of Frédéric Chopin

April 1912

The train line linking Palma with Sóller opens; poor roads across the mountains had made it easier for the people of Sóller to travel north by sea to France than south by land to Palma.

June 1922

The first postal service flight takes place between Barcelona and Palma. The service would use flying boats parked in hangars at Es Jonquet in Palma.

On 9 August 1936 a Catalan-Valencian force (apparently without approval from central command) retook Ibiza from Franco and then landed at Porto Cristo on the 16th. So taken aback were they by the lack of resistance that they failed to press home the advantage of surprise. A Nationalist counter-attack begun on 3 September, backed by Italian planes, pushed the hapless (and ill-equipped) invaders back into the sea. Soon thereafter the Republicans also abandoned Ibiza and Formentera. Of the Balearic Islands, only Menorca remained loyal to the Republic throughout the war.

An asteroid discovered by Mallorcan astronomers in 1997 was named 9900 Ramon Llull after the island's great medieval philosopher, writer and evangelist.

With Franco's victory in 1939, life in Mallorca followed that of the mainland: use of Catalan in public announcements, signs, education and so on was banned. Rationing was introduced in 1940 and stayed in place until 1952. Of the nine mayors the city had from 1936 to 1976, four were military men and the others conservative.

Boom Times

In 1950 the first charter flight landed on a small airstrip on Mallorca. No-one could have perceived the implications. By 1955 central Palma had a dozen hotels and others stretched along the waterfront towards Cala Major.

The 1960s and 1970s brought an extraordinary urban revolution as mass tourism took off. The barely controlled high-rise expansion around

A RIGHT ROYAL DILETTANTE

As the first battles of the Italian campaign raged in 1915, Archduke Ludwig Salvator sat frustrated in Brandeis Castle in Bohemia, writing furiously but impeded by the fighting from returning to his beloved Balearic Islands. He died in October that year of blood poisoning after an operation on his leg.

Ludwig had been born in 1847 in Florence, the fourth son of Grand Duke Leopold II. He was soon travelling, studying and visiting cities all over Europe. From the outset he wrote of what he saw. His first books were published one year after his first visit to the Balearic Islands in 1867. He returned to Mallorca in 1871 and the following year bought Miramar. He decided to make Mallorca his main base – a lifestyle choice that many northern Europeans would seek to imitate over a century later.

Salvator was an insatiable traveller. In his private steam-driven yacht Nixe (and its successors) and other forms of transport, he visited places as far apart as Cyprus and Tasmania. Hardly a year passed in which he didn't publish a book on his travels and studies, possibly the best known of which are his weighty tomes on *Die Balearen* (The Balearics). His love remained Mallorca (where royals and other VIPs visited him regularly) and, in 1877, local deputies awarded him the title of Adopted Son of the Balearic Islands. Four years later he was made an honorary member of the Royal Geographic Society in London.

19 July 1936

The army and right-wing militias take control of Mallorca for General Franco as he launches his military uprising against the Republican government in Madrid.

1 April 1939

Franco claims victory in a nationally televised radio speech, three days after Madrid had fallen to Nationalist troops and bringing to an end almost three years of conflict.

1952

After almost 12 years, post–Civil War rationing finally ends on the island. Although many Mallorquins continue to live subsistence lives, the tourism boom will soon transform the island forever.

1960

An estimated 500,000 tourists visit the island, marking the beginning of mass tourism on the island. These figures would increase 50 times over during the decades that followed.

the bay in both directions, and later behind other beaches around the coast, was the result of a deliberate policy by Franco's central government to encourage tourism in coastal areas. Many of the more awful hotels built in this period have since been closed or recycled as apartment or office blocks.

The islanders now enjoy – by some estimates – the highest standard of living in Spain, but 80% of their economy is based on tourism. This has led to thoughtless construction on the islands and frequent anxiety attacks whenever a season doesn't meet expectations. The term *balearización* has been coined to illustrate this short-termism and wanton destruction of the area's prime resource – its beautiful coastlines.

In regional elections held in May 2007, PP leader, Jaume Matas, fell short of an absolute majority by just one seat, but he found himself on the outer as the remaining six parties joined forces to create a coalition under the Socialists of Francesc Antich. Antich's key ally is the conservative autonomy-oriented Unió Mallorquina, formerly aligned with the PP.

1983

The autonomy statute for Balearic Islands region (together with those of other Spanish regions) is approved eight years after the death of Franco.

May 2007

Mallorcan Socialist Francesc Antich ends right-wing Partido Popular rule after regional elections by forming a coalition government with promises to put a brake on construction projects.

2009

The Basque separatist group ETA detonates a series of bombs, killing two policemen and causing havoc at the height of Mallorca's July and August summer tourist seasons.

May 2011

The conservative Partido Popular (PP) storms back into power, winning an absolute majority in regional elections. The kingmakers in 2007, the Unió Mallorquina, loses all its seats.

Landscape & Wildlife

Mallorca is an incredibly diverse island where limestone cliffs, spectacular caves and sandy coves meet blooming fields of wild flowers, eerie olive groves and damp forests to form one of the Med's most storied landscapes.

Mallorca's Landscape

Mallorca, shaped like a rough trapezoid, is the largest island of the Balearic archipelago. Technically. The island chain is an extension of mainland Spain's Sistema Penibético (Beltic mountain range), which dips close to 1.5km below the Mediterranean and peeks up again to form the islands of Mallorca, Menorca, Ibiza and Formentera. The stretch of water between the archipelago and the mainland is called the Balearic Sea.

Among the most complete guides available to Mallorca's caves are the *Cuadernos de Espeleogía I and II* (Speology Notebooks I & II), by José Bermejo.

The Coast

Mallorca's coastline is punctuated for the most part by small coves, save for three major bays. The Badia de Palma in the south is the most densely populated corner of the island. The two large, shell-shaped bays of the north, the Badia de Pollença and Badia d'Alcúdia, are enclosed by a series of dramatic headlands, Cap de Formentor, Cap des Pinar and Cap Ferrutx.

A series of plunging cliffs interspersed with calm bays marks the south, which is where you'll also find Mallorca's two main island networks: the Illa de Sa Dragonera (offshore from Sant Elm) and the 19-island Parc Nacional Marítim-Terrestre de l'Arxipèlag de Cabrera (from Colònia de Sant Jordi).

Mountains

The island's defining geographic feature is the 90km-long Serra de Tramuntana, which begins close to Andratx in the southwest and reaches its dramatic finale in the northern Cap de Formentor. The highest peaks are in the centre of the range, northeast of Sóller, but the steep-sided western flanks that rise abruptly from the Mediterranean shore and shelter numerous villages, give the appearance of being higher than they really are. The range is for the most part characterised by forested hillsides (terraced with agriculture in some areas) and bald limestone peaks. A

MALLORCA'S GEOGRAPHY: THE STATS

- Area: 3636 sq km
- Coastline: 550km
- Closest distance to mainland Spain: 175km
- Highest point: Puig Major de Son Torrella (1445m)
- Highest accessible point: Puig de Massanella (1365m)

number of tributary ranges, such as the Serra d'Alfabia and Els Cornadors, both close to Sóller, are sometimes named separately.

On the other side of the island, the less-dramatic Serra de Llevant extends from Cap Ferrutx in the north to Cap de Ses Salines in the south; the offshore Illa de Cabrera is considered an extension of the range. It's highest point is the easily accessible Santuari de Sant Salvador (509m), while the range dominates the Parc Natural de la Península de Llevant, north of Artà.

Between the two, in the centre of the island, extends the vast fertile plain known as Es Pla.

The web forum www.birdforum.net has an extensive listing of Balearic birdwatching sites. Also good is Birding in Spain (www.birdingin-spain.com); click on 'Birding Mallorca' for links to organised tours as well as a list of bird species at major birdwatching sites around the island.

Caves

Mallorca, particularly along its eastern and southern coasts, is drilled with caves created by erosion, waves or water drainage. The caves range from tiny well-like dugouts to vast kilometres-long tunnels replete with lakes, rivers and astounding shapes sculptured by nature's hand. Although underground, most of the caves actually sit above sea level. The best-known caves are the Coves del Drac (p145) and Coves dels Hams (p145), both outside Porto Cristo, Coves d'Artà (p143) in Platja de Canyamel, Coves de Campanet (p127) in Campanet, and Coves de Gènova (p76), which are close to Palma.

Wildlife

Mallorca's animal population is fairly modest in both numbers and variety, but this is more than compensated for by the abundant birdlife which makes the island a major Mediterranean destination for twitchers.

Land Animals

The most charismatic (and easily visible) of Mallorca's land species is the Mallorcan wild goat *(Capra ageagrus hircus)*, which survives in reasonable numbers only in the Serra de Tramuntana, Cap des Pinar and Parc Natural de la Península de Llevant.

Other mammals include feral cats (a serious threat to bird populations), ferrets, rabbits and hedgehogs. Lizards, turtles, frogs and bats make up the bulk of the native populations. Lizards thrive on Mallorca's islands due to the lack of human population and introduced species, particularly on the Illa de Sa Dragonera, where they have the run of the island, and the Illa de Cabrera; the latter provides a refuge for 80% of the last surviving Balearic lizards *(Podarcis lilfordi)*.

You'll also find spiders, more than 300 moth species and 30 kinds of butterflies.

Marine Mammals

Sperm whales, pilot whales and finback whales feed not far offshore. Also swimming here are bottlenose dolphins, white-sided dolphins and other species. Scuba divers often spot barracuda, octopus, moray eels, grouper, cardinal fish, damsel fish, starfish, sea urchins, sponges and corals.

Birds

As a natural resting point between Europe and Africa, and as one of the few Mediterranean islands with considerable wetlands, Mallorca is a wonderful birdwatching destination and coastal regions in particular draw hundreds of resident and migratory species, especially during the migration periods in spring and autumn.

With more than 200 species it's all but impossible to predict what you'll see. The birds can be divided into three categories: sedentary (those that live on the island year-round), seasonal (those that migrate south after hatching chicks or to escape the cold winters in northern Europe) and migratory (those that rest briefly in Mallorca before continuing their journey).

Try birdwatching field guides such as *Collins Field Guide: Birds of Britain & Europe*, by Roger Tory Peterson, Guy Mountfort and PAD Hollom, or the slimmer *Collins Bird Guide: The Most Complete Guide to the Birds of Britain & Europe*, by Lars Svensson et al.

Endangered Species

The populations of Mallorca's threatened species of Mediterranean birds, tortoises and toads are recovering thanks to the conservation and controlled breeding efforts of Mallorca's parks and natural areas.

Endangered species here include the spur-thighed tortoise and Hermann's tortoise, the only two tortoises found in Spain, and bird species such as the red kite.

Among the programs showing results, the endemic Mallorcan midwife toad's status was in 2006 changed to 'vulnerable' from 'critically endangered' on the IUCN Red List of Threatened Species. But there's not such good news about the Balearic shearwater, a water bird that has suffered greatly because of feral cats; IUCN lists it as 'critically endangered'.

Plants

The Balearic Islands claim more than 100 endemic species and provide a fertile home to countless more.

Mountain & Plains Species

On the peaks of the Serra de Tramuntana, Mallorca's hardy mountain flora survives harsh sun and wind. Thriving species tend to be ground-huggers or cliff species such as *Scabiosa cretica* (with exotic-looking lilac blooms), which burrow into rock fissures to keep their roots well drained and cool.

On Mallorca's rocky hillsides and flat plains, where oak forests once grew before being burned or destroyed to create farmland, drought-resistant scrubland flora now thrives. Expect to see evergreen shrubs like wild olives and dwarf fan palms, as well as herbs like rosemary, thyme and lavender. Other plants include heather, broom, prickly pear (which can be made into jam) and 60 species of orchids.

Endemic plants include the lovely *Paeonia cambessedesii,* a pink peony that lives in the shade of some Serra de Tramuntana gullies, and *Naufraga balearica,* a clover-like plant found on shady Tramuntana slopes.

BIRDWATCHING SITES

Just about anywhere on the island is good for birdwatching, but the best places are along the northern, eastern and southern coasts.

» **Parc Natural de S'Albufera** A marshy birdwatchers' paradise where some 230 species, including moustached warblers and shoveler ducks, vie for your attention. The park is home to no less than two-thirds of the species that live permanently or winter on Mallorca and is a Ramsar Wetland of International Importance.

» **Parc Nacional Marítim-Terrestre de l'Arxipèlag de Cabrera** These protected offshore islands draw marine birds, migrants and birds of prey, including fisher eagles, endangered Balearic shearwaters, Audouin's gulls, Cory's shearwaters, shags, ospreys, Eleonora's falcons and peregrine falcons.

» **Parc Natural de la Península de Llevant** Watch for cormorants and Audouin's gulls in this rugged promontory north of Artà.

» **Parc Natural de Mondragó** Falcons, turtle doves and coastal species are the major draws here.

» **Embassament de Cúber** In the shadow of the Puig Major de Son Torrella, watch for raptors and other mountain species.

» **Vall de Bóquer** Near Port Pollença, this rocky valley is home to warblers, Eurasian Scops owls, red-legged partridges, peregrine falcons, and other predominantly mountain and migratory species.

» **Cap de Formentor** Species on this dramatic peninsula include all manner of warblers, blue rock thrushes, crag martins, Eleonora's falcons, pallid swifts, migratring raptors and, if you're lucky, the Balearic shearwater.

AGE ARCHITECTURE

ages of Mallorca's west and north are a striking counterpoint to the concrete mon-
es that too often predominate in the resort towns of the south and east. That's pri-
because the villages – among them Fornalutx, Biniaraix, Valldemossa, Deià and Ori-
re built using local stone. The stone, which can take on red or yellow hues depending
time of day, ensures a rare harmony between the natural and man-made landscapes.

Modernisme

Towards the end of the 19th century, the Catalan version of art nouveau architecture was all the rage in Barcelona, and whatever was happening in the Catalan capital at the time was sure to influence architectural styles in Mallorca. Symbolised by Antoni Gaudí, who worked on the renovation of Palma's Catedral (p42) and was the man behind Barcelona's unfinished La Sagrada Família, the eclectic style soon had its adepts, both local and Catalan, in Mallorca. They sought inspiration in nature and the past (especially Gothic and mudéjar influences), and developed a new freedom and individual creativity.

Palma

Like most islandwide phenomena, Palma is the centrepiece of Mallorca's Modernista period. A contemporary of Gaudí, Lluís Domènech i Montaner (1850–1923) was another great Catalan Modernista architect who left his mark on the magnificent former Grand Hotel, now the CaixaForum (p53).

The undulating facade of Can Casasayas (p50), built for the wealthy Casasayas family known for their historic Confitería Frasquet (p60) sweets shop, is a typical feature of Modernisme. One half of the building is residential and the other now houses offices. In the original design they were to be joined by a bridge.

Another eminent and influential figure in the history of Mallorcan Modernisme was Gaspar Bennàssar (1869–1933). Unlike many other other Catalan architects who worked on the island, Bennàssar was born in Palma and he played with various styles during his long career, including Modernisme. An outstanding example of this is the Almacenes El Águila (p53), built in 1908 at the height of Modernisme's glory. Each of the three floors is different and the generous use of wrought iron in the main facade is a herald of the style. Next door the use of *trencadís* (ceramic shards) in the Can Forteza Rey (p50) facade is classic Gaudí-esque. Can Corbella (p50), on the other hand, dates from roughly the same period but is dominated by a neomudéjar look.

The seat of the Balearic Islands Parliament is located in the Círculo Mallorquin, a high society club on Carrer del Conquistador that local Modernista architect Miquel Madorell i Rius (1869–1936) renovated in 1913.

Sóller

Provincial Sóller can't rival Palma for the breadth of its Modernista buildings, but it does have some outstanding examples of the genre. Most of it is attributable to Joan Rubió, an acolyte of Antoni Gaudí, and the most eye-catching example is his unusual early-20th-century Modernist facade grafted onto the 18th-century Església de Sant Bartomeu (p92). The adjacent and extravagant Banco de Sóller (p92) is a typically bold example of his approach. Nearby, the Ca'n Prunera – Museu Modernista (p92) sports a typically delicate stone facade with muted wrought ironwork; it's also unusual on Mallorca in that it allows you to step beyond the Modernist facade and see the genre's influence upon early-20th-century interiors.

u can
many
patis,
e buffs
to be
during
hristi
n many
erwise-
rtyards
to the
c.

GREEN CARD (TARGETA VERDE)

In 2004 the nonprofit Fundació pel Desenvolupament Sostenible de les Illes Balears (Sustainable Development Foundation for the Balearic Islands) was set up. It introduced the **Targeta Verda** (Green Card; ☎800 401 112; www.balears-sostenible.com) in 2005. Anyone can buy the card (€10) from various locations around the island such as rural hotels, airline desks, newspaper stands and post offices. It entitles holders to discounts at many sights, restaurants and shops throughout the Balearic Islands, including the free use of binoculars in the Parc Natural de S'Albufera. Proceeds go to environmental protection and sustainable projects, such as the improvement of infrastructure and protection at the Parc Natural de S'Albufera.

Forests & Ferns

Where evergreen oak forests have managed to survive you'll find holly oaks, kermes oaks and holm oaks growing alongside smaller, less noticeable species like violets, heather and butcher's broom. Most interesting to botanists are endangered endemic species like the shiny-leaved box *(Buxux balearica)* and the needled yew *(Taxus baccata)*, a perennial tree that can grow for hundreds of years. A specimen in Esporles is thought to be more than 2000 years old.

Humidity-seeking ferns (more than 40 species of them) have found marvellous habitats near Mallorca's caves, gorges and streams. In other damp areas, clusters of poplars, elms and ash trees, all introduced species, form small forests.

Coastal Species

Along the shore, plants have had to adapt to constant sea spray, salt deposits and strong winds. One of Mallorca's most beloved coastal species is samphire *(fonoll marí)*, a leafy coastal herb that was given to sailors as a source of scurvy-preventing vitamin C. These days it's marinated and used in salads. Other common species are the spiny cushion-like *Launaea cervicornis*, and *Senecio rodriguezii*, whose purple, daisy-like flowers earned it the nickname of *margalideta de la mar* (little daisy of the sea).

In the wetlands, marshes and dunes of Mallorca, a variety of coastal freshwater flora prosper. Duckweed is one of the most common plants here, though it is often kept company by bulrush, yellow flag iris, sedge and mint. These sand-dwelling species often have white or pale-green leaves and an extensive root system that helps keep them anchored in the shifting sands.

The *Plants of the Balearic Islands*, by Anthony Bonner, is the definitive guide to Mallorca's fauna and the ideal companion for budding botanists who plan to spend lots of time hiking.

Environmental Threats

The uninhibited construction that began in the 1960s and 1970s has influenced everything from birds' nesting habits to plant habitats, rainwater runoff and water shortages. Although the government is more environmentally aware than in decades past, the relationship between development and environmental protection remains uneasy.

One of the most pressing concerns for environmentalists is the prevalence of invasive plant species. Many destructive species were first introduced in local gardens but have found such a good home in Mallorca that they're crowding out endemic species. A good example is *Carpobrotus edulis*, called 'sour fig' in England and locally dubbed *patata frita* (french fry) or *dent de león* (lion's tooth) because of its long, slender leaves. A robust low-lying plant, it chokes native species wherever it goes.

Mallorcan Architecture

Sampling Mallorca's surprising breadth of architectural styles is one of the highlights of any visit to the island. Mallorca's architectural story begins with the mysterious prehistoric settlements that predated the Roman arrival on the island, remnants of which survive around the island's interior; you'll also find more recent trends represented in the villages built of local stone all over the island. Palma is the undoubted star of Mallorca's architectural show with Modernista mansions and the lovely former homes of Mallorca's nobility among the highlights.

The next chapter in the story is still to be written: the wave of innovation sweeping contemporary Spanish architectural circles has largely passed Mallorca by.

Buildings of Muslim Mallorca

» Banys Àrabs
» Jardins d'Alfàbia
» Arc del Wali
» Arco de l'Almudaina
» Palma's Remnants of 12th-century Arab Wall
» Castell de Santueri

First Beginnings

Remains of the *talayots* (enigmatic, tower-like structures) of the Balearic peoples are found at a few archaeological sites around the island, although little is known about the purpose of these structures and the wider lives who inhabited the towns. Most settlements of these so-called Talayotic cultures were encircled by high stone walls, within which were numerous dwellings and the towers which were built of stone, usually without the use of mortar; it is thought that some of the towers may have served as watchtowers, others tombs. Although these cultures survived roughly until the Roman arrival on the island in 123 BC, many of the structures seen today date back to 1000 BC. The best preserved Talayotic sites are at Ses Païsses (p137) and Capocorb Vell (p152).

Despite ruling over Mallorca for more than two centuries and despite their reputation as mighty builders, the Romans left behind surprisingly few signposts to their presence. This dearth of Roman ruins on Mallorca is most likely attributable to the fact that the Romans, unlike their predecessors, occupied the prime patches of coastal real estate, which was later built over by subsequent civilisations. The only meaningful extant Roman site in Mallorca – Pol·lentia (p112), in Alcúdia in the island's north – is also believed to have been its largest city.

Muslim Mallorca

Mallorca has remarkably little to show for its three centuries of Muslim rule, not least because the mosques they built were invariably occupied by conquering Christian armies in the 13th century, and were subsequently converted into churches. Palma's Catedral (p42) and Església de Sant Miquel (p52) are two buildings to have suffered this fate; no evidence of their original purpose survives. And mosques were not the only buildings to be appropriated by the new Christian rulers and trans-

formed beyond recognition – the Palau de l'Almudaina was first the Romans, adapted by a succession of Muslim governors befor ing the seat of royal (Christian) power on the island.

Defensive fortresses on strategically sited hilltops were anc ture of the Islamic occupation, but again most were taken over a modified by Christian forces in the centuries that followed. C Capdepera (p139) is perhaps the most impressive example.

Mallorcan Gothic

The Catalan slant on the Gothic style, with its broad, low-slu ing church entrances and sober adornment, inevitably predom Catalan-conquered Mallorca. Guillem Sagrera (c 1380–1456), a architect and sculptor who had previously worked in Perpign; in France), moved to Mallorca in 1420 to take over the directio on the Catedral (p42), the island's foremost Gothic structure. S considered to be the greatest architect and sculptor of the peric lorca. He designed one of the Catedral's chapels and the Gothic house, and, more importantly, he raised Sa Llotja (p55), Mallor stand-out Gothic monument.

As in other parts of Spain, Islamic influences were evident aspects of building through the Gothic period. In Mallorca this style is not immediately evident in external facades, but a h beautiful *artesonados* (coffered wood ceilings) remain. Those i Palau de l'Almudaina (p46) are outstanding. The beautiful *arte* the manor house at the Jardins d'Alfàbia (p99) appears to be a relic.

Renaissance & Baroque

Renaissance building had a rational impulse founded on the ture of classical antiquity, but it seems to have largely passed by. Some exceptions confirm the rule, such as the (later re; main entrance to Palma's Catedral (p42), the Consolat de I building and the mostly Renaissance-era sea walls. Althou rated in baroque fashion, the Monestir de Lluc (p102) is bas Renaissance, and was designed by sculptor and architect Jau quer (c 1578–1636).

The more curvaceous and, many would say, less attra cessor to the Renaissance was a moderate, islandwide bar rarely reached the florid extremes that one encounters els: Europe. It is most often manifest in the large churches t; nate inland towns. In many of the churches, existing Got tures received a serious reworking, evident in such element; vaulting, circular windows, and bloated and curvaceous p columns. Church exteriors are in the main sober (with the c gaudy facade). An exception can be found in the *retablos* (; Catalan), the grand sculptural altarpieces in most churches. and swirling with ornament, this was where baroque sculp; let their imaginations run wild.

Yet perhaps the most pleasing examples of Mallorca's interp; the baroque style comes in the *patis* (courtyards) that grace (mansions. Drawing on Islamic/Andalusian and Roman influ; tated by a warm Mediterranean climate, they represent one; most subtle baroque forms. Although baroque is the predomi; a handful of noble Palma houses betray Renaissance influe; as the facade of the Cal Marquès del Palmer (p50); standir; of this building, you might for the briefest of moments thi; transported to Medici Florence.

The stro ma ent on I

While peer ir of Palm architect will wa in Palm Corpu (p59) w of the o closed c are oper pu

Arts & Crafts

Literature

For centuries, Mallorca's writers have not only strived for literary excellence, but have sought to deploy such excellence in promoting Catalan or Mallorquin as powerful forms of cultural expression. Many of the works have now been translated, and reading just a few will initiate you into a rich literary scene little known beyond the Catalan-speaking world.

Those curious to find out more about authors writing in Catalan, in Mallorca and elsewhere in the Catalan-speaking world, should check out www.escriptors.cat, the website of the Association of Catalan Language Writers.

The Early Centuries

In one sense Mallorcan literature began with the island's medieval conqueror, Jaume I (1208–76), who recorded his daring deeds in *El Llibre dels Fets* (The Book of Deeds). He wrote in Catalan, a language that the Palma-born poet and visionary evangeliser Ramon Llull (1232–1316) would elevate to a powerful literary tool. A controversial figure, who many feel should be declared a saint (he has only made it to beatification), Llull has long been canonised as the father of the literary Catalan tongue.

Few Mallorquins grapple with Llull's medieval texts but most know at least one poem by Miquel Costa i Llobera (1854–1922), a theologian and poet. His *El Pi de Fomentor* (The Formentor Pinetree, 1907), which eulogises Mallorcan landscapes through a pine on the Formentor peninsula, is *the* Mallorcan poem.

The 20th Century

One of the island's greatest poets was the reclusive Miquel Bauça (1940–2005). His *Una Bella Història* (1962–85) is a major anthology. Llorenç

WRITINGS ABOUT MALLORCA

Mallorca has long been a favourite for foreign writers, both in providing a place in which to write and yielding up rich subject matter for the stories themselves.

» *Snowball Oranges* (2000), *Mañana Mañana* (2001), *Viva Mallorca* (2004) and *A Basketful of Snowflakes* (2007), by Peter Kerr

» *Tuning Up At Dawn* (2004) and *Bread and Oil: Majorcan Culture's Last Stand* (2006), by Robert Graves' son, Tomás

» *Un Hiver à Mallorque* (A Winter in Mallorca, 1839), by the 19th-century French novelist George Sand (actually Amandine-Aurore-Lucille Dupin)

» *Jogging Around Mallorca* (1929), by Gordon West

» *British Travellers in Mallorca in the Nineteenth Century* (2006), edited by Brian J Dendle and Shelby Thacker

» *Letters From Mallorca* (1887), by Charles W Wood

» *Die Insel des Zweiten Gesichts* (The Island of the Second Vision, 1953), by German writer Albert Vigoleis Thelen (1903–89)

Anaïs Nin set an erotic short story, 'Mallorca', in Deià. It appeared in the volume *Delta of Venus* and deals with a local girl who gets into an erotic tangle with a pair of foreigners and pays a high price. Nin stayed in Deià for a year in 1941.

Villalonga (1897–1980), born into an elite Palma family and trained in medicine, was one of Mallorca's top 20th-century novelists. Many of his works, including his most successful novel, *Bearn* (1952), portray the decay of the island's landed nobility.

Baltasar Porcel (b 1937, Andratx) is the doyen of contemporary Mallorcan literature. *L'Emperador o l'Ull del Vent* (The Emperor or the Eye of the Wind, 2001) is a dramatic tale about the imprisonment of thousands of Napoleon's soldiers on Illa de Cabrera.

Carme Riera (b 1948, Palma) has churned out an impressive series of novels, short stories, scripts and more. Her latest novel, *L'Estiu de l'Anglès* (The English Summer, 2006), tells of a frustrated Barcelona estate agent's decision to spend a month learning English in a middle-of-nowhere UK town.

Guillem Frontera (b 1945, Ariany) has produced some engaging crime novels, particularly the 1980 *La Ruta dels Cangurs* (The Kangaroo Route), in which the murder of the detective's ex-girlfriend muddies his Mallorca holiday plans.

Music

Folk Music

Mallorca, like any other part of Spain, has a rich heritage in folk songs and ballads sung in Mallorquin. At many traditional *festes* in Mallorcan towns you'll hear the sounds of the *xeremiers,* a duo of ambling musicians, one of whom plays the *xeremia* (similar to the bagpipes) and the other a *flabiol* (a high-pitched pipe). Younger bands sometimes give these Mallorcan songs a bit of a rough-edged rock sound.

Contemporary Music

In 1936, inspired by a stay in the then little-known town of Pollença, Agatha Christie wrote the short crime thriller *Problem at Pollensa Bay,* which would later be the title for a volume of eight short crime mysteries.

Los Valldemossa, who sang Mallorcan folk songs with a jazz feel in Palma's clubs, had some success overseas – they wound up playing the London circuit and, in 1969, won the Eurovision Song Contest, which back then actually meant something. They stopped playing in 2001 but their CDs still abound.

The island's best-known singer-songwriter is Palma's Maria del Mar Bonet i Verdaguer (b 1947). She moved to Barcelona at the age of 20 to join the Nova Cançó Catalana movement, which promoted singers and bands working in Catalan. Bonet became an international success and is known for her interpretations of Mediterranean folk music, French *chanson* (Jacques Brel and company) and experiments with jazz and Brazilian music.

An altogether different performer is Concha Buika. Of Equatorial Guinean origins, she was born in Palma in 1972 and rose through the Palma club circuit with her very personal brand of music, ranging from hip-hop to flamenco to soul. Her second CD, *Mi Niña Lola,* came out in 2007, followed by *Niña de Fuego* a year later, and in 2009 *El Ultimo Trago,* a collaboration with Chucho Valdés, the renowned Cuban jazz pianist.

Argentine-born, Mallorca-based starlet Chenoa got her break when she stunned all in the TV talent show *Operación Triunfo.* Since 2002 she has churned out four albums and has become one of the most popular voices in Spanish-Latin pop.

Painting & Sculpture

The Early Centuries

Subsumed after the 1229 conquest into the Catalan world of the Crown of Aragón, Mallorca lay at a strategic point on sea routes in a Catalan lake. This fostered the movement of artists and not a few were attracted from the mainland, particularly Valencia, to Mallorca.

The earliest works from this revival of Catalan culture, transmitted by Catalan artists, were influenced by the Gothic art of the Sienese school in Italy. Later, International Gothic began to filter through, notably under the influence of the Valencian artist Francesc Comes, who was at work in Mallorca from 1390 to 1415.

Important artists around the mid-15th century include Rafel Mòger (c 1424–70) and Frenchman Pere Niçard, who worked in Mallorca from 1468 to 1470. They created one of the era's most important works, *Sant Jordi,* now housed in Palma's Museu Diocesà. The outstanding sculptor of this time was Guillem Sagrera, who did much of the detail work on Sa Llotja.

Pere Terrencs (active c 1479–1528) returned from a study stint in Valencia with the technique of oil painting – the death knell for egg-based pigments. His was a transitional style between late Gothic and the Renaissance. In a similar category was Córdoba-born Mateu López (d 1581), who trained in the prestigious Valencia workshops of father and son Vicent Macip and Joan de Joanes (aka Joan Vicent Macip, 1523–79), both signal artists. In 1544 López landed in Mallorca where he and his son became senior painters.

Gaspar Oms (c 1540–1614) was Mallorca's most outstanding late-Renaissance painter. The Oms clan, from Valencia, dominated the Mallorcan art scene throughout the 17th and 18th centuries.

Miquel Bestard (1592–1633) created major baroque canvases for churches, such as the Convento de Santa Clara and the Església de Monte-Sion, in Palma. Guillem Mesquida Munar (1675–1747) concentrated on religious motifs and scenes from classical mythology.

For those who thought Ibiza was the exclusive Mediterranean home of club sounds, Daniel Vulic (DJ and German radio director in Mallorca) brought out *Cool Vibes Vol 1,* a compilation of strictly Mallorcan chillout and club music in 2007.

19th- & 20th-century Mallorcan Art

The 19th century brought a wave of landscape artists to Mallorca. Many came from mainland Spain, particularly Catalonia, but the island produced its own painters, too. More than half a dozen notables were born and raised in Palma. Joan O'Neille Rosiñol (1828–1907) is considered the founder of the island's landscape movement. He and his younger contemporaries Ricard Anckermann Riera (1842–1907) and Antoni Ribas Oliver (1845–1911), both from Palma, were among the first to cast their artistic eyes over the island and infuse it with romantic lyricism. The latter two concentrated particularly on coastal scenes.

From 1890 a flood of Modernista artists from Catalonia 'discovered' Mallorca and brought new influences to the island. Some of them, such as Santiago Rusiñol (1861–1931), had spent time in Paris, which was then the hotbed of the art world. Locals enthusiastically joined in the Modernista movement. Palma-born Antoni Gelabert Massot (1877–1932) became a key figure, depicting his home city in paintings such as *Murada i Catedral a Entrada de Fosc* (1902–04). Other artists caught up in this wave were Joan Fuster Bonnín (1870–1943) and Llorenç Cerdà i Bispal (1862–1955), born in Pollença.

Meanwhile Llorenç Rosselló (1867–1902) was shaping up to be the island's most prominent sculptor until his early death. A handful of Rosselló's bronzes as well as a selection of works by many of the painters mentioned here can be seen in Es Baluard (p54).

By the 1910s and 1920s symbolism began to creep into local artists' vocabulary. Two important names in Mallorca painting from this period are Joan Antoni Fuster Valiente (1892–1964) and Ramón Nadal (1913–99), both from Palma.

Best Niche Galleries

- Es Baluard
- Casa-Museu Dionís Bennàssar
- Casa-Museu Joaquim Torrents Lladò
- Ca'n Prunera – Museu Modernista

Contemporary

Towering above everyone else in modern Mallorcan art is local hero and art icon, Miquel Barceló (b 1957, Felanitx). His profile has been especially sharp in his island home after the unveiling in 2007 of one of his more controversial masterpieces, a ceramic depiction of the miracle of the loaves and fishes housed in Palma's Catedral (p42). The artist, who divides his time between Paris and Mali's Dogon Country, has a studio in Naples and was a rising star by the age of 25. Although he is best known as a painter, Barceló has worked with ceramics since the late 1990s. However, the commission for the Catedral was on a hitherto unimagined scale for the artist.

Less well known but nonetheless prolific is Palma-born Ferran García Sevilla (b 1949), whose canvases are frequently full of primal colour and strong shapes and images. Since the early 1980s he has exhibited in galleries throughout Europe. Joan Costa (b 1961, Palma) is one of the island's key contemporary sculptors, who also indulges in occasional brushwork.

One cannot leave out 20th-century Catalan icon, Joan Miró (1893–1983). His mother came from Sóller and he lived the last 27 years of his life in Cala Major, just outside Palma, where his former home is now a museum, the Fundació Pilar i Joan Miró (p75). Working there in a huge studio, he maintained a prolific turn-out of canvases, ceramics, statuary, textiles and more, faithful to his particular motifs of women, birds and the cosmos.

Crafts

Tourism may have led to the overdevelopment of the Mallorcan coast, but it has enabled the revival of many traditional crafts and artisan workshops, among them those working with metal, ceramics, paper, glass, leather and jewellery.

The Consell de Mallorca tourist office (p72), its airport branch and some municipal tourist offices around the island have a fine little brochure entitled *Map of Arts & Crafts in Majorca*, pinpointing 21 artisan producers working in a range of materials.

Top Craft Shops

» Artesania

» Estel@rt

» Oliv-Art

» Teixits Vicens

» Temps era Temps

» Típika

Glasswork

Glasswork was first produced on the island way back in the 2nd century BC and its artisans were part of a network of glass production and trade with its centre on Murano, in Venice. Mallorcan glass manufacturing reached its highpoint in the 18th century, whereafter the industry fell into decline. But one family, the Gordiolas who first entered the industry back in the 18th century, were almost singlehandedly responsible for glassmaking's revival in the mid- to late-20th-century. Although you'll find smaller artisans working with glass, the Museu de Gordiola (p129) near Algaida is the largest producer and here you can watch traditional glass-blowing techniques.

Leatherwork

Thanks to its world-famous shoe manufacturers like Camper, Mallorca's leather-making industries have become renowned worldwide for their quality. Although smaller traditional manufacturers tend to get drowned out by the larger companies, there's no denying that this industry has become a stunning Mallorcan success story. Inca is the capital of Mallorcan shoe-making with a host of factories and outlets; the latter are open to the public.

Well aware of its pulling power, the industry has produced two useful brochures which you may find in some tourist offices around the island: *Mallorca Mapa Turístico – Ruta de Calzado* (Mallorca Tourist Map – Shoe Route) and *Industry Tour of Majorcan Footwear – Guide to Footwear Manufacturers.*

Survival Guide

DIRECTORY A–Z . . . 200
Business Hours 200
Customs Regulations . . . 200
Discount Cards. 200
Electricity 200
Gay & Lesbian Travellers 200
Climate. 201
Health. 201
Insurance. 202
Internet Access. 202
Language Courses 202
Legal Matters 202
Maps. 202
Money. 203
Post. 203
Public Holidays. 203
Safe Travel. 204
Telephone 204
Time 204
Toilets. 205
Tourist Information 205
Travellers with Disabilities. 205
Visas. 205
Women Travellers. 206
Work 206

TRANSPORT 207
GETTING THERE & AWAY 207
Entering Mallorca. 207
Air 207
Sea 208
Tours. 208
GETTING AROUND. 208
Bicycle 208
Bus 208
Car & Motorcycle. 209
Local Transport. 210
Train 210

LANGUAGE 211

Directory A–Z

Business Hours

Reviews in this guidebook won't list business hours unless they differ from the following standards.

TYPE OF BUSINESS	STANDARD OPENING HOURS
Banks	8.30am-2pm Mon-Fri; some also open 4-7pm Thu and 9am-1pm Sat
Central post offices	8.30am-9.30pm Mon-Fri, 8.30am-2pm Sat
Nightclubs	midnight-6am
Restaurants	lunch: 1-3.30pm, dinner: 7.30-11pm
Shops	10am-2pm & 4.30-7.30pm or 5-8pm Mon-Sat; big supermarkets and department stores generally open 10am-9pm Mon-Sat

Customs Regulations

Duty-free allowances for travellers entering Spain from outside the EU include 2L of wine (or 1L of wine and 1L of spirits), and 200 cigarettes or 50 cigars or 250g of tobacco.

There are no duty-free allowances for travel between EU countries and there are no restrictions on the import of duty-paid items into Spain from other EU countries for personal use. It is also possible to buy VAT-free articles at airport shops when travelling between EU countries.

Discount Cards

At museums, never hesitate to ask if there are discounts for students, young people, children, families or the elderly. See also p191 for details about Mallorca's Targeta Verde.

» **Senior Cards**: Reduced prices for people over 60, 63 or 65 (depending on the place) at various museums and attractions (sometimes restricted to EU citizens only) and occasionally reduced costs on transport.

» **Student Cards**: An ISIC (International Student Identity Card; www.isic.org) may come in handy (there is also a teachers' version, ITIC), although about all it's officially good for is a discount on Avis car rental and Palma's city sightseeing bus.

» **Youth Card**: Travel, sights and youth hostel discounts with the Euro<26 (www.euro26.org) card (known as Carnet Joven in Spain). The International Youth Travel Card (IYTC; www.istc.org) offers similar benefits. You can find comprehensive lists on the website.

Electricity

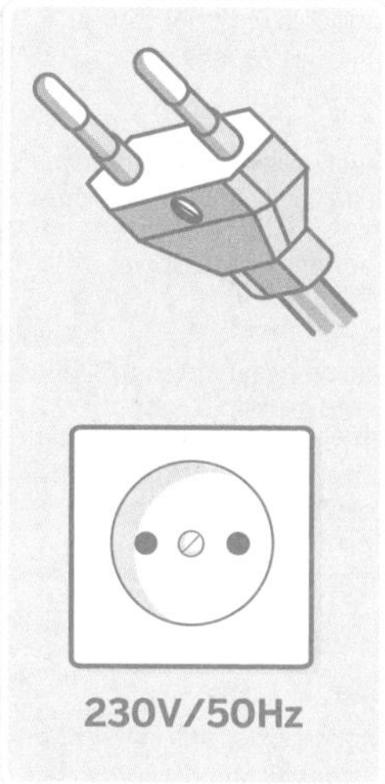

Gay & Lesbian Travellers

Homosexuality is legal in Spain. In 2005 the Socialist president of Spain, José Luis Rodríguez Zapatero, gave the conservative Catholic foundations of the country a shake with the legalisation of same-sex marriages. In Mallorca the bulk of the gay scene takes place in and around Palma (p68).

Useful resources and organisations:

Climate

Palma

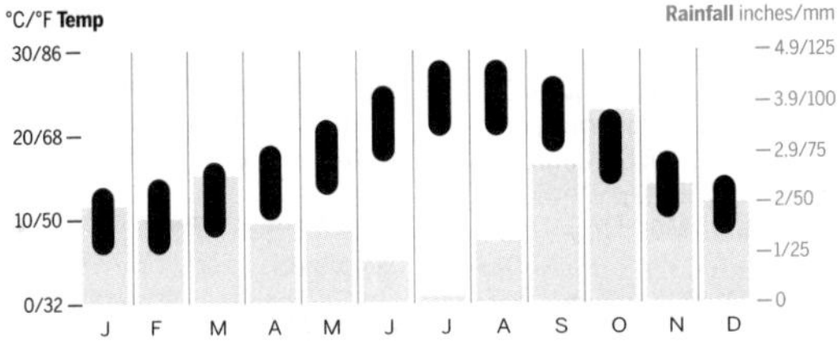

» **Ben Amics** (☎971 715 670; www.benamics.com; Carrer del Conquistador 2; ⏰9am-3pm) The island's umbrella association for gays, lesbians and transsexuals.

» **Gay Mallorca** (www.gay-mallorca.blogspot.com, in Spanish) Weekly events listings.

» **Guía Gay de España** (guia.universogay.com/palmademallorca, in Spanish) More useful listings of cafes, saunas, nightclubs and restaurants.

» **Mallorca Gay Map** (www.mallorcagaymap.com) A handy guide to gay-friendly attractions (restaurants, hotels, clubs etc); a paper version is available from some municipal tourist offices in Palma.

Health

Mallorca doesn't present any particular health dangers.

Before You Go

INSURANCE

If you're an EU citizen, a European Health Insurance Card (EHIC), available from health centres or, in the UK, post offices, covers you for most medical care. It will not cover you for non-emergencies or emergency repatriation. Citizens from other countries should find out if there is a reciprocal arrangement for free medical care between their country and Spain.

RECOMMENDED VACCINATIONS

No jabs are necessary for Mallorca but the WHO recommends that all travellers be covered for diphtheria, tetanus, measles, mumps, rubella and polio, regardless of their destination.

In Mallorca

AVAILABILITY OF HEALTH CARE

If you need an ambulance call ☎061. For emergency treatment go straight to the *urgencias* (casualty) section of the nearest hospital. The island's main hospital is Palma's **Hospital Son Dureta** (☎971 175 000; Carrer de Andrea Doria 55), but other important ones are based in Inca and Manacor. At the main coastal tourist resorts you will generally find clinics with English- and German-speaking staff.

Farmacias (pharmacies) offer valuable advice and sell over-the-counter medication, and a system of *farmacias de guardia* (duty pharmacies) operates: when a pharmacy is closed it posts the name of the nearest open one on the door.

ENVIRONMENTAL HAZARDS

» Heat exhaustion occurs following excessive fluid loss with inadequate replacement of fluids and salts. Symptoms include headache, dizziness and tiredness. To treat heat exhaustion, replace lost fluids by drinking water and/or fruit juice, and cool the body with cold water and fans.

» Heat stroke is much more serious, resulting in irrational and hyperactive behaviour and eventually loss of consciousness and death. Rapid cooling by spraying the body with water and fanning is ideal.

» If you have a severe allergy to bee or wasp stings, carry an 'epipen' or similar adrenaline injection.

» In forested areas watch out for the hairy reddish-brown caterpillars of the pine processionary moth. They live in silvery nests up in the pine trees and, come spring, they leave the nest to march in long lines (hence the name). Touching the caterpillars' hairs sets off a severely irritating allergic skin reaction.

» Some Spanish centipedes have a very nasty but non-fatal sting. The ones to watch out for are those with clearly defined segments, which may be patterned with, for instance, black and yellow stripes.

» In summer, waves of stingers (jellyfish) can appear on the island's beaches and there's not much you can do about them. There are two basic types of stinger, the *Rhizostoma pulmo* and *Pelagia noctiluca*. Traditionally the best method for easing the pain is to rub vinegar in, although Epsom salts are better for the *Pelagia noctiluca*. A bag of ice also soothes the pain. If none of these options are available, rub in salt water; fresh water can stimulate the sting. Head to a Red Cross stand (they are usually present on the main beaches) if you are stung.

» Sandflies are found on many Mallorcan beaches. They usually cause only a nasty itchy bite but can carry occasionally a rare skin disorder called cutaneous leishmaniasis.

» Tap water is generally safe to drink in Mallorca but rarely tastes very good, which is why most locals buy bottled mineral water. Do not drink water from rivers or lakes as it may contain bacteria or viruses that can cause diarrhoea or vomiting.

Insurance

A travel-insurance policy to cover theft, loss and medical problems is a good idea. It may also cover you for cancellation or delays to your travel arrangements. EU citizens are entitled to the full range of health-care services in public hospitals, but you will need to present your European Health Insurance Card (inquire at your national health service before leaving home). Private insurance is still a good idea, however. Check that the policy covers ambulances or an emergency flight home.

Worldwide travel insurance is available at www.lonelyplanet.com/travel_services. You can buy, extend and claim online anytime – even if you're already on the road.

Internet Access

Wireless internet (wi-fi) access is widespread in hotels and some cafes and is usually (but not always) free. You'll find that in many hotels the signal doesn't extend beyond the lobby, and in-room wi-fi is not nearly as common as you might expect.

There are cybercafes in Palma and the main coastal resorts and towns, but few last for more than a year or two; ask at the tourist office for the nearest place. Internet cafes typically charge about €1.50 to €3 per hour.

Language Courses

Palma is the main place to learn Spanish, but Sóller is an appealing alternative. The better places include the following:

» **Dialog** (☎971 719 994; www.dialog-palma.com; Carrer del Carme 14, Palma; 2-week course €395; ⏰9am-2pm & 4.30-8.30pm Mon-Fri, 10am-1.30pm Sat)

» **Die Akademie** (☎971 718 290; www.dieakademie.com; Carrer de Morei 8, Palma; per week €175-195; ⏰9am-1.30pm & 5-7.30pm Mon-Fri)

» **Estudi Lul·lià de Mallorca** (☎971 711 988; www.estudigeneral.com; Carrer de Sant Roc 4, Palma; courses from €400)

» **Academia Sóller** (☎971 634 149; www.academiasoller.com; 2nd fl, Plaça de la Constitució 8, Sóller; weekly intensive courses from €240-450)

Legal Matters

If you're arrested you will be allotted the free services of a duty solicitor *(abogado de oficio)*, who may speak only Spanish (and Mallorquin). You're also entitled to make a phone call. If you use this to contact your embassy or consulate, the staff will probably be able to do no more than refer you to a lawyer who speaks your language. If you end up in court, the authorities are obliged to provide a translator.

In theory you are supposed to have your national ID card or passport with you at all times. If asked for it by the police, you're supposed to be able to produce it on the spot. In practice it's rarely an issue and many people choose (understandably) to leave passports in hotel safes.

Cannabis is legal but only for personal use and in very small quantities. Public consumption of any drug is illegal.

Police

The Policía Local or Policía Municipal operates at a local level and deals with such issues as traffic infringements and minor crime. The Policía Nacional (☎091) is the state police force, dealing with major crime and operating primarily in the cities. The military-linked Guardia Civil (created in the 19th century to deal with banditry) is largely responsible for highway patrols, borders, security, major crime and terrorism.

Maps

City Maps

The free maps handed out by tourist offices in Mallorca's towns are generally adequate. In Palma, the tourist office map is OK and has a map of the island on the reverse side. The free map produced by the department store El Corte Inglés is excellent for central Palma.

Island Maps

Among the better and clearer island maps:

» Freytag and Berndt's *Mallorca* (1:100,000)

» Michelin's No.579 *Balears/Balearics* (1:140,000)

» Marco Polo's *Mallorca* (1:175,000)

Walking Maps

Walking maps need to be scaled at least at 1:25,000. Anything bigger is near useless.

Alpina Editorial produces three such maps to the Serra de Tramuntana range (*Mallorca Tramuntana Sud*, *Mallorca Tramuntana Central* and *Mallorca Tramuntana Nord*). These come with detailed walk descriptions in a solid booklet. The first two are in Catalan and Spanish with English and German summaries, while the third is in Catalan and German only.

The *Kompass Wanderbuch 942 Mallorca* (in German), by Wolfgang Heizmann, comes with detailed walking maps.

Walk! Mallorca (North & Mountains), by Charles Davis, is packed with walks, basic maps and GPS aid. You'll need to buy maps though.

Spain's **Centro Nacional de Información Geográfica** (CNIG; www.cnig.es) covers a good part of the island in 1:25,000 scale sheets.

Some of these maps are available in Palma at **La Casa del Mapa** (971 225 945; casamapa@imi.a-palma.es; Carrer de Sant Domingo 11, Palma; 9.30am-2pm Mon-Fri), while some map specialists in other countries, such as **Stanfords** (020-7836 1321; www.stanfords.co.uk; 12-14 Long Acre, London WC2E 9LP) in the UK, have a good range.

Money

As in 16 other EU nations, the euro is Spain's currency.

ATMs

Cajeros automáticos are widespread around the island, although it's best to stock up on funds in larger towns or major resorts; look for ATMs that display the relevant symbols such as Visa, MasterCard, Cirrus etc. Remember that there is usually a charge (around 1.5% to 2%) on ATM cash withdrawals abroad.

Cash

Most banks exchange major foreign currencies and offer the best rates, although there's little advantage in bringing foreign cash into Spain, which you can't replace if lost or stolen. Ask about commissions and take your passport. Also, ask about commissions before changing money in exchange bureaux (look for the sign 'cambio'), which tend to open longer hours but can charge outrageous amounts. You'll find some in central Palma and the main resorts.

Credit & Debit Cards

Can be used to pay for most purchases. You'll often be asked to show your passport or some other form of photo ID. Among the most widely accepted are Visa, MasterCard, American Express (Amex), Cirrus, Maestro, Plus, Diners Club and JCB. If your card is lost, stolen or swallowed by an ATM, you can call the following telephone numbers toll free to have an immediate stop put on its use: **Amex** (902 375 637 or 900 994 426), **Diners Club** (901 101 011), **MasterCard** (900 971 231) and **Visa** (900 991 216, 900 991 124).

Taxes & Refunds

In Spain, value-added tax (VAT) is known as IVA *(ee-ba; impuesto sobre el valor añadido)*. To ask 'Is IVA included?', say '*¿Está incluido el IVA?*'

Visitors are entitled to a refund of the 18% IVA on purchases costing more than €90.16 from any shop if they are taking them out of the EU within three months. Ask the shop for a cash back (or similar) refund form showing the price and IVA paid for each item, and identifying the vendor and purchaser. Then present the refund form to the customs booth for IVA refunds at the airport, port or border from which you leave the EU. For more information, see www.spainrefund.com.

Tipping

Menu prices include a service charge. Most people leave some small change if they're satisfied: 5% is normally fine and 10% extremely generous. Porters will generally be happy with €1. Taxi drivers don't have to be tipped but a little rounding up won't go amiss.

Travellers Cheques

Most people are perfectly happy to wander around Mallorca with plastic. The advantage of travellers cheques is that they can be replaced if lost or stolen and so it might not be a bad idea to carry some of your money in this form. Visa, Amex and Travelex are widely accepted brands with (usually) efficient replacement policies: ask for their emergency phone numbers in Spain when you purchase the cheques. It's vital to keep your initial receipt, and a record of your cheque numbers. Take along your ID when you cash travellers cheques.

Post

The Spanish postal system, **Correos** (902 197 197; www.correos.es), is generally reliable, if a little slow at times.

Postal Rates

Sellos (stamps) are sold at most *estancos* (tobacconists' shops with 'Tabacos' in yellow letters on a maroon background), as well as post offices. A postcard or letter weighing up to 20g costs €1.07 from Spain to other European countries, and €1.38 to the rest of the world. For a full list of prices for certified *(certificado)* and express post *(urgente)*, go to www.correos.es (in Spanish) and click on 'Calculador de Tarifas'.

Sending Mail

Delivery times are erratic but ordinary mail to other Western European countries can take up to a week (although as little as three days); to North America up to 10 days; and to Australia or New Zealand (NZ) between 10 days and three weeks.

Public Holidays

The two main periods when Spaniards (and Mallorquins are no real exception) go on holiday are Semana Santa (the week leading up to Easter Sunday) and August, at precisely the same moment when half of Europe descends on Mallorca. Accommodation can be hard to find and transport is put under strain.

There are 14 official holidays a year, to which most

towns add at least one to mark their patron saint's day. Some places have several traditional feast days, not all of which are official holidays, but which are often a reason for partying.

The main islandwide public holidays:

» **Cap d'Any** (New Year's Day) 1 January

» **Epifania del Senyor** (Epiphany) 6 January – in Palma a landing of the Three Wise Men (Reis Mags) is staged in the port, followed by a procession

» **Dia de les Illes Balears** (Balearic Islands Day) 1 March

» **Dijous Santa** (Holy Thursday) March/April

» **Divendres Sant** (Good Friday) March/April

» **Diumenge de Pasqua** (Easter Sunday) March/April

» **Festa del Treball** (Labour Day) 1 May

» **L'Assumpció** (Feast of the Assumption) 15 August

» **Festa Nacional d'Espanya** (Spanish National Day) 12 October

» **Tots Sants** (All Saints) 1 November

» **Dia de la Constitució** (Constitution Day) 6 December

» **L'Immacula da Concepció** (Feast of the Immaculate Conception) 8 December

» **Nadal** (Christmas) 25 December

» **Segona Festa de Nadal** (Boxing Day) 26 December

Safe Travel

Mallorca is safe. The main thing to be wary of is petty theft. Most visitors to Mallorca never feel remotely threatened, but that's no reason not to exercise the usual caution.

Theft & Scams

Theft is mostly a risk in the busier resort areas and Palma. You are at your most vulnerable when dragging around luggage to or from your hotel. Watch for pickpockets and bag snatchers and for an old classic: ladies offering flowers (the so-called *claveleras*, because they usually offer *claveles*, ie carnations) for good luck. We don't know how they do it, but if you get too involved in a friendly chat with these people, your pockets always wind up empty.

Carry valuables under your clothes if possible – not in a back pocket, daypack or anything easily snatched away. Keep a firm grip on daypacks and bags at all times. Anything left on the beach can disappear in a flash when your back is turned.

Report thefts to the national police. It is unlikely that you will recover your goods but you need to make a formal *denuncia* for insurance purposes. To avoid endless queues at the police station *(comisaría)*, you can make the report by phone (☎902 102 112) in various languages or on the web at www.policia.es (click on 'Denuncias'). The following day go to the police station of your choice to pick up and sign the report, without queuing.

Telephone

Blue payphones are easy to use for international and domestic calls. They accept coins, *tarjetas telefónicas* (phonecards issued by the national phone company Telefónica) and, in some cases, credit cards. *Tarjetas telefónicas* come in €6 and €12 denominations and are sold at post offices and tobacconists.

Area Codes

All telephone numbers in Mallorca (including for mobiles) have nine digits. Almost all fixed-line telephone numbers in Mallorca begin with 971, although a small number begin with 871. Numbers starting with a '6' are for mobile phones.

Numbers starting with 900 are national toll-free numbers, while those starting 901 to 905 come with varying costs. A common one is 902, which is a national standard rate number, but which can only be dialled from within Spain. In a similar category are numbers starting with 800, 803, 806 and 807.

It is possible to dial an operator in your country of residence at no cost to make a reverse-charge call (*una llamada a cobro revertido*) – pick up the number before you leave home. You can usually get an English-speaking Spanish international operator on 1008 (for calls within Europe) or 1005 (rest of the world).

Mobile Phones

Spain uses GSM 900/1800, which is compatible with the rest of Europe and Australia but not with the North American GSM 1900 or the totally different system used in Japan. If your phone is tri- or quadriband, you will probably be fine. Shops on every high street sell *teléfonos móviles* with prepaid cards from around €80 for the most basic models.

Phonecards

Cut-rate phonecards from private companies can be good value for international calls. They can be bought from *estancos*, newsstands and *locutorios* (call centres), especially in Palma and coastal resorts – compare rates if possible.

Time

» **Time zone** Same as most of Western Europe (GMT/UTC plus one hour during winter and GMT/UTC plus two hours during the daylight-saving period)

» **Daylight-saving** From last Sunday in March to last Sunday in October.

» **UK, Ireland, Portugal & Canary Islands** One hour behind mainland Spain.

» **USA** Spanish time is USA Eastern Time plus six hours and USA Pacific Time plus nine hours.

» **Australia** During the Australian winter (Spanish summer), subtract eight hours from Australian Eastern Standard Time to get Spanish time; during the Australian summer, subtract 10 hours.

Toilets

Toilets are of the sit-down variety, although public toilets are rare to nonexistant across the island. If you find yourself in need of the facilities, remember that most bars and restaurants will expect you to purchase something before or after you use the toilet; the busier the place, the less likely you are to be detected.

Tourist Information

Most towns (including many small villages) have an *oficina de turismo* or *oficina de información turística* for local information. Those in coastal areas usually open from Easter or May until October and keep surprisingly short hours: most employees are government functionaries and work hours that are more generous to the workers than they are to visitors seeking information. If you do find them open, they're usually helpful and overflowing with useful brochures.

In Palma you'll find numerous municipal tourist offices which focus on information about Palma and the immediate surrounds. There's also the **Consell de Mallorca tourist office** (☎971 712 216; www.infomallorca.net; Plaça de la Reina 2, Palma; ⌚8am-8pm Mon-Fri, 9am-2pm Sat), which covers the whole island.

Travellers with Disabilities

Mallorca is not overly disabled-friendly but some things are slowly changing. Disabled access to some museums, official buildings and hotels represents something of a sea change in local thinking, although it remains very much a minority phenomenon. You need to be circumspect about hotels advertising themselves as disabled-friendly, as this can mean as little as wide doors to rooms and bathrooms, a ramp into reception or other token efforts. Palma city buses are equipped for wheelchair access, as are some of those that travel around the island. Some taxi companies run adapted taxis – they must be booked in advance.

Organisations

» **Accessible Travel & Leisure** (☎01452-729739; www.accessibletravel.co.uk) Claims to be the biggest UK travel agent dealing with travel for the disabled and encourages the disabled to travel independently.

» **Associació Balear de Persones amb Discapacitat Física** (Asprom; ☎971 289 052; www.asprom.net; Carrer de Pasqual Ribot 6) The island's disabled persons' organisation is more of a lobby group than a source of practical holiday information.

» **Discount Mobility** (☎966 445 812; www.mobilitymallorca.com) Hires out mobility scooters for the disabled.

» **Easy Rider** (☎606 543 099; www.easyridermobilityhire.com) A Port d'Alcúdia-based outfit hiring mobility scooters.

» **Mobility Scooters** (☎971 132 538; www.mobilityscootersmallorca.com) Delivers mobility scooters for hire to customers around the island.

Visas

Spain is one of 25 member countries of the Schengen Convention, under which 22 EU countries (all but Bulgaria, Cyprus, Ireland, Romania and the UK) plus Iceland, Norway and Switzerland have abolished checks at common borders. Cyprus has signed the Schengen agreement, but full membership has been postponed.

The visa situation for entering Spain is as follows:

» **Citizens or residents of EU & Schengen countries** No visa required.

» **Citizens or residents of Australia, Canada, Israel, Japan, NZ and the USA** No visa required for tourist visits of up to 90 days.

» **Other countries** Check with a Spanish embassy or consulate.

» **To work or study in Spain** A special visa may be required – contact a Spanish embassy or consulate before travel.

Extensions & Residence

Schengen visas cannot be extended. You can apply for no more than two visas in any 12-month period and they are not renewable once in Spain. Nationals of EU countries, Iceland, Norway and Switzerland can enter and leave Spain at will and don't need to apply for a *tarjeta de residencia* (residence card), although they are supposed to apply for residence papers.

People of other nationalities who want to stay in Spain longer than 90 days require a residence card; getting one can be a drawn-out process, starting with an appropriate visa issued by a Spanish consulate in their country of residence. Start the process well in advance.

Women Travellers

Travelling in Mallorca is largely as easy as travelling anywhere else in the Western world. However, you may still occasionally find yourself the object of staring, catcalls and unnecessary comments. Simply ignoring them is sufficient, but learn the word for 'help' *(socorro)* in case you need to draw other people's attention. Remember that eye-to-eye contact and flirting is part of daily Spanish life and need not be offensive.

By and large, Spanish women have a highly developed sense of style and put considerable effort into looking their best. While topless bathing and skimpy clothes are in fashion on the island's coastal resorts, people tend to dress more modestly in the towns and inland.

Work

Nationals of EU countries, Switzerland, Norway and Iceland may work freely in Spain, and hence, Mallorca. If you are offered a contract, your employer will normally steer you through any bureaucracy.

Virtually everyone else needs to obtain, from a Spanish consulate in their country of residence, a work permit and, if they plan to stay more than 90 days, a residence visa. These procedures are well-nigh impossible unless you have a job contract lined up beforehand.

You can start a job search on the web, for instance at **Think Spain** (www.thinkspain.com). Translating and interpreting could be an option if you are fluent both in Spanish and a language in demand. Teaching English and some other languages is another option if you are qualified. Language schools are listed under 'Academias de Idiomas' in the Yellow Pages. Check the work conditions carefully before signing up.

Many bars (especially of the UK and Irish persuasion), restaurants and other businesses are run by foreigners and look for temporary staff in summer. Check any local press in foreign languages, which carry ads for waiters, nannies, chefs, babysitters, cleaners and the like.

It's also possible to stumble upon work as crew on yachts and cruisers. Check out the situation in the port of Palma de Mallorca.

Transport

GETTING THERE & AWAY

Most visitors to Mallorca fly into Palma's international airport, though it's possible to arrive by ferry from points along the Spanish coast (Alicante, Barcelona, Denia and Valencia). The neighbouring islands of Ibiza and Menorca are also linked to Mallorca by air and ferry. Flights, tours and rail tickets can be booked online at www.lonelyplanet.com/travel_services.

Entering Mallorca

Passport

Citizens of most of the 27 EU member states and Switzerland can travel to Spain with their national identity card. Citizens of countries that don't issue ID cards, such as the UK, need a full passport. All other nationalities must have a full valid passport.

If applying for a visa, check that your passport's expiry date is at least six months away. Non-EU citizens must fill out a landing card.

By law you are supposed to carry your passport or ID card with you at all times.

Air

Airports

Palma de Mallorca's **Son Sant Joan Airport** (☎902 404 704; www.aena.es) is 8km east of Palma de Mallorca. In summer especially, masses of charter and regular flights form an air bridge to Palma from around Europe, among them many low-cost airlines. In 2010, Sant Joan received 21.12 million incoming passengers, making it Spain's third-busiest airport.

The arrivals hall is on the ground floor of the main terminal building, where you'll find a tourist information office, money-exchange offices, car hire, tour operators and hotel-booking stands. Departures are on the 2nd floor.

Airlines

Airlines serving Palma include the following:

» **AerLingus** (www.aerlingus.com) From Dublin.

» **Air Berlin** (www.airberlin.com) From London (Stansted), dozens of cities all over Germany and elsewhere in mainland Europe.

» **AirEuropa** (www.aireuropa.com) From Paris, and 10 Spanish cities.

» **British Airways** (www.britishairways.com) From London.

» **Brussels Airlines** (www.brusselsairlines.com) From Brussels.

» **Condor** (www.condor.com) From various German cities.

» **EasyJet** (www.easyjet.com) From 10 UK airports and seven in mainland Europe.

» **Germanwings** (www.germanwings.com) From dozens of UK and mainland Europe airports.

» **Iberia** (www.iberia.es) With its subsidiary Air Nostrum, flies from many mainland Spanish cities.

» **Jet2** (www.jet2.com) From Belfast, Leeds, Edinburgh and Newcastle.

» **Jetair** (www.jetairfly.com) From three Belgian cities.

» **Lufthansa** (www.lufthansa.com) From nine central European cities.

» **Monarch** (www.flymonarch.com) Scheduled and charter flights from London (Luton), Edinburgh, Birmingham and Manchester.

» **Niki** (www.flyniki.com) From dozens of Spanish and European cities.

» **Ryanair** (www.ryanair.com) From numerous UK and mainland European airports.

» **Spanair** (www.spanair.com) From most mainland Spanish centres and a handful of European cities.

» **Cimber Sterling** (www.cimber.com) From Copenhagen and Aalborg.

» **Swiss** (www.swiss.com) From Zürich.

» **Thomson Fly** (www.thomson.co.uk) From many UK cities.

» **Transavia** (www.transavia.com) From Paris, Nantes, Eindhoven and Amsterdam.

» **Vueling** (www.vueling.com) Dozens of flights from mainland Spain and further afield.

Tickets

Full-time students and those under 26 can sometimes get discounted fares. Other

CLIMATE CHANGE & TRAVEL

Every form of transport that relies on carbon-based fuel generates CO_2, the main cause of human-induced climate change. Modern travel is dependent on aeroplanes, which might use less fuel per kilometre per person than most cars but travel much greater distances. The altitude at which aircraft emit gases (including CO_2) and particles also contributes to their climate change impact. Many websites offer 'carbon calculators' that allow people to estimate the carbon emissions generated by their journey and, for those who wish to do so, to offset the impact of the greenhouse gases emitted with contributions to portfolios of climate-friendly initiatives throughout the world. Lonely Planet offsets the carbon footprint of all staff and author travel.

cheap deals include discounted tickets released to travel agents and specialist agencies. Also check online for well-priced tickets direct from low-cost carriers.

Sea

Ferry services connect Mallorca to the Spanish mainland and to Menorca, Ibiza and Formentera. Most services operate only from Easter to late October, and those services that continue into the winter reduce their departure times. Most ferry companies allow you to transport vehicles on longer routes.

A good place to start is to check routes and compare prices at **Direct Ferries** (www.directferries.co.uk).

Ferry companies that operate to and from Mallorca include the following:

» **Acciona Trasmediterránea** (☎902 454 645; www.trasmediterranea.es)

» **Baleària** (☎902 160 180; www.balearia.com)

» **Interilles** (☎902 100 444; www.interilles.es, in Spanish)

» **Iscomar** (☎902 119 128; www.iscomar.com)

Tours

Joining an organised tour to Mallorca is certainly not necessary – it's an easy destination for independent travel. But some companies offer specialist tours that make it so much easier to indulge your passions.

» **Balearic Discovery** (☎971 875 395; www.balearicdiscovery.com) Choose from tailor-made trips that allow you to build your own itinerary or a set activities trip where you can choose activities from sea kayaking to horse riding.

» **Headwater** (☎in UK 01606 720119; www.headwater.com) Eight-day 'Backroads of Mallorca Cyling Tour' with stays in a local rural estate.

» **Mallorca Muntanya** (☎639 713 212; www.mallorcamuntanya.com) Trekking tours, mostly in the Serra de Tramuntana.

» **Mar y Roc** (☎971 235 853; www.mallorca-wandern.de) Group hiking tours in Mallorca.

» **Naturetrek** (☎in UK 01962 733051; www.naturetrek.co.uk) Eight-day birdwatching tour.

» **Unicorn Trails** (☎in UK 01762 600606; www.unicorn-trails.com) Two weeklong horse-riding tours to choose from.

» **Vuelta** (☎in Germany 0511 21 57 101; http://vuelta.de, in German) Hiking and biking tours.

GETTING AROUND

Bicycle

Mallorca is one of Europe's most popular cycling destinations. Although the going can be tough in the mountainous areas, particularly along the island's western and northwestern coasts, much of the island is reasonably flat and can be easily explored by bike. You can take your own or hire one once you arrive. Tourist authorities publish a booklet called *Cicloturismo* (Cycling Tourism), which you can also see on the web (www.illesbalears.es; click on 'Sport Tourism'). It has numerous routes across the island. Signposts have been put up across much of rural Mallorca indicating cycling routes (usually secondary roads between towns and villages). In the northeast, you can get on to a network of so-called Ecovies.

Hire

Bike-hire places are scattered around the main resorts of the island, including Palma, and are usually highly professional.

Bus

The island is roughly divided into five zones radiating from Palma.

Bus line numbers in the 100s cover the southwest, the 200s the west (as far as Sóller), the 300s the northeast and much of the centre, the 400s a wedge of the centre and east coast and the 500s the south. These services are run by a phalanx of small bus companies, but you can get route and timetable information for all by contacting **Transport de les Illes Balears** (☎971 177 777; http://tib.caib.es).

Most of the island is accessible by bus from Palma.

All buses depart from (or near) Palma's bus station (Carrer d'Eusebi Estada). Not all lines are especially frequent, however, and services slow to a trickle on weekends. Frequency to many coastal areas also drops from November to April and some lines are cut altogether (such as those between Ca'n Picafort and Sa Calobra or Sóller).

Although services in most parts of the island are adequate, more-out-of-the-way places can also be tedious to reach and getting around the Serra de Tramuntana by bus, while possible, isn't always easy. Bus 200 from Palma runs to Estellencs via Banyalbufar for example, while bus 210 runs to Valldemossa and then, less frequently, on to Deià and Sóller. Nothing makes the connection between Estellencs and Valldemossa and all but the Palma–Valldemossa run are infrequent.

Fares are not especially onerous. One-way fares from Palma include Cala Ratjada (€10.15), Pollença (€4.90), Sóller (€2.35) and Cala d'Or (€7.80) with very few services taking longer than two hours to reach their destinations.

Car & Motorcycle

Although you can get about much of the island by bus and train, having your own vehicle allows you far greater freedom, and most visitors rent their own cars. Mallorca, especially on the west and north coasts, and along narrow country roads in the centre of the island, is ideal for motorcycle touring.

Automobile Associations

The **Real Automóvil Club de España** (RACE; ☎902 404 545; www.race.es; Calle de Eloy Gonzalo 32, Madrid) is the national automobile club. They may well come to assist you in case of breakdown, but in any event you should obtain an emergency telephone number for Spain from your own insurer. Its **local office** (☎971 715 140; Avinguda Conde Sallent 7) in Mallorca is in Palma.

Bring Your Own Vehicle

Always carry proof of ownership of a private vehicle.

Every vehicle should display a nationality plate of its country of registration. It is compulsory in Spain to carry a warning triangle (to be used in case of breakdown)

FERRY SERVICES TO MALLORCA

TO	FROM	COMPANY	PRICE	FREQUENCY	DURATION (HR)	SLEEPER BERTH
Palma	Barcelona	Acciona Trasmediterránea, Baleària	seat from €53-60, sleeper from €62	one or two daily	seven	yes
Palma	Denia	Baleària	seat from €37, sleeper €119	two daily	two to five	yes
Palma	Formentera	Baleària	€98	one daily	4½	no
Palma	Ibiza (Ibiza City)	Acciona Trasmediterránea	from €49	Fri & Sat	four	yes
Palma	Maó (Menorca)	Acciona Trasmediterránea	from €49	Sun	3½	yes
Palma	Valencia	Acciona Trasmediterránea	seat €60, sleeper from €98	one daily	eight	yes
Port d'Alcúdia	Barcelona	Baleària	seat from €48	one daily	seven	yes
Port d'Alcúdia	Ciutatdella (Menorca)	Baleària	€37-68	two daily	one to two	no
Cala Ratjada	Ciutatdella (Menorca)	Interilles	€60	one daily	one	no

and a reflective jacket. Recommended accessories include a first-aid kit, spare-bulb kit and fire extinguisher.

Driving Licences

All EU member state driving licences are recognised throughout Europe. Those with a non-EU licence are supposed to obtain a 12-month International Driver's Permit (IDP) from their home automobile association to accompany their national licence. In practice, national licences from countries such as Australia, Canada, New Zealand and the USA are usually accepted.

Fuel

Petrol *(gasolina)* prices vary between service stations *(gasolineras)*. Lead free *(sin plomo;* 95 octane) costs an average €1.35/L. A 98-octane variant costs €1.46/L. Diesel *(gasóleo)* comes in at around €1.30/L.

You can pay with major credit cards at most service stations.

Hire

About 30 vehicle-hire agencies are based in Palma and plenty more operate around the island, from international companies to local shopfronts that may offer cheaper rates. To rent a car you have to have a licence, be aged 21 or over and, for the major companies at least, have a credit card.

A word of advice: renting cars in Mallorca can be expensive, and some agencies try to make even more money by charging a €90 fee for fuel, instead of asking you to bring it back with a full tank. Always read the fine print carefully before signing off. If you're willing to wait until you arrive on the island, forsake the larger international companies and try one of the local companies in the area you're staying – rates are generally cheaper but always make sure you're fully insured.

The Consell de Mallorca tourist office in Palma or Sant Joan Airport should have a copy of the useful *Lloguer de Vehicles (Rent a Car)* pamphlet which lists dozens of car- and motorcycle-hire companies around the island.

Insurance

Third-party motor insurance is a minimum requirement in Spain and throughout Europe. Ask your insurer for a European Accident Statement form, which can simplify matters in the event of an accident. A European breakdown-assistance policy such as the AA Five Star Service or RAC Eurocover Motoring Assistance is a good investment.

Car-hire companies also provide this minimum insurance, but be careful to understand what your liabilities and excess are, and what waivers you're entitled to in case of an accident or damage to the hire vehicle.

Road Rules

» **Blood-alcohol limit** 0.05%. If found to be over the limit you can be judged, fined and deprived of your licence within 24 hours. Fines range up to around €600 for serious offences. Nonresident foreigners will be required to pay up on the spot (at 30% off the full fine).

» **Legal driving age for cars** 18

» **Legal driving age for motorcycles & scooters** 16 (80cc and over) or 14 (50cc and under). A licence is required.

» **Motorcyclists** Must use headlights at all times and wear a helmet if riding a bike of 125cc or more.

» **Overtaking** Spanish truck drivers often have the courtesy to turn on their right indicator to show that the way ahead of them is clear for overtaking (and the left one if it is not and you are attempting this manoeuvre).

» **Roundabouts (traffic circles)** Vehicles already in the circle have the right of way.

» **Side of the road** Drive on the right.

» **Speed limits** In built-up areas, 50km/h, which increases to 100km/h on major roads and up to 110km/h on the four-lane highways leading out of Palma.

Local Transport

Palma is the only centre with its own local transport system. Buses are the main way around, although a new metro line (of more interest to commuters in the suburbs than to visitors) runs from the centre to the university.

It's easy to get around Palma (especially the old centre) by bicycle, although cycling lanes are limited (the main one runs along the shoreline).

Palma is well supplied with taxis, with several stands around the city. Elsewhere on the island, you may not necessarily find them waiting when you need them, but generally they're fairly easy to order by phone; ask at your hotel or local tourist office.

Train

Two train lines run from Plaça d'Espanya in Palma de Mallorca.

One heads north to Sóller and is a panoramic excursion in an antique wooden train, and is one of Palma's most popular day trips.

The other line heads inland to Inca, where the line splits to serve Sa Pobla and Manacor. Prices are generally cheaper than buses (€1.80 to Inca and €2.40 to Manacor) and departures are frequent throughout the day. There are plans underway to extend the line from Manacor to Artà (which train services used to reach), although no-one could tell us when the extension would be completed.

Language

WANT MORE?

For in-depth language information and handy phrases, check out Lonely Planet's *Spanish phrasebook*. You'll find it at **shop.lonelyplanet.com**, or you can buy Lonely Planet's iPhone phrasebooks at the Apple App Store.

Mallorca is a bilingual island, at least on paper. Since the Balearic Islands received their autonomy statute in the 1980s, the islanders' native Catalan (*català*) has recovered its official status alongside Spanish. This signified a reversal of Francoist policy which had largely eliminated minority languages from public life and schools. This said, it would be pushing a point to say that Catalan, or its local dialect, *mallorquí*, had again become the primary language of Mallorca or the rest of the Balearic Islands. Today, despite the broad schooling in Catalan, many locals choose to speak Spanish (Castilian) anyway and overall, Spanish remains the lingua franca, especially between Mallorquins and other Spaniards or foreigners. You'll often hear and read Catalan on Mallorca, and locals will be pleasantly surprised to hear you trying your hand at it, but just making the effort in Spanish will please most.

Spanish pronunciation is straightforward as most Spanish sounds are pronounced the same as their English counterparts. Note that the kh in our pronunciation guides is a guttural sound (like the 'ch' in the Scottish *loch*), ly is pronounced as the 'lli' in 'million', ny as the 'ni' in 'onion', th is pronounced with a lisp, and r is strongly rolled. In our pronunciation guides, the stressed syllables are in italics. If you follow our pronunciation guides given with each phrase in this chapter, you'll be understood just fine.

Spanish nouns (and the adjectives that go with them) are marked for gender – feminine nouns generally end with *-a* and masculine ones with *-o*. Where necessary, both forms are given for the words and phrases in this chapter, separated by a slash and with the masculine form first, eg *perdido/a* (m/f).

Also note that Spanish has two words for the English 'you': when talking to people familiar to you or younger than you, use the informal form, *tú*, rather than the polite form *Usted*. The polite form is used in the phrases provided in this chapter; where both options are given, they are indicated by the abbreviations 'pol' and 'inf'.

BASICS

Hello./Goodbye.	*Hola./Adiós.*	o·la/a·*dyos*
How are you?	*¿Qué tal?*	ke tal
Fine, thanks.	*Bien, gracias.*	byen *gra*·thyas
Excuse me.	*Perdón.*	per·*don*
Sorry.	*Lo siento.*	lo *syen*·to
Yes./No.	*Sí./No.*	see/no
Please.	*Por favor.*	por fa·*vor*
Thank you.	*Gracias.*	*gra*·thyas
You're welcome.	*De nada.*	de *na*·da

My name is ...
Me llamo ... — me *lya*·mo ...

What's your name?
¿Cómo se llama Usted? — *ko*·mo se *lya*·ma oo·*ste*

Do you speak (English)?
¿Habla (inglés)? — *a*·bla (een·*gles*)

I (don't) understand.
Yo (no) entiendo. — yo (no) en·*tyen*·do

ACCOMMODATION

I'd like to book a room.
Quisiera reservar una habitación. — kee·*sye*·ra re·ser·*var* oo·na a·bee·ta·*thyon*

How much is it per night/person?
¿Cuánto cuesta por noche/persona? — *kwan*·to *kwes*·ta por *no*·che/per·*so*·na

air-con	*aire acondicionado*	ai·re a·kon·dee·thyo·*na*·do
bathroom	*baño*	*ba*·nyo
bed	*cama*	*ka*·ma
campsite	*terreno de cámping*	te·*re*·no de *kam*·peeng
double room	*habitación doble*	a·bee·ta·*thyon* *do*·ble
guesthouse	*pensión*	pen·*syon*
hotel	*hotel*	o·*tel*
single room	*habitación individual*	a·bee·ta·*thyon* een·dee·vee·*dwal*
window	*ventana*	ven·*ta*·na
youth hostel	*albergue juvenil*	al·*ber*·ge khoo·ve·*neel*

DIRECTIONS

Where's ...?
¿Dónde está ...? don·de es·*ta* ...

What's the address?
¿Cuál es la dirección? *kwal* es la dee·rek·*thyon*

Could you please write it down?
¿Puede escribirlo, por favor? *pwe*·de es·kree·*beer*·lo por fa·*vor*

Can you show me (on the map)?
¿Me lo puede indicar (en el mapa)? me lo *pwe*·de een·dee·*kar* (en el *ma*·pa)

behind ...	*detrás de ...*	de·*tras* de ...
far away	*lejos*	*le*·khos
in front of ...	*enfrente de ...*	en·*fren*·te de ...
left	*izquierda*	eeth·*kyer*·da
near	*cerca*	*ther*·ka
next to ...	*al lado de ...*	al *la*·do de ...
opposite ...	*frente a ...*	*fren*·te a ...
right	*derecha*	de·*re*·cha

EATING & DRINKING

I'd like to book a table.
Quisiera reservar una mesa. kee·*sye*·ra re·ser·*var* *oo*·na *me*·sa

What would you recommend?
¿Qué recomienda? ke re·ko·*myen*·da

What's in that dish?
¿Que lleva ese plato? ke *lye*·va *e*·se *pla*·to

I don't eat ...
No como ... no *ko*·mo ...

That was delicious!
¡Estaba buenísimo! es·*ta*·ba bwe·*nee*·see·mo

Please bring the bill.
Por favor nos trae la cuenta. por fa·*vor* nos *tra*·e la *kwen*·ta

Cheers!
¡Salud! sa·*loo*

KEY PATTERNS

To get by in Spanish, mix and match these simple patterns with words of your choice:

When's (the next flight)?
¿Cuándo sale (el próximo vuelo)? *kwan*·do *sa*·le (el *prok*·see·mo *vwe*·lo)

Where's (the station)?
¿Dónde está (la estación)? *don*·de es·*ta* (la es·ta·*thyon*)

Where can I (buy a ticket)?
¿Dónde puedo (comprar un billete)? *don*·de *pwe*·do (kom·*prar* oon bee·*lye*·te)

Do you have (a map)?
¿Tiene (un mapa)? *tye*·ne (oon *ma*·pa)

Is there (a toilet)?
¿Hay (servicios)? ai (ser·*vee*·thyos)

I'd like (a coffee).
Quisiera (un café). kee·*sye*·ra (oon ka·*fe*)

Could you please (help me)?
¿Puede (ayudarme), por favor? *pwe*·de (a·yoo·*dar*·me) por fa·*vor*

Key Words

appetisers	*aperitivos*	a·pe·ree·*tee*·vos
bar	*bar*	bar
bottle	*botella*	bo·*te*·lya
breakfast	*desayuno*	de·sa·*yoo*·no
cafe	*café*	ka·*fe*
children's menu	*menú infantil*	me·*noo* een·fan·*teel*
cold	*frío*	*free*·o
dinner	*cena*	*the*·na
food	*comida*	ko·*mee*·da
fork	*tenedor*	te·ne·*dor*
glass	*vaso*	*va*·so
highchair	*trona*	*tro*·na
hot (warm)	*caliente*	ka·*lyen*·te
knife	*cuchillo*	koo·*chee*·lyo
lunch	*comida*	ko·*mee*·da
main course	*segundo plato*	se·*goon*·do *pla*·to
market	*mercado*	mer·*ka*·do
menu (in English)	*menú (en inglés)*	me·*noo* (en een·*gles*)
plate	*plato*	*pla*·to
restaurant	*restaurante*	res·tow·*ran*·te
spoon	*cuchara*	koo·*cha*·ra
supermarket	*supermercado*	soo·per·mer·*ka*·do
with/without	*con/sin*	kon/seen
vegetarian food	*comida vegetariana*	ko·*mee*·da ve·khe·ta·*rya*·na

Signs

Abierto	Open
Cerrado	Closed
Entrada	Entrance
Hombres	Men
Mujeres	Women
Prohibido	Prohibited
Salida	Exit
Servicios/Aseos	Toilets

Meat & Fish

beef	*carne de vaca*	*kar*·ne de *va*·ka
chicken	*pollo*	*po*·lyo
duck	*pato*	*pa*·to
fish	*pescado*	pes·*ka*·do
lamb	*cordero*	kor·*de*·ro
pork	*cerdo*	*ther*·do
turkey	*pavo*	*pa*·vo
veal	*ternera*	ter·*ne*·ra

Fruit & Vegetables

apple	*manzana*	man·*tha*·na
apricot	*albaricoque*	al·ba·ree·*ko*·ke
artichoke	*alcachofa*	al·ka·*cho*·fa
asparagus	*espárragos*	es·*pa*·ra·gos
banana	*plátano*	*pla*·ta·no
beans	*judías*	khoo·*dee*·as
beetroot	*remolacha*	re·mo·*la*·cha
cabbage	*col*	kol
carrot	*zanahoria*	tha·na·o·rya
cherry	*cereza*	the·*re*·tha
corn	*maíz*	ma·*eeth*
cucumber	*pepino*	pe·*pee*·no
fruit	*fruta*	*froo*·ta
grape	*uvas*	*oo*·vas
lemon	*limón*	lee·*mon*
lentils	*lentejas*	len·*te*·khas
lettuce	*lechuga*	le·*choo*·ga
mushroom	*champiñón*	cham·pee·*nyon*
nuts	*nueces*	*nwe*·thes
onion	*cebolla*	the·*bo*·lya
orange	*naranja*	na·*ran*·kha
peach	*melocotón*	me·lo·ko·*ton*
peas	*guisantes*	gee·*san*·tes
(red/green) pepper	*pimiento (rojo/verde)*	pee·*myen*·to (*ro*·kho/*ver*·de)
pineapple	*piña*	*pee*·nya
plum	*ciruela*	theer·*we*·la
potato	*patata*	pa·*ta*·ta
pumpkin	*calabaza*	ka·la·*ba*·tha
spinach	*espinacas*	es·pee·*na*·kas
strawberry	*fresa*	*fre*·sa
tomato	*tomate*	to·*ma*·te
vegetable	*verdura*	ver·*doo*·ra
watermelon	*sandía*	san·*dee*·a

Other

bread	*pan*	pan
butter	*mantequilla*	man·te·*kee*·lya
cheese	*queso*	*ke*·so
egg	*huevo*	*we*·vo
honey	*miel*	myel
jam	*mermelada*	mer·me·*la*·da
oil	*aceite*	a·*they*·te
pepper	*pimienta*	pee·*myen*·ta
rice	*arroz*	a·*roth*
salt	*sal*	sal
sugar	*azúcar*	a·*thoo*·kar
vinegar	*vinagre*	vee·*na*·gre

Drinks

beer	*cerveza*	ther·*ve*·tha
coffee	*café*	ka·*fe*
(orange) juice	*zumo (de naranja)*	*thoo*·mo (de na·*ran*·kha)
milk	*leche*	*le*·che
tea	*té*	te
(mineral) water	*agua (mineral)*	*a*·gwa (mee·ne·*ral*)
(red) wine	*vino (tinto)*	*vee*·no (*teen*·to)
(white) wine	*vino (blanco)*	*vee*·no (*blan*·ko)

Catalan – Basics

Good morning.	*Bon dia.*	bon *dee*·a
Good afternoon.	*Bona tarda.*	*bo*·na *tar*·da
Good evening.	*Bon vespre.*	bon *bes*·pra
Goodbye.	*Adéu.*	a·the·oo
Please.	*Sisplau.*	sees·*pla*·oo
Thank you.	*Gràcies.*	*gra*·see·a
You're welcome.	*De res.*	de res
Excuse me.	*Perdoni.*	par·*tho*·nee
I'm sorry.	*Ho sento.*	oo *sen*·to
How are you?	*Com estàs?*	kom as·*tas*
(Very) Well.	*(Molt) Bé.*	(mol) be

EMERGENCIES

Help!
¡Socorro! so·*ko*·ro

Go away!
¡Vete! *ve*·te

Call a doctor!
¡Llame a un médico! *lya*·me a oon *me*·dee·ko

Call the police!
¡Llame a la policía! *lya*·me a la po·lee·*thee*·a

I'm lost.
Estoy perdido/a. es·*toy* per·*dee*·do/a (m/f)

I'm ill.
Estoy enfermo/a. es·*toy* en·*fer*·mo/a (m/f)

Where are the toilets?
¿Dónde están los baños? *don*·de es·*tan* los *ba*·nyos

NUMBERS

1	*uno*	*oo*·no
2	*dos*	dos
3	*tres*	tres
4	*cuatro*	*kwa*·tro
5	*cinco*	*theen*·ko
6	*seis*	seys
7	*siete*	*sye*·te
8	*ocho*	*o*·cho
9	*nueve*	*nwe*·ve
10	*diez*	dyeth
20	*veinte*	*veyn*·te
30	*treinta*	*treyn*·ta
40	*cuarenta*	kwa·*ren*·ta
50	*cincuenta*	theen·*kwen*·ta
60	*sesenta*	se·*sen*·ta
70	*setenta*	se·*ten*·ta
80	*ochenta*	o·*chen*·ta
90	*noventa*	no·*ven*·ta
100	*cien*	thyen
1000	*mil*	meel

SHOPPING & SERVICES

I'd like to buy ...
Quisiera comprar ... kee·*sye*·ra kom·*prar* ...

May I look at it?
¿Puedo verlo? *pwe*·do *ver*·lo

How much is it?
¿Cuánto cuesta? *kwan*·to *kwes*·ta

That's too/very expensive.
Es muy caro. es mooy *ka*·ro

Can you lower the price?
¿Podría bajar un poco el precio? po·*dree*·a ba·*khar* oon *po*·ko el *pre*·thyo

There's a mistake in the bill.
Hay un error en la cuenta. ai oon e·*ror* en la *kwen*·ta

ATM	*cajero automático*	ka·*khe*·ro ow·to·*ma*·tee·ko
credit card	*tarjeta de crédito*	tar·*khe*·ta de *kre*·dee·to
internet cafe	*cibercafé*	thee·ber·ka·*fe*
post office	*correos*	ko·*re*·os
tourist office	*oficina de turismo*	o·fee·*thee*·na de too·*rees*·mo

TIME & DATES

What time is it?
¿Qué hora es? ke *o*·ra es

It's (10) o'clock.
Son (las diez). son (las dyeth)

Half past (one).
Es (la una) y media. es (la *oo*·na) ee *me*·dya

morning	*mañana*	ma·*nya*·na
afternoon	*tarde*	*tar*·de
evening	*noche*	*no*·che
yesterday	*ayer*	a·*yer*
today	*hoy*	oy
tomorrow	*mañana*	ma·*nya*·na

Monday	*lunes*	*loo*·nes
Tuesday	*martes*	*mar*·tes
Wednesday	*miércoles*	*myer*·ko·les
Thursday	*jueves*	*khwe*·bes
Friday	*viernes*	*vyer*·nes
Saturday	*sábado*	*sa*·ba·do
Sunday	*domingo*	do·*meen*·go

TRANSPORT

I want to go to ...
Quisiera ir a ... kee·*sye*·ra eer a ...

What time does it arrive/leave?
¿A qué hora llega/sale? a ke *o*·ra *lye*·ga/*sa*·le

I want to get off here.
Quiero bajarme aquí. *kye*·ro ba·*khar*·me a·*kee*

1st-class	*primera clase*	pree·*me*·ra *kla*·se
2nd-class	*segunda clase*	se·*goon*·da *kla*·se
bicycle	*bicicleta*	bee·thee·*kle*·ta
boat	*barco*	*bar*·ko
bus	*autobús*	ow·to·*boos*
car	*coche*	*ko*·che
cancelled	*cancelado*	kan·the·*la*·do
delayed	*retrasado*	re·tra·*sa*·do
motorcycle	*moto*	*mo*·to
one-way	*ida*	*ee*·da
plane	*avión*	a·*vyon*
return	*ida y vuelta*	*ee*·da ee *vwel*·ta
ticket	*billete*	bee·*lye*·te
ticket office	*taquilla*	ta·*kee*·lya
timetable	*horario*	o·*ra*·ryo
train	*tren*	tren

GLOSSARY

Most of the following terms are in Castilian Spanish which is fully understood around the island. A handful of specialised terms in Catalan (C) also appear. No distinction has been made for any Mallorcan dialect variations.

agroturisme (C) – rural tourism
ajuntament (C) – city or town hall
alquería – Muslim-era farmstead
avenida – avenue
avinguda (C) – see *avenida*

baño completo – full bathroom with toilet, shower and/or bath
bodega – cellar (especially wine cellar)
bomberos – fire brigade

cala – cove
call (C) – Jewish quarter in Palma, Inca and some other Mallorcan towns
cambio – change; also currency exchange
caña – small glass of beer
canguro – babysitter
capilla – chapel
carrer (C) – street
carretera – highway
carta – menu
castell (C) – castle
castellano – Castilian; used in preference to '*Español*' to describe the national language
català – Catalan language; a native of Catalonia. The Mallorcan dialect is Mallorquin
celler – (C) wine cellars turned into restaurants
cervecería – beer bar
comisaría – police station
conquistador – conqueror
converso – Jew who converted to Christianity in medieval Spain
correos – post office
cortado – short black coffee with a little milk
costa – coast
cuenta – bill, cheque

ensaïmada (C) – Mallorcan pastry
entrada – entrance, ticket
ermita – small hermitage or country chapel
església (C) – see *iglesia*
estació (C) – see *estación*
estación – station
estanco – tobacconist shop

farmacia – pharmacy
faro – lighthouse
fiesta – festival, public holiday or party
finca – farmhouse

gasolina – petrol
guardía civil – military police

habitaciones libres – literally 'rooms available'
hostal – see *pensión*

iglesia – church
IVA – *impuesto sobre el valor añadido*, or value-added tax

lavabo – washbasin
librería – bookshop
lista de correos – poste restante
locutorio – telephone centre

marisquería – seafood eatery
menú del día – menu of the day
mercat (C) – market
mirador – lookout point
Modernisme – the Catalan version of the art nouveau architectural and artistic style
monestir (C) – monastery
museo – museum
museu (C) – see *museo*

objetos perdidos – lost-and-found
oficina de turismo – tourist office; also *oficina de información turística*

palacio – palace, grand mansion or noble house
palau (C) – see *palacio*
pensión – small family-run hotel
plaça (C) – see *plaza*
platja (C) – see *playa*
playa – beach
plaza – square
port (C) – see *puerto*
possessió (C) – typical Mallorcan farmhouse
PP – Partido Popular (People's Party)
puente – bridge
puerto – port
puig (C) – mountain peak

rambla – avenue or riverbed
refugis (C) – hikers' huts
retablo – altarpiece
retaule (C) – see *retablo*
robes de llengües (C) – traditional striped Mallorcan fabrics

santuari (C) – shrine or sanctuary, hermitage
según precio del mercado – on menus, 'according to market price' (often written 'spm')
Semana Santa – Holy Week
serra (C) – mountain range
servicios – toilets

tafona (C) – traditional oil press found on most Mallorcan farms
talayot (C) – ancient watchtower
tarjeta de crédito – credit card
tarjeta de residencia – residence card
tarjeta telefónica – phonecard
terraza – terrace; pavement cafe
torre – tower
turismo – tourism or saloon car

urgencia – emergency

behind the scenes

SEND US YOUR FEEDBACK

We love to hear from travellers – your comments keep us on our toes and help make our books better. Our well-travelled team reads every word on what you loved or loathed about this book. Although we cannot reply individually to postal submissions, we always guarantee that your feedback goes straight to the appropriate authors, in time for the next edition. Each person who sends us information is thanked in the next edition – and the most useful submissions are rewarded with a free book.

Visit **lonelyplanet.com/contact** to submit your updates and suggestions or to ask for help. Our award-winning website also features inspirational travel stories, news and discussions.

Note: We may edit, reproduce and incorporate your comments in Lonely Planet products such as guidebooks, websites and digital products, so let us know if you don't want your comments reproduced or your name acknowledged. For a copy of our privacy policy visit lonelyplanet.com/privacy.

OUR READERS

Many thanks to the travellers who used the last edition and wrote to us with helpful hints, useful advice and interesting anecdotes: Andy, Nikki Buran, Martina Doherty, Mark Gorst, Matt Heason, Holger and Uscha, John and Sue Holwill, Delyth Morton, Linda Nijlunsing, Erik Vloeberghs

AUTHOR THANKS

Anthony Ham

In nine years of living in Spain, I have been welcomed and assisted by too many people to name and whose lives and stories have become a treasured part of the fabric of my own. A huge thank you to Dora Whitaker, Daniel Corbett, Martine Power and the wonderful LPOS team at Lonely Planet. It was my great fortune to explore Mallorca with my wife and soul mate, Marina, and with Carlota and Valentina, the most special little people a father could ever wish for.

ACKNOWLEDGMENTS

Climate map data adapted from Peel MC, Finlayson BL & McMahon TA (2007) 'Updated World Map of the Köppen-Geiger Climate Classification', *Hydrology and Earth System Sciences*, 11, 163344.

Cover photograph: Stone hermitage near Valldemossa, Mallorca, Schmid Reinhard/4Corners.

Many of the images in this guide are available for licensing from Lonely Planet Images: www.lonelyplanetimages.com.

This Book

This 2nd edition of Lonely Planet's *Mallorca* guide was researched and written by Anthony Ham. The 1st edition was written by Damien Simonis and Sarah Andrews, with contributions from Sally Schafer. This guidebook was commissioned in Lonely Planet's London office, and produced by the following:

Commissioning Editor Dora Whitaker

Coordinating Editor Martine Power

Coordinating Cartographer Corey Hutchison

Coordinating Layout Designer Carlos Solarte

Managing Editors Sasha Baskett, Annelies Mertens, Kirsten Rawlings, Tasmin Waby McNaughtan

Managing Cartographers David Connolly, Amanda Sierp

Managing Layout Designers Chris Girdler, Jane Hart

Assisting Editors Jackey Coyle, Kate Daly

Cover Research Naomi Parker

Internal Image Research Sabrina Dalbesio

Language Content Branislava Vladisavljevic

Thanks to Chris Aitchison, Merlin Ananth, Sudha Ananth, Dan Austin, Karthick Balakrishnan, Gus Balbontin, Anitha Bharanidharan, Sophia Cangan, David Carroll, Alan Castles, Lena Chan, Rebecca Chau, Gordon Christie, Helen Christinis, Daniel Corbett, Melanie Dankel, Ryan Evans, Tobias Gattineau, Michelle Glynn, Satishna Gokuldas, Vasanthi Govindarajulu, Daniel Heath, David Hodges, Ken Hoetmer, Manju Krishnan, Sandeep Krishnan, Vijay Kumar, David Kunjumon, Anthony Langhorne, Ali Lemer, Ross Macaw, Ioomi Manners, Rowan McKinnon, Erin McManus, Darren O'Connell, Sunny Or, Krishnaprasad Palani, Jani Patokallio, Trent Paton, Suresh Ramani, Anthony Reinbach, Jon Ricketson, Averil Robertson, Luke Robins, Vaneesa Rowe, Sally Schafer, Fiona Siseman, Brent Snook, Laura Stansfeld, Satish Thayagu, Angela Tinson, Boopathi Vasan, Kavitha Velu, Sue Visic, Gerard Walker, Justin Wark

index

A

accommodation 162-74
costs 162
Eastern Mallorca 172-3
Interior, the 171-2
internet resources 163
monasteries 164
Northern Mallorca 169-71
Palma & the Badia de Palma 164-5
Southern Mallorca 174
Western Mallorca 165-9
activities 19-20, 23-8, *see also individual activities*
air travel 207-8
airlines 207
airports 207
Alaró 100-1
Alcúdia 112-14
Algaida 129-30
Alomar, Francisco 128
amusement parks
Aqualand 73
Hidropark 115
Marineland 77
Natura Parc 124
Western Water Park 77
Andratx 79
animals 117, 189, *see also* birdwatching
aquariums, *see also* zoos
Centro de Visitantes Ses Salines 153
Palma Aquarium 73
archaeological sites 18, *see also talayots*
Pol·lentia 112-13
architecture 192-4
baroque 193
Gothic 193
Modernisme 194
Modernista buildings 50
Muslim 192-3
Renaissance 193
Roman 192
area codes 15, 204
art galleries, *see* museums & galleries
Artà 12, 136-8, **136**, 12
arts 195-8
ATMs 203

000 Map pages
000 Photo pages

B

Badia d'Alcúdia 112-18
Badia de Palma 72-7
ballooning 24
Banyalbufar 85-6
Banys Àrabs 49
Barceló, Miquel 43, 197-8
bathrooms 205
beaches & coves 16
Cala Barques 109
Cala Carbó 109
Cala Clara 109
Cala d'Estellencs 84
Cala d'Or 160
Cala de Banyalbufar 85
Cala de Deià 91
Cala es Conills 83
Cala Estreta 144
Cala Figuera 159
Cala Gat 140
Cala Llamp 82
Cala Llombards 157
Cala Magraner 146
Cala Marçal 147
Cala Matzoc 144
Cala Mesquida 144, 9
Cala Millor 144
Cala Mitjana 144
Cala Molins 109
Cala Mondragó 159
Cala Pi 152
Cala Romántica 146
Cala s'Arenal 147
Cala Sa Nau 147
Cala Santanyí 157
Cala Sequer 146
Cala Torta 144
Cala Varques 146
Caló des Màrmols 156
Cova de Sa Plana 156
Cova de Sant Martí 114
Cova del Pilar 146
Font de Sa Cala 140
Platja d'Almunia 156
Platja d'en Repic 96
Platja d'es Port 96
Platja de Ca'n Pastilla 73
Platja de Cala Agulla 140
Platja de Canyamel 143
Platja de Formentor 112
Platja de la Colònia de Sant Pere 119
Platja de Palma 73
Platja de Sa Canova 119
Platja de Santa Margalida 118
Platja de Ses Covetes 152
Platja de Son Bauló 118
Platja de Son Moll 140
Platja de Son Real 118
Platja des Coll Baix 13, 117, 13
Platja des Trenc 155
Port de Pollença 110
Portocolom 147
Sa Plageta 154
Sant Elm 83
Ses Casetes dels Capellans 118
S'Espalmador 154
Bendinat 76
Bennàssar, Gaspar 194
Betlem 119
bicycle travel, *see* cycling
Biniaraix 8, 98, 8
Binibona 127
Binissalem 121-4
birds 189-90, *see also* animals
birdwatching 190
Illa de Cabrera 154-5
Parc Natural de la Península de Llevant 138
Parc Natural de Mondragó 159
Parc Natural de S'Albufera 117-18
boat travel 208, 209
boat trips 24, *see also* sailing
Cala d'Or 160
Cala Ratjada 140-1
Illa de Cabrera 154-5
Port d'Alcúdia 114-15
Port de Pollença 110
Porto Cristo 146-7
Sant Elm 83
books 176, 195
botifarra 30
budget 14
buildings & structures, *see also* castles, mansions, towers
Ajuntament (Palma) 51
Arc del Wali 51
Arco de l'Almudaina 49
Banco de Sóller 92
Casa de la Vila 121
Casa Natal de Santa Catalina Thomàs 87
Consolat de Mar 55
Els Calderers 130-1, 3
Finca Pública de Son Real 118
Medieval Walls 113
Miramar 88
Pont de Sa Roca 117

Sa Llotja 55
Son Marroig 88
Walls & Parc de la Mar 51
Bunyola 99
bus travel 208-9
bushwalking, *see* hiking
business hours 200

C

Ca'n Pastilla 73-5
Ca'n Picafort 118-19
Cala Blava 73
Cala de Deià 91
Cala de Sa Calobra 101
Cala d'En Basset 84
Cala d'Or 160-1, **161**
Cala Figuera 159
Cala Llamp 82
Cala Major 75-6
Cala Millor 144-5
Cala Pi 152
Cala Portals Vells 79
Cala Ratjada 140-3, **142**
Cala Sant Vicenç 109-10, **2**
Cala Tuent 101
Calvari 106
Campanet 127
canyoning 24, 100
Cap Blanc 153
Cap de Cala Figuera 79
Cap de Formentor 10, 111, 112, **10**
Cap des Pinar 115-17
Cap Ferrutx 119, 138
Capdepera 139-40
Capocorb Vell 152
car travel 15, 209-10, *see also* driving tours
driving licences 210
hire 210
road distance chart 5
rules 210
castles 18, *see also* buildings & structures, mansions, towers
Castell d'Alaró 100-1
Castell de Bellver 56
Castell de Capdepera 139
Castell de n'Amer 144
Castell de Sant Carles 58
Castell de Santueri 133
Castell de Son Mas 79
Santuari de Sant Salvador 137
Catedral (Palma) 8, 42-3, 46, **8**
cathedrals, *see* churches & cathedrals
caves 18
Cova des Pas de Vallgornera 152-3
Coves Blanques 145
Coves d'Artà 143-4
Coves de Campanet 127
Coves de Gènova 76
Coves de L'Alzineret 109
Coves del Drac 145
Coves dels Hams 145
Sa Cova Blava 155
caving 24-5
cell phones 15, 204
cellers 125-6
children, travel with 33-5, 58
Chopin, Frédéric 87, 89
churches & cathedrals, *see also* convents & monasteries
Basílica de Sant Francesc 49-51
Catedral (Palma) 8, 42-3, 46, **8**
Església de la Mare de Déu deis Àngels 106-7
Església de la Nativitat de Nostra Senyora 98
Església de la Verge del Carme 79
Església de Nostra Senyora de les Robines 121
Església de Nostra Senyora Verge dels Dolors 132
Església de Sant Bartomeu 87, 92
Església de Sant Crist de la Sang 54
Església de Sant Feliu 127
Església de Sant Jaume 53-4
Església de Sant Joan Baptista 90
Església de Sant Mateu 99
Església de Sant Miquel 52, 133
Església de Sant Pere i Sant Pau 129
Església de Sant Vicenç Ferrer 132
Església de Santa Creu 55
Església de Santa Eulàlia 49
Església de Santa Magdalena 54
Església de Santa Maria 128
Església de Santa María d'Andratx 79
Església de Santa Maria de Déu de Roser 107
Església de Sants Cosme i Damià 130
Església del Monti-Sion 51
Oratori de Santa Caterina d'Alexandria 96
Santuari de Sant Salvador 137
Transfiguració del Senyor 137
Civil War 185-6
climate 14, 19-20, 201, *see also individual regions*
Colònia de Sant Jordi 153-4
Colònia de Sant Pere 119
convents & monasteries 164, *see also* churches & cathedrals
Antic Monestir de Nostra Senyora de Soledad 121
Convent de la Concepció 128
Convent de Santa Clara 51
Convent dels Mínims 128
Ermita de Betlem 139
Ermita de la Mare de Déu de Bonany 131
Ermita de Santa Magdalena 125
La Trapa 84
Monestir de Lluc 102
Real Cartuja de Valldemossa 87
Santuari de la Mare de Déu des Puig 107
Santuari de Nostra Senyora de Cura 130
Santuari de Sant Salvador 133
costs 14
courses 202
courtyards 50
coves, *see* beaches & coves
Coves d'Artà 143-4
crafts 128, 195-8
credit cards 203
cultural centres
Casal Solleric 55
Centre Cultural Contemporani Pelaires 51
Costa Nord 87
Fundació Sa Nostra 53
culture 176-7
currency 14
customs regulations 200
cycling 25, 208, *see also* cycling tours
Artà 137-8
Cala d'Or 160
Cala Ratjada 141
Northern Mallorca 109
Parc Natural de la Península de Llevant 138
Portocolom 147
cycling tours 74, 116, *see also* driving tours, walking tours

D

dangers, *see* safety
Deià 7, 90-2, **7**
development (construction) 176, 177
disabilities, travellers with 205
discounts 200
diving 27-8
Cala Ratjada 141
Port d'Alcúdia 115
Port d'Andratx 82
Port de Pollença 110
Port de Sóller 96
Porto Cristo 146
Portocolom 147
Sant Elm 83
Domènech i Montaner, Lluís 194
Douglas, Michael 87

drinks 31, 124
driving, *see* car travel
driving tours 16, 97, *see also* cycling tours, walking tours

E

Eastern Mallorca 37, 134-49, **135**
accommodation 134, 172-3
climate 134
food 134
highlights 135
travel seasons 134
economy 187
Ecovies 109
electricity 200
Els Calderers 130-1, 3
emergencies 15, 71
endangered species 190
ensaïmades 31, 61
environmental issues 177, 191
Es Baluard 54-5, 10
Es Caló 119
Es Firó 19
Estellencs 84-5
events 19-20
exchange rates 15

F

Felanitx 133
ferries 208, 209
Festes de la Patrona 20, 108
Festes de la Verema 20
festivals 19-20
films 176-7
food 29-32
botifarra 30
eating out 31-2
ensaïmades 31, 61
frit Mallorquí 30
markets 60, 71
pa amb oli 30
sobrassada 30
vegetarian 32
Fornalutx 8, 98-9
Franco, General Francisco 185-6
frit Mallorquí 30
Fundació Pilar i Joan Miró 75-6

G

galleries, *see* museums & galleries
gardens, *see* parks & gardens
Gaudí, Antoni 43
gay travellers 68, 200-1
Gènova 76
geography 188-9
glassmaking 128, 198
golf 25, 139
Graves, Robert 90-1

H

health 201-2
hermitages, *see* convents & monasteries
hiking 17, 25-6, 202-3, *see also* walking tours
Artà 137
Cala d'Or 160
Cala Ratjada 141
Cap de Formentor 111
Deià Coastal Path 91
Finca Pública de Son Real 118
Illa de Cabrera 154-5
Northern Mallorca 111
Parc Natural de la Península de Llevant 138
Portocolom 147
Ruta de Pedra en Sec 83
Sóller 94
history 178-87
Civil War 185-6
Jaume I 183-5
Jews 182
Muslim rule 181-3
Roman rule 180-1
Talayotic period 179-80
holidays 203-4
horse riding 26, 141
hostales 163
hot-air ballooning 24
hotels 163

I

Illa de Cabrera 11, 154-5, 11
Illa de Sa Dragonera 83
Illa Es Pantaleu 83
immigration 207
Inca 125-6, **125**
insurance
car 210
health 201
travel 202
Interior, the 120-33, **122-3**
accommodation 120, 171-2
climate 120
food 120
highlights 122-3
travel seasons 120
internet access 202
internet resources 15
accommodation 163
birdwatching 189
Catalan literature 195
children 35
gay travellers 201
lesbian travellers 201
itineraries 21-2, **21**, **22**, *see also* cycling tours, driving tours, walking tours

J

Jardins d'Alfàbia 99
Jaume I 183-5

K

kayaking 28, 110, 147, 160
kite surfing 28, 115

L

La Ruta Martiana 65
landscape 188-91
language 14, 176-7, 211-15
courses 202
leatherwork 198
legal matters 202
lesbian travellers 68, 200-1
literature 195-6, *see also* books
Lloseta 126-7
Llubí 127
Lluc Alcari 91
Llull, Ramon 184, 195
lookouts
Mirador de Sa Creueta 112
Mirador de Ses Barques 101
Miranda dels Lledoners 87

M

Magaluf 76-7
Manacor 131-3, **132**
mansions 17, 50, 127, *see also* buildings & structures, castles
Alcúdia 114
Almacenes El Águila 53
Can Bordils 49
Can Marquès 48
Casal Solleric 55
La Granja 86
Raixa 99
maps 202-3
marine mammals 189
markets 60, 71
medical services 201
Miramar 88
Miró, Joan 75-6, 198
mobile phones 15, 204
Modernisme 194
Modernista buildings 50
monasteries, *see* convents & monasteries

000 Map pages
000 Photo pages

money 14, 15, 203
Montuïri 130-1
motorcycle travel 209-10
Muro 129
Museu Fundación Juan March 52
museums & galleries 10, 17
  Ca'n Prunera - Museu Modernista 92
  CaixaForum 53
  Can Planes 129
  Casa-Museu Dionís Bennàssar 107
  Casa-Museu Joaquim Torrents Lladó 49
  Casa-Museu Llorenç Villalonga 121, 124
  Círculo de Bellas Artes 53
  Claustre de Sant Antoniet 52-3
  Els Calderers 130-1
  Es Baluard 54-5, 10
  Fundació Pilar i Joan Miró 75-6
  Fundació Sa Nostra 53
  Fundación Yannick y Ben Jakober 113-14
  Galeria K 55
  Galeria La Caja Blanca 55
  Joan Guaita Art 55
  Museo de Muñecas 48
  Museo Liedtke 79
  Museu Arqueològic de Son Fornés 130
  Museu Balear de Ciències Naturals 93-4
  Museu d'Art Contemporani 129
  Museu d'Història de la Ciutat 56
  Museu de Gordiola 129-30
  Museu de la Catedral 43
  Museu de la Mar 96
  Museu de Mallorca 49
  Museu de Pollença 107
  Museu de Sa Jugueta Antiga 129
  Museu de Sant Jaume 113
  Museu Diocesà 47-8
  Museu Fra Junípera Serra 131
  Museu Fundación Juan March 52
  Museu Krekovic 56
  Museu Martí Vicenç 107
  Museu Monogràfic de Pol·lentia 112-13
  Palau March 48
  Poble Espanyol 56
  Posada de Biniatró 127
  Sa Torre Cega 140
  Sala Pelaires 55
  Sala Picasso & Sala Miró 92
  S'Estació Contemporary Art Museum 128
  Torre de Ses Puntes 132
music 177, 196

N

Nadal, Rafael 131
Nit de Sant Joan 20
Northern Mallorca 36, 103-19, **104-5**
  accommodation 103, 169-71
  climate 103
  food 103
  highlights 104-5
  travel seasons 103

O

opening hours 200
Orient 99-100
ostrich riding 156

P

pa amb oli 30
painting 196-8
Palau de l'Almudaina 46-7
Palau March 48
Palma & the Badia de Palma 36, 40-77, **41**
  accommodation 40, 164-5
  climate 40
  food 40
  highlights 41
  travel seasons 40
Palma de Mallorca 8, 42-72, **42**, **44-5**, **52**, **57**, 8
  activities 56-8
  courses 58
  drinking 65-7
  emergencies 71
  entertainment 67-9
  festivals 58-60
  food 60-5
  for children 58
  history 42
  itineraries 43
  medical services 71
  safe travel 71
  shopping 69-71
  sights 42-56
  tourist information 72
  tours 58
  travel to/from 72
  travel within 72
Palma, *see* Palma de Mallorca
Palmanova 76-7
paragliding 26, 115
Parc Nacional Marítim-Terrestre de l'Arxipèlag de Cabrera 154-5
Parc Natural de la Península de Llevant 138-9
Parc Natural de Mondragó 159
Parc Natural de S'Albufera 12, 117-18, 12
parks & gardens 18, 27
  Botanicactus 156
  Fundación Yannick y Ben Jakober 113-14
  Jardí Botànic 93-4
  Jardí del Bisbe 48
  Jardins d'Alfàbia 99
  Monestir de Lluc 102
  Parc Nacional Marítim-Terrestre de l'Arxipèlag de Cabrera 154-5
  Parc Natural de la Península de Llevant 138-9
  Parc Natural de Mondragó 159
  Parc Natural de S'Albufera 12, 117-18, 12
  Walls & Parc de la Mar 51
passports 207
patis 50
Petra 131
phonecards 204
Pina 130
Plaça de la Constitució 92
planning, *see also individual regions*
  accommodation 163
  activities 23-8
  budgeting 14-15
  calendar of events 19-20
  children 33-5
  food 29-32
  internet resources 15
  itineraries 21-2
  Mallorca basics 14-15
  Mallorca's regions 36-7
  travel seasons 14, 19-20
plants 110, 190-1
Platja de Canyamel 143-4
Platja des Coll Baix 13, 117, 13
Platja des Trenc 155
Pollença 9, 106-9, **106**, 9
Pol·lentia 112-13
population 176
Porreres 130
Port d'Alcúdia 114-15
Port d'Andratx 79-83
Port de Pollença 110-12
Port de Sóller 95-8
Port de Valldemossa 90
Portals Nous 76
Portals Vells 79
Porto Cristo 145-7, **146**
Portocolom 147-9
Portopetro 159-60
poseidon grass 110
possessions 17, 127
  Jardins d'Alfàbia 99
  La Granja 86
postal services 203
public holidays 203-4
Puerto Portals 76

R

Ramon Llull 88
refugis 163
religion 177
Reserva Marina del Migjorn de Mallorca 152
resorts, *see* accommodation
road distances 5
road rules 210
Rubió, Joan 194
ruins, *see* archaeological sites, *talayots*
Ruta de Pedra en Sec 83

S

Sa Calobra 6, 101, 6
Sa Cova Blava 155
Sa Fira 19
Sa Pobla 129
Sa Ràpita 152-3
safety 71, 204
sailing 26-7, 59, 86, 96, *see also* boat trips
Salvator, Archduke Ludwig 186
Sand, George 87, 89
Sant Elm 83-4
Santa Maria del Camí 121
Santanyí 157-9
Santuari de Nostra Senyora de Cura 130
Santuari de Sant Salvador 133
S'Arenal 73-5
scams 204
scuba diving, *see* diving
sculpture 196-8
sea kayaking, *see* kayaking
seafood 10, 30, 10
Serra de Tramuntana 84-102
Ses Covetes 152
Ses Illetes 76
Ses Salines 155-7
shopping 60, 71
Sineu 128-9
snorkelling 27-8
sobrassada 30
Sóller 92-5, **93**
Son Bauló 118-19
Son Serra de Marina 119
Southern Mallorca 37, 150-61, **151**
- accommodation 150, 174
- climate 150
- food 150
- highlights 151
- travel seasons 150

structures, *see* buildings & structures

T

Tayalotic period 179-80
talayots 179, 192, *see also* archaeological sites
- Capocorb Vell 152
- Es Figueral de Son Real 118
- Illot dels Porros 118
- Museu Arqueològic de Son Fornés 130
- Necròpolis de Son Real 118
- Poblat Talaiòtic dels Antigors 156
- Ses Païsses 137
- Talaia d'Albercuix 112

taxes 203
taxis 210
telephone services 15, 204
theft 204
time 204-5
tipping 203
toilets 205
Torre des Verger 85
tourism 176
tourist information 205
tours 208, *see also* cycling tours, driving tours, walking tours
towers, *see also* buildings & structures, castles
- Sa Torre Cega 140
- Torre de Canyamel 144
- Torre del Palau 132
- Torre des Verger 85
- Torre Miquel Nunis 139

train travel 11, 63, 210, 11
travel to/from Mallorca 207-8
travel within Mallorca 208-10
travellers cheques 203
trekking, *see* hiking

V

vacations 203-4
vaccinations 201
Valldemossa 13, 87-90, **88**, 13
value-added tax (VAT) 203
vegetarian travellers 32
visas 15, 205

W

walking, *see* hiking
walking tours 148, 158, *see also* cycling tours, driving tours
water sports 12, 12, *see also* diving, kayaking, kitesurfing, sailing, windsurfing
weather 14, 19-20, 201, *see also* *individual regions*
websites, *see* internet resources
Western Mallorca 36, 78-102, **80-1**
- accommodation 78, 165-9
- climate 78
- food 78
- highlights 80-1
- travel seasons 78

wi-fi access 202
wildlife 188-91
windsurfing 12, 28, 110, 115, 12
wine 31
wineries 124
- Bodega Son Vives 85
- Bodegas Castell Miquel 126
- Bodegas Crestatx 129
- Bodegas Macià Batle 121
- Bodegas Miquel Oliver 131
- Celler Tianna Negre 121
- Jaume Mesquida Winery 130
- José Luis Ferrer 121
- Toni Gelabert 132

women travellers 206
work 206

Z

zoos, *see also* aquariums
- Natura Parc 124
- Safari-Zoo 145

000 Map pages
000 Photo pages

how to use this book

These symbols will help you find the listings you want:

- Sights
- Beaches
- Activities
- Courses
- Tours
- Festivals & Events
- Sleeping
- Eating
- Drinking
- Entertainment
- Shopping
- Information/ Transport

These symbols give you the vital information for each listing:

- Telephone Numbers
- Opening Hours
- Parking
- Nonsmoking
- Air-Conditioning
- Internet Access
- Wi-Fi Access
- Swimming Pool
- Vegetarian Selection
- English-Language Menu
- Family-Friendly
- Pet-Friendly
- Bus
- Ferry
- Metro
- Subway
- London Tube
- Tram
- Train

Reviews are organised by author preference.

Look out for these icons:

TOP CHOICE Our author's recommendation

FREE No payment required

A green or sustainable option

Our authors have nominated these places as demonstrating a strong commitment to sustainability – for example by supporting local communities and producers, operating in an environmentally friendly way, or supporting conservation projects.

Map Legend

Sights
- Beach
- Buddhist
- Castle
- Christian
- Hindu
- Islamic
- Jewish
- Monument
- Museum/Gallery
- Ruin
- Winery/Vineyard
- Zoo
- Other Sight

Activities, Courses & Tours
- Diving/Snorkelling
- Canoeing/Kayaking
- Skiing
- Surfing
- Swimming/Pool
- Walking
- Windsurfing
- Other Activity/ Course/Tour

Sleeping
- Sleeping
- Camping

Eating
- Eating

Drinking
- Drinking
- Cafe

Entertainment
- Entertainment

Shopping
- Shopping

Information
- Post Office
- Tourist Information

Transport
- Airport
- Border Crossing
- Bus
- Cable Car/ Funicular
- Cycling
- Ferry
- Metro
- Monorail
- Parking
- S-Bahn
- Taxi
- Train/Railway
- Tram
- Tube Station
- U-Bahn
- Other Transport

Routes
- Tollway
- Freeway
- Primary
- Secondary
- Tertiary
- Lane
- Unsealed Road
- Plaza/Mall
- Steps
- Tunnel
- Pedestrian Overpass
- Walking Tour
- Walking Tour Detour
- Path

Boundaries
- International
- State/Province
- Disputed
- Regional/Suburb
- Marine Park
- Cliff
- Wall

Population
- Capital (National)
- Capital (State/Province)
- City/Large Town
- Town/Village

Geographic
- Hut/Shelter
- Lighthouse
- Lookout
- Mountain/Volcano
- Oasis
- Park
- Pass
- Picnic Area
- Waterfall

Hydrography
- River/Creek
- Intermittent River
- Swamp/Mangrove
- Reef
- Canal
- Water
- Dry/Salt/ Intermittent Lake
- Glacier

Areas
- Beach/Desert
- Cemetery (Christian)
- Cemetery (Other)
- Park/Forest
- Sportsground
- Sight (Building)
- Top Sight (Building)

OUR STORY

A beat-up old car, a few dollars in the pocket and a sense of adventure. In 1972 that's all Tony and Maureen Wheeler needed for the trip of a lifetime – across Europe and Asia overland to Australia. It took several months, and at the end – broke but inspired – they sat at their kitchen table writing and stapling together their first travel guide, *Across Asia on the Cheap*. Within a week they'd sold 1500 copies. Lonely Planet was born.

Today, Lonely Planet has offices in Melbourne, London and Oakland, with more than 600 staff and writers. We share Tony's belief that 'a great guidebook should do three things: inform, educate and amuse'.

OUR WRITERS

Anthony Ham

In 2001 Anthony fell irretrievably in love with Spain on his first visit to Madrid and, less than a year later, he arrived in the Spanish capital on a one-way ticket. A decade later, Madrid is very much home. From there, he spends a significant proportion of every year exploring his adopted country, and has written or co-written Lonely Planet guides to Madrid, Andalucía, Barcelona and Spain. When he's not writing for Lonely Planet, Anthony writes about and photographs Spain, Africa and the Middle East for newspapers and magazines around the world.

Read more about Anthony at:
lonelyplanet.com/members/anthony_ham

Published by Lonely Planet Publications Pty Ltd
ABN 36 005 607 983
2nd edition – Jan 2012
ISBN 978 1 74179 237 9

10 9 8 7 6 5 4 3 2 1
Printed in China